DECODING ALBANIAN ORGANIZED CRIME

DECODING ALBANIAN ORGANIZED CRIME

Culture, Politics, and Globalization

Jana Arsovska

UNIVERSITY OF CALIFORNIA PRESS

University of California Press, one of the most distinguished university presses in the United States, enriches lives around the world by advancing scholarship in the humanities, social sciences, and natural sciences. Its activities are supported by the UC Press Foundation and by philanthropic contributions from individuals and institutions. For more information, visit www.ucpress.edu.

University of California Press
Oakland, California

Library of Congress Cataloging-in-Publication Data

Arsovska, Jana, 1981– author.
    Decoding Albanian organized crime : culture, politics, and globalization / Jana Arsovska.
        pages   cm
    Includes bibliographical references and index.
    ISBN 978-0-520-28280-3 (cloth) — ISBN 978-0-520-28281-0 (pbk. : alk. paper) — ISBN 978-0-520-95871-5 (ebook)
    1. Organized crime—Albania.   2. Organized crime—Balkan Peninsula.   3. Organized crime—Europe, Western.   4. Organized crime—United States.   5. Transnational crime.   I. Title.
    HV6453.A38A77   2015
    364.106094965—dc23

                                                        2014029706

23   22   21   20   19   18   17   16   15
10   9   8   7   6   5   4   3   2   1

To my parents, for showing me the way; to my husband, for showing me that the sky is the limit; and to caffeine, my companion through many long days and nights of writing

CONTENTS

LIST OF ILLUSTRATIONS

FIGURES

TABLES

PREFACE

Kur shqiptari te jep fjalen, ai te jep djalin.
When the Albanian gives his word, he gives his son.

—ALBANIAN PROVERB

BALKAN TRAGEDY

The Roman philosopher Marcus Tullius Cicero once wrote: "During war, laws are silent" (*Silent leges inter arma*). Only strength, physical might, and power can establish "moral right." The use of violence is always concealed by lies, and the lies are maintained by violence. In the Balkans, the 1990s will be remembered as the *decade horribilis:* one of silent laws, bloody wars, deception, and crime.

I was eleven years old when the Socialist Federal Republic of Yugoslavia was drawn into a highly destructive conflict. Men with much to lose from a peaceful transition to free-market democracy killed off Yugoslavia; the federation did not die a natural, or historically inevitable, death. In part, the origins of the war can be traced back to the rise of Serbian nationalism among Belgrade intellectuals in the mid-1980s, and to former Serbian president Slobodan Milošević's conscious use of nationalism as a vehicle to achieve power.

In 1991 the collapse of the federal state culminated in the secession of its more developed republics, Slovenia and Croatia. By 1992 the struggle had shifted to Bosnia-Herzegovina, and Europe experienced the bloodiest war on its territory since World War II. In less than three years, more than 2.2 million Bosnian citizens were displaced, between one hundred thousand and a quarter of a million were killed, and an estimated twenty thousand to fifty thousand women were raped (Siebert 1997). The Muslims, unprepared for conflict, were to become the biggest victims—driven from their homes, their cultural heritage obliterated.

At the same time, in neighboring Albania, the government's laxity in economic regulation allowed fraudulent financial pyramid schemes, known as Ponzi schemes, to proliferate. The inevitable collapse of these schemes in 1997 eradicated the savings of a large section of the Albanian population. By January 1997 the people of Albania, who had lost about 1.2 billion dollars over the previous couple of years, took to the streets. Thousands of citizens launched daily protests demanding reimbursement by the government, which they believed was profiting from the schemes. Foreign countries began to evacuate their citizens from Albania. The pyramid-scheme crisis led to an outburst of anger and destruction that resulted in the deaths of almost two thousand Albanians. During the turbulent 1990s, Albania experienced some of the world's highest emigration rates. Some six to seven hundred thousand Albanians, or almost one-fourth of the population, emigrated mainly to Italy and Greece, driven by the economic and sociopolitical problems in their country (Martin et al. 2002; UNDP 2000).

Images of desperate refugees crowding into trucks and speedboats, angry street demonstrations, and destruction of property faithfully conveyed the anguish of the time. Newspapers also started writing about weapons moving from Albania to Kosovo, to be used in support of rising ethnic Albanian paramilitaries and criminal-terrorist movements. By March 1998 the situation in Kosovo had become highly unstable. The Balkan region witnessed the birth of a militant underground movement, known as the KLA (Kosovo Liberation Army, Ushtria Çlirimtare e Kosovës or UÇK) fighting against the abusive regime of Slobodan Milošević, and later for Kosovo's independence as well.

The international press labeled Macedonia, my native country, the Balkan "oasis of peace" because it wasn't as affected by the regional wars as the other republics. Once the conflict spread to Kosovo, however, it became clear that regional conflict would have serious consequences for Macedonia as well. Against the backdrop of a rising fear among the population in Macedonia, in July 1998 my parents sent me to Tennessee as an exchange student. I was sixteen at the time.

"It is the right thing to do!" my heartbroken mother said. "You will see the world . . . improve your English. You never know what will happen tomorrow here."

Soon after I left for the United States, several terrifying events brought the situation in Kosovo to the breaking point. The KLA attacks and the Serbian reprisals culminated with the Račak incident on January 15, 1999, during which forty-five Kosovo Albanians were killed in the village of Račak (Reçak) in central Kosovo. Various reports, including those prepared by Human Rights Watch, the Organization for Security and Cooperation in Europe (OSCE), and the International Criminal Tribunal of Yugoslavia (ICTY), characterized the killings as a deliberate massacre of civilians by Serbian police forces. The Yugoslav government maintained that the casualties were all members of the KLA killed in a clash with state security forces.

The Račak massacre became one of the main causes for the subsequent NATO bombing of Yugoslavia, a campaign that lasted from March 24 to June 11, 1999.

Every day during that year I spent endless hours in front of the television, anxiously watching the news reports about this unfolding Balkan tragedy. Critics were arguing that the West had failed to intervene decisively and with sufficient will and vigor. Others were criticizing NATO's military intervention, arguing that what occurred in Yugoslavia was not the international community's business. And while diplomats and politicians were arguing over the role of the international community in ending the war, the war was pursued with terrifying rationality by protagonists playing long-term power games. By April 1999, the United Nations reported that 850,000 people, most of whom were ethnic Albanians, had fled their homes. Western Europe, the United States, and Canada experienced a vast increase in ethnic Albanian refugees.

By this point, thousands of people had lost their lives. My hosts in Tennessee were a Baptist preacher and his family. We traveled from city to city, village to village, to listen to my host father preaching. "Send prayers to Jana and her family. Her country is at war, and her people need your prayers," he used to tell the passionate crowds. Coming from a postcommunist country, I did not understand religion well. There were many sad days, however, when I found comfort in it.

I returned to Macedonia in June 1999. NATO's intervention was concluding, and the conflict allegedly had ended. However, the problems were far from over, as the war crossed the border to Macedonia. The first actions by ethnic Albanians in Macedonia occurred in 2000, mainly along Macedonia's border with Kosovo. Between 2001 and 2002, ethnic killings intensified and a group of ethnic Albanians calling itself the National Liberation Army (NLA) appeared. The NLA claimed responsibility for attacks on Macedonian police forces, and we witnessed the Kosovo conflict being repeated on our territory.

According to the Macedonian government and media reports, in the period between 2001 and 2003 gas stations around the city of Tetovo were repeatedly robbed, vehicles were stoned while trying to leave the city, tollbooths on the Tetovo–Gostivar road were destroyed, and armed and uniformed Albanians were harassing ethnic Macedonian drivers at an impromptu "checkpoint" set up near the village of Poroj. The TV news regularly reported on incidents of kidnappings and torture in parts of Macedonia. Consequently, the government advised us residents not to leave our cities and to avoid traveling on specific roads.

While many people suffered during the Yugoslav conflicts, there is no doubt that some benefited from this ten-year cycle of war that swept the Balkan peripheries. Local newspapers claimed that the lack of regulations in the region allowed for the rise of a violent "Albanian mafia" and that the growing illegal trade in drugs, arms, and human beings made Kosovo, Albania, and Macedonia "hotbeds of organized crime." Starting around the turn of the twenty-first century, the so-called Albanian mafia went global. Many are familiar with the legendary Italian mafia and its notorious players—such as Al Capone, who ruled Chicago's underworld in the 1920s, and "Lucky" Luciano, who established the first US crime syndicate a decade later. Now the newspapers were noting that another powerful organized crime group, comprised of ethnic Albanians, was gaining prominence in the global criminal underworld and threatening the West. The international press frequently portrayed the Albanian mafia as the "new Sicilian mafia"—a highly secretive, brutal, and clan-based organization. Common people did not know much about the nature of this so-called sinister entity (Raufer and Quéré 2006), yet many felt threatened by it.

Throughout the Balkan region, as well as in many Western European countries, the rise of the Albanian mafia became a topic of great interest. During these lawless times, I opened a café bar (ironically called Decorum, meaning "dignity, politeness, and order") in Macedonia. What was I thinking? It should come as no surprise that four months into operating the business I became a victim of violence and extortion by local criminal groups. However, I learned a great deal from my unpleasant experience, and I turned it into something positive. Today, as a professor of international criminal justice, I specialize in Balkan organized crime. That is the irony of life.

FACING THE "ENEMY"

Café Bar Decorum

The café bar Decorum came to life in January 2001. At that time, the local Macedonian newspapers were writing about the spread of interethnic violence in the country, the uncertain future of the Balkan region, and the rise of ethnic Albanian rebels and mobsters retaliating against the Macedonian authorities and taking advantage of their compatriots. The following extracts are some examples of the events that were taking place at the time[1]:

January 22, 2001—A group of armed Albanians attacked a police station in the village of Tearce, near Tetovo, killing a police officer and injuring three others.

March 5, 2001—A soldier of the Macedonian army, Teodor Stojanovski, died after being shot by a sniper at the Tanusevci watchtower. Two other soldiers were killed and one seriously wounded when their vehicle hit a mine on the road leading from Skopje to the rebel-controlled village of Tanusevci.

March 14, 2001—Yesterday morning at 10:30, a group of armed and disguised people attacked a police patrol near the city of Tetovo.

April 28, 2001—Eight Macedonian police officers were killed in an NLA ambush, and their bodies were mutilated. The ambush was executed by Komandants Hoxha, Qori and Brada—all veterans of the KLA. Komandant Brada was a member of the Kosovo Intelligence Agency and was one of the main organizers of weapons smuggling in Kosovo.

These were terrible times for most small businesses in the Balkan region, but my acquaintance Vlado and I were optimistic about opening a café bar in Macedonia. "We will make a lot of money out of selling water!" Vlado used to say. For a few months the business went surprisingly well. It seemed that good company, music, and alcohol helped people to escape the harsh reality of poverty, war, and violence.

One night a group of men, known in our city to be thugs, racketeers, and "tough guys," visited our bar. They were powerfully built, with shaved heads and heavy gold chains around their necks. They drank good-quality Scotch whisky for almost two hours and then asked for the check. Because we were aware of their reputation for violence, we instructed the waitress not to charge them anything, hoping they would leave without causing trouble.

"It's on the house," she told them anxiously.

One of the guys, however, insisted on paying the bill. He acted as if he did not understand why we would let him drink for free.

"OK, please give me a moment and I will bring you the check. No problem," the waitress responded in a wobbly voice.

As soon as he paid the bill, the man approached my partner, Vlado, and asked him to step outside the bar. The man was in his early thirties, around five feet eight, with a large build and short, dark hair. His beard was fringed, and there was a visible scar on his face. He was certainly not a typical Decorum customer. In fact, he was reputed to be one of the leaders of a spectacularly elusive and violent gang of thieves and extortionists operating in our city. His name was Berisha.

Vlado and Berisha went outside to "chat." When Vlado came back, he looked very worried. And he was becoming visibly angry and upset over Berisha's bogus claims that we had "dishonored" him. "When he asked for the bill, he didn't expect that he would have to pay for the drinks of everyone else in this bar," Vlado said dryly, his eyes clouding over for a moment. Trouble was on its way.

Berisha demanded that we pay him two thousand euros for this "dishonor," and he threatened my partner: "I will be back for the money tomorrow. Have it ready or else. . . ."

Berisha and his group left. We were puzzled. What now? Vlado called a friend for advice.

"Just give them the money. They will not leave you alone otherwise," the friend advised. "Then just hope that they stay away for at least some time. But be aware that they will ask again for money in the future. They do this with other bars as well. And don't bother with the police. They can't do much."

"Why not the police?" Vlado asked, although he already knew the answer.

"Even if they take one in for questioning, the other guys will demolish your bar in a second. You will go out of business in the blink of an eye. It's not worth the trouble, trust me!"

I remember vividly the two days following that incident. To avoid a confrontation, Vlado and I did not go to the bar. Instead we stayed in Vlado's apartment. Every time he called the bar, the waitress informed him that someone from the group had paid a visit and "was looking for us." We also saw Berisha and his crew driving around Vlado's apartment a few times. I knew that we could not hide forever. Something had to be done.

On the third day after the incident at the bar, I called Tiger, an old acquaintance of mine from the city. Tiger was a tough street guy, a boxer. He knew everyone in town and could set up an appointment with Berisha. Vlado disliked my plan, but I assured him that confronting Berisha would be better than any other scenario we could think of. Tiger arranged the meeting.

It was a Friday evening, around 7:45. I found myself waiting alone in front of a church not far from Decorum, in the center of Macedonia's capital, Skopje. A few moments before 8 P.M., a black Mercedes pulled up in front of the church. Three big men were sitting in the car. In the front seat was Berisha. The back door of the car opened and an unfamiliar man told me to get in.

For a few moments no one said a word to me. The guys were having a conversation among themselves.

"Did you see the guy with the newspaper?" Berisha asked the driver, with a sarcastic smile on his face. "No doubt a secret agent. I can smell them from miles away."

Berisha then turned his head and finally started talking to me. "Why did you want to meet with us? And where is that gay friend of yours that sends his woman to deal with us? What a loser!"

Everyone started laughing. My head was spinning.

"The bar is mine," I finally said in a shaky voice. "Vlado has been helping me because I am often away in Greece for my studies, but the bar is mine. He has nothing to do with it, so it is pointless to ask him for money. I will give you the money if you think this is the right thing to do."

I stopped for a second to catch my breath. I was getting very nervous.

"But two thousand euros is a lot of money!" I continued. "I don't make that much profit, and it will be impossible to give you so much money. There are more expenses than profit for me at this point. But I will give you some money every month. Maybe one or two hundred euros every month? Will that work?"

Another brief moment of silence passed before I continued. I think it was easier for me to talk rather than to stop and listen to what Berisha had to say. I was afraid of his answer.

"But please leave Vlado alone. You are right that he is a coward, so there is no point in wasting your time dealing with a small fish like him. I am the bar owner, and I will give you the money. Let him go."

"What a loser this guy is!" the man sitting next to me interrupted. "Do you hear this, Berisha?"

Berisha and the driver were laughing. They seemed entertained.

"OK." Berisha finally got serious. "But tell that disgusting pig that if he tells anyone that we let him go like this, his family will find him in a box. Two feet underground! You hear me? He must say that he paid the money for dishonoring us. Every cent! Let me tell you, if I ever hear from anyone that Vlado said he didn't pay, you don't know what will happen to him. People will laugh at me if I let him go just like that! Take note of what I say to you."

Berisha stopped for a moment and muttered, "I can't even believe I am doing this. So, you will pay the money, huh?"

"Every cent," I replied. "As long as you give me enough time. And don't worry about Vlado. He knows better than to squeal."

We had been driving for almost forty minutes, although it seemed like just seconds to me. I had no idea where we were heading. It was somewhere on the outskirts of the city. Berisha had mentioned Kili's house. I'd heard Kili's name before, but I had never met him. "The head of their gang," I was thinking to myself.

The car pulled up in front of a big, old house in the middle of nowhere, with only dirt roads and miles of grapevines nearby. On the porch, at least ten men were playing cards and smoking cigarettes. At the sound of our car pulling into the driveway, the men moved around anxiously, until the moment they recognized the car and realized it was Berisha. We all got out of the car. Weapons lay on the floor next to the card table. Berisha told me to stay close to the car and wait. Everyone else went to shake hands with the men playing cards.

I could hear the crew laughing. Berisha and a short man went inside the house. Fifteen minutes later everyone was back in the car.

"Nice talking to you, m'lady," Berisha said after dropping me off at my apartment. "Call me when you have the money. This is my number. Call me if you need me for anything else, too."

The problem was solved. At least, I thought it was. I called Berisha three weeks after our first meeting to give him 150 euros. He seemed happy to hear my voice and invited me to an elite restaurant, where he and his group hung out most of the time.

"M'lady!" he shouted when he saw me enter the restaurant. "How have you been? Glad to see you, and glad you are keeping your word, m'lady."

I had lunch with Berisha and his crew. Afterward, he offered to bring me back home. I insisted on taking a taxi.

"You want to dishonor me again? I don't think so. My driver and I will take you home. Get in the car."

As we were driving, I took the money out of my pocket and gave it to him. Berisha looked embarrassed and humiliated.

"Hey, look at me. Big mafioso getting pennies from you. Now this feels like a joke. I am ashamed. Take your money back. No need for this. Just don't say to anyone that the bar didn't pay its dues. I have a business to run."

I remember feeling so proud of myself. I rushed to call Vlado as soon as I got home, just to tell him what had happened. He was not pleased at all, and I was not sure why. But I soon understood. Berisha and his crew had become regular customers at our bar. They stayed at the bar for hours. Although they always paid their bill, they sat with their weapons on the table. We lost all our other customers in less than three months.

The bar could not survive on the profits made from these fifteen tough guys, yet I felt as if I owed Berisha something. I often had to sit with his crew and listen to their bizarre stories. It was the most uncomfortable experience of my life. So many times I wished he had taken the money and left us alone. Berisha would call me at any time of the day, asking if I would come to the bar to keep him company.

"Why you are not at Decorum, m'lady?" he used to ask, as if he owned me. One day the waitress told me that Berisha had visited the bar and left a gold bracelet set with shiny diamonds. "A sign of his appreciation for your hospitality and friendship," the waitress quoted as she handed me the bracelet.

I did not accept the present, although I wondered how Berisha would react to this rejection. "Tell him that being hospitable and friendly is part of my job, and there is no need for gifts. The thought is what counts."

I avoided coming to the bar for about a week, so I would not have to confront Berisha. When I returned, he and I did not mention the bracelet. We pretended the whole situation had never happened. In these lawless years, many bar owners in our town were paying "protection" money to different criminal groups. I learned this the hard way.

Life in Greece

Eventually, the daily pressure became too much to handle. I started spending more of my time in Greece, where I was attending university. My aim was to distance myself from the troubles at home. But I couldn't bury my past. One night in early June 2001, after my summer classes were over, I received a phone call from an anonymous number.

"M'lady! Is that you? It is me, Berisha! I hope you didn't forget your old friend. I am here with Tiger, and he gave me your number. We just wanted to see how you're doing. Are you in Thessaloniki?"

I could not believe my ears. "What do they want now?" I thought to myself.

"M'lady, Tiger has some business in Khalkidhiki, close to where you are, so he will need to stay in Thessaloniki for a day or two. We were wondering if he could stay for a night at your place?"

"Sure, no problem." The words flew out of my mouth. I could not think fast enough to come up with a good excuse as to why he couldn't stay with me.

The next day Tiger arrived in Thessaloniki. We arranged to meet in a local tavern known for its superb seafood dishes. I arrived a bit early and, although I wasn't hungry, I ordered a Greek salad so my plate would not be empty. After fifteen minutes I looked up. Tiger was standing over my left shoulder with a smile on his face.

"Jana! I am so thrilled to see you! It has been such a long time."

"Not long enough," I thought to myself. I greeted him with a fake smile.

Every two or three weeks for the next two months, someone from Berisha's group had to stay at my apartment "for a night or two."

"My guys have to finish some work there, but they will be out of your way in no time," Berisha would tell me.

I was not sure what the nature of their business was, but from time to time I could overhear parts of telephone conversations. References were made to businesspeople in Khalkidhiki who wanted to transport cigarettes to Macedonia, and to credit cards stolen in Italy and Greece and used to purchase expensive clothes that could be resold in Macedonia. I heard mentions of loan sharking, extortion, smuggling luxury cars, and buying Italian passports. I never knew what these stories really meant and which parts were actually true.

Each time I entered the room, the conversations would end abruptly. I felt like a guest in my own apartment. It all felt like a bad dream—one in which I was watching my life fall apart before my eyes. "Eventually all this will stop," I reminded myself.

One day, right after my class, I received a phone call from Berisha. He told me that he and his crew had some business with Bosnian businessmen in Greece, and that they were all having dinner at the tavern Porto di Mare in Kalamaria.

"I expect you to come and see us. We are saving some seafood for you," said Berisha.

I did not even try to come up with an excuse. I just got into my car and drove to Porto di Mare. Seven men were sitting at a large table full of food. Calamari, *tzaziki,* eggplant, octopus, *kolokithakia,* fish, pitas . . .

Among the seven men I recognized the face of Kili, the man I'd met the day I had first negotiated with Berisha. He was one of the group's bosses. The men didn't discuss their business directly at the table. Yet on a few occasions they did mention Bosnian businessmen who were to deliver cigarettes for them, and they gossiped about the kidnapping of the son of a well-known businessman in Macedonia because of "unpaid bills." I stayed for about forty-five minutes, so I wouldn't "dishonor" Berisha, and then said I had to leave to finish a homework assignment.

The shocking news came in July, several days after Kili, Berisha, Tiger, and the other unknown men left Thessaloniki and went back to Skopje. My friend Mia called me from Macedonia to tell me the news. "A little before midnight, Marjan and his driver were shot dead in cold blood!"

Marjan, who was one of Kili's rivals—although some claim he was "friend and an associate"—and his driver had been killed in a busy area close to the center of Skopje. Two (some say three) men shot them as they were walking toward their car after they left the café bar Vitraz and had a quick stop in the nearby café bar Zoo (also known as Panta rei). The first man allegedly shot "the boss," Marjan, in his leg, and then in his chest and head. Eleven bullets were fired. A witness reported that Marjan begged him to stop but the assassin put his gun inside Marjan's mouth and fired (Popovski 2006). The driver started to run in panic. The second assassin shot him in the back as he was trying to climb over the parking lot fence.

According to witnesses, the assassins were professionals and left the scene quickly, so it was difficult to identify them (Popovski 2006; *Vest* 2001). When the police arrived, they found a black bag with two fully loaded guns, a Browning and a Russian-made Zastava, next to the bloody bodies. The victims never got a chance to use them.

But who killed Marjan and his driver? At that time no one knew who the killers were, yet gossip quickly started spreading. Marjan had a long police record and too many rivals. He was known as one of the most dangerous racketeers in the city and was doing the same work as Berisha and Kili. He was particularly infamous for shooting the owner of a famous restaurant in Macedonia; he'd fired nine bullets, aiming to kill, but luckily only one found its mark, ending up in the restaurant owner's foot.

"Marjan had a lot of enemies. He extorted shop owners in the shopping mall Beverly Hills. Everyone was paying him money. Major companies were paying big money, too," a friend of Marjan's told me (interview, Macedonia, 2001). "He injured the owner of a local café bar who refused to give him ten thousand euros. . . . Sorry, he refused to 'lend' him money. He also took six thousand euros from the owner of a music shop, and was asking for sixty thousand euros from one big businessman. He was no doubt blacklisted. Maybe this was the ultimate revenge of the local businesspeople."

I don't know if what he was telling me was the truth, but his words made me think of Decorum. Could Berisha or Kili have arranged this assassination? Alex, an old friend of mine, said, "Hey, today you can hire assassins for two or three hundred bucks. Albanians from the north of Albania are the best in this business. Life is very cheap nowadays! I am telling you, it's a sad reality for our region."

However, there was more support for the claim that the men involved in Marjan's shooting were professional assassins from Serbia and Montenegro. One scenario linked the shooting to Ljube Boshkovski, then the Macedonian minister of interior. The minister seemed to have been a close friend of Marjan, and he had helped him create the special police force called the Lions—a unit in which many criminals took an active role during the 2001 interethnic conflict. Marjan's father told a reporter for Macedonian newspaper *Utrinski Vensik* that the minister had promised Marjan that he'd make him the chief of the police station in Skopje if he brought him votes and helped him with the Lions (Popovski 2006; MKnews 2012). But then the brother-in-law of the minister was kidnapped and brutally injured, and many people speculated that Marjan had something to do with it because of a money-related dispute with the former minister. Allegedly, the minister and the chief of his security personnel promised one hundred thousand euros to Marjan if he burns the property of a well-known Macedonian businessman for insurance purposes. "These people had a lot of disputes. A lot of promises were made. Promises were not delivered. There was a lot of deception and behind-closed-doors talks. This is what happens when you mix politics with criminals," an insider told me.[2]

After Marjan's assassination neither Berisha nor Tiger contacted me again. They simply disappeared. Several months later, Vlado and I closed Decorum.

Empty Promises

Not long after the deaths of Marjan and his driver, my cousin introduced me to an ethnic Albanian man from Macedonia named Artan. Artan's family sold alcohol and cigarettes in Macedonia and along the Macedonia-Kosovo border. People close to Artan once told me that one of his family's small storefronts in the duty-free zone made more money than the entire Frankfurt Airport in Germany. This may have been an exaggeration, yet Artan's family was undoubtedly one of the wealthiest in our country.

Artan's older brother was kidnapped for ransom in 2002, and his family sent Artan to study in Greece in order to protect him from future troubles. In Macedonia, kidnappings of wealthy individuals were common around this time.

I was studying international relations and foreign affairs at the same university where Artan was due to start. My cousin asked me if Artan could stay at my apartment until he found a place of his own. Artan seemed like a pleasant person, so letting him stay at my place for a few weeks was not a problem.

Toward the end of 2002, Artan introduced me to his good friend Vuli, whose family owned a luxury car dealership in Macedonia. Vuli and I became fast friends. He was an adventurous and charismatic young man, fun to be around. Some people disapproved of my friendship with Vuli because he was ethnic Albanian. Some also said that he was a manipulative con artist who bought stolen jewelry from Kosovo, smuggled it across the borders, and resold it in Macedonia. I thought this was just gossip. "How far would people go to discredit someone because of his ethnicity?" I used to wonder.

With time, and through Vuli, I met many Albanians who were doing all sorts of jobs, some indeed illegal. Their businesses varied from loan sharking and selling forged university diplomas to dealing contraband cigarettes and stolen cars. In those days, I didn't care too much about how people made their living. According to the NGO Transparency International, 80 percent of the Albanian economy is a "parallel" one; for every hundred euros of documented capital, another eighty euros are never accounted for. Most of this undocumented capital comes from organized crime activities. At that time, the situation in countries such as Kosovo and Macedonia was not much different; many people were engaging in some form of illegal business to make ends meet.

In 2003 I graduated from university and returned to Macedonia, hoping to find a good job. Having a university degree, though, meant little. Only active membership in a political party mattered. I managed to get an entry-level, low-paying job as an office manager in a local NGO focusing on Euro-Atlantic integration. I worked for 130 dollars per month, enough to cover my parking expenses. By late 2003, I had had enough of the situation and decided to pursue my education abroad. I applied for a master's degree program in European criminology in Belgium.

After selling my car—a present from my parents—to finance my studies, I had some money left over that I felt I should invest somewhere.

"Listen," Vuli told me one day. "I can help you double your money if you want me to. I know you have plans, and you have been struggling with your job, so I would like to help out."

"How?" I asked, excited.

"I don't need to give you any details," he told me in a friendly voice. "Just give me whatever you have left, and every month you will get good interest on your money. In one year you will double your money—trust me."

Vuli promised that by the time I returned from Belgium I would be—in his words—a "rich girl," a dream for many young, ambitious Macedonians, including myself.

"You have my word, and my word is harder than a stone," Vuli reassured me. "Handshake?"

He gave me his *besa*—a word of honor and inviolable trust. As an old Albanian proverb goes, when an Albanian gives his *besa,* he would sooner lose his son than break his word. *Besa* is a sacred promise and it means more than any written contract.

I left for Belgium in September 2003. By the following month Vuli and my money were gone. I called and texted Vuli every morning and every evening for a couple of months, but no one ever picked up the phone. Eventually the number was disconnected.

My cousin knew an influential ethnic Albanian man called "Komandant Cati" who was willing to help me with my problem with Vuli. People called him "Komandant," or Commander, because he had taken an active part in the 2001 conflict in Macedonia and supported the Albanian national cause. He promised to get my money back for a "reasonable" 30 percent of the total amount, and he asked me to write on a piece of paper that the money Vuli had taken from me was actually his.

"This way I can deal with Vuli as if he owes me money personally," he explained. "If they ask you anything, you just say, 'Deal with Komandant Cati; that is his money.'" He gave me his *besa* too, assuring me that the problem would be solved.

After two months, Komandant Cati told my cousin that he couldn't betray his "own kind." Vuli was the son of a well-known Albanian "businessman," and Komandant Cati did not want to start a blood feud or enter into troubles for a "Macedonian girl."

At first, I was furious. "Empty promises, lies, and deception," I thought. Albanian honor culture, *besa,* and blood feuds—all were words without meaning. But then my anger turned into a curiosity about Albanian criminality and the causes of organized crime. I became more intrigued than dismayed. Berisha, Vuli, Artan, and Komandant Cati were no longer my enemies; I wanted to understand why they did what they did. How did we all get here? Who were these people? I felt a pressing need to make sense of the mythology surrounding ethnic Albanian organized crime. I needed to reflect on its reality—its origin, its nature, and its impact. With these questions in mind, I started my doctoral dissertation at the University of Leuven in 2004.

· · ·

The narratives presented in this book are about the dynamic relationship between culture, politics, and organized crime. They are based on more than a decade of empirical and ethnographic research on the causes, codes of conduct, activities, and structure of ethnic Albanian organized crime groups in the Balkans, Western Europe, and the United States. Most importantly, however, these narratives also are based on my own personal experiences and relationships with people from the Balkan region—something that no short-term empirical research can grasp.

Decoding Albanian Organized Crime is a book about the nature of Albanian organized crime and my experience as a researcher trying to conduct an objective study on an entity concealed in the criminal underworld. It is an attempt to identify and analyze, clinically and dispassionately, the crucial events and milestones that led to the rise of ethnic Albanian organized crime, and to reconstruct some of those events through the accounts of the people who took part in them.

ACKNOWLEDGMENTS

It would not have been possible to put this book together if many compassionate people from various countries—academics, practitioners, and common folks—had not shared their stories, knowledge, and experiences with me. My first acknowledgment goes to the Albanian people about whom I write. I have met so many hospitable Albanian men and women during the past two decades. My hope is that this book accurately reflects some of the truths, hurts, and passions that these people shared with me. I am very grateful to those whose life experiences fill these pages.

This project was first conceived at Leuven University in Belgium, and I am eternally thankful to my doctoral committee supervisors, Frank Verbruggen, Letizia Paoli, and Johan Leman, for their guidance and words of encouragement. I am also especially grateful to Cyrille Fijnaut and Henk van de Bunt for sharing their academic advice at times when I really needed it. I would like to extend my deepest gratitude to a friend and colleague, Stef Janssens, an analyst at the Human Trafficking Unit at the Center for Equal Opportunities and Combating Racism (CEOOR), for his support.

When I arrived in New York, I was lucky to meet Rosemary Barberet, an inspiring scholar and exceptional human being. She has been my mentor for the past five years, and there are no words to describe how grateful I am for her support and advice. There is nothing like having the help of mentors in facing the challenges of an academic career.

I am greatly indebted to a number of law enforcement officials for their participation in my research, and for sometimes going above and beyond to help a young scholar. In particular, I wish to thank Laurent Sartorius, Philippe Leys, Bruno Frans, and François Farcy from the Belgian Federal Police; Rene Bulstra from the

Amsterdam Police; Roger Stubberud, Pål Meland, Reidar Syversen, Bard Henriksen, Kai Holm, and Christian Berg from the Oslo Police; Siri Frigaard from the Prosecution Office in Oslo; Besim Klemendi from the Anti-Corruption Agency in Kosovo; Fatos Hajziri and Haxhi Krasniqi from the Directorate against Organized Crime within the Kosovo Police Service; Ardian Visha from the Public Prosecutor's Office in Tirana; Rosario Aitala from the EU Police Mission PAMECA in Albania; Vladimir Sharovic from the Unit on Violent and Serious Crimes within the Ministry of Interior of Macedonia; and Filip de Ceuninck from the EU Police Mission Proxima in Macedonia.

I would also like to extend my thanks to Haki Demolli from Prishtina University in Kosovo, Teuta Starova from Tirana University in Albania, and Borbala Fellegi from ELTE University in Hungary for their participation in the cross-national public survey I conducted in 2006–2007. They helped me greatly in the execution of this project, which was partially supported by a grant from the CERGE-EI Foundation under a program of the Global Development Network.

Several other people of great importance in my career are Arben Tabaku, former senior analyst at the EU Police Mission PAMECA in Albania; Patsy Sörensen, director of the Victim Shelter Payoke in Belgium; and Fatmir Qollakaj, from the Ministry of Social Affairs in Kosovo. Each has been a source of support. Also, special thanks to Elizabeta Nikoloska for familiarizing me with INTERPOL's Kanun Project.

Much appreciation is due to my colleagues at John Jay College of Criminal Justice, particularly Dr. Mangai Natarajan, with whom I have had numerous fruitful discussions over the years. I would also like to thank my research assistants and former students Michael Temple, Irini Gjoka, Adriana Michilli, Dimal Basha, Jeff Walden, Lauren Paradis, Malvina Selmanaj, and Armand Alia.

Moreover, I am extremely thankful to University of California Press editors Maura Roessner and Jack Young, who believed in my book project and made the publishing process smooth and pleasant. Special thanks to the reviewers, John Cencich and Phill Williams, for their valuable feedback on earlier drafts of this book. Working with my editor, Christine Kindl, has been a true pleasure. Her eye for detail is exceptional. I would also like to thank photographer Laurent Piolanti for the outstanding photography presented in this book. His photos tell a powerful story.

My sincere gratitude goes to those ethnic Albanian offenders who were willing to share some personal stories with me. This book tries to understand their actions and behaviors, not to judge them or the Albanian people.

Parts of the research presented in this book have been financially supported by various grants and agencies. This project was supported by Award No. 2012-IJ-CX-0004, granted by the National Institute of Justice, Office of Justice Programs, US Department of Justice. The opinions, findings, and conclusions expressed in this publication are, of course, mine and do not necessarily reflect those of the Department of Justice or the other funding agencies. The project also was supported financially by the Research Council of the University of Leuven and by the Open Society Institute (Supplementary Grant Program). Moreover, the Office for Sponsored Programs support for this project was provided by a PSC-CUNY Award, jointly funded by the Professional Staff Congress and the City University of New York. Funding for this work was also provided by a grant from the Office for the Advancement of Research at John Jay College. Without their generous financial support, this work never would have been done.

Last, but not least, I am eternally grateful to the people who give meaning to my life and who share with me all the little ups and downs that make life worth living. I thank my father, Nikola; my mother, Jelica; and my husband, Elie, not only for their endless encouragement and words of wisdom, but also for their critical reflections on parts of my work. They have been my greatest source of strength and inspiration.

I do not believe that people are either good or bad, criminals or law-abiding citizens. Crime is not always an objective truth that can be discovered, and rational thought is only one way of thinking. While some people conceive of things as either black or white, I believe that we live in a gray zone.

The scientist and writer Primo Levi challenged the tendency to oversimplify and gloss over unpleasant truths. He outlined the coercive conditions that cause people to become so demoralized that they will harm one another just to survive. He described the power of the situation that gives meaning to certain actions and subsequently changes people.[1] In anthropology, the term *liminality* ("a threshold") is used to describe a state of ambiguity or disorientation that occurs during rituals or rites of passage, but also during periods of rapid political and sociocultural change. During liminal stages, participants "stand at the threshold" between their previous way of structuring their identity, time, or community, and a new way, which the ritual establishes. The gray zone and the liminal stage have the power to change people's lives.

In my view, to be a cultural relativist and critical criminologist is a gift, but also a curse. This book tries to acknowledge and validate numerous "truths" about Albanian organized crime, and Albanian criminality in general. Some of these truths may anger the offenders because they do not glorify their actions—they are simple stories about crooks. Other accounts may anger law enforcement agents who believe these accounts seek to justify the actions of criminals or to shift the blame to a dysfunctional society. Some Albanian people may feel stigmatized by the book, while non-Albanians may believe me to be a great sympathizer and apologist for the Albanian people. Members of the media may believe this book criticizes their work, which I often describe as sensational. Some politicians may be upset because this book explains why certain versions of the "truth" have been presented to the public while others have been dismissed or ignored.

I can offer one partial solution to this multiple-reality "problem." I encourage readers to read the entire book with an open mind before rushing to any conclusions. Different truths are presented because I believe that crime means different things to different people. This book triangulates perspectives from numerous sources—from state agencies to victims, offenders to ordinary people—in order to present my own interpretation of the "truth." I can only hope that my version of the truth is acceptable to most of my readers, and particularly to the Albanian people about whom I write.

While studying criminology at the University of Leuven in Belgium, I developed a passion for qualitative and ethnographic research. It was there that I met the late professor William J. Chambliss, who gave a guest lecture on his paradigm-changing book *On the Take* and noted: "Going to the streets of the city, rather than [to] the records, may bring the role of corruption and complicity between political, economic, and criminal interests into sharp relief." I came to know Bill as an inspiring scholar who took to the streets and hung out with organized crime figures, as well as with drug dealers and petty criminals. Unafraid, he had a gift for seeking out those who were on the receiving end of an exploitive social system.

Like Bill, I wanted to meet the people I was writing about—and to talk with some of those people—in order to better understand their actions. Some of the names and identities in this book have been changed, mainly for safety reasons. I also disguised a few locations and altered the titles of certain groups and organizations. But the people, places, and groups are all real, and the material is based on written field notes whenever possible. A few of the stories go back to my teenage years in Macedonia, and these have been reconstructed from memory. Nevertheless, I have tried my best to reproduce conversations and events as faithfully and authentically as possible.

It should be noted that some of the claims expressly stated or implied in this book, with reference to certain suspects' involvement in criminal acts, may later have been dismissed by courts. No person mentioned in the context of an alleged offense, directly or indirectly, should be considered guilty unless a formal court verdict of guilt has been issued. Although this book refers to numerous court verdicts, and most of the Albanian offenders discussed have served or are still serving prison sentences, some criminal cases nevertheless have been described to illustrate the arguments of the theoretical framework based on anecdotal evidence and a de facto presumption of guilt. Not all of the cases discussed are necessarily supported by a de jure sentence—and that is the only legal condition to validate the involvement of a suspect in an offense.

I hope this book leaves you with much to think about, and that you enjoy reading it as much as I enjoyed writing it.

Chapter 1

INTRODUCTION

Ethnic Mob on the Rise

We had a sense they were an organization, but we were surprised at how aggressively they challenged New York's Italian organized crime families. They started taking territory, beating up "made men."

—FBI AGENT ASSIGNED TO THE RUDAJ INVESTIGATION (FBI 2006)

By 2004 the Balkan wars were officially over and the region seemed to be stabilizing. But mediators and politicians who initially took pride in bringing an end to the Yugoslav wars now were asking themselves if this newfound peace in the Balkans would be sustainable, or if it would devolve into another wave of wrenching violence. Some believed that what had been achieved in the Balkan region had nothing to do with a commitment to the peace process, or to a change of heart among rival leaders with conflicting visions. They feared that greed and violence still hung heavy in the air, and that the warlords and powerful criminals who benefited from lawlessness would be the ultimate victors. Talk about the creation of "mafia states" was not uncommon.

By the turn of the century, concerns about the rise of Albanian organized crime had spread beyond the Balkan region. "Genovese, Gambino, Bonanno, Colombo and Lucchese are nowadays called Hasani, Dzelilji, Fteja, Keka, Mehmedovici and Cakoni," observed French criminologists Raufer and Quéré (2006, 160). A number of reports published by reputable international magazines and institutions between 1990 and 2005 described the expansion of the "Albanian mafia" into continental Europe and the United States as a security threat.[1] Powerful organized crime groups comprised of Albanian-speaking criminals were gaining prominence in the global criminal underworld, they concluded. "Hollywood had created Tony Soprano," *The Times* reported, "but had failed to give the world a Toni Sapunxiu" (Pavia 2011).

Kosovo, in particular, was described as the nexus of human trafficking and the place where cartels directed illegal drugs, arms, diamonds, and human organs to the rest of Europe.[2] Newspapers and lighter publications repeatedly drew on the themes of ethnic homogeneity and extreme violence in the Albanian criminal

1

underworld.[3] Consequently, numerous myths arose about a ruthless, hierarchically structured and ethnically homogenous Albanian mafia that was moving easily across territories.

THE "NEW MAFIA" THREAT
Sex, Drugs, and Politics

Trafficking and smuggling flourished in the Balkan region during the 1990s. A number of nightclubs arose in western Balkan areas, in which large numbers of girls were kept in custody by the local bar owners. The town of Veleshta in Macedonia epitomized the problem. Beyond the busy central market, with its signs for ironmongers and butchers, were businesses with names like Bela Dona and Safari Club—brothels that give Veleshta and other towns in the Balkans a bad reputation. From Bosnia to Serbia, Montenegro to Albania, bars like those in Veleshta were packed with women and girls—mostly from Moldova, Ukraine, and Romania—who were tricked or kidnapped by traffickers and forced to work as prostitutes. For years, nothing was done about these so-called "sexual slavery" rackets. According to interviewed law enforcement officials from the EU Police Mission in Macedonia (Eupol Proxima), traffickers put corrupt local police, prosecutors, and judges on their payrolls, and it seemed that people did not care much about what was going on behind closed doors (interview, Macedonia, 2006).[4]

In Macedonia, the NGO Coalition All for Fair Trials reported that in 2005, nearly three-fourths of those convicted in Macedonia of human trafficking were of Albanian ethnicity.[5] There was evidence that the victims were traded first in Kosovo, then transported to Macedonia, and eventually returned to Kosovo (IOM 2004). These ethnic Albanian international human trafficking networks quickly gained a reputation for being exceptionally violent.

Drug trafficking and extortion rackets were another growing problem. The drug trade via the Balkan route was run largely by ethnic Albanian groups from Albania and Kosovo, and from Arachinovo and Kondovo in Macedonia.[6] In Macedonia, criminal groups such as one that went by the name "the Colombians," as well as the crews led by Dzjelal Ajeti, Zija Asani, Bajrush Sejdiu, Agim Krasniqi, and Arslan Nuishi, gained their criminal reputation in the 1990s and, according to reports, demanded a share of the Balkan criminal underworld. Naser Kelmendi, of Kosovo, and Lulzim Berisha, of Albania, were among the Albanian drug traffickers whose names became well known. For years, some of these groups had been involved in illegal trafficking of heroin and cocaine; illegal manufacturing, possession, and trafficking of weapons and explosive materials; and trade in stolen luxury cars and counterfeit cigarettes, as well as extortion and loan sharking. Also in Albania, the outlaw village Lazarat (Gjirokastra), which was reputed to be Albania's drug capital and off-limits to the police, has built a fortune from the cultivation of cannabis. According to the Italian financial police, the annual crop earns the traffickers almost six billion dollars, almost half of Albania's total GDP (Likmeta 2013b).

The ties between the Kosovo Liberation Army (KLA) and drug trafficking became another prominent topic in the press. Newspaper articles referred to intelligence documents showing that the KLA had aligned itself with an organized crime network centered in Albania that was smuggling heroin and cocaine to buyers throughout Western Europe and, to a lesser extent, the United States. Newspapers repeatedly argued that this Albanian criminal network was one of the most powerful heroin smuggling organizations in the world, and that much of its profits were being diverted to the KLA to buy weapons.[7]

The French criminologist Xavier Raufer (2002) also claimed that the only purpose of military operations led by the Liberation Army of Presevo, Medvedja, and Bujanovac (LAPMB) in southern Serbia and the National Liberation Army (NLA) in Macedonia was to keep heroin trafficking routes open. Raufer referred to the roads between southern Serbia and Macedonia that led to Kosovo as the "Balkan Golden Triangle." Similarly, according to Anastasijevic (2006), Kosovo was an ideal strategic location to store drugs smuggled from Macedonia, which then could be repackaged and sent to the West through Serbia or Montenegro.

Alarming the West

The rise of Albanian organized crime was of concern not only in the Balkan region. By the late 1990s, some 70 percent of the heroin reaching Germany and Switzerland was believed to have been transported through Albania or by Albanian groups, and the figure for Greece may have been closer to 85 percent (Galeotti 2001; Ghosh 2012). In November 2001, a report by Europol (Raufer 2007) estimated that 40 percent of the heroin on the streets in Europe was sold by Albanians. In 2005 the Italian Ministry of Social Solidarity reported that about 40 percent of the heroin trade in Europe was controlled by Albanian nationals, and in 2006 the Italian Central Directorate for Antidrug Services stated that Albanian nationals controlled 80 percent of Europe's heroin trade. One of the first scholars writing on this topic, Mark Galeotti, reported that ethnic Albanian communities in Europe provide street-level distribution networks. This, he observed, was especially important in Belgium, Germany, Switzerland, and Greece, which collectively have absorbed an estimated three hundred thousand illegal Albanian immigrants since 1991 (Galeotti 2001).

Researchers Alison Jamieson and Alessandro Sily argued that in Italy, of the mafias of foreign origin (such as the Russian, the Chinese, and the Nigerian organized criminal enterprises), the "Albanian mafia is considered the most powerful" (Jamieson and Sily 1998). In an interview with the BBC in 2000, one of Italy's top prosecutors, Cataldo Motta, added that Albanian organized crime had become "a point of reference for all criminal activity today" (Barron 2000). Writing for *The Times* (2000), Allan Hall and John Philips cited Piero Luigi Vigna, an Italian law enforcement officer, who stated that "Albanian clans are really the heirs to the ancient Sicilian Mob" (Hall and Philips 2000).

An officer of an elite group of the Italian gendarmerie noted that ethnic Albanians are among the most dangerous dealers of drugs and weapons—determined, ruthless, and capable of the worst when it comes to achieving their goals. According to a report from Marco Ludovico, Albanian criminals gradually formed alliances and accords with the Sicilian mafia; the Camorra, a similar group in Naples and Campania; and the 'Ndrangheta, or Calabrian mafia. In the words of the Italian intelligence agency SISDE,

> Dotted here and there, and based on a system of mutual aid, the Albanian presence is elusive, marked by internal solidarity, grid-like in its structure, flexible in its activities, very fast in its movements, and capable of gradually capitalizing the criminal profits which it makes. This is shown by its leading position in the sex market in Italy, in which the Albanians not only run the racket in their young female compatriots, but also now have control over other illegal immigrants from the Balkans. In the exploitation of prostitution, they have to stand against the Nigerians, the other powerful foreign mafia-style association which is present—and there has been no shortage of clashes. (BBC Monitoring 2005)

According to *Washington Quarterly* writers Cilluffo and Salmoiraghi (1999) Albanians have come to dominate smuggling within Europe, overshadowing their erstwhile mentors, the Italian mafia. Many countries have witnessed the rise of Albanian criminal organizations. European intelligence services have identified about fifteen mafia-style clans operating in northern Albania and involved in smuggling heroin throughout Western Europe. In 2001 and 2002, *The Independent* and *The Times,* referring to a UK Home Office briefing, wrote that the "tightening grip" of Albanian gangs on the vice trade was "changing the landscape" of Britain's sex industry (Burrell 2001). In Scotland, detectives have been particularly concerned about the arrival of the "ultra-violent" Albanian mafia. The Scottish Crime and Drug Enforcement Agency (SCDEA) noted that among all "non-indigenous" crime groups, ethnic Albanian groups pose the greatest threat. Former SCDEA director Graeme Pearson said: "The Albanians are a bit of a challenge because they have a military background in their homelands, and their criminal elements have a very violent history. They are very difficult groups to penetrate" (Laing 2012).

By the end of 2003, addressing ethnic Albanian organized crime was high on the agendas of many Western countries. In reports on organized crime prepared by the Council of Europe and Europol, it was noted time and again that ethnic Albanian organized crime groups constituted a major threat to the European Union and Norway because of their extreme violence and the fact that they had graduated from simple criminal service providers to working within the highest echelons of international organized crime.[8]

Ethnic Albanian criminal groups were, in fact, the only ethnic groups discussed in the 2006 Europol publication *The Threat from Organised Crime*. Also, the report *EU Organized Crime Threat Assessment* (Europol 2011) argues that Albanian criminal organizations play a significant role in the transport of cannabis in southeastern Europe. According to that report, the cannabis is grown in Albania and the surrounding region. From there it is sent to Greece, Italy, Slovenia, Hungary, and Turkey, where it is traded for heroin that is distributed in Western Europe.

In December 2000 Ralf Mutschke, assistant director of the Criminal Intelligence Directorate of INTERPOL, discussed the problems related to Balkan organized crime at a hearing of the Committee on the Judiciary Subcommittee on Crime.[9] He stated that future threats posed by Albanian organized crime groups were realistic given the ruthlessness displayed by these groups, the international links they already had established, the professionalism that characterized most of their activities, and the strong ties created by their ethnic Albanian origins. INTERPOL has since been active in collecting information on Albanian organized crime figures, and in 2006 it opened two new working files, "Kanun" and "Besa," focusing exclusively on ethnic Albanian criminals and drug traffickers. More than five hundred ethnic Albanians were listed in the INTERPOL reports as "wanted" on serious drug trafficking charges, which points to the significant involvement of Albanians in this highly profitable illegal market.

Although the drug estimates vary, a 2008 UNODC report on crime in the Western Balkans concludes, "There is round consensus that Balkan organised crime groups, and particularly ethnic Albanian groups, are a hazard in West Europe. Arguably, Albanian heroin dealers are the single most notorious Balkan organised crime phenomenon" (UNODC 2008).

Of course, Albanian organized crime is not just a European phenomenon; it has raised concerns among US law enforcement officials as well. The US Department of Justice, in its 2005 intelligence report, quoted Grant D. Ashley (2003), assistant director of the criminal investigative division of the Federal Bureau of Investigation (FBI), who stated that Balkan organized crime groups, particularly those comprised of ethnic Albanians, have expanded rapidly to Italy, Germany, Switzerland, Great Britain, and the Scandinavian countries, and are beginning to gain a strong foothold in the United States. Ashley added that these groups have been successful in their criminal endeavors both internationally and domestically, and that their illegal operations have increased at an alarming rate.

Special Agent Jim Farley, of the FBI office in Newark, New Jersey, led the bureau's Operation Black Eagle, which targeted Albanian drug traffickers in 2009. He noted that, in addition to Italian and Russian organized crime gangs, Albanians had begun moving expensive heroin into the United States. In 2004 the

Albanian-led Rudaj organization, known as "the Corporation," was labeled the "sixth crime family" in New York City, joining the five major Italian American crime families that have dominated New York's organized crime scene since the 1930s.[10] And when thirty-seven members of an Albanian criminal organization were arrested in 2011 for smuggling large quantities of cocaine and pills hidden in secret compartments inside luxury cars, court documents described the organization as being comprised of several ethnic Albanian immigrant families with a code of honor, strong ties to the homeland, and a record of ruthless violence (Pavia 2011).

The "Mafia" Characters

A number of so-called Albanian mafia bosses made a name for themselves, both in Europe and in the United States. For instance, Kapllan Murat, a Belgian criminal of Albanian descent, was the driver for the notorious Haemers gang, which kidnapped former Belgian prime minister Paul Vanden Boeynants in 1989. Murat worked closely with Basri Bajrami, an ethnic Albanian man from Macedonia. In 1993, Kapllan Murat and Basri Bajrami escaped from the Saint-Gilles prison in Belgium with Philippe Lacroix, another Haemers member. The trio demanded that a stolen BMW be driven inside the prison gates, to be used as an escape vehicle. They tied a prison guard and the prison director to the roof of the car, and the Belgian gendarmerie could do nothing but watch the convicted men flee the scene. Between 2003 and 2008 Murat was jailed and released several more times in Belgium, mainly for stealing CDs and burglarizing a store. In 2008 he left the prison of Nivelles after being granted a conditional early release.

During the 1990s, according to newspaper articles and police statements, Kosovo Albanian offender Viktor Hoxha was considered the new "boss" of the Albanian mafia in Belgium. He was known as the leader of an ethnic Albanian criminal group comprising about twenty members who specialized in extortion rackets and prostitution in Antwerp, Belgium. He also presided over a "security" team whose members worked the front doors of several nightclubs in Antwerp's Central Station area. In 1998 he was sentenced to fifteen and a half years in prison. After serving half of the sentence, he was paroled on the condition that he return to Kosovo and never come back to Belgium.

A Kosovo Albanian man known as Princ Dobroshi also captured the world's attention. Dobroshi was considered the leader of an Albanian drug gang in Kosovo. For years he controlled the northern path of the Balkan heroin trade route, and in 1993 he was arrested in Norway for trafficking heroin. In 1997 he escaped from the Ullersmo prison in Oslo until he was found, arrested, and prosecuted in 1999.

Then there was Agim Gashi. In July 1998 the special anti-mafia unit of the Italian carabinieri, known as the ROS, launched Operation Africa, aimed at dismantling an important Albanian criminal network that was trafficking drugs and weapons. At the head of the group was Gashi, an Albanian from Kosovo who had established close professional links with the 'Ndrangheta, or Calabrian mafia. Gashi was convicted in March 1999 in Milan. The newspaper *Corriere della Sera* (1998) cited an officer of the Italian ROS who said that Kosovo Albanians were among the most dangerous traffickers in drugs and arms: "These men are determined, violent, and capable of the worst" (Raufer 2002).

Another Albanian, Luan Plakici, used a false British passport to find the "poor, naïve, and gullible" (BBC 2003a) in Eastern Europe and traffic them to Western Europe for the purpose of sexual exploitation. He even married one teenage girl before telling her that she would be spending her wedding night working as a prostitute. Detectives said that Plakici was involved in the biggest case of human trafficking for prostitution seen in the United Kingdom, supplying women to brothels in north London, Bedford, Luton, and Reading (BBC 2003a).

In Albania the name Aldo Bare and the Lushnje gang (Banda e Lushnjës) makes many people anxious even today. During the late 1990s, Bare and his associates beheaded people, burned houses, produced and smuggled drugs, and threatened and killed both police officers and prosecutors. The gang members paradoxically called themselves "guarantors of the law" and "untouchables." Bare was best known for killing his rival Artur Daja in 1998.

During the first decade of the twenty-first century, some more "sophisticated" organized crime figures emerged. On March 26, 2011, Tirana's Serious Crimes Court ordered the detention of Albanian businessman Dhimiter Harizaj on charges of involvement in international drug trafficking. The arrest followed the seizure of two hundred kilograms of cocaine, which had been found mixed into a shipment of palm oil. Harizaj said he had purchased only the palm oil and knew nothing about the concealed cocaine. The stash, seized in Gjirokastra, was the largest quantity of smuggled cocaine the Albanian authorities had ever found (Karadaku 2011).

The list of characters does not end here, of course. Hundreds of notorious ethnic Albanian offenders have been involved in transnational crimes and are considered highly dangerous by the international community. Albanian crime figures have appeared in popular culture, too. They are the main characters in films such as *Taken* and *Taken II*, *Casino Royale*, *The Nest*, *Pusher III*, *Dossier K*, *In with Thieves*, and *The Brooklyn Connection*. As one Internet blogger wrote in 2008 on the forum Streetgangs.com, "It is crazy how every thread on gangs and crime that has nothing to do with the Albanians ends with the rise of the Albanian mafia."

The underlying contradiction is that although the Albanian crime phenomenon has been extensively publicized in the last decade, there has been limited scientific research explaining it in a methodical manner. Existing studies on the topic appear to be fragmented and outdated, and they rely too heavily on unsubstantiated media accounts.

Today the impression remains that Albanian organized crime is becoming more powerful, that Albanians have formed alliances and accords with the Sicilian mafia and La Cosa Nostra (LCN), and that the Albanian mafia is marked by internal solidarity and grid-like structures. The Albanian mafia has diversified its criminal portfolio and is now involved in activities ranging from drug, weapon, organ, and human trafficking to extortion, credit card fraud, counterfeiting, and theft. Honor codes, *besa,* secrecy, hierarchy, brutality, ethnic homogeneity, and revenge killings remain key attributes associated with the Albanian mob.

THE BOOK AND THE MYTHS

Several conclusions emerge regularly in the existing literature on Albanian organized crime: first, that the Albanian mafia is composed of some fifteen to twenty clan-based or kinship-based "families" that strictly obey traditional codes of conduct; second, that it is a hierarchically structured, extremely violent, and highly secretive organization; and third, that it poses a serious threat to Western societies because of its ability to learn, adjust, and grow.[11]

This depiction of Albanian organized crime as a family-based bureaucracy imported from mysterious foreign regions resembles that of La Cosa Nostra, as presented by the first American *pentito* (insider or a defector), Joseph Valachi; the criminologist Donald Cressey (1969); and Mario Puzo's film *The Godfather* (1972). But is this an accurate portrayal? This image of fifteen strategic and brutal Albanian mafia families that strictly obey the ancient Kanun laws and send their "soldiers" to advanced market economies to expand their criminal empire certainly needs further analysis.

Decoding Albanian Organized Crime is an empirically based and theoretically founded book about the causes, culture, structure, politics, action, and migration of ethnic Albanian organized crime groups operating in Western societies and the Balkan region. It attempts to make sense of the mythology surrounding the topic of ethnic Albanian organized crime, although its implications are much wider. To that end, I examine some of the most widespread myths about the so-called Albanian mafia:

- that the traditional Albanian "culture of violence" and the customary Kanun laws have led to a drastic increase in organized crime in Albania;
- that the Albanian mafia is the new Sicilian mafia;
- that there is one nationwide Albanian mafia;
- that this Albanian mafia is hierarchically structured, with families, bosses, and underbosses;
- that this organization adheres to the ancient Albanian customary Kanun laws (code of conduct);

- that Albanian mafia ties are those of blood (homogeneous groups based on blood ties);
- that this criminal organization is extremely violent;
- that the Albanian mafia is highly secretive and impossible to infiltrate;
- that the organization is hypersophisticated, rational, and able to easily adjust to its environment;
- that the Albanian mafia is able to move easily across territories and gain control of foreign territories; and
- that politicians in the countries of origin (Albania and Kosovo) control the Albanian mafia.

On a broader level, this book contributes to the cultural and critical dimension of criminological and sociological theory, as well as to the debate on organized crime.

THE CHALLENGES

Many scholars have argued that organized crime is a topic beyond objective measure. Indeed, it is difficult to conduct reliable empirical research on an entity concealed in the criminal underworld. Only rarely can law enforcement officers and researchers observe the activities of a criminal group directly.[12] Even if it were possible to interview offenders, one should remain skeptical about the reliability and validity of the data collected. Some authors have maintained that accounts given by offenders and informers are often self-glorifying fantasies (Potter and Jenkins 1985).

Because it is almost impossible to gain direct access to the internal dynamics of a criminal organization, social scientists are forced to rely on accounts supplied by police, judicial authorities, and the media, and on reports from key witnesses. Gaining access to police files and interviewing victims or witnesses, however, is far from a simple task. The police are not eager to give up their information, and victims are often reluctant to say a word. Also, as collaborators in the judicial process, police informants are often entitled to police protection, living allowances, and a reduction in their prison terms, which might affect the reliability of their testimonies.

Collecting scientific data on organized crime in a variety of jurisdictions is also difficult because of definitional problems and language barriers. And there is no guarantee that official agencies concentrate on the most serious crime problems.

Clearly, the reality of organized crime is not easy to discover. As noted previously, the situation is made even more challenging by the fact that writers looking to sell newspapers and lightweight academic publications sometimes accept poor empirical data without question. Organized crime as a research topic, nevertheless, offers an exceptional opportunity to utilize a truly interdisciplinary research methodology.

Decoding Albanian Organized Crime is based on research conducted over a period of ten years, and the method used is that of triangulation—the application and combination of several research methodologies in the study of the same phenomenon. The purpose of triangulation is to obtain confirmation of findings by comparing different perspectives. By turning to multiple observers, theories, and empirical materials, criminologists can hope to overcome the intrinsic biases linked to single-method studies.

This book therefore combines different qualitative and quantitative approaches to exploit the strengths of each. In the course of my research, I have traveled to eleven countries across two continents and interviewed more than seventy law enforcement officials. I have conducted in-depth interviews with prosecutors, judges, and police from Belgium, the Netherlands, Norway, Italy, the United Kingdom, Switzerland, the United States, Albania, Kosovo, Greece, and Macedonia, among other countries. The stories told by these experts are one part of this book.

I also interviewed representatives of NGOs, victims shelters, and international organizations, as well as journalists, academics, and victims of trafficking and smuggling. I spent a total of two years in Albania, Kosovo, and Macedonia solely for the purpose of completing these interviews.

Additionally, I looked into more than fifty police files and court cases from Belgium that involved ethnic Albanian criminals who were active mainly (but not exclusively) in prostitution and in trafficking and smuggling human beings between 1992 and 2009. Some of these Albanian-speaking offenders also were involved in illegal drug trade, arms trafficking, extortion, and organized theft. Based on these police files, I helped to develop a comprehensive database with 259 criminal profiles that allowed me to observe how some of the groups' characteristics changed over time.[13] A brief analysis of statements given by victims of Albanian traffickers was undertaken as well, and some of their stories are presented in this book.

The conclusions in this book also are based on an additional thirty-seven court cases from the United States involving ethnic Albanian offenders who were prosecuted for various organized crime activities committed between 1975 and 2013. Based on these files, I have created a single comprehensive database with an additional 237 criminal profiles categorized by twenty criteria.

In 2006 and 2007 I conducted a cross-national public survey, with 864 ethnic Albanian respondents from Albania, Macedonia, and Kosovo, on the meaning of violence and crime in an ethnic Albanian context.[14] Structured questionnaires and extensive face-to-face interviews were used. I postulated that cultural norms promoted by the Kanun of Lek Dukagjini, a foundation of traditional Albanian culture, play a significant role in shaping ethnic Albanians' perceptions of violence

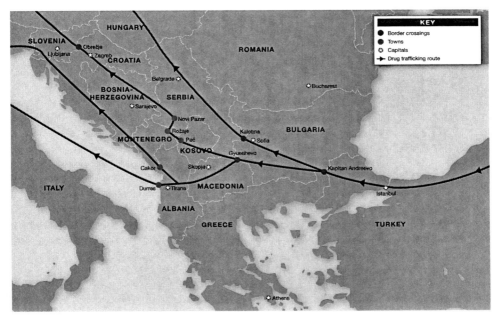

FIGURE 1. Drug trafficking routes in the Balkans used by ethnic Albanian organized crime groups.
Source: Jane's Intelligence Review, 2009.

and crime. Thus the survey questionnaire was aimed at assessing the importance of the customary Kanun laws among ethnic Albanians, as well as the respondents' knowledge about the laws.

From January to April 2009, I also underwent training at INTERPOL's Criminal Analysis Unit in Lyon, France, and familiarized myself with the project "Kanun," dealing with ethnic Albanian criminals and drug trafficking. Most of the information I gathered there is confidential and thus not cited in this book, but the training helped me to better understand the magnitude of Albanian organized crime around the world.

Twelve semi-structured interviews were conducted with less accessible research subjects—the organized crime offenders themselves. A few of those interviews were conducted with convicted offenders in a prison setting. In order to understand the offenders' actions, it is useful to consider the self-created narratives that help to give form and significance to those actions. As a result of these interviews, the stories of some Albanian offenders depicted in the media as Albanian mafia bosses are also a part of this book. I have used aliases and changed some of their real names to preserve anonymity.

My research does not stop here. Since 2012 I have been actively studying the migration patterns of Albanian organized crime groups to foreign territories, focusing on their expansion to the New York/New Jersey area. This study, supported by the National Institute of Justice, is based on interviews with ethnic Albanian offenders, law enforcement officials, and people from the ethnic Albanian diaspora who live and work in and around New York City. More than sixty in-depth interviews were conducted with Albanian migrants, both legal and illegal, in New York on the topics of migration, crime, culture, and social exclusion.

Collecting reliable information on organized crime is a challenging job. In Albania, Kosovo, and Macedonia, official data on organized crime are often unavailable or unreliable. Victims and the general public are afraid to talk because they fear revenge. Moreover, the lack of previous research on the topic has made it difficult, if not impossible, for me to compare my conclusions with previous findings. Despite these obstacles, I am hopeful that this book will provide readers with a detailed, nuanced, and objective picture of Albanian organized crime.

Chapter 2

WHY WE DO WHAT WE DO

*In a society such as ours where emotions stand against the rational and
material world, those without wealth are left only with the world of emotions
to express their hurts, their injustices and their identity.*
—MIKE PRESDEE, *CULTURAL CRIMINOLOGY* (1999, 4)

Most conventional perspectives on organized crime start with the assumption that
criminals are "rational" and approach their crimes in the calculating spirit of making money. But are Albanian criminals strategic players motivated by economic
payoffs, or are their decisions based on normative-affective considerations? Might
organized crime be as much about emotions—hatred, anger, frustration, excitement, and love—as it is about poverty, possession, and wealth?

In 2005, when Sali Berisha became Albania's prime minister, the Albanian government clamped down on key organized crime figures. Twelve of the largest
criminal clans in the country were investigated in 2005, and more than 150 members of so-called "mafia families" were arrested (World Bank 2010). Primarily as a
result of the pressure that the European Union and the United States put on the
Balkan region to reduce organized crime, major crime figures were arrested in
neighboring Kosovo, Macedonia, and Bosnia-Herzegovina.

The convictions of notorious ethnic Albanian organized crime figures such as
Aldo Bare, Lulzim Berisha, Dritan Dajti, and Naser Kelmendi between 2005 and
2013 prompted a closer look at some common assumptions about the origins and
nature of these groups. In particular, it brought into question the notion that
organized crime figures are rational, or at least exhibit limited rationality, and that
the reemergence of the traditional Albanian culture of violence and crime might
be an important factor in explaining the rising tide of criminality in contemporary
Albanian society.

But what can a study of societies permeated by a history of violence, patri·
and incomplete modernization tell us about the motivations and
processes of Albanian organized crime figures? The complex

operational context—political, sociocultural, and economic—in which some of these organized crime groups flourished should be studied prudently in order to understand the decision-making processes of Albanian offenders, as well as their cognitive limitations and extremes in emotional arousal. A systematic analysis of the political dimension of Albanian organized crime—as well as the contribution of social forces including anomie, strain, and "culture conflict" to the formation of predatory criminals—may provide answers to pressing questions such as: What turned many Albanians to a life of crime, and at what point in their life? Are Albanian organized crime offenders amenable to long-term incentives for abandoning crime? Do they desire instantaneous, rather than delayed, gratification? Do they seek political power and influence over the way state institutions set and enforce the rules of the market within which they operate, or do they use violence and other tactics mostly to enlarge their profits? What role do history, values, and emotions play in their decision-making processes?

LIFE, PEOPLE, AND SITUATIONS
Albania: The Vengeful "Professor"

Alfred Shkurti (known as "the Professor"), who in 1998 changed his name to Aldo Bare, is recognized as the leader of the notorious Lushnje gang (Banda e Lushnjës), which was formed in 1997 in the city of Lushnje, in western Albania. Over his fourteen-year career, Bare became a high-profile figure in Albania. Beginning in the late 1990s, he and his associates committed murders, manufactured explosives in their own laboratories, threw grenades at the properties of their rivals and victims, produced and smuggled drugs, killed police officers, and extorted and kidnapped people for money.

In the early 1990s, Bare was a police officer in Albania. Amid the postcommunist turbulence of 1992, he was suspected of killing an Albanian citizen during a police riot in the Albanian city of Durrës. His guilt in this case, however, was never legally proven. In 1993 Bare fled to Greece and then to Italy, along with tens of thousands of Albanians who migrated to these neighboring countries to escape chaos and poverty in their homeland. Not much is known about Bare's life between 1993 and 1997, although it appears that he may have taken up crime during this period.

Patriotic feelings grew among some ethnic Albanian expatriates during the late 1990s because of the instability in Albania and Kosovo and the suffering of the Albanian people; consequently, some returned to the region to fight while others financed political parties from abroad. These were some of the most unstable years in recent Albanian history, and proactive criminals also saw an opportunity to establish ties with politicians in Albania. Bare came back to Lushnje in 1997, during the collapse of the Albanian pyramid schemes—a time when people were losing not only their money but also their lives.

It seems that a new stage in Bare's criminal career—as we know it today—began in the summer of 1997, after his brother Ramadan Shkurti was killed by an Albanian man known as Artur Ahmet Daja. Police sources indicate that the conflict between the Bare brothers and Daja might have started years earlier over arguments related to the control of the drug market in Italy. However, it was in June 1997 that Bare, with his brother and cousins, damaged the cars of Daja and his associates. This resulted in an exchange of gunfire that left Daja wounded and his friend Genci Kashari dead. In the crossfire, Daja ended up killing Bare's brother and cousin and seriously injuring another cousin.

Bare then created his own group of about fifteen heavily armed Albanians, Banda e Lushnjës, to avenge the death of his brother. According to police sources, this feud led to the disappearance or death of approximately twenty-five additional people, as well as many kidnappings and cases of torture, some of which took place in Bare's garage, referred to as Station No. 2. After much bloodshed, in October 1998, Bare found, brutally killed, and decapitated Daja, his brother's alleged killer.

After 1998, at the beginning of the Kosovo conflict, Bare's group grew in strength, and it became involved in the drug trafficking business in Turkey, Bulgaria, Macedonia, and Romania. By 2002 Bare was known as one of the most dangerous Albanian crime bosses.

Bare allegedly had close connections with politicians in Albania and, according to local sources, rode in Albanian police cars. "Police officers and judges were on his payroll," locals used to say. In an interview from 2010, a local police officer noted that around the turn of the century, a few honest Albanian police officers tried to bring Bare down, but they were never successful. Bare was always "set free" or "left alone" by judges and prosecutors because of his political connections and violent reputation (interview, Albania, 2010).

Bare, the former police officer, targeted police, members of the secret service, politicians, businessmen, and rival gang leaders. For years no institution in Albania wanted to deal with Banda e Lushnjës, for fear of reprisal. This allowed the group to operate with impunity and to terrorize the people of Lushnje until 2006, when Bare and seven members of the group finally were arrested. Bare was arrested in Ankara, Turkey, and was extradited to Albania in November 2009.

After more than a decade of criminal activity, Bare was convicted on March 28, 2011, by the High Court of Serious Crimes of Albania for organizing a criminal syndicate, committing seven murders, destroying property, illegally possessing firearms, desecrating graves, trafficking drugs, and committing crimes through his criminal organization.[1] His group was accused of ordering the murder of local police officers and state officials and bombing the houses of various poli~ who were investigating its criminal activity. Petrit Lici, one of Bare's group who later provided evidence against other membe

Judge Artan Gjermeni, who had been working on Bare's case, was corrupt and linked to the group.[2]

Bare continued to make threats even while he was in custody during his trial. He was brought to the courtroom under heavy guard and was held behind bars, even inside the courtroom, for "security reasons." He showed no remorse and threatened anyone who interfered with the properties he had acquired through crime. The following is an extract (translated from Albanian) from a conversation between Bare and Judge Hajdari during his trial.

> *Bare:* There is no motherf . . . who can take the Lagoon from me. I would f . . . Sali Berisha's mother and anyone else who would touch that property!
>
> *Judge Hajdari:* Calm down and don't intimidate in the courtroom.
>
> *Judge Hajdari:* Sit down and stop threatening people.
>
> *Bare:* Whilst I am alive, no one will enjoy the Lagoon! Not even Sali Berisha, nor any court, nor any other person!
>
> *Judge Hajdari (to the police):* Take him out. Cuff him and take him out for court disorder.
>
> *Bare:* I will kill, even from the position I am in, anyone who touches my property!
>
> *Police:* Come on, move! (*They handcuff him.*)
>
> *Bare:* And you, why do you look at me like that? I can straighten you out too, you . . . (*He curses at a staring police officer.*)[3]

Bare, who did not seem to care much about consequences, was sentenced to life in prison. When Judge Fatmira Hajdari read the sentence, the silent, calm, and cold Aldo Bare did not make any declarations or jokes, as he had done throughout his trial. His only reaction was a disapproving facial expression. When the judge read the words "to be served in a high-security prison," the former Lushnje gang leader just smiled (see chapter 5 for a more detailed discussion of Bare's criminal career).

Kosovo: The Calculating Businessman

In neighboring Kosovo, another ethnic Albanian organized crime figure was on the rise: Naser Kelmendi, a wealthy businessman. Although on the surface Kelmendi's operational methods appear different than those of Aldo Bare, these two organized crime figures started their criminal careers in similar highly politicized, unstable, and emotionally charged environments. Police, including INTERPOL, have repeatedly claimed that Kelmendi runs a major cocaine and heroin trafficking organization out of a family-owned hotel in the Bosnian capital, Sarajevo. In 2012, the US Treasury barred American citizens from doing business with Kelmendi and placed his name on a list that allows authorities to freeze any of his US assets. Kelmendi has dual Kosovo and Bosnian citizenship, and he is wanted by

Bosnian authorities in connection with at least six murders, as well as illegal money transfers and drug trafficking.

To understand better who Kelmendi is, we need to look at his past. During the early 1990s, police reports show, he was involved in the cigarette smuggling business in Kosovo, although no charges were brought against him. In 2001 UN Mission in Kosovo (UNMIK) police confiscated contraband cigarettes belonging to Kelmendi and his associate Ekrem Luka—a wealthy, powerful, and controversial Kosovo businessman—in the village of Zahać in Kosovo. The value of the cigarettes was estimated at thousands of euros. In October 2002 members of the Italian police, while trying to disrupt the main cigarette smuggling routes in Kosovo, searched Luka's business premises in Zahać and seized approximately 280 tons of cigarettes. Luka and Kelmendi were taken into custody on charges of illegal tobacco production and sale of counterfeit cigarettes, although no trial was subsequently held (CIR 2009). Confidential sources indicate that a large part of the illicit proceeds from the cigarette sales came into the hands of the Kosovo Liberation Army (KLA), which points to political-criminal ties during the period of armed conflict in the region. Kelmendi was known by local and Western law enforcement agencies as a KLA financier, and this may have been one of the reasons he was able to operate in the country for so many years (JIR 2009; CIR 2009).

When UNMIK began focusing its attention on his Kosovo operations, Kelmendi moved his criminal empire to Bosnia-Herzegovina. Drug trafficking, particularly heroin trafficking, became his primary criminal activity in the early years of the twenty-first century, when a number of powerful and well-connected individuals who had controlled the cigarette smuggling market used the same routes and connections to move into the more lucrative drug trade.[4] In 2009 Saud Bulić, the former chief of police in Novi Pazar, Montenegro, noted that, for the previous seven years, drug clans from his city had sent between twenty and thirty kilograms of heroin to Sarajevo each week. Sarajevo had become a safe haven for Balkan criminals (CIR 2009).

In 2008 Western law enforcement agencies noticed that Kelmendi was relocating his criminal activities from Bosnia to Kosovo and Montenegro. Competition with Bosnian criminal groups, as well as intensive police operations targeting Kelmendi's operations, appeared to be behind the move. In order to ensure immunity and gain political support for his criminal activities in Kosovo, Kelmendi used an intermediary to deliver 1,000–1,500 euros to politicians in Kosovo, allegedly to strengthen his contacts with them and with former members of the KLA. Intelligence also showed that Kelmendi had strong ties with the Kosovo police. Since his arrest in Kosovo in May 2013, members of the media wondered if Kelmendi will be extradited to Bosnia-Herzegovina (*The Guardian* 2013).

Kelmendi's son Elvis, also a member of the group, was arre
police in 2012 on an arrest warrant issued in Bosnia, but he later wa

police custody. The EU authorities that deal with serious crimes in Kosovo detained Elvis Kelmendi immediately after the Kosovo police let him go, and they held and subsequently sentenced him to four years in prison for the attempted murder of Elvis Hodzic, in 2010.

Macedonia: The Daring Chameleon

And then there is Basri Bajrami, an ethnic Albanian from Macedonia who left his native country in the late 1970s, when he was in his twenties, in a search for a better life in the West. En route to the United States he stopped in Belgium, where he ended up spending the next thirty years of his life—fifteen in prison and fifteen as a free man. In Belgium, Basri started a life as a businessman. In his own words, he owned shares of a well-known casino in Brussels, at the Sheraton hotel. For the first few years business was good, but Basri had issues with paying taxes he claims he shouldn't have paid, and argued that the Belgian government "extorted" money from him. He blamed the prime minister at the time, Paul Vanden Boeynants, who himself was convicted in 1986 for fraud and tax evasion.

Basri's life changed significantly around 1985 when he was accused of an armed robbery, although he claims that he never committed the robbery, and that the arrest was a setup. He was convicted and sent to prison in Belgium, where he began to establish new criminal connections. After his release, Basri helped Patrick Haemers, a fellow prisoner and future criminal associate, to escape from prison. Then, along with Haemers, Kapllan Murat, a Belgian offender of Albanian origin, Denise Tyack, and Philippe Lacroix, he started planning the kidnapping of the former prime minister whom he blamed for extorting money from him and from the casino.

For nearly five months, Basri Bajrami and his group patiently followed the prime minister. Finally, Vanden Boeynants was kidnapped on January 14, 1989. Three days later, the criminals published a note in the leading Brussels newspaper, *Le Soir*, demanding thirty million Belgian francs (one million dollars) in ransom. Basri himself noted that the group initially demanded twenty million German marks (about thirteen million dollars) but decided to take five million German marks (about three million dollars) because, in his own words, "it is easy to kidnap someone but it is difficult to get large sums of money" (Lupevska 2009). Vanden Boeynants was released (physically unharmed) a month later, when, according to Basri Bajrami, the ransom of five million German marks was paid to the perpetrators.

Soon after, Patrick Haemers, Kapllan Murat, and Basri Bajrami were arrested. While in prison they carefully planned their sensational escape from St. Gilles prison. Haemers hanged himself in his jail cell in 1993, but the other two managed to escape. Basri Bajrami fled to Macedonia, where he started a new life, again as a businessman. The Macedonian government, however, extradited him to Belgium to serve his sentence, but he is now back in Macedonia, where he is a wealthy businessman, with strong political connections in Kosovo and Albania. He says he is just a regular family guy who got himself into a messy situation for a period of time. "I have no problem with the law. I have been in Macedonia for four years now, and I don't even have a parking ticket" (interview with Lupevska 2009).[5]

"IT AIN'T ALL ABOUT THE MONEY"

There are many theories about the causes of organized crime and the ways organized crime figures make decisions. As mentioned earlier, some scholars argue that criminals are rational and intelligent decision makers who carefully calculate costs and benefits, while others claim they are like billiard balls, pushed and pulled into a life of crime. These seemingly conflicting perspectives should not be treated as mutually exclusive.

Scholars who subscribe to rational choice theory (RCT) start by making a number of assumptions about the purposefulness and rationality of social action. They assume, for example, that actors have clearly formulated goals, that in the light of such goals they evaluate alternative courses of action, and that they apply rational criteria when choosing the courses of action for obtaining their ultimate goals (see figure 2). The RCT criminological tradition owes its origins to the eighteenth-century "classical" ideas of Cesare Beccaria and Jeremy Bentham and to the utilitarian philosophies of John Locke and David Hume. Central to these philosophers' accounts of criminality was the belief that human nature is predicated on the search for pleasure and the avoidance of pain, and that, consequently, human action is organized around calculative strategies aimed at maximizing utility.

Rationality is also one of the major themes in the works of German sociologist and philosopher Max Weber, who criticized the simple models of rational decision making and differentiated between decision-making processes rooted in interests and those driven by values (Weber [1921] 1976). Becker (1976) and his followers (Eide 1994) also criticized the inability of ultra-positivist economic research to grasp norm-guided rational behavior. Much of the economic research considers norms as static and often identical among individuals. According to Becker (1976, 5), "Since economists generally have had little to contribute . . . to the understanding of how preferences are formed, preferences are assumed not to change substantially over time, nor [to] be very different between wealthy and poor persons, or even between persons in different societies and culture[s]." Becker studied criminals' backgrounds and whether they had sufficient information about the environment and the outcomes of their actions to be able to make rational choices. He concluded that the rationality of individuals is limited by the information th[ey] have and the time pressures they may experience when making [deci]offenders stick to "satisficing" and not to maximization.[6]

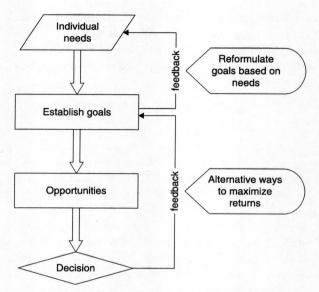

FIGURE 2. Diagram of rational decision-making process.
Source: Arsovska & Kostakos, 2008.

In the years since Becker's study, the concept of *limited* or *bounded rationality* (also known as "bounded self-interest" and "bounded willpower") firmly established itself in the sociology literature. The assumption that actors do not always behave rationally, in the economic sense, raises the possibility that different people in different social contexts have different perceptions about the probable consequences of a specific behavior. People also develop different perceptions regarding the risk, effort, and reward entailed in criminal behavior.

Ideas of limited or bounded rationality in general relate to two aspects, one arising from cognitive limitations and the other from extremes in emotional arousal; however, scholars who study human choices generally have placed too little attention on the role of emotions, the power of situations, and the symbolic meaning of crime to those who sell and buy illegal products. The last decades of the twentieth century finally saw the emergence of the schools of symbolic interactionism and cultural criminology, which focus more on the division between "interests" (rational behavior) and "passions/emotions" (impulsive action).[7] According to these schools of thought, emotional factors are often so powerful that they seem to make various modes of rational decision making inconceivable.

Many people seek out the feeling of "getting away with it," the excitement of wrongdoing—of living on the edge of law and order. Scholars have argued that these emotions transgress the rules of rationality, and that consumer culture has cultivated a desire for immediate, rather than delayed, gratification (Hayward 2007). As seen in this chapter's epigraph, particularly people who seemingly don't have much to lose often express their injustices through emotions, and sometimes act in ways that are not considered rational. Rage, excitement, pride, fear, and hatred therefore should be considered commonplace characteristics in the performance of crime.

In the field of consumer research, similarly, consumer choices traditionally have been understood via rational choice models that explain purchases in terms of the costs and benefits of alternatives as weighed by consumers. In these normative models—just as in RCTs of crime—consumers are viewed as dispassionate information processors (Katona 1975). Such purely rational models, however, have proven unable to answer an important question: Why do consumers frequently act against their own better judgment and engage in spending they later regret? Relatedly, why do intelligent people who understand the health risks nevertheless choose to overeat or smoke?

Consider also the following scenario, which sheds some light on the symbolic and subjective meaning of crime to the offender. In research conducted by sociologist Jack Katz (1990), one of his subjects, John Allen, a career stickup man, said the following about why he chose robberies over safer, more lucrative forms of crime: "For a man, pimping is a good way of making money, but the fastest way is narcotics, and the safest and best way of all is numbers. Even though my whores were making a lot of money, I just didn't like pimping that much. It ain't my style . . . I missed stickup quite a bit. . . . What I really missed was the excitement of sticking up and the planning and the getting away with it" (Katz 1990, 166).

Katz, along with other cultural criminologists, challenges the conventional view that criminals approach their crimes in the calculating spirit of making money.[8] By the time stickup man Allen was thirty-four, he had spent more than fourteen years behind bars and was crippled for life after being shot by police. Yet he persisted, committing at least one robbery even after he was confined to a wheelchair.

Katz also argues that Allen's experience is by no means unusual. Where career offenders are concerned, there is considerable support for the maxim that "crime doesn't pay." In addition, the spending patterns of criminals support the contention that material deprivation is not their primary motive for committing crime. In Allen's words, "I get lots of things I don't need." Often, much of the take is spent on others or simply given away. "It ain't the money or the cars or the women. It's about all that but ain't what it's deep down about. . . . The money ain't noth¹⁻ the money to make your play. To show people you are the best" (Ka

It appears, then, that crime is not necessarily "functional," and it does not always make sense in terms of personal economic efficiency. On the contrary, it often occurs, or at least continues to reoccur, because of less material and sometimes seemingly "absurd" motives linked to culture (or the lack of it), religion, status, emotions, networks, or prestige.

In particular, people going through a liminal period seem increasingly separated from prevailing normative values. Originating from anthropological research of the early twentieth century, the concept of *liminality* refers to a stage of ambiguity or disorientation that occurs during rituals. For ethnographer Arnold van Gennep ([1909] 1960) *rites de passage* consist of three stages: first, the separation, in which a subject is detached from its stabilized environment; second, the margin, in which the subject is in an ambiguous state; and, third, the aggregation, in which the passage has been completed and the subject has crossed the threshold into a new, fixed, stabilized state.

During the liminal stage, participants, that is, *liminal personae*, "stand at the threshold" between their previous way of structuring their identity, time, or community, and the "new way" (van Gennep 1960). Turner describes the state of liminal personae as somewhat "dissolved" during the liminal period. They are "transitional-beings" characterized by a series of contradictions. Having departed but not yet arrived, liminal personae are "at once no longer classified and not yet classified . . . neither one thing nor another; or may be both; or neither here nor there; or may even be nowhere" (Turner 1967, 97).

Diverging from its originally narrow sense, *liminality* has both spatial and temporal dimensions, and the term can be applied to a variety of subjects: individuals, larger groups, or even the whole of society. From this point of view, liminal periods lead to substantial changes in preferences over time, and they illustrate that norms are not static and that emotions and situations are important to understanding changes in preferences. During liminal periods of all kinds, social hierarchies may be reversed or temporarily dissolved, continuity of tradition may become uncertain, and future outcomes, once taken for granted, may be thrown into doubt. Liminal experiences can last for a moment, a finite period, or a lifetime. Wars and (ethnic) conflicts, enduring political instability, and prolonged economic crises, as well as incomplete modernization, have the potential to result in "permanent liminality," in which the suspended character of social life takes on a more fixed character.

Thus, the normative–affective model of "rationality" essentially illustrates that the majority of human choices are defined by normative factors and affect, and that instrumental thinking and logical, empirical analysis seldom factor into decisions. Human beings, particularly those in the midst of liminal periods, are highly sensitive to initial conditions—an effect popularly referred to as the "butterfly effect."[9] For such dynamic systems, small differences in initial conditions have the potential to yield widely diverging outcomes, rendering long-term prediction impossible. People do not respond directly to some universal objective reality; rather, they respond to their particular social understanding of that reality.

Criminologist Jay Albanese (2000) presented a model of organized crime group interaction in which he discussed opportunity factors that should be taken into consideration when studying the "causes" of crime. These factors include economic conditions, government regulation, enforcement effectiveness, demand for a product or service, technical and language skills, and criminal environments (preexisting networks). He argued that such opportunity factors are of key importance, since crime-prone individuals or organizations move to exploit changing criminal opportunities.

Although most of the factors presented in Albanese's opportunity model are no doubt relevant to the Albanian situation, one could easily add to the list many equally important, nonopportunity and noneconomic factors that some may consider "irrational" or "emotional."

Criminologist Peter Lupsha (1983), for instance, questioned the rationality of organized crime figures: why would a mafioso who already has made millions of dollars from illegal activities risk paying for his dinner with a stolen credit card? In fact, economic payoffs and rationality paired with the power of emotions and noneconomic interests—products of society, history, culture, and human emotions—provide a more accurate picture of the causes of organized crime (see table 1). Over the years, there has been an effort to construct more rounded conceptualizations of human choice that go beyond straightforward consideration of exogenous factors to consider internal psychic–emotive processes, and this effort should continue.

Four important factors may help us to better understand the origins of ethnic Albanian organized crime groups in the Balkan region. First is the role of criminal opportunities and preexisting networks in the region, including criminal-political ties that developed during the communist era. Second is the political and conflict situation in the postcommunist Balkan region. Third is the overall sociocultural confusion ("culture conflict") and normlessness within the society, and fourth is the economic strain on the society combined with an extreme drive to make money fast (anomie/strain and "the culture of now"). It is essential that we understand the impact of these factors on the human decision-making process, and how sensual experiences, frustration, trauma, and materialistic rewards all help to explain both the absurd and rational behaviors of Albanian organized crime figures.

Also, although the traditional scholarly view is that organized crime pursues goals that are economic, rather than political, social, or cultural, the question remains whether and to what degree Albanian criminal organizations are guided by choices not just to enlarge their profits but also to create political power, earn respect and a better position in society, or simply act in accordance with cultural interpretations of masculinity. This chapter focuses predominantly o~ ·· of Albanian organized crime in the Balkans and its political dimen.

TABLE 1 Multiple registers of rationality: An overview of external factors, inner containments, and circumstances that may influence an offender's decision making

1. Rational choice–inspired decision making	Overview of factors and circumstances that may affect people's decision to commit organized crime	Albanian organized crime (impact and relevance of factors as illustrated in the following chapters)
Deterrence	Cost (e.g., certain, severe, and swift punishment)-benefit (e.g., profit)	Weak (less concerned about formal consequences, for example, long prison sentence, or unaware of the extent of their crime)
Opportunity	Availability of target; life events and situations that provide easy access to organized crime; lack of capable guardians	Medium to weak (situations that provide access to organized crime, such as social networks, are important although Albanian offenders are pro-active and create new opportunities; also, capable guardians have not deterred them from committing crimes)
Skills, knowledge	"Know-how"; language; technical skills	Medium importance (if they are not experts, they train hard to learn skills and techniques)
2. Normative-affective considerations (macro and micro)		
Politics	Distrust of the system; patriotism; dedication to a political party	Strong (particularly in the Balkan context; less relevant abroad)
Culture conflict	Confusion; normlessness	Strong
Relative poverty	Economic strain	At the beginning of the criminal career very strong but then less relevant
Networks	Peer/family pressure	Strong
Culture/religion	Values/beliefs	Weak
History	Conflict mentality	Medium
Personality; emotions; situations; inner containments	Situational meaning and interpretation	Strong, particularly pride

Of course, not all illegal activities are so thick with meaning. Many do indeed resemble simple market transactions in which little more is involved than the sale of illegal goods by one party to another, primarily for profit. Also, to say that crime is motivated by emotions is not to say that it never makes sense from a materialist perspective as well.

PREEXISTING TIES: ORGANIZED CRIME DURING COMMUNISM

It is important to acknowledge that preexisting criminal networks, special skills, and access to the means of carrying out criminal activities are important opportunity factors that explain, in part, the rise of Albanian organized crime after the fall of communism in 1991. Like most postcommunist countries, Albania was home to a vast network of people who previously had worked for national military services, secret security services, or the police (see figure 3). In fact, internal security police and intelligence agencies were a key part of the absolutist communist regime.

According to a UN Office on Drugs and Crime (UNODC) report from 2008, the state security police in Albania and other Balkan countries operated largely above the law. And with time, underground operators and the security services in that region joined forces through the creation of an extensive informant apparatus.[10]

Communist-era security agencies also commonly retained professional criminals, including many based in Western Europe, informally as informants or operatives (Leman and Janssens 2006). According to police reports, these men were used for a variety of state security tasks, such as smuggling oil, arms, and drugs, and assassinating expatriate dissidents. In Serbia, for example, things eventually got so bad that the Zemun Clan, one of the country's top drug-peddling groups, essentially merged with the JSO—an elite special operations unit—and had its own artillery, armored vehicles, and helicopters (Samuels 2010).

In Albania, some organized crime activities, although not defined as such, were tolerated by the state even during communist times because they generated extra money for the state, supplied consumer needs unmet by the official economy, and helped to destabilize capitalist societies. The internal security services often took part in these illicit activities.

For example, although not well documented, it seems that relations existed between the Albanian secret police Sigurimi and organized crime (Leman and Janssens 2006; CSD 2004). A confidential intelligence report prepared by a Belgian liaison officer in 2008 shows that, as far back as the 1960s, the Albanian communist state made secret arrangements with some Italian criminal organizations, enabling them to smuggle cigarettes on Albanian territory.

The intelligence report indicates that in 1966, Albania provided Italian criminals with escape routes via the Adriatic Sea. Italian mafiosi also were allowed to make use of Albanian airports, where they stored smuggled cigarettes. The agreement between the Sigurimi and the Italian criminal organizations was approved by the political bureau and Albania's dictator, Enver Hoxha. On the basis of this agreement a special unit, "101K," was created in Albania. Stationed in the village of Rrushbull, five kilometers from the Durrës port, the unit was composed of offic··· ' from the Albanian border police. The 101K guarded ships full of ··

FIGURE 3. Years after the fall of communism, bunkers (*bunkerët*) such as this one are still a ubiquitous sight in Albania, with an average of twenty-four bunkers per square kilometer. Most are now derelict, though some have been reused for residential accommodation, cafés, storehouses, and shelters for animals or the homeless (2007). Copyright © Jana Arsovska.

were departing from Durrës, and it kept an eye on the cigarette storage houses located in Rrushbull.

According to the report, Mustafaraj Ilir, a former Albanian vice minister, reported that during a single year in the late 1960s the Italian mafia paid twenty-two million dollars in cash to the Albanian state. The money went into the state budget, and some of it ended up in the budget of the Ministry of Interior. In fact, the report notes that the Alouette helicopters that are still used in Albania today were bought in the 1980s with money from the Italian mafia.

Rama Mersin, whose son Rama Luan served as Albania's minister of interior from 2002 to 2003, was commandant of the elite 101K. The agreement between the Italian mobsters and the Albanian state allegedly was negotiated between Myftin Qazim and Nenshati Lorenc, two important agents of the Albanian Sigurimi who later immigrated to Switzerland and were granted political asylum.

Based on the Belgian intelligence report, it appears that another criminal activity in Albania was the cultivation of *Papaver somniferum*, the poppy plant from which opium and many refined opiates are extracted. Once farmers collected the opium, it was delivered to the communist state. Officially, the communist state reported that the drug was to be used for medical purposes, but internal reports note that the quantity of opium cultivated far exceeded the legitimate medical needs of the Albanian population. Witnesses report that the crop was intended for export to other countries, and the Belgian investigative report claims that the communist leadership argued it should be used "to poison the capitalist societies, so that Communism will triumph."

Other forms of organized crime also flourished in Albania during the communist era. For example, well-connected people established parallel systems for the distribution of food, which was scarce at the time, moving it from storehouses to consumers for much higher prices. Collaboration between various actors— producers, chauffeurs, storehouse managers, local shops, clients, and so on—was required in order to set up such food distribution systems. In an interview, a Belgian diplomat working in Tirana noted that the criminal groups organizing these parallel systems were "very complex but efficient" (interview, Albania, 2007).

Even seemingly "official" organizations sometimes engaged in illicit operations. The Albanian national transport company Park of the Export was a state-owned firm that transported minerals, agriculture products, cigarettes, and other goods all over Europe. Yet internal reports point out that sometimes the drivers jointly smuggled goods without the knowledge of the state. The truckers established strong links with the Albanian diaspora, and in Albania the state granted them many privileges. When the communist regime collapsed, many of these well-connected drivers became the new elite of Albania (see, e.g., UNODC 2008).

Of course, not all Albanian organized crime figures during the 1970s and 1980s worked for the communist Albanian state. In the United States, a prosecutor's memo indicates that in 1979 a kilogram of heroin was distributed by an Albanian man called Xhevdet Lika, who made New York City's Lower East Side his area of operation. According to federal court testimony and his sentencing report, Lika regularly traveled to Turkey and Yugoslavia to arrange drug shipments.

Xhevdet Lika's partner-in-crime, an Albanian named Xhevdet Mustafa, went on the run from US law enforcement officials in 1982, after he also was charged with drug trafficking. Mustafa first fled Albania in 1964 and moved to Staten Island, New York, where he operated an auto body shop and later joined Xhevdet Lika. Some of his business operations were allegedly financed by the exiled Leka, Crown Prince of Albania, a friend. Once his million-dollar bail had been paid, Mustafa fled the United States, first to New Zealand and then to southern Italy.

Mustafa was a strong supporter of the deposed Albanian monarch King Zog, who had died in 1961. After fleeing the United States Mustafa allegedly led an unsuccessful coup in Albania that aimed to restore the monarchy. In reality, he was part of a four-person group called Banda Mustafaj that planned the assass¬ of Enver Hoxha in 1982. The other members were Sabaudin Hazned

Haznedari), Halit Bajram (aka Halit Eid), and Fadil "Fred" Kaceli, a nightclub manager with property in New Zealand (Bacelli n.d.).

It appears that Halit was an informant who obtained approval from the Albanian secret service Sigurimi to participate in this mission. Halit planned to secure the group's capture by sending information to Sigurimi's headquarters. The group's planning and preparation stages took place in southern Italy, and the coup involved a startling array of intelligence services, including the CIA, MI6, the New Zealand Secret Service, and the Australian Secret Service. The operation was also thought to have been backed by Yugoslavia as retaliation against the 1981 protests in Kosovo (Pearson 2006; Bacelli n.d.).

The assassination attempt was ultimately unsuccessful, and President Hoxha claimed that the invaders were "liquidated" (Bacelli n.d.; Kamm 1982). Fadil was injured before the launch of the speedboat that was supposed to bring the four men across the Strait of Otranto to Albania. Albanian forces had been tipped off by Halit and were looking for the group (Pearson 2006). A couple of days later Sabaudin was allegedly shot by riflemen in a firefight, and Xhevdet Mustafa carjacked a car and drove southwest to Lushnje. He hid in a residence, taking one family hostage. Allegedly, Xhevdet shot himself as an armored vehicle knocked down one of the house walls. Halit, the sole survivor, was held in protective custody and testified in 1983 against the former Albanian minister of defense, Kadri Hazbiu, who was suspected of working for Yugoslavia and the CIA. Hazbiu was convicted of abuse of office and executed in 1983. Halit Bajrami was released and returned to his home in New Zealand. The exiled Leka, Crown Prince of Albania, denied authorizing the operation.[11]

In the late 1980s, with communism in decline, members of the secret police and their criminal allies were well placed to profit from the capitalist economy that emerged in Eastern Europe. They had the know-how and the right connections. Research from Albania, and from the Balkans in general, shows that party functionaries frequently were awarded state-owned companies at noncompetitive rates (CSD 2004; Kokalari 2007). In the Balkans, these functionaries were often secret police officers, who "teamed their clandestine skills with their criminal contacts to create local monopolies and shady multinational conglomerates" (UNODC 2008).

Between 1991 and 1997, postcommunist government policy deprioritized core state functions, and public spending drastically declined. In Albania, the abolition of the secret service Sigurimi in 1991 left about ten thousand agents unemployed, and some of them became involved in organized crime activities.[12] In 1996, one analyst (cited in UNODC 2008, 50) noted that postcommunist liberalization had brought with it corruption and profiteering by ruthless men. In 1992 and 1993, the analyst said, "the Albanian government removed nearly two thirds of [Sigurimi] personnel. Many of the ex-Sigurimi agents, once in feared positions of power, now found themselves unemployed, stripped of their state pensions." Antagonistic toward the new government, these individuals offered their services to those willing and capable of paying for them: organized crime figures.

At the time, the UN sanctions imposed on neighboring Yugoslavia offered an immediate opportunity as well—organizing smuggling channels to supply Yugoslavia with oil. Oil smuggling initially was organized by the Serbian State Security Service (Sluzba drzavne bezbednosti, or SDB), but many former Sigurimi agents and police officers also became involved in the business. Large-scale smuggling of cigarettes and coffee to Montenegro, using the oil smuggling routes, followed in 1993. People working for the security services later began using some state-controlled channels to smuggle drugs, stolen vehicles, contraband goods, and people. By the early 1990s, in Albania, the political, commercial, and criminal had merged.

PATRIOTISM AND CONFLICT MENTALITY

The Failure of Democracy

The collapse of the communist regime in 1991 brought numerous changes to the Balkan region and its governments and led to a decade-long era of lawlessness, confusion, and feelings of insecurity among residents of the region. In fact, the "democratization" of Yugoslavia and Albania coincided with an increase in violence and crime in these countries. Many organized crime groups were formed during this time, and they operated in the region for more than a decade with very few obstacles. This was in part due to a failed process of political and economic modernization, a lack of consistent government regulation and political willpower to deal with organized crime cases, and a dearth of effective and motivated law enforcement agencies. Government, police, judicial, and military reforms in the postcommunist Balkan region were slow in coming, and fighting organized crime was not seen as a priority for a long time.

Many Balkan countries were unable to achieve political modernization during the 1990s. This failure lies not only in the backward character of representative institutions and their inability to look beyond populist collectivism and a managed form of participatory democracy, but also in the lack of civil society and the related failure to develop a sense of citizenship among residents of these nations.

A critical aspect of the development of an effective civil society is the establishment of a strong and independent judiciary. In a modern society, an independent judiciary is particularly important because it offers norms of rationality as the basis for the regulation of relations between groups and individuals. Without strong and independent courts, liberty cannot be realized.

In spite of its significance, however, the law received hardly any attention in the Balkan countries during the communist era or immediately thereafter. The judicial sector of the state bureaucracy and the elite bureaucrats who functioned in that sector were ineffective, and a corrupt judiciary contributed to feelings of in lack of a rule of law, and the creation of strong criminal-political ties throughout Eastern Europe.

Another obstacle that had a lasting impact on governance during the postcommunist era was the partial retreat of the state from other core functions, including economic regulation and strategic infrastructure development. Until 1991, Albania, Kosovo, and Macedonia were communist-socialist countries with planned economic systems in which the government controlled all major sectors of the economy. After 1991, however, the welfare state that had cared for citizens "from cradle to grave" was replaced by a "pay-as-you-go" social service system. This drastic change made the public feel uncertain and fostered the perception of a lack of human security. Under the new social order, residents no longer could take for granted "freedom from want"—for example, economic security, health care, food security, and environmental security—and "freedom from fear"—personal and political security, stability of tenure, and so on. This insecurity further contributed to the existing lawlessness and booming crime rates.

According to reports from the World Bank (2010), this lawlessness manifested itself in a number of governance failures: high levels of corruption in the delivery of public services, large-scale illegal occupation of land and construction, and the resurgence of blood feuds as a mechanism for settling disputes. The lack of government supervision of the banking sector also resulted in the creation and then collapse of several Albanian pyramid savings schemes in 1997, which in turn caused thousands of Albanians to lose their savings and subsequently their lives, because of the chaos it created in the country.

The violent conflicts that took place between 1998 and 2001 in Kosovo and Macedonia in the name of nation building and ethnic survival further reinforced criminal ties to politics, increased public feelings of personal and political insecurity, and provided justification for all sorts of criminal behavior. This was a period of strengthening nationalistic and patriotic feelings, clientelism, and endemic corruption—factors that can help us understand the increase in organized crime in the Albanian context.

The Pyramid Schemes

After the collapse of communism, Albania was engulfed by deep conflict and political, social, economic, and security disturbances. The country's transition from totalitarian regime to democracy led to corruption, privatization fraud, protection rackets, violence, and other forms of organized crime. Between 1990 and 1991 the number of homicides doubled, and armed robberies tripled.

The Albanian government, influenced by the democratic West, allowed opposition parties to arise in the early 1990s. The Democratic Party (DP), led by Sali Berisha (see figure 4), won the election in March 1992, and Berisha served as president from April 1992 to March 1997. When the multiparty system was introduced

FIGURE 4. Former president Sali Berisha at a political meeting in Skanderbeg Square (Tirana, Albania, 1997). Copyright © Laurent Piolanti.

in Albania, the Albanian diaspora started financing the DP. The party was in great need of funds, so financial contributions from the diaspora were vital to its functioning and growth. However, some of these funds were contributed by Albanian offenders who lived and operated abroad.

For example, funds were transferred to the DP by a man listed as a defendant in the Belgian Federal Prosecution Service's Albanian case "Gazmen," which involved human smuggling and trafficking. The defendant, a former officer in President Berisha's republican guard (CEOOR 2006), had a diplomatic passport when he lived in Brussels. After being convicted in an Albanian smuggling case in Dendermonde, he continued his criminal activities from prison.

Such political-criminal entanglements left a legacy of institutional ambivalence toward illicit activities in Albania. Not only did financial support for political parties originate in criminal activities, but politicians sometimes were accused of, and linked to, various organized crime activities. During the UN embargo imposed on Yugoslavia from 1992 to 1995, the Albanian state set up a company called Shqiponija ("The Eagle"). The company was a property of the Democratic Party, and its director was Shehu Tritan, the vice minister of foreign affairs. Intelligence indicated that Tritan developed a monopoly in the transport of oil and violated the UN embargo for about three years. Under pressure from the international community,

Shqiponija was eventually closed down, but its financial statements were never found.

During these same years, criminal clans from Berat, in south-central Albania, engaged in numerous criminal activities. According to intelligence, organized crime in Berat had a political aspect. Between 1993 and 1996, Albania's minister of interior, a DP supporter named Musarah Agron, allegedly provided criminal clans from Berat with immunity for their operations in return for their votes and political support.

An anonymous author, at the behest of the Centro Gino Germani in Rome, argued that as soon as Berisha took office, he ensured that the native Gheg clans, or *fares,* from the northern part of the country to which he belonged, were given control of all the country's key posts in the ministries, the police, and the secret police (SHIK, or Shërbimi Informativ Kombëtar), whose principal objective was to neutralize the political opposition represented by the Socialist Party (Jamieson and Sily 1998). Also, an Albanian interviewee noted that a lot of the Albanian intellectuals left Albania during the 1990s, and "many people from the north who had no education, or proper job qualifications, took over key government positions" (interview, New York, 2014). The state arms company Meico, for example, was sold off in 1994 to Albania's largest privately owned company, Vefa Holdings, whose controversial chairman, Vehbi Allmucaj, was a close personal friend of Defense Minister Safet Zhulali (Jamieson and Sily 1998). Allmucaj was the single largest donor to Berisha's Democratic Party in the May 1996 parliamentary elections, which, according to media accounts, took place against a background of considerable electoral bribery.

In the Albanian context of the 1990s, it was often argued that if a member of a clan entered into politics, he (often male) would receive the support of the people associated with his clan, village, city, or even subethnicity, irrespective of his political ideology. The loyal clan members would bring him votes, and in return they would receive many benefits from the politician they had endorsed. With such political support the criminal groups were able to operate without hindrance.

Social relations of this sort alleviate the problem of distrust not only because of their "social embeddedness" (Kleemans and van de Bunt 1999) but also because of the "temporal embeddedness" of the behavior of the cooperating actors. As Kleemans and van de Bunt (1999) explain, criminal actors have a common history, and they act in the shadow of a common future. Cooperation problems between criminal actors decrease, because the offenders have information about one another's histories. Both have invested in the relationship, and they know they probably will meet again. This "temporal embeddedness" discourages opportunistic and selfish actions, and it has a stabilizing effect on criminal-political cooperation, in particular. Criminals support politicians and politicians return favors, but they all try to "honor" their agreements because they are aware of the nature of their "cooperation." This leads to severe forms of clientelism, nepotism, and favoritism—all frequent phenomena in the Balkans during the 1990s.

Criminal-political ties in Albania grew stronger through the mid-1990s and culminated in 1997 with the collapse of many pyramid savings schemes that yielded "an estimated USD 13 million in illegal proceeds" (Hysi 2005). As Albania's economy liberalized, its rudimentary financial system had become dominated by Ponzi schemes endorsed by government officials. By January 1997, the number of investors had grown to include two-thirds of Albania's population. It is estimated that more than 1.2 billion dollars was invested in companies offering monthly interest rates ranging from 10 percent to 25 percent, while the average monthly income was around eighty dollars (Jarvis 2000). People sold their homes to invest money, and immigrants working in Greece and Italy transferred money to the schemes back home in Albania (Lushnje 1997). Although functioning as bankers, the pyramid operators had no concrete investment pool from which to collect money and apparently did not lend.

The first pyramid scheme, which started in 1991, was run by Hajdin Sejdia (Sejdisë), a businessman from Kosovo who raised millions of dollars from ordinary Albanians to build a luxury hotel. He then escaped with the money and left not a hotel, but an enormous hole in the center of Tirana (Lushnje 1997). Between 1993 and 1997 many "companies" emerged and offered tempting interest rates. Despite the advice of the International Monetary Fund (IMF) to shut down these schemes, the Albanian democratic government continued to allow them. In fact, a number of government officials were involved in the schemes and profited from them personally. In January 1997, the majority of the pyramid schemes collapsed, taking with them the life savings of many Albanians.

In Lushnje, Hajdin Sejdia's hometown, half the population ended up living with the other half because their houses had been sold and the proceeds lost (Lushnje 1997). People marched in the streets to protest the government's support of the schemes, and the protest descended into violence. Tritan Shehu, chairman of the DP, was sent to Lushnje to resolve the situation; however, protesters assaulted him and held him hostage at City Stadium. State Special Forces intervened to rescue Shehu. By morning, every government institution in the city had been looted and burned.

Only a couple of days later, violence erupted in other southern towns, including several on the coast. About fifty students from the University of Vlore initiated a hunger strike on campus on February 20, 1997. The demonstrators, many of whom had sunk their life savings into the schemes, demanded their money back and called for the resignation of the government led by President Berisha. On February 26, thousands of people joined the protest and surrounded the university to defend the protestors from a feared attack by the National Intelligence Service, or SHIK. Some of the demonstrators, without warning, attacked the SHIK building. During

FIGURE 5. Smuggling of weapons looted during the collapse of Albania in 1996–1997 (Shkodër, Albania, 1997). Copyright © Laurent Piolanti.

the fight between the so-called "rebels" and the government forces, six officers and three civilians were killed (Nelan 1997).

Soon after, tales of the pyramid schemes spread throughout the country. Tensions continued to rise. It was almost impossible to find an Albanian who had not put some money into the schemes. One story described a young man who wanted to get married but did not have the money to do it. He raised seventeen hundred dollars from his friends, then went to Bashkim Driza, head of the Populli pyramid scheme, to arrange an "investment." Driza, a personal friend, gave him twenty-six hundred dollars as an instant payback and sent him on his way. But as the young man left the Populli office, he saw the huge crowd of investors outside, yielded to temptation, and put all his money back into the scheme. He was left broke and unable to get married (Lushnje 1997).

The failed pyramid savings schemes unleashed a flood of weapons in Albania (see figure 5). More than 550,000 small arms, 839 million rounds of ammunition, and 16 million explosive devices were looted from army stockpiles during the protests (Khakee and Florquin 2003; Zaborskiy 2007). Some sources estimate that the 1997 Albanian pyramid crisis led to 1 million light weapons and 1.5 billion rounds of ammunition becoming available on the black market in southeastern and central Europe, with obvious security implications (Smith and Sagramoso 1999;

Anastasijevic 2006). Hundreds of thousands of Chinese-made AK-47s and other small arms ended up in the hands of criminal groups and paramilitaries.

"Down with Berisha"

The effect of the pyramid crisis was less than salutary. Apart from recurring riots sparked by frustration and anger, there is a sense that Albanians have become more greedy and selfish since the schemes' collapse. As Vasilika Hysi, a professor at the University of Tirana in Albania, argues: "After their collapse, Albanian criminal groups [but also common people] became intensively involved in illegal activities and organized crime, trying to recover their lost money" (Hysi 2005, 540).

In 2006 an elderly man named Xzaferi (pseudonym), of Saranda in southern Albania, recalled that chaotic period: "In 1997 everyone was broke, everyone had invested in the pyramids and lost money. Berisha won the fraudulent elections of 1996 and fooled us all. They took everything. Marks, dollars, drachmas, everything. Services, factories, and shops were all closed down. The state was the mafia, not the people, but people also started doing all sorts of jobs that thrive under these conditions. We all had to make it somehow. Some became greedy and some justified crime and violence" (interview, Albania, 2006).

One young couple had lost fifty thousand dollars at that time. They said "their furniture import business had ground to a halt because customs policemen—no doubt themselves losers to the schemes—were demanding bribes to allow the wares into the country and often 'confiscated' the goods for themselves" (Lushnje 1997).

"People that lost money were ready to fight," Xzaferi added during our interview. "They had had enough. Armed rebels were waiting in the hills to repel the army of Berisha. You [could] hear young insurgents everywhere. They [would] fire their weapons in the air and shout, 'Down with Berisha'." He continued: "By March 1997 the city of Saranda was captured by rebels, and Vlore was controlled by gangs. They were burning government buildings and broke into the detention facility and took guns. People were angry with Berisha and the killings continued throughout southern Albania" (interview, Albania, 2006).

Many Albanians lost their jobs in 1997, when hundreds of state-run factories closed down, and criminal figures took over state-owned agricultural companies. While ordinary Albanians were struggling to survive, disorganized and highly corrupt privatization began (see figure 6). Violent groups created small armies for protection and to impose their influence on Albanian citizens, and rivalries between criminal gangs and individuals increased. Extortion, kidnapping, and corruption became common.

The deteriorating domestic situation in Albania also resulted in the development of smuggling channels and a massive exodus of refugees to Western Europe. During the 1990s, an estimated six hundred thousand Albanians emigrated to Italy

FIGURE 6. During the 1990s, Albania underwent an economic crisis and people were starving. International agencies donated food. This photo was taken before the gates were opened for food distribution to the most deprived (Tirana, Albania, 1996). Copyright © Laurent Piolanti.

and Greece, driven by the economic crisis. Many drowned in the deep Adriatic waters as they tried to make the crossing.

To prevent the unauthorized entry of illegal migrants into Italy, the Italian Navy boarded Albanian vessels whenever they encountered them, implementing a de facto blockade. In one tragic incident, as the Italian naval vessel Sibilia boarded the Albanian ship Kateri i Radës in the Strait of Otranto, the vessels collided, the Kateri i Radës capsized, and as many as eighty-three Albanians lost their lives.

As desperate Albanians fled their homeland, some members of Albanian émigré communities with shady backgrounds and strong patriotic feelings returned to Albania (see figure 7). Aldo Bare was one of them, but the list is very long. These ethnic Albanians often returned to establish alliances with local criminals, to help certain political parties gain power, and to "support" their country.

After Prime Minister Aleksandër Meksi resigned and President Berisha declared a state of emergency in Albania on March 2, 1997, Albania's Socialist Party (SP) won a victory. However, the transfer of power did not stop the unrest, and protests spread to northern Albania. The DP then reelected Berisha as president with the votes of the DP members of the Parliament alone. This led to massive riots in southern and central Albania.

FIGURE 7. During the breakdown of the pyramid schemes, Albania fell into anarchy. This military base was occupied by so-called local mafias (Shkodër area, Albania, 1996). Copyright © Laurent Piolanti.

On March 5, the Committee of Public Salvation (Salvation Committee) formed in Vlore.[13] This committee began to act as a parallel government, and rebels in the south launched a wave of destruction. Prominent crime figures escaped from prisons in Greece and Albania, and organized gangs took control of many areas. Gangs looted banks and took hostages. President Berisha decided to open the weapon depots in the north and to allow civilians in the north to arm themselves, for protection against the violence of the south. When southern Albanian bases were looted, it was estimated that, on average, every male over the age of ten possessed at least one firearm.

During the June 1997 election for Parliament, more than sixty people were killed. SP allies won the election, and as the SP came to power in July 1997, Fatos Nano, a moderate communist, was elected prime minister. Berisha was replaced by the socialist Rexhep Meidani, who became the new president. Many members of the Salvation Committee ran for office, despite earlier promises to remain out of politics. Taking advantage of the situation, criminal groups seized control of entire cities.

Overall, this period in Albania was marked by exceptionally high levels of violent crime, extreme poverty, and corruption. In 1997 alone, the Albanian police reported 1,542 murders, a total unprecedented in the nation's history (see figure 8).

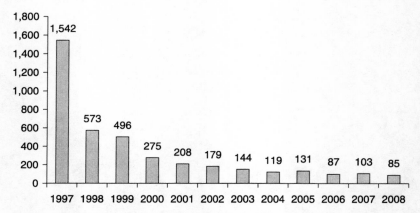

FIGURE 8. Murder rates in Albania. Source: Albanian Ministry of Interior (2009).

The UN Mission in Kosovo reported that in the late 1990s, Albania experienced the highest murder rate in the entire Balkan region (12.2 per 100,000 people). In 2002, the World Health Organization (WHO) ranked Albania fifth in the world for murders committed by youths (28 per 100,000). Between 1998 and 2004, the Albanian police reported 1,994 murders, of which 9 percent were "blood feuds" or revenge killings. In the period from 1992 to 1996, some 10 percent of all murders were blood feuds.

"I think all politicians that got hold of power at that time had some criminal connections," said Bledar, another man from Saranda. He related a story from the late 1990s, when Albanian police attempted to arrest a crime suspect in his neighborhood: "Ardi was a known criminal. When the police started approaching him, he shouted: 'Stop, don't shoot! I am a supporter of the Socialist Party!'" (interview, Albania, 2006).

"Stop, Don't Shoot! I Am a Supporter of the Socialist Party"

Clientelism was not typical of the DP alone. The SP also supported a number of criminal figures who in turn ensured that the party garnered votes during elections. The notorious gang leader Zani Myrteza Çaushi led dozens of armed bandits in Vlore during the March 1997 uprising. His group was known as the Gang of Çole (Banda e Çoles, or Banda e Zani Çaushit), after a neighborhood in the city of Vlore. Before he established his criminal organization along with some friends from his neighborhood, Çaushi had been convicted of serious offenses and imprisoned in a high-security prison in Greece (Larissa).

In February 1997 he escaped and returned to southern Albania. Çaushi and his Banda e Çoles became the primary supporters of the Salvation Committee of

Vlore, mentioned earlier, whose political aim was to usurp the functions of the Albanian state.

Çaushi retained delegates from across the country, and he was the bodyguard of Italian prime minister Romano Prodi during his visit to southern Albania in April 1997, after the Otranto tragedy.[14] In actuality, Çaushi seemed to be supportive of the SP and an opponent of Berisha. He also served as the bodyguard of Skender Gjinushi, an Albanian politician and later also a leader of the SP, during the campaign for the June 1997 elections.

But Çaushi and his group soon became known throughout the country for committing heinous crimes. He was suspected of killing at least four people and kidnapping six. Unofficially, he also was linked to a number of drug trafficking offenses, and he was arrested on September 28, 1997. In July 1998, General Prosecutor Arben Rakipi reported that he did not have enough evidence to launch legal proceedings against the imprisoned gang leader. Ultimately Çaushi did face trial, but he was found guilty only of illegal possession of weapons, and his sentence was equated with the time of his detention. The court ordered his release in the courtroom. For illegal possession of arms, the court declared guilty four more defendants, who also were sentenced only to time served. These were all key players in Çaushi's notorious group, and all of them were set free.

Soon after his release, Çaushi participated in a shootout in which three people died. The media argued that Çaushi's gang was powerful because of the support of the leader Fatos Nano and the Socialist Party.

Finally, in 1999, Çaushi was arrested and sentenced to life imprisonment for murder, robbery, weapons possession, and rape. Various members of his group also ended up in prison after being convicted of creation of a criminal group, possession of military vehicles, homicides, kidnappings, destruction of state institutions, and drug trafficking..

A man who knew Çaushi described his motives: "He didn't do what he did for money or protection. It was more than that. He wanted to be admired, known, feared. Always trying to show people who is the best. He didn't care if he lost his life. Most of the members of his group ended up dead. Zani was known as 'the strongman of Vlore'" (interview, Albania, 2006).

Çaushi, who is currently serving a prison sentence at the same prison as Aldo Bare, was not the only criminal figure linked to the SP. The list is long. For example, Altin Dardha ruled in Berat and committed murders during 1997 and 1998. The publicly known justification for his criminal organization was to avenge the murder of his father. Altin Dardha and his group have killed 120 people, and sources point out that 63 were executed by Altin Dardha himself (Hoxha 2008). Altin Dardha's main rivalry, with Lulzim Caka, another local offender, was largely political: Altin Dardha was a supporter of the SP whereas Lulzim Caka was an alleged supporter of the DP.

Furthermore, on March 29, 2003, the businessman Fatmir Rama was gunned down outside Kartodrom 2000, an entertainment complex he owned on the outskirts of Tirana. He had the private telephone numbers of senior politicians stored in his cell phone. Media reports claimed that he had connections within the SP. Even though there was an international arrest warrant issued against him (by Italy, on charges of drug trafficking), he was able to freely conduct business in Albania in the late 1990s. Just a month after Rama was killed, rival politicians started trading blame over his death.

In the same period, iron tycoon Florian Vila was shot dead outside his house in a Tirana neighborhood, and in the city of Vlore the nephew of leading cement dealer Sulo Shehu was kidnapped. Shehu's nephew was released within four days, after a police raid that netted six suspects, including one policeman.

The DP started arguing that the ruling socialists must protect legitimate businesses from the upsurge in violence. In a press conference on April 28, 2003, Sali Berisha said his party had prepared a resolution that would "denounce the indifferent attitude of the government and its probable links with such (criminal) acts" (Bregu 2005). The SP responded by saying Berisha was trying to capitalize on a string of unrelated gangland attacks. Berisha's case rested on his claim that both Florian Vila and Sulo Shehu were affiliated with the DP. Shehu had funded the party in the past, while Vila was known for his right-wing views.

Eight years later, in Tirana Court, Lavderim Tufa was sentenced to twenty years as a collaborator in the murder of Fatmir Rama. He was accused of being one of two hitmen who had murdered Rama, Kristaq Cami, and Julian Durishti and wounded two other men. The motive remains unknown; Tufa claimed innocence and insisted the case was a political setup. According to Top Chanel (2011), his father has said, "The state knows very well who the murderer is, but they don't want to go there."

The assassination of DP lawmaker Azem Hajdari in September 1998 and the assassination of SP lawmaker Fatmir Xhindi in 2009 also point to the complex relationships among politics, business, and organized crime in Albania. The catalogue of events raises questions of what "justice" really meant in an Albanian context, particularly prior to 2005.

Links have been established not only between criminals and political parties, but also between public servants and criminals on all levels. In 2003 former minister of interior Luan Rama said that authorities knew of policemen and prosecutors who were either directly involved in human trafficking or who maintained links with organized crime figures involved in such crimes. In one case, seven repatriated Albanians (who were detained in Belgrade en route to the United States) claimed they were supposed to pay seven thousand euros to crime members, including police officers from Tirana's Rinas Airport, when they landed on US soil.

At the end of 2003, Albanian Bledar Mane, who had been convicted of human trafficking by a court in London, wrote a letter to an Albanian daily newspaper in which he elaborated on his work and the relationships that facilitated his smuggling business. Mane was of the opinion that the Albanian authorities would not be able to suppress human trafficking, because high-ranking individuals from the judiciary, police, customs, and administration were heavily involved in it.

The Criminogenic Society

There is no doubt that the dysfunctional state and the growing accommodations between Albanian authorities and organized crime figures in the 1990s fostered the development of a secretive society permeated by crime. In this society, being an "organized crime figure" did not have a negative connotation, at least not until the early twenty-first century. Only after the fall of communism did Albania start to recognize several new forms of crime, particularly the smuggling of people and commodities. Neither state bodies nor the public were prepared for these new forms of crime, and so they were not acknowledged officially by politicians and state representatives. Criminologist Vasilika Hysi (2005, 541) explains: "In most cases, entrepreneurial illicit activities were not even identified as offences, and in the rare cases in which investigation was started, they were hardly ever classified as 'organized crime.'"

In addition, common people sometimes saw economic crime as beneficial to their own personal welfare, as well as to the development of the failing state. For example, Lazarat, a municipality in southern Albania close to the Greek border, is known as the cannabis capital of Albania and, now, Europe (Likmeta 2013a). It is estimated that Lazarat may produce as much as six billion dollars' worth of marijuana every year. To put that in perspective, the annual GDP of the entire Albanian economy is about thirteen billion dollars. Some reports note that up to 90 percent of village residents—six to seven thousand in all—are believed to take part in the business, making marijuana production their main source of income. Intelligence reports suggest that the village cultivated more than sixty acres of land in 2013, an estimated three hundred thousand plants that could yield as much as five hundred tons of marijuana (about nine hundred metric tons of cannabis a year, as reported by *The Guardian* on June 16, 2014).

Lazarat is not easily accessible to outsiders, and political will to deal with this issue is lacking, possibly because of the income cannabis cultivation generates. In one incident from 2012, when officers began cutting down cannabis plants, villagers starting firing. "We were drawing indiscriminate fire from twenty positions, including heavy machine guns and antitank missiles," the police commissioner explained in an interview. "I saw a seventy-year-old grandmother shooting at us with a heavy machine gun. I thought I was going to die" (Likmeta 2013a). It appears that drugs traffickers have taken advantage of a political power vacuum, and that organized crime has become part of the daily life of the farmers in Lazarat.

Similarly, in June 2014, hundreds of lightly armed police officers stormed the village after suspected marijuana growers fired machine guns at officers during an earlier raid. The police exchanged fire with nearly thirty armed men (*The Guardian* 2014). It appears that drugs traffickers have taken advantage of a political power vacuum, and that organized crime has become part of the daily lives of the farmers in Lazarat. During a personal discussion from June 2014, one Albanian prosecutor noted that the offenders in this village often used women and children as a shield, making it difficult for police officers to take control of the village.

In parts of the Balkan region during the 1990s, organized crime was often perceived as an "institution" that fostered social mobility, capital accumulation, economic prosperity, and nation building—not as a serious threat, as many interpret it today. In these turbulent times, crime offered people an escape from cruel reality and an unpleasant economic situation, and the possibility of "making one's name" and building a formidable personal reputation.

Kosovo's "Shadow Government"

The Balkan conflicts, including the Kosovo conflict of 1998–1999, also provided a significant opportunity for committing crime, neutralizing and justifying criminal behavior, and establishing criminal-political alliances. Kosovo was central to the Serbian nationalist narrative. The alleged suffering of Serbs residing in the area became the focus of the reemerging Serbian nationalist movement in the late 1980s. This provoked an ethnic Albanian counterreaction. The rise of the KLA fighter remains a powerful image of the desperation of Kosovo Albanians after a decade of oppression by Yugoslav president Slobodan Milošević and his followers.

The Kosovo conflict arose mainly over control of the territory of Kosovo, which both Serbs and Albanians had regarded as their own historical space. Despite its ethnic Albanian majority, Kosovo became part of Serbia in 1913, following the Balkan wars. Later it became part of Yugoslavia. Toward the end of the 1960s, the repressive Yugoslav policy toward Kosovo became more tolerant. Under the 1974 Yugoslav Constitution, Kosovo became an autonomous province within Serbia. After the disintegration of Yugoslavia in 1981, both Serbian and Albanian ethnonationalistic movements strengthened in Kosovo.

The Memorandum of the Serbian Academy of Sciences and Arts (1986), later used by the young Serbian Party chief Milošević to justify his actions, catalogued the Serbs' nationalist grievances. Although the memorandum did not create nationalism, it tapped sentiments that ran deep among the Serbs but had been suppressed by communism. In 1987 Milošević rose to prominence in Serbian politics partly by exploiting the growing discontent over the situation of Serbs in Kosovo. There was nothing about the Serbian communist leader's visit to Kosovo Polje in April 24, 1987, to suggest it would change the course of history. But for the first time Milošević donned the mantle of protector of all Serbs. "No one should dare beat you," he told a large group of angry Serbs who claimed to have been mis-treated by the Albanians.

> You should stay here. This is your land. These are your houses. Your meadows and gardens. Your memories. You shouldn't abandon your land just because it's difficult to live, because you are pressured by injustice and degradation. It was never part of the Serbian and Montenegrin character to give up in the face of obstacles, to demo-bilize when it's time to fight. . . . You should stay here for the sake of your ancestors and descendants. Otherwise your ancestors would be defiled and descendants disap-pointed. But I don't suggest that you stay, endure, and tolerate a situation you're not satisfied with. (Siebert and Little 1997)

Milošević gave this infamous speech at the Gazimestan field in Kosovo (Kosovo Polje), the site of a 1939 battle between Serbs and Turks. The speech came on the heels of a new constitution pushed through by Milošević in early 1989 that drasti-cally reduced the autonomy of the region, leading to extensive protests in Kosovo. After Kosovo's autonomy was revoked, the political situation worsened. The cul-mination of the disagreement came in 1998–1999, resulting in open armed conflict between ethnic Albanians and Serbs and subsequent NATO intervention.

Throughout 1990 and 1991 thousands of Kosovo Albanians lost their jobs, and Serbian police violence against them increased. Most Albanians were purged from the security apparatus, and the few who remained were automatically branded as traitors and of no real value to the Serb-run police. Various unconfirmed Albanian sources claimed hundreds of thousands of cases of official police harassment since 1981 (MSF 2014).

In 1989 literary scholar Ibrahim Rugova assumed leadership of the Democratic League of Kosovo (LDK), a newly formed party that resisted the nullification of Kosovo's autonomy. Under Rugova, the LDK pursued a strategy of passive resist-ance against the Serbian state. LDK members practiced a policy of nonviolent civil resistance and, importantly, established a "shadow government" system of unoffi-cial, parallel institutions in the health care and education sectors. The fact that the demands of the Kosovo Albanians were not heard during the Dayton negotiations of 1995, when Bosnia-Herzegovina's future was decided, led to further radicaliza-tion of the ethnic Albanian population in Kosovo. The Dayton Agreement failed to reward the patient resistance of the Kosovo Albanians, which led to widespread political dissatisfaction (Heinemann-Grüder and Paes 2001).

The KLA was created parallel to the LDK in 1993. The KLA brought together a variety of militant groups and individuals that sought the liberation of Kosovo through organized armed struggle. Its ranks were filled with a diverse set of char-acters, ranging from established organized criminals to Marxist-Leninist followers of the late Albanian president Enver Hoxha's ideals of a Greater Albania. It seems that a majority of KLA members were young Kosovo Albanians or exiles with no experience of the Yugoslavian political life. This contributed to their more militant strategy and uncompromising approach to Serbian authority in Kosovo.

The number of armed incidents involving the two ethnic communities was in fact very low in the period from 1992 to 1995, and their intensity was limited to short exchanges of fire. Although official Serbian data records 136 attacks on the police in the first eighteen months after the declaration of the Republic of Kosovo, the only major (and known) action was an attack on a vehicle of the Serbian Interior Ministry (Ministarstvo unutrasnjih poslova, or MUP) in 1993, in which two policemen were killed and five were wounded.

The strengthening of the anti-Serbian attitude culminated on April 22, 1996, when four attacks in separate locations took place within less than two hours. One of them, in which three Serbian civilians were killed, may have been a revenge attack. But the attacks in Stimlje, Pec, and Kosovska Mitrovica targeted uniformed MUP personnel; two police officers were killed and another three were wounded (JIR 2008). At the time, no organization claimed responsibility for the attacks. The existence of a "Kosovo liberation movement" was at first just a rumor, but continued attacks and a consistent modus operandi made it clear that such an organization existed.

Attacks continued at a steady rate, targeting Serbs and ethnic Albanians who pledged their loyalty to the Serbian administration. In early 1997, Albanian-language media started receiving faxes from an organization calling itself Ushtria Çlirimtare e Kosovës (Kosovo Liberation Army, or KLA), which admitted responsibility for the attacks. After a series of executions of "loyal Albanians," Serbian authorities arrested sixty Albanians in late January 1997. Although President Milošević claimed that "terrorism in Kosovo had been cut in its roots," reality proved him wrong.[15]

The series of attacks that gave the KLA credibility took place in a four-hour span on the night of September 10, 1997. No fewer than ten coordinated actions in locations up to 150 kilometers apart, mostly targeting police barracks and vehicles, proved the existence of a well-organized force that had the knowledge and resources to plan and execute relatively complex attacks. The attacks escalated further when antitank weapons were used for the first time to penetrate the wall of a building in a night attack in the village of Babaloc, near Decani. However, the event that was to make the KLA a household name was the first public appearance of one of its members on November 28, 1997, a date observed by Albanians in Kosovo, as well as their kin in Albania, as Flag Day, a holiday of great patriotic significance.

The KLA's Dark Side

Most Albanians perceived KLA members as legitimate freedom fighters, while the Yugoslav government called them terrorists.[16] By granting support and legitimacy to the KLA, Kosovo Albanians unwittingly contributed to the development of a criminal-political nexus. Large amounts of money were needed for the Kosovo shadow government to function and the KLA to arm itself. The KLA was not supported formally by any state, so it had to rely on alternative sources of funding. The bulk of the financing for the KLA seems to have originated from two sources: drug-related operations and Kosovo Albanian settlers in the West (Jonsson 2013; Alexe 1998).

John Cencich, a war crimes investigator who worked for the International Criminal Tribunal for the Former Yugoslavia (ICTY), has described his experiences investigating war crimes in Bosnia-Herzegovina and Kosovo as follows:

> The KLA members I encountered during my missions appeared to be either ragtag fighters or mobbed-up gangsters. We exchanged glances before we spoke, and these men were easy to size up. . . . On the surface, the KLA operated openly as freedom fighters, but the group had a darker side. . . . Certainly the Western intelligence community knew what the KLA was really into. As in Afghanistan during its conflict with the Soviets, the CIA had a hand in helping the KLA too.
>
> This wasn't just a war zone; it was also the underworld. I was smack in the middle of major auto theft, heroin smuggling, and human trafficking for purposes of prostitution. Narcotics trafficking throughout the Balkans funded many of the KLA operations. In fact, many KLA members were directly linked to syndicated crime in Albania. They also were involved in arms smuggling and had connections to the Italian mafia.
>
> On top of all that, the KLA ran extortion rackets. It is important to remember that while I was in Kosovo there was virtually no border between Kosovo and Albania, which made smuggling, trafficking, and other forms of transnational crime relatively risk-free endeavors. This was a lawless state, and the only trained criminal investigators . . . were focused on crimes against humanity, such as murder, rape, and torture. Consequently, the KLA was free to run whatever rackets it wanted with impunity. (Cencich 2013, 77)

But why did the KLA have links with organized crime figures? Why did the international community turn a blind eye for so long? The former Yugoslavia has always been on the main European drug-transit route, and there are more than five hundred thousand Kosovo Albanians in the West, mostly in Europe and the United States. The "shadow" institutions in Kosovo and the functioning of the KLA were largely funded through the "three percent fund," which received donations from the Kosovo Albanian diaspora in Western Europe and the United States (Sullivan 2004). Money was collected through fundraisers among the diaspora, with individuals expected to pay up to 10 percent of their profits from companies they owned, or 3 percent of their wages.

The Luzern-based LPK, led by Ibrahim Kelmendi, was the first organization to claim a direct connection with the KLA and openly collect funds. However, it seems that after an initial fundraising success, the LPK was not able to convince donors of its connection with armed elements. Its reputation was further damaged by revelations that the former head of logistics for the KLA, Xhavit Haliti, was believed to have been an informant to the Serbian authorities beginning in the early 1980s (KFOR 2004).

Consequently, although there seems to have been a willingness on the part of Kosovo Albanians to contribute to the cause, people were skeptical, demanding concrete proof of KLA connections before donating money. Many Kosovo Albanians proved incapable or unwilling to aid the "Kosovo cause." Therefore, according to a KFOR (NATO-led Kosovo Force) intelligence assessment, Haliti, who was responsible for the Homeland Calling Fund, "turned to organized crime on a grand scale as a source of recruits, funding and ammunition."[17]

Financial support for the KLA started coming through the extortion of Albanian immigrants abroad, and the KLA depended on the financing provided by patriotic bandits across Europe and the United States. According to investigative police files and interviews with Belgian law enforcement officials, a well-known Albanian mafia boss threatened people from the Albanian diaspora in order to collect "voluntary" taxes on behalf of the KLA.

Support for the KLA was not limited to money alone. Drug traffickers also sent armed men to fight alongside the KLA (Heinemann-Grüder and Paes 2001). Court cases from Germany, Italy, Belgium, and the Czech Republic point to a connection between drug traffickers and the KLA, either in the form of monetary support or the purchase of weaponry.[18]

Although more than twenty thousand Albanians reach military age each year, as late as 1997 the KLA was estimated to have no more than 150 full-time, armed members (Jonsson 2013). Training presented a major problem: Until 1990, basic rifle training was provided by the Yugoslav National Army, or JNA. Since that year, however, Albanian conscripts have not been required to serve in the JNA. Large basic training camps could not be established either in Kosovo or in Western Europe, forcing the KLA to limit its size. Several specialized training camps had existed in Albania since the postwar rule, and at least two (in Fushe Kruje and Bajram Curri) are believed to have remained well into the Berisha regime (Heinemann-Grüder and Paes 2001; del Ponte 2008). Although Fatos Nano's government has officially acknowledged Kosovo to be a part of Serbia and stated its commitment to a peaceful solution to the autonomy and ethnic problems, it is possible that unconfirmed reports of a training camp in Lhibrazd may be true as well.

Until the spring 1997 chaos in Albania, Kosovo Albanians could count on only a limited number of weapons. The reserves of the Kosovo Territorial Defense had been taken away after riots in 1981, and arms supplies were limited. However, the wide availability of weapons after the start of the conflict in the former Yugoslavia brought a steady trickle of arms to Kosovo. Many were sold by the Serbs themselves. Following the looting of Albanian Army barracks and depots in February and March 1997, weapons became even more readily available. There is little doubt that the seclusion of Albanians from the formal state apparatus, as well as the maintenance of a shadow government, all played a causal role in the rise of organized crime in Kosovo.

Patriotic Bandits

Ethnic conflict and the deteriorating economic situation supported Kosovo's corrupt criminal-political nexus. Developments were legitimized in the name of "nation building" and "ethnic survival." Personal interviews with organized crime figures from Kosovo, conducted between 2006 and 2010, reveal that many offenders used the conflict as a justification for their own criminal behavior. One former prisoner, Ilir (pseudonym), convicted in a Western European country for extortion, human trafficking, and prostitution, reported: "Committing crime in the West doesn't mean much to me. Who cares? I care about my own people in Kosovo. . . . Don't ask how much money I sent back to Kosovo during the war. I also wanted to come and fight together with the KLA, but I ended up in prison. But I don't care, because it was for the good of my people. I wouldn't commit the same crimes here in Kosovo and harm my own people" (interview, Kosovo, 2007).

It appeared that Ilir's situation arose from a complex web of contempt for Serbia and the developing European Union. Those committing crimes, such as prisoner X, found ways to neutralize the devastating effects of their crimes by appealing to higher loyalties, denying injury, or denying their victims. The conflict allowed many common people to believe they had a temporary reprieve from morality and to accept, and even participate in, illegal activities. In the words of a young Albanian teenager, an alleged gang member living in the Bronx: "Everyone hates us. . . and we give as good as we get" (Filkins 2001). Yet as one Kosovo Albanian man stated, "It's wrong to speak of these criminals as Albanian patriots. They don't care about their country, although they pretend to be patriots. They just give us a bad name" (interview, New York, 2013).

Besmir   During the mid-1990s, according to police sources, Besmir (pseudonym), a Kosovo Albanian man, was considered one of the "bosses" of the Albanian mafia in one Western European country. Besmir was known to be the leader of a notorious ethnic Albanian criminal group, composed of about twenty members, that specialized in extortion of nightclubs. Around this time, politicians in this country began to admit that they had a serious problem with Albanian organized crime. In the late 1990s Besmir was sentenced to prison on several charges, including being a member of a criminal organization, trafficking women, mediating in prostitution, kidnapping, racketeering, extortion, fighting, and possessing an illegal weapon. He also was suspected of financing the KLA, controlling his gang from prison, and committing a murder. He was freed eight years later on the condition that he return to Kosovo and never travel to the European Union again.

Besmir described how he ended up in Western Europe: "I had nine years of school when the troubles in Kosovo started. I was participating in some demonstrations against Milošević's regime and was arrested by the Serbs and put in prison for several months. Only Serbian judges were there. No other ethnicities. The police had to release me eventually because I was a minor at the time. Then my father decided to send me abroad because under these circumstances I could have been imprisoned for thirty or more years" (interview, 2007).

According to police files, after Besmir (and, several years later, his family) left Kosovo they founded an organization that I will call TAPI, which collected "voluntary" tax money from the Kosovo diaspora in their country of residence. The funds helped to finance the KLA.

Besmir and his family appeared to be great patriots who sought to reunite ethnic Albanian people into one state. Besmir resembled the many young supporters of the KLA who favored a militant strategy and armed resistance. The irony is that Besmir and his family left Kosovo in its most turbulent times, yet they presented their collection of tax money from the diaspora as a demonstration of patriotism. As a social organization, TAPI worked with Vendlinja Therret Asbl (Homeland Calling), and the eagle seen on the Albanian flag was the symbol imprinted on the club's membership cards.

According to anonymous case agents, Besmir's family collected some fifteen thousand euros for the KLA each month. A bullet was left in front of the doors of those who hadn't paid, as a threat. Vast sums of money from clubs, discotheques, racketeering and protection operations, and exploitation came into the hands of the increasingly notorious Besmir and his family.

In addition, Besmir provided security or protection to sex workers in the city in which he lived for about twenty-five to thirty euros per day. "They charged clients twenty-five euros for ten minutes. So my price was reasonable," he said. Some of the sex workers had his name tattooed on their vaginas. This basically meant, "Don't mess with me! Besmir has my back." Some of the local brothels had photos of Besmir with the brothel owners hanging near the entrance, again as a sign that the premises were protected. But, in Besmir's own words, most of the money he made went to the KLA. "Also, when the prostitutes decided to become my girlfriends, I stopped charging them for protection. I didn't care about the money any more" (interview, Kosovo, 2006).

Clearly Besmir was not in the criminal underworld only for personal gain. While searching the house where Besmir and his father lived, police found evidence of transactions between TAPI and Homeland Calling, linking them to the KLA.

Princ Dobroshi   Princ Dobroshi was allegedly the leader of an Albanian drug gang in Kosovo. For years he controlled the northern path of the heroin trade's "Balkans route," which included Turkey, the Balkan region, the Czech Republic, and the Nordic countries. In 1993 Dobroshi was caught in Norway, and in 1994 he was sentenced to jail for heroin trafficking. In a well-coordinated operation in January 1997, he bribed a guard and escaped from the Ullersmo prison in Oslo. He then traveled to Croatia and underwent facial plastic surgery. From there Dobroshi moved to the Czech Republic, where he continued his drug trafficking business.

On February 23, 1999, Dobroshi was arrested in Prague in a joint operation conducted by Czech, Norwegian, Danish, and Swedish law enforcement agencies that resulted in more than forty arrests. A note from the Czech special services (BIS) stated that some of the drug money that Dobroshi had earned in the Czech Republic had gone toward buying arms for the KLA. When the Czechs decided to extradite Dobroshi to Norway to complete his earlier sentence, the Norwegian police chose to fly him to Oslo in a private plane, because "it would be too dangerous to transport him on a commercial flight due to his close links with the UCK" (Raufer 2003, 71).

In January 2005, Dobroshi was paroled and deported to Kosovo. He now splits his time between Kosovo and Spain. Personal interviews indicate that both Besmir and Dobroshi continue to provide financial support to KLA veterans in Kosovo.

Agim Gashi   The Italian police investigation Operation Africa sheds some light on the sophistication of a heroin smuggling organization and its political and economic base. The operation was aimed at dismantling an important Albanian criminal network that was trafficking heroin in Italy during the 1990s.[19] At the head of the group was Agim Gashi, an Albanian from Kosovo. In Italy, Gashi established close professional links with the 'Ndrangheta, or Calabrian mafia.

Gashi's organization transported heroin, as well as cocaine and arms, through a series of intertwined networks centered in Milan and linking France, Switzerland, Spain, Germany, Slovakia, Albania, Kosovo, Turkey, and Egypt. The networks allegedly enjoyed the discreet support of corrupt officials from Italian intelligence agencies, and they had direct involvement with politicians, who were not arrested because of their diplomatic immunity (Raufer 2003, 71).

Gashi lived the high life in a luxurious villa in Milan. Nevertheless, as a good "patriotic bandit" he did not forget his country. He was arrested just as he was buying two hundred automatic rifles equipped with night-vision devices. "When war broke out in Kosovo, Kosovar criminals planted in Italy suddenly took an interest in arms trafficking," said Carlos De Donno, commander of the carabinieri intelligence unit. "Up until then, they only trafficked in drugs" (Raufer 2003, 71).

The Milanese newspaper *Corriere della Sera* reported on January 19, 1999, that "Gashi supplied his brothers in Kosovo with Kalashnikov rifles, bazookas, and hand grenades. He controlled the heroin market, and at least part of the billions he made from it was used to buy weapons for the 'resistance' movement of the Albanian Kosovo community."

During this investigation, the special antimafia unit of the Italian carabinieri, the ROS, used wiretaps to uncover the nature of Gashi's sophisticated criminal group. Investigators found that Gashi was in communication with arms dealers from Bulgaria, Romania, and Albania to buy automatic weapons, rocket launchers, and grenades.[20] He was convicted and received a heavy sentence in Milan in March 1999.

Changing Hats

Western intelligence agencies that recurrently turned a blind eye to the emerging criminal-political nexus in Kosovo in its early years also inadvertently contributed to the rise in organized crime and a crime-permeated society. Thus, many KLA soldiers, whose primary aim may have been a free and independent Kosovo, gradually established close connections with organized crime figures from the diaspora. Many agencies became aware of the connection between the KLA and drug traffickers in the early 1990s, and in 1999, former US president Bill Clinton admitted that the DEA and CIA knew that drug traffickers "contributed at least limited funds and possibly small arms to the KLA" (Klebnikov 2000). However, despite some talk in the press about the KLA's shady practices and criminal ties, no one seems to have paid much attention to this growing nexus.

The criminal-political links that developed blurred the lines between the formal and the informal, and right and wrong, in postconflict Kosovo. After the war ended, the problem of drug trafficking became more visible in Kosovo. Yet the Serbian police withdrew and KFOR did not seek to tackle the drugs trade properly (Klebnikov 2000; Jonsson 2013). Although the KLA was formally disbanded after the conflict, some former KLA commanders simply changed hats and moved into politics. For example, KLA spokesperson Hashim Thaçi, known to be one of the central figures of organized crime in Kosovo (Lewis 2011; Jonsson 2013) became the head of the Kosovo Democratic Party (PDK) and, in 2008, the prime minister of Kosovo. According to an interview with an international police advisor, Filip de Ceuninck, from EU Proxima in Macedonia, "With politics came crime, as well as corruption."

One bone of contention was a sixty-seven-page analysis of organized crime in Kosovo produced by Germany's Bundesnachrichtendienst (BND, or Secret Service) in February 2005 and reported by Frankfurt journalist Jürgen Roth in weekly magazine *Die Weltwoche* later that year. The report accused Ramush Haradinaj, head of the Kosovo government from December 2004 to March 2005; Prime Minister

Thaçi; and Xhavit Haliti, who sits in the parliament presidium, of being deeply implicated in the drug trade.

According to this German police report, Thaçi was one of the leaders of Kosovo's Drenica Group, which was involved in organized crime (Schwarz 2008). *Die Weltwoche* summarized the results of the study, saying, "Key players like Thaçi are responsible for the close links between politics, business and internationally operating mafia structures. Political recognition has awarded Thaçi, other representatives of the KLA and former terrorists with a previously unsurpassed authority" (Schwartz 2008).

A report written by the Swiss parliamentarian Dick Marty and adopted by the Council of Europe confirmed many of these findings (Marty 2010). The report accused many other former KLA commanders of serious human rights abuses, including trafficking in body organs, drugs, and human beings.

Ramush Haradinaj, for example, was the regional commander of the Dukagijn zone in Kosovo during the war. After the war he became the leader of the Alliance for the Future of Kosovo (AAK), the second major party of the KLA, and in 2004 he was elected prime minister of Kosovo. In 2005, however, the International Criminal Tribunal for the Former Yugoslavia (ICTY) indicted him for war crimes, so he had to step down from his position. Haradinaj was acquitted because of insufficient evidence, although this may have been due to witness intimidation (Brunnwasser 2011). Former KLA fighters were reportedly among the witnesses who were intimidated (Jonsson 2013).[21] During this time, however, the media and Western law enforcement agencies continued accusing Haradinaj of involvement in organized crime—something that was atypical during the 1990s (Schwartz 2008).[22]

Fatmir Limaj, a former commander of the KLA and deputy president of the PDK, also was tried by the ICTY, but he was acquitted on all charges in 2005. Between 2008 and 2010 he served as minister of transport and telecommunication in Kosovo. EULEX (the European Union Rule of Law Mission) investigated him on fraud and corruption charges for several tenders relating to the construction of roads. In order to avoid criminal prosecution, he was offered a diplomatic post outside of Kosovo (International Crisis Group 2010).

One of the potential key witnesses against Limaj was found dead in Germany. German authorities recorded his death as a suicide, although before his demise the witness had reported being threatened by Limaj's brother. If he testified, the witness said, Limaj's brother would "blow up him and his entire family" (Nimoni 2011). Despite the accusations against him, Limaj was always greeted with street celebrations when he visited Prishtina (BBC 2005; McKinna 2011). In March 2011, however, Limaj was placed under house arrest after a court ruling found that government officials are not immune from prosecution.

When the war in Kosovo ended, the number of KLA fighters was estimated to be around twenty thousand. About half went back to their previous occupations, and five thousand were integrated into the Kosovo Protection Corps (KPC), an organization with an ambiguous mandate (Jonsson 2013).[23] Since its establishment the KPC frequently has been accused of extorting money from businessmen under the guise of "taxes" for Thaçi's government (BBC 2000). After the conflict, KFOR appeared reluctant to tackle crimes perpetrated by KPC members. This created an impression that former KLA commanders were untouchable.

Also after the war, some twenty-five hundred former KLA combatants were integrated into the Kosovo Police Service, some into its unofficial "intelligence arm," SHIK, or K-SHIK (Kosovo's National Intelligence Service). SHIK was formed during the Kosovo war with the assistance of the United States and possibly other intelligence services, and then became the intelligence arm of the now-ruling Democratic Party of Kosovo, the PDK. After the war, however, SHIK established strong links to criminal organizations and turned its guns against its political competitors, including even moderate politicians in Kosovo. The Democratic League of Kosovo, LDK, has accused SHIK in the past of being behind the assassinations of its members, but these claims were rejected by SHIK's former director Kadri Vesel (Xharra 2005; Aliu 2012; KFOR 2004).[24]

The reintegration of former combatants into key positions in police and army units during the demobilization stage of a postconflict settlement became a problem in Kosovo because it supported patronage networks with the potential to increase levels of corruption and compromise the independence of the police and judiciary. The fact that many former combatants and police officers became involved in organized crime confused the local population and contributed to doubts about the future of their country.

Some of the most notorious Albanian organized crime figures, who were known to have financed the KLA during the 1990s, were deported to Kosovo after serving part of their prison sentences in Western Europe. After their return to Kosovo some reported in personal interviews that they expected "special treatment" from the former KLA leadership that was now in a position of power. The situation was similar to that in Albania, where clientelism and "the need to give back" no doubt affected the "rationality" of some decision makers.

Journalist Peter Schwartz, referring to the German Secret Service (BDN) report findings from February 2005, writes: "Former [Kosovo Albanian] criminals have won a reputation as politicians abroad, and enjoy parliamentary immunity at home, and the protection of international law abroad. This enables them to operate largely unchallenged in Kosovo and to put pressure on political opponents with the help of—officially forbidden—party secret service operations" (Schwarz 2008).

The clientelism did not stop here. Over time, police agencies have become more aware of the perplexing criminal-political ties in Kosovo and their negative impact on the country's future. Still, there have been accusations of improper cooperation between Western countries that have added to the political ambivalence in Kosovo. A report published by the Berlin Institute for European Policy in 2007 notes that the intelligence report published by the German secret service (BND) is particularly critical of the United States, which obstructed European investigations and was opened up to political extortion by the existence of secret CIA detention centers on the grounds of Camp Bondsteel in Kosovo. According to the Institute for European Policy, "Doubts are growing about the American methods and also as a result of the 'serious' description of a high-ranking German UN police officer [who said] that the main task of UNMIK's second in command, American Steve Schook, is 'to get drunk with Ramush Haradinaj once a week.'" (Schwarz 2008).

These statements came after the arrest of three German secret service agents in Kosovo for corruption, organized crime, and secret service plots (Kulish and Mekhennet 2008; Adams 2008). The affair began on November 14, 2008, when a bomb exploded outside the office of EU special representative Pieter Feith in Kosovo's capital, Prishtina. The building was damaged, but no one was hurt. Immediately afterward, in a neighboring building, a German man known as A.J. was questioned by the Kosovo security forces and revealed to be an agent of Germany's BND. This is according to the public prosecutor's office; German sources claim that A.J. arrived at the scene four hours after the explosion, to take photographs (Schwarz 2008; Fitsanakis 2008).

Fear, insecurity, patriotism, distrust, social trauma, and political ambivalence are all factors that have unquestionably affected the decisions of those who supply and demand illicit products in the Balkans—anything from arms and drugs to sex and protection. The multifaceted political and historical contexts described above illustrate how, in addition to economic payoffs, certain emotions—often a result of unfortunate events—led people to develop seemingly absurd needs and get involved in organized crime. One should never forget that both in Albania and Kosovo, a generation of young people grew up in states run by thieves and murderers, which no doubt affected their outlook and contributed to the creation of so-called criminogenic, or crime-permeated, societies. Consequently, today a thin line divides politics, business, and organized crime structures in Kosovo and Albania.

The National Liberation Army in Macedonia

In 2001, the Republic of Macedonia faced one of the most serious threats to its sovereignty and territorial integrity, caused by the open aggression of an armed paramilitary group called the NLA, or National Liberation Army. Ivan Babanovski (2002, 201) defines the NLA as "a terrorist organization which by using organized violence, terror, kidnapping, and intimidation is trying to change the constitutional order in the Republic, to jeopardize its security, achieving its goal through the conquest of territory." However, as scholars have recognized, a thin line divides freedom fighters from terrorists.

Between February and November 2001, the NLA occupied the northwestern area of Macedonia, where Macedonia borders Kosovo and Albania. Experts agree that a small number of Albanian political leaders in Kosovo, Albania, and Macedonia, who publicly encouraged the idea of so-called Greater Albania and provided financial support to the NLA, played a major role in the creation of the paramilitary group.[25] These political leaders' main interest in starting conflicts, according to Daskalovski (2004) and Babanovski (2002), was the profit generated by regional criminal activities, although this remains a controversial statement.

A report of the UNODC (2008) says that the village of Tanusevci, where the conflict began in 2001, was the main channel for arms for the KLA in the early 1990s. The report gives particular importance to the occupation of Arachinovo, which is located ten kilometers from Skopje, Macedonia's capital. According to the report, during this period Arachinovo—similarly to Lazarat in Albania—turned into "a hotbed of Albanian mafia activities" (Ilievski and Dobovšek 2013).

The NLA was led by Ermush Xemaili; Ali Ahmeti, the group's political representative; Fazli Veliu, who was responsible for the diaspora; and Gezim Ostreni, its chief military commander. Ahmeti is a Macedonian of ethnic Albanian origin who during his studies participated in the Albanian separatist movement in Kosovo, for which he was imprisoned for a year (European Stability Initiative 2008). From 1988 to 1989 he was one of the leaders of the student protests against the Milošević government. In 2001 Ahmeti told Macedonia's daily newspaper *Utrinski Vesnik* that ethnic Albanians in Macedonia were forced to go to war because no government official wanted to sit down with the Albanians to discuss their needs and demands (BETA 2001).

Veliu, Ahmeti's uncle, was arrested by the German police for terrorist activities. He also had close ties with the Kosovo criminal clan Jashari, a clan connected with Hashim Thaçi, the prime minister of Kosovo. Ostreni was a senior official in the KLA (Ilievski and Dobovšek 2013). Close relations between the NLA and KLA members set the groundwork for assumptions that the NLA was created following the KLA example.

The similarities between Kosovo's KLA and NLA lie not only in the groups' structure and function but also in their transformations. After the dissolution of the KLA in Kosovo, Hashim Thaçi founded the Democratic Party of Kosovo and was elected prime minister on November 17, 2007. Ali Ahmeti founded the Democratic Party of Integration (DUI) only a year after the conflict in Macedonia; according to Ilievski and Dobovšek (2013), there is no difference between the leadership of the NLA and the political party. People closest to the NLA occupied the highest positions in the party: Musa Xhaferi, a senior military commander, became general secretary of the party, while Fazli Veliu, senior commander of the NLA, became vice president of the DUI (Tsaliki 2011).

Three months after the formation of the new Albanian DUI party, parliamentary elections were held in Macedonia. The party of Ali Ahmeti won 102,038 votes, or 12 percent of the voting electorate—in other words, the majority of the Albanian population (Macedonia's State Election Commission 2012). Ethnic Albanians continue to support the party. In fact, since 2002, Ahmeti's party has received the greatest support of any of the Albanian parties in Macedonia.

Agim Krasniqi is another prominent ethnic Albanian criminal-political figure from Macedonia. He was one of the commanders of the Albanian National Army (ANA)—officially declared a terrorist organization by UNMIK in 2003—active in Macedonia in 2001. He remained the leader of an armed group even after the Ohrid Peace Agreement was signed on August 13, 2001.[26] While Ali Ahmeti disarmed the NLA in September 2001 and became engaged in the political process of implementing the Ohrid Agreement, Agim Krasniqi did not join this newly created party and continued with some criminal activities.

Krasniqi and his group continued to control the village of Kondovo (first between July and December 2004, and later between February and August 2005). Starting in September 2004, arrest warrants were issued against him for illegal possession of weapons, kidnapping, and theft. In February 2007 Krasniqi and his group pleaded not guilty on charges of acts of terror.

Despite his violent methods and criminal ties, Krasniqi had support from some Albanians in Macedonia and elsewhere. Nevertheless, the Albanian intellectual elite saw his actions as unjustified, because of the exaggerated use of violence. Some serious acts of violence conducted by his group occurred during the 2008 parliamentary elections in Macedonia. Krasniqi was specifically involved in several election incidents and was accused of "stealing votes" in villages populated with Albanians around Skopje and in Tetovo. Currently he is serving a prison sentence in Macedonia.

Although forming a paramilitary organization is a punishable offense, Ali Ahmeti, on the other hand, achieved much for the Albanian people and members of the NLA through his presence in the government. In July 2011, with the support of sixty-three ministers of parliament, the Macedonian Parliament voted for amnesty for a group of NLA terrorists charged with war crimes in 2001 (Murusic 2011). The cases were connected to the kidnapping and liquidation of twelve civilians, as well as to inhumane behavior during the conflict in 2001. However, the amnesty rules did not apply to ethnic Macedonian authorities, and some were prosecuted by the International Criminal Tribunal for the former Yugoslavia (ICTY).[27] Such double standards, occurring often as a result of conflict situations, caused further tensions among the already divided population and led to overall distrust in the system.

GOD, KANUN, AND THE WEST
Global Anomie, Risk, and "Culture Conflict"

Although it is not the only element worthy of critical inquiry, the absence of smooth political "modernization" and "democratization" in the Balkan region is one important factor in understanding Albanian criminality. While some scholars have pointed to cultural norms that are supportive of crime as a catalyst for criminal behavior, others have argued that the lack of consistent cultural codes and regulations necessary for ordering human behavior causes crime. The latter contend that culture and society must be regarded as mechanisms of social control, because humans depend on culture and society to order their behavior. During periods of conflict, however, social bonds and overall trust in the system weaken.

Emile Durkheim (1965b, 204) argued that "where interest is the only ruling force each individual finds himself in a state of war with every other since nothing comes to mollify the egos." Durkheim saw crime as a natural human condition associated with a breakdown of social norms that he called *anomie*. Society in general functions because of conformity through consensus, but once the structure is subject to rapid social change and conflict, people, neighborhoods, and nation-states have difficulty adapting to the new social environment.

The social self of human beings, or the aspect of self that is a product of socialization and cultivation of human potentials (the "civilized" member of a community), is suddenly lost, and the egotistic or primal self that is full of impulses knowing no natural limits takes over. Social solidarity based on integration and regulation, which allows the more primal self to become fully humanized in a life shared with others on moral common ground, declines during liminal periods.

In general, the weakening of formal and informal regulative mechanisms in the postcommunist Albanian context is an important macro-level factor for understanding the rapid increase in crime. During times of rapid change—when countries open borders and are subject to extensive foreign influences—traditional social controls often are undermined. Weakened controls and a lack of clear norms can lead to lawlessness, culture conflict, and overall confusion. In unstable periods, conflict also intensifies between the values present in society. Conduct norms that mirror the sociocultural values of the less influential groups often enter into conflict with the governing norms, leading to an increase in crime rates and systematic criminal behavior (Sutherland 1939; Sellin 1938).

In criminology, "social disorganization" and "culture conflict" explanations frequently have been applied to elucidate various forms of conflict such as crime, war, racial tensions, and suicide. A cultural system can be disorganized in the sense that there are conflicts among values, norms, and beliefs within a widely shared, dominant culture. Thorsten Sellin (1938), the father of culture conflict theory, argued that criminal law contains crime norms that primarily reflect the values of the group(s) successful in achieving control of legislative processes. Conversely, conduct norms mirror the sociocultural values of other, less influential groups. These norms often enter into conflict with the governing norms. For example, if the legal norms of one group are extended over areas that formerly were not cognizant of them, this might cause confusion and violation of these norms by individuals living in the area newly subjected to these norms.

Critics have argued that globalization has enabled the dominant Western norms to gain control of legislative processes in non-Western societies, causing sociocultural confusion and a breakdown of values, which has led to a further increase in crime (Black 1993). The so-called modernization process also has led to the development of new risks and to changes in the perceptions of "risks" in general.

Ulrich Beck and Anthony Giddens, the two most prominent risk society theorists, argue that we are moving from an "industrial society" to a "risk society" characterized by new uncertainties, rising individualism, and basic changes in major social institutions (Beck 1992, 21). They identify how the progress of science and technology, intended to reduce risks and increase stability, instead (often ironically) leads to instability, unpredictability, and new types of risk. This, in turn, leads to the development of a new breed of risk takers.

It is also important to note that culture affects the degree to which we are willing to take a risk. Mary Douglas argued that risk cannot be defined only objectively, since what counts as a risk depends on the values held by groups or individuals (Douglas 1985, 84). One of Douglas's key insights is that real risks do exist, but our perception of them is culturally biased. Culture and "culture conflict," history and prior experiences, media, economic and personal situations, and other factors affect both our willingness to get involved in "risky" businesses and the degree to which we care about consequences.

Identity Crisis in a Multi-Loyalty System

Despite the strong ethnic and cultural ties among Albanians, numerous historical and ethnographic studies point out that the Albanian population traditionally has been divided into two major subgroups, Ghegs and Tosks, based on their dialects. There are an estimated 2.9 million Tosk speakers and 300,000 Gheg speakers in Albania. The majority of Gheg speakers (between 1.4 million and 2 million) live in Kosovo. In Macedonia a small percentage of the population are Tosks, and the dominant Albanian population (about 242,250) is Gheg. The Ghegs in Albania live in the northern region of the country.

The Ghegs and Tosks have many social differences, according to public perceptions. The Ghegs are stereotyped as stern and courageous people, while the Tosks are viewed as friendly and better educated. In general, Tosks are considered more open-minded than Ghegs, perhaps because of the greater foreign influence in southern Albania, as compared to the isolated, mountainous north. The respondents in Zhelyazkova's (1999) study reported that they believe the Tosks are the intellectuals, the real politicians and creators, while the Ghegs have always been military men, the class of soldiers and police.

Before the changes introduced by the communist regime, Albanians were tribal people. Albania had broken away from the Ottoman Empire in 1912. It was then overrun by successive armies in World War I, and in 1928 it became a kingdom under King Zog I. Mussolini's Italy occupied the country in World War II, and King Zog fled to Britain. The Albanian Communist Party, founded by Enver Hoxha, led the resistance against first the Italians and then the Germans. A provisional government was formed in 1944, and by January 1946, the People's Republic of Albania was proclaimed. Hoxha became president and remained in power until his death in 1985.

When the Communist Party took power, Albanians' traditional lifestyles began to change drastically. Hoxha, a Tosk, believed that national unity could be achieved only if differences in tribe, religion, culture, and tradition were abolished. Therefore, his government suppressed cultural, linguistic, and economic differences between the south and the north. In 1967 Albania declared itself the world's first atheistic state, and it closed its borders to any foreign influence. Albanians born during that period (1967–1985) were never taught about religion, so many grew up either atheist or agnostic. During the communist regime, the ruling party also prohibited the use of traditional Kanun laws.

Sigurimi, the Albanian secret service, was the ultimate agent of social control. With its pervasive and secretive nature, it had a huge impact on the everyday life of Albanians during the communist era. Some statistics show that every third Albanian was questioned or arrested by the Sigurimi during the years of communist rule (Zickel and Iwaskiw 1992; O'Donnell 1995). As a result, many Albanians became private and distrustful, seeing a potential enemy in everything and everyone. This exacerbated the friend-enemy dichotomy in Albania, so that many people trusted only family members and close associates.

The collapse of the communist regime brought numerous rapid changes. Southerners reported that after the fall of communism and during the presidency of Sali Berisha, a Gheg from northern Albania, they were ousted from key state positions and highlanders from the north flooded Tirana. Differences in tribe, religion, and politics regained importance. This left many people angry, confused, and lost as they sought to reconcile loyalties based on formal laws, religion, and culture.

With the process of globalization, new laws emerging from the dominant Western value system were imposed on Albania, Kosovo, and Macedonia. This legal framework and value system did not arise naturally from within Albanian society. The gap between the people and the "state" remained wide, and research indicates that society was not organized with reference to the values expressed in law (Valinas and Arsovska 2008). Various Balkan governments ratified Western laws in order to align their countries more closely with the European Union and NATO. However, these governments did not always understand the values behind the new laws. Many organizations have pointed out that the Albanian population has not internalized the democratic values promoted by the West because the country itself has no heritage of democratic norms.

For example, according to a study conducted by the World Bank (2010), Albania's democratic transition did not follow a clear path in the 1990s, but instead oscillated toward an authoritarian leadership model. During his tenure as president from 1992 to 1997, Sali Berisha used his powers under the provisional constitution to push through a radical reform program, including the privatization of state property. As president, Berisha displayed some authoritarian tendencies, not only in his treatment of political opponents and critics from the press, but also in the manner in which he passed reforms without debate in Parliament, where his Democratic Party enjoyed a majority until mid-1997.

Although many Albanians were great admirers of the US political system and its policies, it appears that the West's top-down approach to leadership left Albanian society misaligned with the values expressed in its laws during this modernization process.

From "Albanianism" to Fundamentalist Islam

In their struggle to find their identity after the fall of communism, many Albanians returned to religion. Albanians are descendants of the Illyrians, who did not espouse any particular religion. Christianity was introduced to the region in the first century A.D. In the fourth century A.D., when the Roman Empire experienced a schism between East and West, Christians in southern Albania (primarily Tosks) identified with the Eastern Orthodox Church, while those in northern Albania (primarily Ghegs) embraced Roman Catholicism. This division continued until the early fifteenth century, when the Ottoman Empire conquered the Balkans (Gjonça 1995). Historically, Albania was a mostly Roman Catholic country, and Orthodox Christians, the second largest group, constituted about 20 percent of the Albanian population.

After the conquest of the Balkans by the Ottoman Empire, Albanians were introduced to Islam, but they were slow to adopt this religion. From the mid-seventeenth century onward, persecution by Ottoman Turkish landlords prompted mass conversions of entire villages to Islam. Conversions were particularly common in southern Albania and among Orthodox Christians. The Roman Catholic religion remained stronger in Albania's more isolated north.

Heavy taxes imposed on Christians under Ottoman rule led to the massive conversion of Christians to Islam during this period (Jacques 1995). To make the situation even more complex, the Muslims of Albania are divided into two main communities: those associated with Sunni Islam and those associated with the Bektashi, a mystic Dervish order that came to Albania through the Ottoman Janissaries.

Today, Islam is the most widely practiced religion in Albania, as well as among ethnic Albanians from Kosovo and Macedonia, followed by Orthodox Christianity and Roman Catholicism. Generally speaking, before the rise of communism, religious pragmatism was a distinctive trait of Albanian society. Edith Durham, who is known for her travels in the Balkans in the early twentieth century, noted that interfaith marriage between Albanian Catholics and Muslims took place without quarrels. She also recorded the lack of understanding about religion in many areas: Albanians told her that before they were converted to Christianity, and later Islam, they believed their forebears were Jews because, as she states, they had very little knowledge and "knew of no other" religion. Durham depicted the northern Albanians she encountered during her travels as people who identified themselves as Albanians first and took religion very lightly (Durham 1909).

By 1912, according to author Noel Malcolm (1998), more than 75 percent of Kosovo's population belonged to the Islamic faith. The majority of Muslims inherited the Ottoman Hanafi Islamic legacy, which is part of the Sunni school of thought, while a minority of Bektashi followers became part of the Shia sect. Among the four schools of thought under the umbrella of Islam, the Hanafi school has a reputation for being liberal, and Bektashi historically has favored a tradition of interfaith coexistence and intrareligious pluralism. Pashko Vasa, a famous Albanian poet in the nineteenth century, wrote in 1881 that the faith of Albanians is Albanianism ("Feja e Shqyptarit asht Shqyptaria").

After World War II, Albanians in Kosovo were subsumed again under the newly formed Socialist Federal Republic of Yugoslavia. The socialist system installed a secular state where religion, in many cases, was banned. The struggle for freedom and human rights continued to be a high priority among Albanians, and so religious identity remained subordinate to national identity. This was the case until the collapse of communism and the breakdown of Yugoslavia.

In the postcommunist period of normlessness and confusion, religion was revived and fundamentalist Islam spread (see figure 9). By the turn of the twenty-first century various foreign actors had taken advantage of the fragile postconflict situation in Kosovo and established themselves in the region. Fundamentalist forms of Islam also were imported to Kosovo by Islamic organizations operating under the banners of relief and humanitarian agencies, and by locally trained clerics from various Islamic countries.

Interviews conducted with politicians and law enforcement officials from Kosovo confirm that a number of Islamic organizations have managed to create influential social networks aimed at penetrating Kosovo's Islamic community and reshaping the Albanian national identity into a religious one (Basha 2013). Irfan al-Alawi, director of the Islamic Heritage Research Foundation, described an Islamic fundamentalism propagated by Salafis that is being imported from Arab countries and threatens the religious harmony that has existed in the region for

FIGURE 9. "Us versus them": a mosque destroyed by Serb forces (Kosovo, 1999). Copyright © Laurent Piolanti.

centuries. In an interview with Basha (2013), a prominent NGO executive and former politician from Kosovo captured some of the internal issues that opened the gates for Islamic fundamentalism: "The conflicts, the shattered social cohesion and family structures, the absence of institutions as well as the influx of religious charity organizations have all fostered the expansion of radical Islam in Kosovo," he said. "During the past decade, Albanians in Kosovo have been growing more conservative and are now turning to religion in greater numbers than ever."

In fact, as a result of the downfall of communism, accompanied by a decline of state authority and sudden relaxation of the coercive power of the state security apparatus, many people in the region found themselves lost in a multi-loyalty system. In countries such as Albania, Bosnia-Montenegro, Macedonia, and Kosovo, where clear norms and regulations were lacking, many people reembraced religion to avoid anarchy. And the new interpretations of Islam that reached Kosovo in the late 1990s created a fresh religious identity crisis.

Islamic-sponsored organizations took advantage of the situation. They built a number of mosques and provided free education and financial support to desperate Albanian youth. "They identified the poorest people in the communities, and offered them a steady salary every month just so long as they take over the ideology and start wearing the veil," said publisher Flaka Surroi, sister of the owner of Kosovo's Koha Media Group (Poggioli 2010).

By 2001, the International Crisis Group warned that more than thirty Islamic NGOs were operating in Kosovo thanks to Saudi, Kuwaiti, or other Gulf state funding. The report also stated, "The UAE has pledged millions of dollars to build some 50 mosques around Kosovo" (International Crisis Group 2001). In addition, the daily *Jeta në Kosovë* reported that more than one hundred mosques in Kosovo had been built illegally. Middle Eastern countries financed many of them, and local governments ignored their unlawful construction (see Basha 2013).

Terrorist groups also have taken advantage of the vulnerability of many Albanians. Foreign-born mujahideen, or holy warriors, first arrived in Bosnia-Herzegovina from countries such as Saudi Arabia, Pakistan, Yemen, and Afghanistan to help their Muslim "brothers," the Bosniaks, in the war against Serbia and Croatia. After the conflict in Bosnia, where Islamic agencies already were well established and operational, the mujahideen moved into Kosovo.

War crimes investigator John Cencich wrote in his book *The Devil's Garden:* "I was in Kosovo a little more than two years before the 9/11 attacks. . . . I, like many of my colleagues, knew little about 'the base' and nothing at all about Osama bin Laden's planning. . . . [but] Al Qaeda members were in the Balkans helping the KLA."

He then explained, "Bin Laden himself is said to have supplied one of his top operatives to assist in their training. In fact, Milošević tried to raise this issue during the trial in an effort to prove that he was fighting terrorists, but as was often the case, the judge shut him down and prevented him from raising potentially relevant issues before the court" (Cencich 2013, 77).

A prominent former politician from Kosovo also claimed in an interview that institutions in that country do not have the means or the political will to confront Islamic fundamentalists. He explained that troops part of KFOR—the multinational military Kosovo Force in charge of maintaining peace and security in the province—have substantial knowledge of Salafi groups operating in Kosovo. For instance, in April 2000, KFOR stormed offices of the Relief Committee, an organization funded by Saudi Arabia, because authorities suspected that members of the SJRC (Saudi Joint Relief Committee) organization were associated with Al Qaeda and were behind attacks on two US embassies. The organization rejected such claims, but a secret document from US intelligence claimed that two leading members of the organization, Adel Muhammad Sadiq Bin Kazem and Wa'el Hamza Jalaidan, were "associates of Osama bin Laden" (Wood 2000).

The Albanian newspaper *Gazeta Shqip* reported in 2011 that the Revival of Islamic Heritage Society, another Islamic organization claiming to do charity work in Kosovo, was actually a Kuwaiti-based NGO listed as a terrorist organization by the United States in 2002 (*Gazeta Shqip Online* 2011; Basha 2013).

According to interviews with local NGO representatives, KFOR allowed Salafi groups to operate freely, because this enabled international security agencies to obtain information about the activities of other radical groups in Europe and the Middle East (Basha 2013).

Islamic agencies acted fast in Kosovo, moving in during the conflict to take advantage of the high unemployment rate among youth and weak social and political institutions that lacked the capacity to prevent radical Islamist movements from infiltrating. More than a decade has passed since the conflict ended in Kosovo, and there are still reports, such as one published by USCIRF (United States Commission on International Religious Freedom) in 2012, stating that oil money from Saudi Arabia and other Islamic countries continues to support agencies that distribute hate literature and spread fundamentalist Islamic beliefs in Kosovo and throughout the region.

As a result of their atheist past, most Albanians today remain moderate, but religious conservativism is on the rise—and increasing fundamentalism forecasts more challenges ahead. Kosovo officials reported in 2012 that as many as fifty thousand residents of Kosovo were following the new, conservative form of Islam. In addition, many Albanian Muslim men reportedly have committed themselves to jihad (Basha 2013). Vedat Xhymshyti, a journalist for *The New York Times* and *The Guardian,* told *Klan TV* that there are two large Albanian groups that fight in Syria against government forces. Xhymshyti reported that the young men join the fighting in Syria because they see it as their sacred Islamic duty, or jihad. But the underlying reason for their participation may go back to the sociocultural confusion that prevails in Albanian society.

The Rebirth of the Kanun

The Kanun of Lekë Dukagjini (and other similar canons) codifies the rules on which traditional Albanian culture is based, primarily focusing on the concepts of personal honor, or *ndera vehtjake;* social honor, or *ndera shoqnore;* hospitality; and the word of honor, or *besa.*[28]

Lekë Dukagjini (1410–1481), a lord of a powerful northern Albanian family, formalized and standardized Albanian oral laws in the fifteenth century, although the practice of these codes of honor may date back two or three thousand years further, or even to the Illyrians of the fifth century B.C. In any case, the Kanun represents the fundamental customary law employed at least since the Middle Ages in almost all areas where Albanians have settled (Fox 1989, xii).

The influence of the Kanun among ethnic Albanians has been enormous, although the impact has been somewhat greater among the Ghegs of northern Albania and Kosovo than among the southern Albanian Tosks. According to Edith Durham (1909), the author of the ethnographic study High Albania, for the ethnic Albanians "Lek said so" obtains far more obedience than the Ten Commandments. "The teachings of Islam and of Christianity, the Sharia and Church law, all have to yield to the Canon of Lek. . . . For all their habits, laws, and

customs, the people, as a rule, have but one explanation: it is in the Canon of Lek"
(Durham 1909, 25).

The Kanun was an oral tradition, and no written version existed until 1913,
when a Franciscan priest from Kosovo, Stjefën Gjecov, started codifying the laws.
The complete Kanun was published for the first time in 1933. The Kanun is a formal
expression of the deeply felt concept of honor widespread among the Albanian
people (Malcolm 1998; Waldmann 2001). Its 1,262 articles have been described as
an expression of the de facto autonomy of the northern Albanian clans during the
Ottoman Empire (Fox 1989; Hasluck 1954). For example, the Kanun details a law
under which a person can protect his community against the attacks of third parties. This protection includes the moral obligation to apply retaliatory attacks until
honor is reestablished.

The Kanun states: "There is no fine for an offense to honor. An offense to honor
is never forgiven" (Fox 1989, 76). One who meets the revenge obligations laid out
in the Kanun is considered "cleansed white." The Kanun also clarifies specifically
how honor should be restored when laws are disobeyed. For specific types of violations it encourages financial compensation, mediation, and reconciliation.

The Kanun comprehensively elucidates the concept of hospitality, which
involves uncompromising protection of a guest, even one with whom the host is in
a state of blood feud. The Kanun also places enormous weight on the submissive
role of women. Albanian society has a long patriarchal history that emphasizes
women's obedience to their husbands (Baban 2004; Minnesota Advocates for
Human Rights 1996). One of the best-known articles (article 29) states: "A woman
is known as a sack, made to endure as long as she lives in her husband's house"
(Fox 1989, 38).

Under communist rule in Albania, from 1944 to 1991, the ruling party prohibited following the Kanun. Communist leader Enver Hoxha described the blood
feud as a legacy of feudalism. Under his regime it was strictly forbidden to defend
the honor of the family. Anyone practicing the customs laid out in the Kanun was
severely punished (Jolis 1997, 30).

The situation in Kosovo and Macedonia was somewhat different than that in
Albania during the communist era. Toward the end of the 1960s the Yugoslav policy toward Kosovo became more tolerant. In the period between 1966 and 1981 the
rights of Albanians were widely guaranteed, and the autonomy of Kosovo within
Yugoslavia was strengthened (Malcolm 1998). Albanians had their own educational system and their own Albanian-led government. Nikolic-Ristanovic (2008)
explains that in Kosovo, "leftovers" of old traditions were very much alive, even
under communism. The Kanun also was followed by parts of the ethnic Albanian
population in Macedonia who lived in remote areas secluded from central govern-
mental control. People needed their own "legal system" to deal with problems that
were not dealt with by the state (see figure 10).

FIGURE 10. The Kanun laws, on sale on the streets of Tirana (Albania, 2007). Copyright © Jana Arsovska.

After the downfall of communism in Albania, it appears that "Kanun morality" experienced a revival in secluded Albanian territories (Waldmann 2001). However, in the past ten years many original elements of the Kanun have been forgotten. Society and culture are not static, and the effects of communism, globalization, modernization, and Westernization have affected the traditional practice of the Kanun. Through oral tradition, ethnic Albanians today are acquainted to some degree with the contents of the code, but few have a thorough understanding of the laws. This naturally leads to individual interpretations of the Kanun, which often are used to justify criminal behavior (Mortimer and Toader 2005; Arsovska and Craig 2006).

But can the Kanun's influence be linked to the increase in crime in Albania after the fall of communism? In a 2006–2007 study of 864 ethnic Albanians from Kosovo, Macedonia, and Albania, respondents were tested on their actual knowledge of the Kanun (see Arsovska and Verduyn 2008). The ethnic Albanian respondents were very supportive of traditional norms, and 79 percent stated that tradition is very important for them. The laws codified in the Kanun are considered the foundation of Albanian culture, and 90 percent of the respondents stated that they had heard about the Kanun. However, just 23 percent of the respondents had read the

Kanun, whereas 71 percent said their knowledge of it was based on oral tradition. As part of the study, the respondents were given nine "Kanun statements" and asked whether they believed these statements to be true or false according to the Kanun. The statements reflected various important elements of Albanian culture, such as honor, hospitality, and revenge.

The scores were more or less normally distributed around point zero, suggesting that respondents' knowledge of the Kanun is quite poor; correct answers may be attributable to random luck instead of real knowledge. The study and the "Kanun knowledge test" point to the conclusion that although some self-selected elements of the Kanun (e.g., an exaggerated sense of honor, gender subordination, and revenge) have remained part of the Albanian mindset, they might not be explicit factors in the rise in crime.

The Confused Albanian

To understand contemporary Albanian culture, one must be aware of how long-held traditions continue to play a role in everyday life. These traditions are not simply customs or blindly followed habits; instead, they are guides that Albanians use, more or less reflexively, to chart a course through life. However, the reawakening of some core traditional values and social institutions in Albanian society—an outcome of the process of "modernization"—has led to the creation of new risks, uncertainties, and overall sociocultural confusion. The following is a representative extract from one of many interviews I conducted with ethnic Albanian people from Kosovo and Albania during 2006 and 2007. It points to the overall sociocultural confusion that characterizes Albanian society.

Q: *Fatmir, what do you think, why do people in Kosovo buy illegal guns, and why do they have a hard time giving up their guns? Is it for security reasons?*

A: No, not for me. I don't think so. You know the proverb, "You can kill an Albanian, but you cannot make him give up his gun."

Q: *So, is it maybe because of culture and tradition? Is it the Kanun laws?*

A: No, the Kanun laws are very old. They are not very important today. I don't think so. If someone were to give me a gun, I would definitely accept it, because it would make me feel safer. It feels good knowing you own a weapon. I need to protect my family.

Q: *Are you religious?*

A: I am a Muslim, but I don't really practice. . . . I think true religion is long gone around here. I guess I am a moderate Muslim.

Q: *What do you think, should the government give people more say? Do you think it is important that everyday citizens express their opinions and influence the government's policies via elections, the media, and community meetings?*

A: Sure, yes, freedom of speech and expressing opinions is very important for development. We need more of that.

Q: *How should one fight organized crime in Kosovo and Albania?*

A: Bring back communism. Harsh penalties. . . . Hang all these criminals on the main square. Only then you will have justice. We need a dictator that will bring back some order in this country. We just talk about human rights, and everyone does what they want.

Q: *What do you think of the death penalty?*

A: Allah gives life and He should take it away. . . . I don't know.

Q: *What would happen if you caught your wife cheating?*

A: Wow. You could kill her. It is part of our tradition. The Kanun allows for it. But I know we can't do it. I don't know. She would not do that. She knows better.

Q: *Do you think you would be able to commit a crime for money if you had to? Let's say a theft.*

A: [*He laughs.*] At times, I feel it's stupid and pathetic to live the way I live. Poor. Earning my bread in a difficult way. Nothing changes for years for me, while some people became millionaires out of crime and lies. I feel I am too honest and too good for this world full of scumbags. I don't know, is my answer.

During this one-hour conversation, Fatmir (pseudonym), a middle-aged man from Kosovo, like many other respondents, gave many contradictory answers. In the 1990s many Albanians—stranded between tradition and modernity, communism and democracy, collectivism and individualism, socialism and materialism, without any proper institutional or social guidance—found themselves lost in a multi-loyalty system. In postcommunist Albanian society, both state organs and social institutions weakened, or were never formed as Western democratic countries imagined, and they subsequently lost their ability to promote social goals adequately.

Broadly speaking, the sociocultural confusion and lack of clear social identity in the ethnic Albanian setting could be observed in the interview subjects' attitudes toward differing ideologies and value systems. In these interviews, 52 percent of ethnic Albanian respondents (strongly) agreed that their "country needs *a strong dictator* and *harsher prison sentences* in order to fight criminality"—a "procommunist attitude"—and 15 percent remained undecided. In a similar survey conducted by World Values Survey (WVS), support for "communist" values also was found.[29] One of the survey questions asked: "What, in your view, is the most important aim of a country: 1) Maintaining order in the nation; 2) Giving people more say; 3) Fighting rising prices; or 4) Protecting freedom of speech." More than forty countries were surveyed in each WVS cycle (survey wave 3: 1995–1999) and (survey wave 4: 2000–2005), but for comparison here, two countries were selected:

Albania (1998 and 2002), a country with a weak democratic heritage, and Belgium (1990 and 1999), a country with a well-established Western democratic system.

While 70 to 85 percent of the Albanians selected "maintaining order in the nation is a country's most important aim"; only 21 to 38 percent of Belgians selected the same option. In 1990, 31 percent of the Belgian respondents stated that "protecting freedom of speech," a democratic value, was the most important aim of a country, and in 1999, 25 percent of the Belgian respondents selected "giving people more say" as their first option. On the other hand, only 1 to 5 percent of the Albanian respondents thought the aim of a state was "to give people more say" and "to protect freedom of speech."

Although a significant number of Albanian survey respondents supported the idea of a dictator, many also supported the idea of democracy—that is, of having a democratic legal system, freedom of speech, and so on. For example, respondents were asked whether they agreed or disagreed with the following statement: "The democratic legal system of the 'Western world' cannot be a model for our country, since it is incompatible with our culture/traditions." While 29 percent (strongly) agreed with the statement, 23 percent remained undecided. When asked whether, in order to achieve development in their country, it was important that everyday citizens express their opinions and influence government's policies via different channels (e.g., elections, the media, and so on), 53 percent of the respondents (strongly) agreed, and 18 percent remained undecided.

Besides supporting communist and democratic values, a significant number of ethnic Albanian respondents also supported traditional values. They were asked whether it would have been useful to build the Kanun laws—the foundation of the traditional Albanian culture—into the legal structure of their country. Although the majority (58 percent) disagreed, 27 percent of respondents said they were undecided. The "Kanun knowledge test" mentioned earlier, however, showed that few people knew the Kanun laws well (Arsovska and Verduyn 2008).

The survey also examined the importance of religion, an issue related to traditional value systems. Although many Albanians appear to be atheists or agnostics, according to the World Values Survey, about 52 to 65 percent of the Albanian population reported deriving comfort and strength from religion. Moreover, when respondents from Albania and thirteen other countries were asked in 2002 whether "it would be better for their country if more people with strong religious beliefs held public office," 37 percent of all Albanian respondents (strongly) agreed with the statement, the highest percentage of the thirteen countries surveyed. While 23 percent neither agreed nor disagreed, 11 percent reported that they did not know. Respondents to the World Values Survey also were asked whether, in their view, "politicians who do not believe in God are unfit for public office." Again, Albanian respondents showed the highest level of agreement with the statement: 41 percent (strongly) agreed, and 25 percent remained undecided. By comparison, only 11 percent of Belgian respondents (strongly) agreed with the statement.

These survey results indicate that social confusion and a breakdown of norms exist in postcommunist Albanian society. As a group, Albanians appear socially confused, as they almost equally support "communist," "democratic," "traditional," and "Western" values, even when those values are incompatible with one another.

Research into the degree of social confusion in Albanian society also has been conducted on a more individual level. Pairs of contradictory statements were presented to 864 ethnic Albanians in order to test the degree of social confusion among Albanian people. As an illustration, the first two statements were the following: (1) "Our country needs a strong dictator and harsher prison sentences in order for the country to be able to fight criminality"; and (2) "In order to achieve development in my country, it is important that the everyday citizens express their opinions and influence government's policies via different channels (e.g., elections, the media, community meetings, and so on)." Although these two statements are contradictory, people supported the first statement (in favor of dictatorship) almost equally as strongly as they did the second statement (in favor of Western democracy). A large number of respondents (78 percent) answered in a confused, inconsistent way and found it difficult to prefer one statement above the other.

The second pair of statements also was based on contradictory views: (1) "It would be useful to build the Kanun laws into the legal structure of the country"; and (2) "The democratic legal system of the Western world cannot be a model for our country since it is incompatible with our culture/traditions." One might expect that people who favored the Kanun laws would not also favor a Western legal system. Yet again, many of the responses indicated that respondents had difficulty choosing one of the two options.

This "sociocultural" confusion combined with political instability and a breakdown of norms has the potential to help us understand the drastic rise of organized crime in the postcommunist Albanian context. This conclusion also has broader implications. For example, Phil Williams (2009) made similar arguments when he tried to identify the roots of organized crime in post-Ba'athist Iraq, an authoritarian and corrupt state dominated by Saddam Hussein and subject to international sanctions. He also explained the rise of organized crime after the US invasion in terms of two distinct waves: a first wave that followed the collapse of the Iraqi state and was accompanied by the breakdown of social control mechanisms and the development of anomie; and a second wave that was driven by anarchy, insecurity, political ambition, and the imperatives of resource generation for militias and insurgents.

MONEY, MONEY, MONEY: MAKING YOUR PLAY

Global Inequality

Another explanation for the drastic increase in economic crime in many postcommunist societies, including the Albanian one, can be found in part in the work of

American sociologist Robert K. Merton (1938) and his contemporaries.[30] Merton argued that there are certain relatively stable conditions associated with higher crime rates in American society. The problem lies in compulsive conformity to conventional American norms and values concerning material success that, in his view, promote dysfunctional changes in noneconomic institutions, and therefore lead to an increase in crime. "Numbers of people become estranged from a society that promises them in principle what they are deprived of in reality," Merton wrote. Basically, the American dream urges all citizens to succeed while distributing the opportunity to succeed unequally.

Scholars have taken Merton's arguments further in order to explain the increase in transnational crimes in postcommunist societies. Some have argued that, through globalization and neoliberalism, structural problems that have been prominent in the United States are now being reproduced throughout the world (Passas 2000; Williams 2009). Country after country has been persuaded (or forced) to promote free trade and consumerism, to reduce government regulation of business, and to adopt the same business model regardless of local, historical, and cultural differences. It is argued that neoliberalism and globalization have contributed to the spread of materialistic values, global anomie, and economic misconduct.

Initially, neoliberal policies were designed to foster economic growth, increased productivity, a better division of labor, lower unemployment, and greater wealth and prosperity, as well as more democracy, less poverty, and fewer inequalities. Unfortunately, in most countries around the world, these results didn't materialize. In fact, inequality has increased around the world in the past three decades. Globalization and neoliberalism have contributed to an overall increase in social expectations that are out of balance with realistic opportunities to reach desired goals. What makes the ideology of the American dream unique is the focus on money and material goods, a strong emphasis on winning by all means, and success for everyone in a society where many opportunities for material advancement are available. However, in reality, legal opportunities are lacking in many countries around the world, and international sanctions and embargoes certainly do not help in such harsh situations.

Criminologist Nikos Passas (2000) argues that economic and power inequalities often have, in fact, widened within and across countries during the past three decades, and promises of increased freedom, prosperity, and happiness for a larger number of people have turned out to be chimerical. Global inequality and the differences between middle- and low-income countries have grown steadily since 1983, although these differences are not as great as those between high-income countries and the rest of the world. Between 1983 and 2009, the average per-person gross national income increased by 297 percent in high-income countries and

60 percent in low-income countries. In 2009, the average person in a high-income country earned roughly 63 times as much as the average person in a low-income country.

As mentioned earlier, until 1991, Albania, Kosovo, and Macedonia were communist-socialist countries with planned economic systems. In contrast to market economies, where private owners make production and pricing decisions, in planned economies the government controls all major sectors of the economy. In Albania and other countries, many public utilities were quickly privatized after the fall of communism, and capitalism and a new market economy led to the creation of competitive and materialistic societies. The privatization process, combined with other drastic changes, led to widespread outbursts and destruction of public property. The extensive damage to the country's infrastructure, from irrigation systems to schools and hospitals, contributed to the economic decline observed in Albania in 1991.

Although Albania's economy showed growth between 1992 and 1997, poverty remained widespread and income-generation opportunities were few, especially in the mountainous areas in the north (World Bank 2010). In fact, Albania in the 1990s was one of the poorest countries in Europe, and Kosovo was the poorest region in the entire former Yugoslavia (UNODC 2008; Cleland et al. 2006). Although experts disagree about the exact level of unemployment in the Balkan region, because of activity within the so-called gray economy, data from Kosovo shows that since 1999 unemployment has soared to 54 percent (Cleland et al. 2006, 26–27), and in 2004, 37 percent of the Macedonian population was considered unemployed. International sanctions and the UN embargo on Yugoslavia in 1992 made the situation even worse, because many people were left without basic resources, including food, clothing, and oil. Smuggling in general became a necessity during this period of conflict.

Regional public surveys show that among a list of primary security concerns, the most important revolve around economics. Although absolute income poverty is rare in most of the countries of southeastern Europe, in some nations a significant share of the population lives on less than $2.15 per person per day, with children being especially affected (UNODC 2008; ISSR 2006). According to UNODC (2008) and UNICEF Report (2006) data, from 2002 to 2003 in Albania, more than 24 percent of the population and more than 30 percent of children were living on less than $2.15 a day.

Real gross domestic product (GDP) per capita in Albania in 1995 was estimated at $2,853, and may have fallen to $1,290 in 1996.[31] The war in Bosnia, the UN sanctions against Yugoslavia, and the fall of the pyramid schemes in Albania all have affected the Albanian economy (see figures 11 and 12).

In the 1990s and early 2000s, Albania's weak economy could not offer people legitimate opportunities to earn money quickly, and its dysfunctional society and

FIGURE 11. Distribution of food tickets by the NGO Première Urgence on the outskirts of Tirana (Albania, 1997). Copyright © Laurent Piolanti.

FIGURE 12. Between poverty, ruin, and modernity: dilapidated buildings against modern billboards on the road from Pogradec to Elbasan, Albania (2008). Copyright © Jana Arsovska.

weak cultural emphasis on nonmonetary goals could not limit or satiate their human appetites, which, as Durkheim argues, are unlimited. This, according to Durkheim, does not necessarily mean that poverty per se causes crime, but that the unregulated desire to be wealthy does. The bottom line is that after the fall of communism, the American preoccupation with economic success that Merton called "pathological materialism" influenced many people living in Albania and Kosovo, causing a state of global anomie. The primal self of some Albanian people, an outcome of years of lawlessness and conflict, simply "wanted what the others had" and did not care much about consequences or moral restrictions.

Global communication and media have played a significant role in this respect. Their influence in shaping the attitudes of many people in the Balkan region should not be underestimated.

One key element of this influence is the possible interrelation between the rise of mass media and increased consumerism (Habermas [1962] 1989). As Hayward (2004, 144) put it, what is unique about the last few decades of the twentieth century is the way that the creation and expression of identity via the display and celebration of consumer goods has triumphed over other, more traditional modes of self-expression. Status differences are generated and maintained via "lifestyle," which in turn is organized through patterns of consumption. Individuals not only recognize themselves but also are recognized by others through their publicly visible consumption choices. Shared consumption practices thus furnish a basis on which class and hierarchical boundaries are drawn between "us" and "them," defining those who are included and those who are excluded from a group's social membership (Southerton 2002; Hayward and Yar 2006). The media, in particular, has played a major role in increasing consumerism.

Research indicates that television viewing might have a significant influence on inducing materialistic attitudes because viewers are constantly making comparisons, and they tend to perceive their own quality of life as lower than that of others. The media continually offer pictures of life and models of behavior in advance of actual experience (McQuail 2005).

The World Values Survey mentioned earlier also provides some interesting insights into the way Albanians think about material possessions. The survey results are based on the responses of 19,729 people to the following question: "If there were less emphasis on money and material possessions, would you consider this to be a good thing, a bad thing, or wouldn't you mind?" The difference in answers between Albanians and Western respondents from fourteen different countries was striking. As can be seen in table 2, the majority of Albanians (37 percent in 2002 and 58 percent in 1998) thought that less emphasis on money and material possessions would be "a bad thing." Additionally, 37 percent in 2002 and 20 percent in 2008 thought it would be "a good thing"; and 26 percent in 2002 and 21 percent in 2008 "did not mind."

TABLE 2 Material possessions and hard work

Q1: Less emphasis on money and material possessions would be a bad thing.		Q2: Less importance placed on work would be a bad thing.	
Nation	Percent saying YES	Nation	Percent saying YES
Albania (2002) [1998]	37.3 [58.4]	Albania (2002) [1998]	79.8 [87.2]
Austria (1999)	28.6	Estonia (1999)	73.8
Estonia (1999)	28.2	Finland (2000)	63.1
Macedonia (2001)	20.7	Italy (1999)	59.4
Finland (2000)	17.6	Macedonia (2001)	55.8
Denmark (1999)	13.3	Austria (1999)	53.1
France (1999)	12.1	Greece (1999)	53.0
Sweden (1999)	11.8	Denmark (1999)	52.9
Greece (1999)	10.5	Spain (1999)	39.2
Belgium (1999)	10.3	Netherlands	38.0
Netherlands (1999)	10.0	USA (1999)	32.4
Italy (1999)	9.0	Belgium (1999)	31.8
Spain (1999)	8.7	Sweden (1999)	31.4
Great Britain (1999)	6.4	Great Britain (1999)	18.8
USA (1999)	5.6	France (1999)	17.2

SOURCE: World Values Survey (1990–2002).

Emblems of Success

Research into the pathological materialism within the Albanian population corresponds with this author's own findings. During one of many visits to Kosovo, I interviewed a Kosovo Albanian man who had spent almost ten years in prison for organized crime activities. We talked about the importance of money and the quality of his life after prison: "I have so many women around, and they are all crazy about me because I have money," he said. "They are not with me because I am some handsome guy but because I spend three hundred euros every day. A few days ago I had four thousand euros in my pocket; now I have one thousand euros left. What else do you want? Life is good" (interview, Kosovo, 2007).

He confirmed that status differences in Kosovo are indeed generated and maintained via "lifestyle." How much money one spends in a bar, what type of car one drives, and what kind of house one owns all matter. Mobile phones, shoes, gold—these "emblems of success" are what people use to identify whether someone is a "success story" or a "loser." It seems as if other, more traditional modes of self-expression have lost their power in postconflict Albanian settlements, and materialistic values have taken precedence.

During my visit to Kosovo in the summer of 2008, a professor at Prishtina University told me that a Westerner in Kosovo during the time of conflict and extreme poverty would not have survived for five days.

For good or bad, people who live here are adaptable to difficult conditions. This is what their harsh life has taught them. Some of the criminals that went to Western countries returned to Kosovo. They attracted attention [by] driving luxury cars and wearing expensive clothes.

These people have broken so many laws, but now they are enjoying their lives and spending money. They became role models here. So people started to despise small people who earned money in a difficult way. They hate the poor for being weak, but they also hate the rich if they can't have what the rich have. This is partially a result of Western influences, because the West showed us what we couldn't have. Many Albanians had very difficult lives growing up, so now they feel they deserve to have what people in other wealthy countries have.

During that same visit I took a taxi from Prishtina to Skopje. My driver was a pleasant, garrulous Kosovo Albanian man, and we discussed values, money, and Western influences. On our way to Skopje, he suggested, "I will take you to one village here in Kosovo, you won't believe it. . . . Every house is one brick bigger than the other. People don't need huge houses, but they build them anyway. It is a symbol of power. They have no money to complete the project and you see red bricks everywhere, but it doesn't matter—they must have the biggest house in their area."

The cultural goal of becoming wealthy was not the only thing that drove Albanians to a life of crime. Another significant element that deserves some attention is the emphasis that Albanian people place on work, as well as their eagerness to work in order to earn money. In the 1998 and 2002 World Values Survey, about 87 percent of Albanian respondents reported that "less emphasis put on work would be a bad thing." Only about 6 percent thought that less emphasis on work would be "a good thing." In contrast, 44 percent of the Belgian respondents in 1999 stated that it would be "a good thing" to put less emphasis on work.

The emphasis that Albanian respondents placed on work may be explained, in part, by the fact that Albania (as well as Kosovo) has one of the highest percentages of young residents in Europe, but it also may be linked to Albania's history and culture. Albania is the youngest country in Europe: just under a third of the population is below the age of fifteen, and the median age is twenty-eight. A UN population survey from 2006 indicated that about 10 percent of the Albanian population consists of males between the ages of fifteen and twenty-five, which is higher than the European average of about 7 percent. If Kosovo and Serbia were considered separately, Kosovo would be an even more extreme outlier, with 57 percent of the population below twenty-five years of age (UNODC 2008; ISSR 2006).

The lack of legitimate work, combined with the desire to work and the youthful population, is a factor that certainly has contributed to the rise of criminality in Albania and Kosovo. For example, since 1999 in Kosovo, 70 percent of sixteen- to twenty-four-year-olds are out of work (ISSR 2006, 26–27). According to EU studies, more than thirty-six thousand young people are entering the employment sector in Kosovo every year—and most of them are unable to find work (ISSR 2006, 50). The situation in the other Balkan countries with high numbers of ethnic Albanians, such as Macedonia and Albania, has been almost identical to that of Kosovo. According to EUROSTAT (2007) and UNODC (2008), in Macedonia about 66 percent of the population under age twenty-five was unemployed in 2004; in Albania, the figure was about 42 percent. In comparison, the average unemployment rate among young people in other postcommunist countries, such as Croatia, Bulgaria, Moldova, and Romania, was between 15 percent and 40 percent for the same year.

Albanian citizens are, on one hand, seeking work and the fulfillment of dreams. On the other hand, they find themselves in a society that fails to provide enough legitimate avenues for the realization of such dreams.

David Samuels, writing for *The New Yorker,* reflected on his encounters with the Pink Panthers, a group of Balkan thieves involved in robberies of jewelry stores across three continents. "Stealing diamonds is a serious crime, but as I paid the check it was difficult for me not to sympathize with these desperate and inventive men. The Pink Panthers were taking revenge on a world that had robbed them blind" (Samuels 2010).

I could not help but agree with him.

. . .

The myth that the traditional Albanian "culture of violence" and the customary Kanun laws have led to a drastic increase in organized crime in Albania is just that, a myth. Instead, it is life events or transitions that have positive or negative effect on people's decision to get involved in organized crime by bringing about changes in both motivation and opportunity structures for crime. In Albania, it is the recurring riots sparked by frustration and anger, a decade of lawlessness, growing patriotic feelings and criminal-political ties, and the disappearance of money that made many ethnic Albanians insecure, angry, and more grasping. These events also refined the country's taste for financial skullduggery, and they changed people's perception of risks and rewards. Materialistic values emerging from the Western value system, in combination with weak social and state institutions and the overall postcommunist confusion, turned many ethnic Albanians toward criminal innovation. The system became unstable and vulnerable, and so did the people.

The social structure in Albania could not offer people legitimate opportunities to earn money, and the dysfunctional society could not limit their human appetites. But even more importantly, social institutions failed to provide alternative definitions of self-worth, so they could not serve as countervailing forces against the anomic pressure of certain neoliberal policies. During this turbulent process of culture and identity formation, many Albanians were indeed left with only the world of emotions to express their hurts and their identity. Culturally specific perceptions of life in Western countries created a thirst for adventure and a pursuit of irrational aims based on distorted ideas about life in the West.

In addition, state institutions in the Balkans were disrespected and often viewed as corrupt. In Albania and Kosovo, a generation of young people grew up in states run by thieves, which no doubt affected their mindset and perception of risk, and contributed to the creation of crime-permeated societies. The shadow economy that persisted in the region empowered a criminal class on which common people depended. This, in turn, generated further cynicism about the rule of law. Because of the overall instability of the system and the growing distrust in state institutions, it all came down to the need for immediate gratification: "Who knows what will happen tomorrow?"

The "games" that some Western countries played in order to protect their own interests did not help these already dysfunctional societies. Normlessness and sociopolitical confusion made many people unable to differentiate right from wrong. The negative influence of this social disruption can be observed especially in societies such as Albania's, where a relatively large, unemployed, and youthful population is in search of its identity. Although certainly not all young and unemployed Albanians resorted to crime and violence, those that did hustled hard, with seemingly no regard for long-term consequences. For these people, however, it was not always about business and money. It was also about pride, and they seemed committed to the criminal life, at all costs.

Chapter 3

ON THE RUN

Albanians Going West

Mafiosi find themselves in the new locale not of their own volition; they have been forced to move there by court orders, to escape justice or mafia infighting and wars. . . . Even if they do not move willingly, they can still . . . chose where to move. . . . They move to places where they had a previous contact, a trusted friend or a relative.

—FEDERICO VARESE, *MAFIAS ON THE MOVE* (2011, 8)

The common perception is that Albanian organized crime groups that now play a significant role in the European and American organized crime scene started to develop rapidly after the fall of communism in the early 1990s. By 1999, as a result of the activities of some Albanian criminal groups and the great deal of international attention these groups received, Albanian criminals were considered to be a dangerous breed, posing a significant threat to Western society. In 2000, one of Italy's top prosecutors, Cataldo Motta, said that Albanian organized crime had become a point of reference for all criminal activity: "Everything passes via the Albanians" (Barron 2000).

However, the relationship between migration and transnational organized crime is complex. On one hand, it is not uncommon to hear stories of young Kosovo refugees and Albanian asylum seekers leaving their war-torn countries in hope of finding a better life in the West, but then turning to a life of crime. Some of these immigrants tried to make the most of bad luck after being forced to move abroad by infighting between gangs, retaliation, or court orders. There also are stories of reverse migration: Albanian criminals who were established in the West and then returned to Albania or Kosovo to escape criminal prosecution. So what might appear to be the product of globalization is, in fact, a consequence of state repression exporting the problem to other countries.[1]

On the other hand, some scholars have speculated that the migration of organized crime groups is more strategic; it is a business choice and a product of globalization, carefully planned and coordinated by powerful and well-connected organized crime figures who reside in Albania and Kosovo. According to this perspective, criminal groups are similar to multinational corporations. They are rational, profit-driven organizations that migrate easily to advanced market economies, where they create long-lasting outposts.[2]

It is widely believed that Albanian offenders gained control over Western markets during the 1990s, and that they remain under the control of powerful groups back in their country of origin. But once organized crime figures find themselves in new territory, under what conditions do they succeed in becoming entrenched? Are Albanian organized crime groups indeed able to reproduce their territorial control in different countries? Do they get support from their ethnic constituencies abroad? In which types of criminal activities are they commonly involved? And are these criminal organizations malleable, learning organizations? Let us explore the migration patterns of Albanian organized crime groups to Western countries, and then study their ability to adapt to their new environments.

STATE OPPRESSION MEETS BLING-BLING

Rags to Riches

As far back as the 1960s, and particularly during the 1990s, a number of Kosovo and Albanian asylum seekers left their unstable countries and migrated to the West. Although most Albanian refugees never engaged in criminal activities and worked hard to earn an honest living, some turned to a life of crime after spending several months or years in their host countries.

"Most of us come from poor families," Vulnet (pseudonym), an Albanian criminal involved in organized theft in Italy, said. "Some of us went to Italy and some to Greece during the conflict to escape the poverty and chaos. We wanted to try our luck abroad. We then saw how people lived there, and we had nothing. And then some of us went insane and tried to have everything at once. We wanted the cars, the women, the lavish lifestyle. . . . We wanted fast money. It sucks to be poor" (interview, Kosovo, 2009).

Arben Dumani started a new life in Scotland in 1999, after he and his family left war-torn Kosovo. The ten-year-old boy began attending school in Glasgow. Language experts and psychologists were on hand to help him settle in to his strange but welcoming new surroundings. Speaking through an interpreter, Dumani said: "It was good. We played football, and we found a lot of friends. I drew pictures of houses, and I am learning the days of the week in English. It was interesting and I was happy" (McCabe 2013).

But thirteen years later Dumani was in prison, convicted of leading a sophisticated organized crime network that plotted to flood Scotland with 1.2 million pounds (two million dollars) of heavily cut cocaine (McCabe 2013). Allegedly,

Dumani's group, composed of ethnic Albanians, drew the attention of the Scottish Crime and Drug Enforcement Agency.

In 2013 Dumani found himself at the High Court in Glasgow, along with his associates Albert Memia, Fabion Ponari, and Gjeorgj Pjetri. The foursome, all originally from Albania and Kosovo and in their twenties, were sentenced to a total of thirty years and six months in prison. They helped to bring about their own downfall by taking photos of themselves with their mobile phones, snorting cocaine laid out to spell their names, and showing off to people in their area.

Dumani's story somewhat resembles that of Luan Plakici. Plakici arrived in Britain in 1996, claiming political asylum as a refugee from Kosovo. In reality he came from Laci, a small city in northern Albania. Plakici drove around London in a battered Ford Fiesta, but his linguistic skills enabled him to find work as an interpreter for Home Office–approved law firms in immigration cases. However, soon after being granted British citizenship in 2001, the twenty-six-year-old Albanian was driving a Ferrari Spider and a BMW convertible and wearing designer clothes, and he had 204,000 euros (340,000 dollars) in his bank accounts. He rented houses in London and began building luxury homes for himself in three European countries, including Albania (McKillop and Wilson 2003; BBC 2003a). In 2001–2002 he identified himself as a self-employed construction worker and declared earnings of 18,000 euros (30,000 dollars). In truth, it is likely that his illegal financial earnings were about 3 million euros (5 million dollars).

Plakici's fortune was built on human trafficking for sexual exploitation. He saw the cash potential when he worked for London law firms specializing in immigration. After securing British citizenship, he headed for Moldova, where he romanced a sixteen-year-old, married her, and brought her back to Britain. On her wedding night she was forced to sell her body to other men; she earned Plakici 144,000 euros (240,000 dollars) in two years (McKillop and Wilson 2003).

Paradoxically, Plakici was arrested just twenty-four hours after buying his dream car, a Ferrari. He was found guilty on seven counts of trafficking and sentenced to twenty-three years in prison.

Viktor Hoxha also turned to crime after arriving in the West. He was born in Podujev in Kosovo. He was about sixteen years old when Yugoslavia started to break down and the troubles in Kosovo commenced. Hoxha was among the young students who participated in early demonstrations against the Milošević regime. Although he was a minor, the Serbs allegedly arrested him and put him in prison. After his release, a lawyer advised his father to send young Hoxha abroad, so when an uncle who had been living in Belgium invited the teen back home with him, Hoxha applied for asylum in Belgium and lived and worked with his uncle, earning good pay.

But when the rest of Hoxha's family arrived in Belgium, he moved with them to another city and had to find a new job. He started working as a bouncer in discotheques and nightclubs. Most of his friends were Albanians, but his network expanded, and he connected with some local tough guys. Soon he was running a protection racket in Antwerp and was involved in both racketeering and prostitution. He also led a "security" team whose members worked the front doors of nightclubs in Antwerp. He was convicted in 1998.

Parid Gjoka had a somewhat similar story. He emigrated to the United States when he was seventeen, with no intention of returning to Albania when his temporary visa expired. He said he came for a better life and started out doing honest work: construction, valet parking, and roofing. But in one of the Albanian coffee shops in Ridgewood, Queens, he met Kujitim Konci, also from Tirana, whom he said had a reputation "as one of the biggest gangsters in Albania" (Heldman 2011a). Envious of Konci's lifestyle, Gjoka started driving to Michigan, picking up forty or fifty pounds of marijuana at a time and taking it back to New York City. Between 2000 and 2008, he was allegedly trafficking fifty to one hundred pounds of weed every ten days, and soon he came to lead an important drug trafficking group in New York. According to journalist Kevin Heldman, Parid Gjoka

> was arrested for a gun charge in 2004, for a D.W.I. in 2005, by immigration in 2007 and for a bar fight in 2008. Just before he was about to be deported the F.B.I. arrested him in this [drug trafficking] case. He signed a cooperation agreement with the government in 2009. I heard a defense lawyer say that Gjoka will have spent $180,000 on him, and that he'll wind up getting a new name, a new identity, and a spot in a special witness-protection program. (Heldman 2011a)

These stories resemble that of the renowned Basri Bajrami, discussed in chapter 1, as well as of other Albanian organized crime figures.

Escaping Communism

A number of Albanian organized crime figures are the sons of Albanian political asylum seekers who tried to escape the harsh Albanian communist regime during the 1960s. They feared for their lives in their own country and sought asylum abroad.

In the United States another criminal, Zef Mustafa, earned a reputation for being ruthless with a baseball bat. Mustafa's Albanian parents had fled communism and brought him from Italy to the United States in 1962. The boy's mother died when he was just two years old, and his father had died by the time he was eleven. Mustafa grew up in an orphanage and dropped out of school by the sixth grade. He spent most of his time hanging around Arthur Avenue in the Bronx, until a local family took him in. Thanks to this family he learned a trade, creating programs in the communications industry. However, Mustafa was also "known for breaking heads," as one Gambino informant told the FBI (Robbins 2005). His alleged prowess with a bat was part of the evidence presented against him by federal prosecutors in Brooklyn.

Mustafa regularly visited the Ravenite Social Club, a hangout on Mulberry Street that was frequented by the Gambino crime family. By 1996, according to court records, Mustafa was working with Salvatore Locascio, the son of Frank "Frankie Loc" Locascio, who took over as the Gambino family's *capo* when his father was sent to prison. Between 1996 and 2002, Mustafa earned as much as 19 million dollars from a telephone and Internet fraud involving sex lines. In 2000 alone, his declared income was 5.9 million dollars, and his tax payments totaled 2.1 million dollars.

Ali Zherka is a friend and associate of Din Celaj. Both were arrested and charged in 2007 with federal crimes. The charges involved stealing safes, breaking into warehouses, and, in one case, holding up a truck driver at a Pennsylvania rest stop who had stashed 420,000 dollars in drug profits inside his rig (Feuer 2007a).

In an interesting coincidence, Ali Zherka's brother is Selim Zherka, a proprietor of high-end New York City strip clubs and publisher of the *Westchester Guardian* weekly newspaper. An online interview in the *New Britain City Journal* described Selim Zherka's upbringing, presumably with his younger brother Ali:

> Born and raised in Bronx, NY, Zherka also obtained his high school education there. He never went to college because he didn't need to. He's a self proclaimed graduate of the Bronx's gritty "sidewalk university." The "school of hard knocks" is the best education anyone can get, according to Zherka. At age 11 he started working at Sal's Pizza on 206th St. in the Bronx as a dishwasher and by age 15, he was looking to buy his own pizza parlor. (Johnson 2012)

Selim Zherka remembers his father waking him up late at night to help him carry an old, dirty couch that was in the garbage several blocks away. "My father had so much pride that he did not want to be seen picking from the garbage during the day so he waited till late at night," he said. "I'm not embarrassed about that. I respect what my parents did to survive and it's what shaped who I am today" (Johnson 2012).

Selim and Ali Zherka's parents, Albanian asylum seekers who tried to escape torture under the harsh regime of Enver Hoxha, came to the United States to secure a better life for their family. But, as seen in numerous other cases of poor migrant families, the new sociocultural environment had its own effects on the children of the migrants, particularly on Ali Zherka.

Albanian offender Kapllan Murat, like Ali Zherka, is the son of UN refugees from Albania who escaped first to Kosovo and then to Italy. It is believed that Murat was born in Italy in 1962; from there his parents reportedly went to Belgium, and their son now is known as a Belgian criminal of Albanian descent. Already a delinquent in his youth, Murat was imprisoned in 1980 after a fight in which one person was killed and others were wounded. A driver for the notorious

Haemers gang, which kidnapped former Belgian prime minister Paul Vanden Boeynants in 1989, he later was nicknamed the "Getaway King" for his multiple successful prison escapes.

On July 2, 2008, Murat left the prison of Nivelles, in Belgium, after being granted a conditional early release.

Escaping Prosecution

Not all Albanian criminals were young and innocent refugees or asylum seekers when they arrived in the United States or Western Europe. Some already had a criminal history, as seen in the case of Din Celaj, Ali Zherka's associate mentioned above. A writer for *The New York Times* stated in 2007 that Celaj "is a young man with a breathtaking criminal past. By his own admission, his first crime was committed at age 10, when he posed as the son of a young couple who were smuggling drugs from Germany past American customs. By 12, he was stealing car radios in the Bronx; by 13, shaking down the owner of a coffee shop. By 15, he owned a .25-caliber Beretta. He used to fire it, he has testified, at ratty old chairs in his basement" (Feuer 2007b).

Ketjol Manoku was a teenager in Albania in 1997 when the pyramid schemes collapsed. He grew up witnessing a lot of violence, corruption, and lawlessness. "In Albania, he said, he was once beaten by police until his grey shirt was bright red, and the cops were paid off the next day and he was let go. He said he fired his first gun at age 11—a Russian version of a .45," Heldman reported in a 2011 article for the New York *Capital* (Heldman 2011a).

Manoku left school at age sixteen or seventeen. At nineteen he spent a year in the army, where he and a friend saw two men get shot. Manoku's friend reached down and took the hat off the dead man's head and put it on his own head. "Man, give the dead man his hat back," Manoku said he told his friend (Heldman 2011a).

Manoku recalls that he went to Greece, got involved in counterfeiting and other crimes, and eventually was deported to Albania. He set out for America in 2001, looking for a new life, and sneaked across the border from Mexico, speaking no English. He had family in Michigan, so he headed there, working in restaurants. He found work in security, helped to organize concerts featuring Albanian singers, and started a small cleaning company. He was also involved in some muscle work. "So, say, an Albanian would be smuggled into America for a fee of $12,000; he'd pay $8,000 up front but once he's here in America he wouldn't want to pay the rest. Manoku would be the guy sent to convince him to settle up" (Heldman 2011a). Since 2002 Manoku has been locked up in prison on ten felony charges, including murder.

Redinel Dervishaj and his brother Plaurent, Albania's most wanted fugitive, also had criminal records when they fled their homeland. On March 15, 2006, Albanian judicial authorities issued arrest warrants for several members of an Albanian organized crime group based in Durrës. Plaurent Dervishaj allegedly had been a leading member of this group since 1997, and he was charged with founding a criminal organization, committing premeditated murder in complicity, and illegally keeping weapons and munitions. Specifically, Plaurent Dervishaj was wanted for murdering at least four rival gang leaders, including one with an antitank weapon, between 1998 and 1999. He also was believed to have been involved in several other murders carried out in Albania as recently as February 2005.

The Dervishaj brothers avoided arrest in Albania by flying from Vienna to New York City on the day Plaurent's arrest warrant was issued. A provisional arrest warrant was issued for him in New Jersey a month later, on the charge of his being a fugitive from a foreign country.

In 2007 Redinel Dervishaj went with another Albanian gangster to a man's house in Queens, New York, threatening to kill the man's family if he didn't give them twenty thousand dollars. The man refused, instead shooting Redinel Dervishaj in the arm and killing his partner. Redinel Dervishaj pleaded guilty to attempted grand larceny and was sentenced to time served. Then, in 2012, a Staten Island grand jury declined to indict him for the March 2012 slaying of Antonio Lacertosa, outside the former Espana Restaurant in Staten Island, New York. Redinel Dervishaj had claimed self-defense. A year later, in 2013, according to authorities, a Staten Island police officer and two associates—including Redinel Dervishaj—shook down a Queens restaurant, demanding cash for "protection" and threatening violence if the victim "didn't play ball" (Donnelly 2013).[3]

Daut Kadriovski is one of the most frequently discussed international drug traffickers and so-called Albanian mafia bosses. Kadriovski is an ethnic Albanian from Macedonia who, during the 1990s, escaped prison multiple times and then, to evade prosecution, moved from country to country. In 1993 he managed to escape a German prison, after which he is believed to have moved to Turkey and then to the United States. Sources indicate that he was trafficking drugs through several types of businesses in New York and Philadelphia, and had close contacts with Albanians living in the Bronx (Williams 2005). Kadriovski gained the attention of the Australian authorities after it was discovered that he had created a drug pipeline through Albania and Croatia to Sydney and Brisbane. He was seen in an embassy in Athens, Greece, trying to obtain an Australian passport. He evaded authorities, and was again seen in Germany under one of his many aliases. Daut had a thick criminal record and was wanted in at least twelve European countries for more than a decade. He was last arrested on drug trafficking charges in September 2001 in Albania, where he seemed to have resided for at least a few years. Allegedly he had received a new passport under the name of Mehmed Haidini, and had had facial surgery (Balkanforum 2013). He was extradited first to Italy, and then to his native Macedonia. Allegedly, because of mental illness and health problems, he was released from prison, and he currently resides in Macedonia (*Albeu* 2010).

False Dreams

And then there are those like John Edward Alite, aka Johnny Alletto, a New York City mobster of Albanian origin. A former member of the Gambino crime family, he was a friend and crew leader for crime boss John A. Gotti in the 1980s and 1990s. Prosecutors accused Alite of heading a unit of the Gambino crime operation in Florida. In 2006 he was convicted on several counts of murder conspiracy, racketeering, and other charges. He was sentenced in 2011 to ten years in prison (of which he had already served six). Because his family is Albanian, not Italian, Alite could not become a made member of the Gambino organization. But he could— and did—serve as a prosecution witness against former associates, including Gotti and Charles Carneglia, in wide-ranging racketeering trials.

Alite grew up in Woodhaven, Queens, and briefly attended the University of Tampa on a baseball scholarship. In court, he testified that he was introduced to organized crime when his uncle took him to a gambling den in the Bronx, accompanied by a made man in the Gambino crime family.

Alite and Gotti met in their teens and moved quickly into criminal enterprises, according to federal prosecutors. Alite testified that he and Gotti ran a cocaine trafficking ring in the Forest Hills neighborhood of Queens and extracted a "tax" from other dealers. By the 1990s, Alite said, the ring was earning one million dollars a month.

According to Alite, his relationship with Gotti and the Gambino leadership soured in 1994, when Alite confronted an associate, Carmine Agnello. Alite allegedly had been having an affair with Agnello's wife, Victoria Gotti, and grew angry when he believed that Agnello was beating her. Victoria Gotti strongly denied the affair. After a tense reconciliation meeting with Gotti, Alite received the family's permission to move to Tampa, where he had an interest in a valet business run by a friend, Ronnie "One Arm" Trucchio, and ran a crew for the Gambino family. In an interview with the *Daily Mail,* Alite said that now his priority was keeping his son John Jr. on the straight and narrow, and disrupting the mob's recruiting pipeline of young men lured by false dreams of money and honor.

"MAFIA" MIGRATION: STRATEGIC OR SPONTANEOUS?

Conspiracy and Alien Invasion

Since the 1950s, major investigative bodies and the Western media have defined organized crime as a nationwide, centralized, criminal organization. A popular theory held that the criminal underworld in the United States was centrally organized by a ruthless Italian organization originating in Sicily and known as the mafia. In the early 1950s, the Federal Bureau of Narcotics was the major proponent of this campaign. With its active support, the Special Committee to Investigate Organized Crime of the Interstate Commerce Commission, chaired by US Senator Estes

Kefauver, became the first congressional body to argue that the mafia is a well-structured, sinister organization—an import of secret criminal societies rooted in foreign cultures (Paoli and Fijnaut 2005). In 1967 the US President's Commission on Law Enforcement and Administration of Justice confirmed the conspiratorial nature of organized crime by announcing that organized crime is "a society that seeks to operate outside the control of the American people and their governments" (President's Commission on Law Enforcement and Administration of Justice 1967).

The testimony of Joseph Valachi, the first organized crime "insider," was the basis for the alien conspiracy model of organized crime. Criminologist Donald Cressey (1969) similarly claimed that organized crime in the United States was composed of a nationwide alliance of twenty-four tightly knit criminal "mafia families." In his book, *The Theft of the Nation,* Cressey adopted the position of law enforcement agencies and argued that La Cosa Nostra (LCN) relied on Sicilian traditional cultural codes but was also a hierarchical and rationally designed organization (Cressey 1969).

Cressey's "modernistic" conceptualization of LCN also reinforced the view, discussed in chapter 2, that organized crime was rationally oriented toward the maximization of profits through illegal business activities. Mario Puzo's 1969 novel *The Godfather,* released in the same year as Cressey's *Theft of a Nation,* and the 1972 film adaptation made by Francis Ford Coppola also had a part in shaping the image of the Italian mafia as a criminal conspiracy. As Paoli (2003) rightly argues, hardly any phenomenon since the Second World War has fascinated the American public more than the Italian mafia as presented in *The Godfather.*

However, in order to understand the transplantation of mafias, we first need to clarify the term. What exactly *is* a mafia group?

In its purest form, "mafia" appears to be a collective term meant to describe the original Italian crime enterprise, the Sicilian mafia, that has existed both in Italy and in the United States, with a smattering of influence elsewhere. But today, the term often is intertwined with other forms of organized crime. While the Italians certainly do not have a monopoly on organized crime, this overuse of the term has made it difficult to define a mafia group, organized crime, or crime in general. The Sicilian mafia proper frequently collaborates or clashes with crime networks originating in other parts of southern Italy. Giovanni Falcone, the antimafia judge murdered by the mafia in 1992, objected to the conflation of the term "mafia" with organized crime in general, arguing in favor of using the term "mafia-type organizations" in order "to clearly distinguish the uniquely Sicilian mafia from other criminal organizations—such as the Camorra [Campania], the 'Ndrangheta [Calabria], the Sacra Corona Unita [Apulia]—that are structured like the Mafia, but are not the Mafia" (Falcone 1992).

The term "mafia" also is applied to organized crime groups that primarily practice protection racketeering—the use of violent intimidation to manipulate local economic activity, especially illicit trade. Secondary activities, such as drug trafficking, loan-sharking, and fraud, also may be part of the picture. Some researchers have argued that the term "mafia" refers to groups of criminals that furnish "extralegal governance and aspire to govern others by providing criminal protection to both the underworld and the upper world" (Varese 2011, 6).

The term also implies a cultural attitude and indicates a sort of political infiltration. These nonstate actors could be regarded as strategic political players, not only as crooks who want to make money. A binding code of honor, in particular the code of silence (or *omertà*, in southern Italy), safeguards the mafia from outside intrusion and law enforcement action. Mafia groups also are typically defined as having a hierarchy of sorts, coupled with control of a defined "turf" or region of a state. As noted, the term originally was applied to the Sicilian mafia, but it has since expanded to encompass other (mafia-type) organizations with similar methods and purposes, such as "the Russian mafia" or "the Japanese mafia."

There are nevertheless contemporary organized crime groups that are more entrepreneurial and less hierarchical, political, and cultural than the stereotypical mafia. These groups are not essentially interested in politics and do not aspire to govern others by providing criminal protection. Albanian organized crime groups that operate across territories often are entrepreneurial organized crime groups whose main criminal activities involve trade in drugs and arms, as well as human trafficking and smuggling. As discussed in chapter 1, although some have argued that Albanian organized crime groups are political and cultural in nature, and thus that they resemble mafia-type organizations, our subsequent analysis will label them "organized crime groups" in order to avoid confusion.

Globalization and Importation

During the 1990s, the problem of organized crime came to the attention of international organizations, state institutions, and the general public. The 2000 UN Convention on Transnational Organized Crime (known as the UN Palermo Convention) also included a definition of "organized criminal group." Article 2(a) of the convention states: " 'Organized criminal group' shall mean: a group of three or more persons that was not randomly formed; existing for a period of time; acting in concert with the aim of committing at least one crime punishable by at least four years' incarceration; in order to obtain, directly or indirectly, a financial or other material benefit" (UN Palermo Convention 2000). Since most "groups" of any sort contain three or more people working in concert and most exist for a period of time, the true defining characteristics of organized crime groups according to the convention are their profit-driven nature and the seriousness of the offenses they commit.

Another important element of this definition is that of "transnationality," since the convention deals only with transnational organized crime. According to the convention, the term "transnational" crime covers not only offenses committed in more than one nation, but also those that take place in one nation but are planned or controlled in another. Despite this broad definition, the perception of organized crime as an imported "entity" (alien conspiracy) remains to this day; the element of transnationality also gives legitimacy to the conspiracy model because it enables more powerful countries to shift blame to less powerful ones.

A moral panic fueled continuing curiosity about "the mafia" and transnational organized crime. In fact, both terms have been used as catchphrases to express the growing anxieties of national and supranational public institutions, as well as private citizens, as illegal markets expand. Dick Ward, executive director for the Office of International Justice, wrote that the Western world has become the primary target of organized crime, but many criminal activities originate in underdeveloped regions.

Although organized crime continues to be depicted as an imported entity in public discourse, there are competing views on the ability of organized crime to take advantage of globalization. The first perspective, which aligns with Cressey's "modernistic" conceptualization of LCN as a rational bureaucracy, holds that criminal groups take advantage of globalization by creating colonies around the world.[4] Author Claire Sterling (1994), in fact, popularized the notion of "Pax Mafiosa," arguing that in the post–Cold War era, international organized crime groups are working together efficiently in an effort to divide the globe among them.

Likewise, Manuel Castells argues that a new phenomenon, "global crime," has now emerged—that is, the "networking of powerful criminal organizations, and their associates, in shared activities throughout the planet" (Castells 2000, 166). Galeotti (2005) also asserts that the increased movement of people has led to internationalization and expansion of organized crime groups, creating a global criminal economy.

According to some scholars, subcontracting and international alliances are common features of international criminal cooperation, and criminal organizations are expanding into new territories.[5] Shelley writes that "just as multinational corporations establish branches around the world to take advantage of attractive labor or raw material markets, so do illicit businesses" (Shelley 2006, 43). This view holds that as globalization progresses, criminal groups increasingly seek to enter attractive markets abroad, putting into action a rational strategy to expand internationally.

According to this "global" view, a number of criminal organizations, such as the Sicilian mafia, the Hong Kong Triads, the Russian mafia, and the Japanese yakuza, are nevertheless part of the same species, often originating from "criminogenic" societies. As Paoli and Reuter (2008) rightly claim, today the list of transnational criminal organizations reads like an inventory of ethnic minorities.

But is there evidence that these groups have indeed transplanted themselves to foreign territories while still working under the umbrella of the same criminal organization? The answer may vary, depending on the criminal organization in question. Considering specifically the migration of ethnic Albanian organized crime groups across territories, should one compare them to multinational corporations and rational bureaucracies? Do they have "offices" around the world while the headquarters remains in the Balkan region? Are Albanian organized crime groups coordinated by a central organization back in the country of origin, and has their migration been rational and strategic?

Local Problems

The second view on "mafia" transplantation focuses on the inability or unwillingness of organized crime groups (especially mafia-type organizations) to move into different illegal economies. Reuter (1985), for instance, argues that illegal enterprise groups (including mafia-type organizations) have difficulty transplanting their operations because violence is expensive and risky, and because large, centralized illegal enterprises are more easily detected by law enforcement. This would seem to be in stark contrast to Shelley's (2006) hypothesis that crime groups make a rational decision to enter into a competing illegal economic market outside of their primary region.

Varese (2011) appears to confirm the view set forth by Reuter (1985) in all but a handful of cases, demonstrating that mafia-type organizations are not successful in transplanting themselves into illegal economies outside their own territories. Specifically, Varese (2011) concludes that such groups (with a few exceptions) make rational decisions not to enter competing markets. When they do find themselves in new markets, it is because of forced migration, a need to escape justice or fighting within their own clans. The claim that mafia-type groups rarely move into criminal economies outside their home region is bolstered by Chambliss and Williams (2012), who argue that there is little evidence that transnational organized crime is hierarchal in nature or transplanted from abroad. According to Williams, contemporary forms of organized crime are decentralized, inherently dispersed, and do not provide obvious loci or centers of gravity (Williams 2001, 71).

This second view maintains that organized crime groups are, in fact, highly localized and stationary. Diego Gambetta writes, "Not only did the [Sicilian] mafia grow mainly in Western Sicily, but, with the exception of Catania, it has remained there to this very day." Organized crime, he adds, "is a difficult industry to export. Not unlike mining, it is heavily dependent on the local environment" (Gambetta 1993, 249, 251). Varese (2011), in his study on mafia migration, has shown that the Russian mafia group known as "Solntsevskaya" did not move its protection racket to Italy. Its core business remained highly dependent on the territory of origin. Similarly, Yiu Kong Chu argues that "Hong Kong Triads are localized and they are not international illegal entrepreneurs whose wealth and connections may enable them to emigrate to Western countries" (Chu 2000, 130).

Peter Hill (2003) dates the beginning of the foreign activities of Japanese yakuza from the 1970s, and concludes that yakuza members' foreign travel was mainly recreational or focused on investing in real estate. Varese (2011) argues that the apparent difficulty faced by a mafia in relocating or expanding its business reflects the high cost of monitoring agents that such a move would entail, as well as the challenges of building a reputation and collecting reliable information in the new territory.

Critical criminologists have taken this argument about the local dimension of organized crime a step further, claiming that the alleged threat posed by "transnational groups" has been exaggerated (Allum and Gilmour 2012). They argue that, for example, the US government and the FBI set out to improve the image of the police by externalizing the problem of organized crime. In order to downplay the involvement of domestic police officers, judges, and politicians in racketeering and other criminal activities, they emphasized the "alien conspiracy" of organized crime (Paoli 2002; Chambliss 1988). Dwight Smith (1991) asked: how better to explain failure (and to prepare the ground for budget increases) than to argue that, dedicated though it might be, the bureau was pressed to overcome an alien, organized, conspiratorial criminal element that had forced its way into an innocent public?

Some criminologists, as mentioned earlier, argue that the success of this "alien" paradigm of organized crime depends on the ability to isolate organized crime from other structures. One way this is achieved is by presenting organized crime as a sinister entity that threatens the civilized (Western) world. The origin of this entity is rather murky, Standing (2003) explains, traced to an alien culture residing in developing countries. What makes this entity particularly threatening is its ability to cross national borders. The critical view argues that this perception of organized crime has its own biases: it allows powerful actors or countries to offer their "services" to Third World countries, and thus to impose their own normative order in these allegedly "criminogenic" regions.

As far as the Albanian case is concerned, it seems that while criminal organizations do exist, there is little likelihood of a grand conspiracy on a global stage, with precontrived networks operating overseas. A further examination of the origins and evolution of Albanian organized crime in Western countries, particularly the EU nations and the United States, may help to explain why.

THE ALBANIAN "WEST SIDE STORY"

There are approximately eight million ethnic Albanians in the world, yet only about 3.2 million live in Albania. The Albanian exodus, caused by the collapse of the communist regime in 1991 and the ensuing economic crisis, is the largest emigration in Europe since the population movements that followed World War II. However, Albanian emigration is nothing new: In the fifteenth century, for example, many

Albanians migrated to Calabria in southern Italy after the defeat of Skanderbeg by Ottoman forces. Turkey and Bulgaria, and later the United States and various South American nations, were other locations favored by Albanian émigrés.

Generally speaking, however, discussions of Albanian emigration today refer to three main phases: an early outflow of emigrants before 1944; another important wave of emigration during the communist era, between 1945 and 1990; and a significant outflow following the 1990 breakdown of the communist leadership that had been in place since 1944.

Before 1944, the United States and some Latin American nations were the primary destination countries for Albanian émigrés. Most of the people who left Albania before 1944 did so for economic reasons, and the Albanian government in power during that time was mostly indifferent to these flows. The second phase of out-migration was prompted largely by political factors. These included disagreements with the country's communist regime and the political pressure that individuals anticipated, in some cases because of their collaboration with Italian and German occupiers during World War II. The Albanian government heavily discouraged this migration by establishing political and legal barriers to emigration and labeling it a crime.

The post-1990 migration can be broken down into the uncontrolled 1991–1992 stream, when approximately 300,000 Albanians left the country; the 1992–1996 stream, when a similar number migrated, most illegally, despite the temporary improvement of the economy and better border controls; and the 1996–1998 stream, which immediately followed the collapse of various pyramid schemes that wiped out the savings of hundreds of thousands of Albanians. In the national unrest that followed, a combination of unemployment, poverty, and economic hardships led some seventy thousand Albanians to migrate within a few months (Barjaba 2004). Overall, from 1989 to 2001, between 600,000 and 800,000 people left Albania, about 440,000 of them settling in Greece, where Albanians make up 60 percent of immigrants.[6] Estimates indicate that about 350,000 Albanians have migrated to Italy since the 1990s.[7]

The situation in Kosovo is similar. Almost one million Albanians have permanently departed Kosovo since the late 1980s, not counting those who fled the war but subsequently returned.[8] Germany and Switzerland have been important destinations for Albanians emigrating from Kosovo. In 2000, for example, about 150,000 Albanians resided in Switzerland, accounting for 6 percent of its total population.

Although little is known about the actual relationship between Albanian organized crime groups operating in Albania and those operating abroad, the scarce literature on the topic suggests that the ethnic Albanian diaspora has played a crucial role in connecting Albanian traffickers worldwide. In 1996, scholar and law enforcement official Gus Xhudo wrote:

Once scattered and disorganized, and working for others, the Albanians have, in the past five to ten years, moved into independent operations, established a vast network of mules and trouble-shooters throughout Western Europe, coordinated activity with supportive émigré communities, and managed to consolidate their operations on both sides of the Atlantic. Indeed, they appear to be growing and expanding their operations at an alarming rate. Authorities both in Europe and the United States are at a loss as to the nature and extent of these groups and have succeeded in making only minor arrests. Highly secretive and ruthless, the Albanians, in some respects, mirror the Sicilian Mafia of years past, with its highly intricate code of honour based upon a patriarchal system of respect. (Xhudo 1996)

By the turn of the century, Albanian organized crime had become a prominent topic of discussion in the West. Reports mentioned that Albanian crime "bosses" resided in the Balkans and sent their "soldiers" to work in the West. The head of the Europol Copper Project reported in an October 2008 meeting in Brussels that ethnic Albanian crime groups operate as oriented clusters—with converging criminal activities and resources—and are led or at least coordinated from the home region. In his speech, he argued that traditional ethnic Albanian crime groups show the following characteristics:

(1) In most cases, only cells are present and visible within the EU, while both leaders and assets are located outside the EU. The visible part of these crime groups shows a low level of organization within the EU; (2) A strong international dimension is found in their activities, which is used to its fullest extent for shielding purposes and to support the criminal activities; (3) The use of legal business structures, corruptive practices against law enforcement, judiciary, public administration, and politics and violence mostly takes place outside the EU.

The official concluded by saying that "these groups exploit the crime markets in the EU only for profit, whilst their strategic center of gravity and interests is situated outside the EU."[9]

Records show that Albanian criminals abroad do indeed send money to their families in Albania; however, this is often to support the family members and not because the "boss" asked them to send money. Also, a number of cases point to links between notorious criminals and powerful politicians and businessmen from the Balkans. Money that Albanian criminals have made in the West has been sent to political parties and to influential members of Albanian society. Such links can be established particularly in relation to the Kosovo Liberation Army, as discussed in the previous chapter. It would be too simplistic, however, to conclude on the basis of such isolated cases that these influential political figures are, in fact, the real bosses of the so-called Albanian mafia.

Interviews with Belgian law enforcement officials point to the core of the problem: "We should be very careful how we use the term 'mafia' and whether the

Albanians really have such a high [level of] organization. We do not have evidence as to whether Albanians from the Balkans are steering the criminal businesses in Belgium and whether they send people [to commit crimes] with specific instructions. We are not clear on whether the groups in Belgium are independent criminal groups or whether mafia bosses from the Balkans control them" (interview, Belgium, 2006).

Research illustrates that most Albanian offenders got involved in organized crime only after they arrived in their new homes, many having fled their country of origin to escape prosecution, retaliation, or war. The cases analyzed indicate that, while ethnic Albanian groups operating in the Balkans tend to be more political and involved to a greater degree in traditional mafia-type activities than some other criminal organizations, this is not the case with Albanian organized crime groups operating abroad.

Major Albanian organized crime groups operating in the West are formed more spontaneously than originally believed, and without the "supervision" or well-considered assistance of groups or politicians in the country of origin. These groups have gotten involved in a variety of criminal markets, depending on available opportunities, demand for products, and members' capabilities. Cases illustrate that Albanians have managed to establish themselves in certain territories, and over time they have come to control some markets; however, there is no evidence to support the argument that their migration and expansion was intentional and well coordinated. Let's examine this further.

TAKING ROOT IN EUROPE

According to media and law enforcement accounts, Albanians who emigrated after 1991, fleeing the collapse of the communist regime and the conflict in Kosovo, brought their so-called culture of violence and crime and their attention-grabbing ways of doing business to their new homes in the West. In the short run, this enabled Albanian criminal organizations to build a reputation in the criminal underworld, but it also attracted significant police attention. By the late 1990s, these groups were mentioned in all major law enforcement reports prepared by national and international law enforcement agencies.

Belgium

Like other Western European countries, Belgium experienced several major waves of Albanian immigration. The first was between 1945 and 1970, when a number of Albanians who opposed the communist regime escaped to Belgium.

According to Laurent Sartorius, a superintendent at the Balkan Unit of the Belgian Federal Police, most of these Albanians émigrés did not cause any major problems. They lived in small communities and married within their own groups.

But after the fall of communism in Albania, another wave of immigrants arrived. "When the new immigrants arrived in Belgium," Sartorius said, "they had support from the old diaspora, since they didn't speak the language and needed help to integrate into the new society. They also settled in communities where the more traditional, older diaspora was living—Antwerp, Liege, and Brussels" (interview, Belgium, 2006). Among this new wave of immigrants were a number of criminals.

Thousands of undocumented young people left Albania in 1991 and 1992. Many of them could not find lucrative work in Western Europe. Some took difficult, low-paying jobs and some became involved in petty crime. Local criminal gangs found it easy to recruit these and other young men who were never properly integrated into Western European society.

According to Sartorius, "The most powerful Albanian organized crime groups rose dramatically between 1998 and 2001, a period that corresponds with the collapse of the pyramid system in Albania and with the Kosovo crisis. They started with activities in the field of exploitation of prostitution, mainly in Brussels" (interview, Belgium, 2006).

Exploitation of prostitution was one of the Albanian groups' core activities, since it did not require a large investment of capital. And this business had been successfully transplanted to other Western European nations in the past. For example, trafficked or prostituted Albanian women began arriving in Italy between 1993 and 1995. Rome and Milan were among the primary destination cities for a large number of these women, and in mid-1996 the Mobile Police Squad of Milan estimated that some three to five hundred Albanian prostitutes worked the city streets each day. A number of these women were then trafficked to Belgium and the United Kingdom. A Home Office briefing, reported by *The Independent* in 2002, stated that Albanian gangs were "changing the landscape" of Britain's sex industry.

Another notable characteristic of Albanian organized crime groups in Western Europe was their readiness to use extreme violence. The media often argued that, between 1998 and 2003, Albanian organized criminal groups rapidly took over certain criminal markets in various parts of Europe, using violence as a primary tactic to drive out competition.

Albanian criminal elements also got involved in illegal migration and the smuggling of people. In order to regulate migration flows from Albania to Italy in the early 1990s, a number of laws and controls were introduced in both nations. This gave rise to Albanian smuggling organizations that sold fake passports and travel documents to people who wanted to leave Albania. Tens of thousands of people emigrated with the help of organized crime groups. Typically, the migrants were hidden in trucks at the Belgian ports of Ostend and Zeebrugge in Belgium, and then ferried to the British ports of Hull and Purfleet, where they applied for political asylum. One ethnic Albanian illegal émigré who left Kosovo in 1998 told this story:

With our fake German visa, from Albania we got to Italy and then we took a train to Belgium. But we wanted to go to the UK because there were more opportunities there. . . . The Albanian smuggler told us that we [were] going to get in a truck in one of those truck stops. I just remember that night the four of us were hiding behind the bushes, and he said, "This is the truck; now you have to go check if the doors are open," and I said, "I'm not going anywhere." The truck driver wasn't aware of this. He was out, having dinner or something. The smuggler said, "You have to jump to this truck if you want to get to England." Then he went to the truck and ripped off a piece from the roof because the doors were closed. That's how we got in. This truck had English license plates. Once we got in, I remember that the truck driver . . . opened up the doors, just to check inside, and he didn't see us hiding inside because it was all washing machines. . . . The next thing I remember, a day later—let's say eight hours— I put my head through the hole on the roof and I remember seeing a sign that says London. . . . That was the happiest moment ever. (interview, New York, 2013)

Between 1998 and 2003, Albanian organized criminal groups in Western Europe expanded their operations and reached a peak of notoriety in the eyes of the public, the media, and law enforcement agencies. At this stage, they did not form significant connections with other ethnic criminal groups. Instead, they carried out their activities in isolation. As a result, Albanian organized criminal groups came to be understood in Western Europe as hierarchical, homogeneous, and ethnic based.

During the Kosovo conflict, an estimated four hundred thousand Kosovo Albanians emigrated from Kosovo as political refugees (see figure 13). In addition, ethnic Albanians from Albania and Macedonia who were not directly affected by the conflict took advantage of the situation and presented themselves as Kosovo refugees. The Belgian and Dutch police often had difficulty determining the real identity of arrested criminals, many of whom claimed they were from Kosovo. Some obtained Greek or Italian visas illegally and presented themselves as EU nationals (CEOOR 2005).

In addition to driving a wave of migration, the conflict in Kosovo also forged links between criminal elements, paramilitary groups, and ordinary people. As a result of Milošević's politics, clandestine groups of nationalist rebels were formed in Kosovo and within the Albanian émigré populations abroad. Fundraising to support the functioning of the Kosovar shadow state was carried out through illegal criminal activities and unofficial "taxation" of the Albanian community abroad. It has been estimated that émigré remittances totaled around three to five hundred million dollars per year, or about 15 to 20 percent of official Albanian gross domestic product in 1995. However, despite some financing of political parties and military formations, there is no evidence that in Belgium the KLA or any other political party or "mafia" clan controlled the activities of Albanian organized crime groups abroad.

FIGURE 13. Massive arrival of the first refugees from Kosovo following the NATO strikes (Kukës, Albania 1999). Copyright © Laurent Piolanti.

Italy

In Italy, officials have reported that the Italian mafia found a partner in Albanian criminal organizations because of the groups' alleged similarities in terms of clan structure, loyalties, code of silence, and distrust of formal justice. One Italian official said: "Until the collapse of communism in Albania, the Albanian 'mafia' was essentially a provider of services to the Italian mafia. However, the balance has shifted as circumstances have brought the Albanians into a position of greater influence. Although there have been contacts with the Sicilian Cosa Nostra, the Napolitan Camorra, and the Calabrian 'Ndrangheta, for reasons of geography the main Italian interlocutor for the Albanian mafia has been the Apulian organised crime group known as the Sacra Corona Unita, or United Holy Crown (UHC)" (Jamieson and Sily 1998).

One of the major waves of ethnic Albanian emigration to Italy occurred after the fall of the communist Enver Hoxha regime in 1991. Albanians had no right to a passport until May 1990. Until the penal code was revised in July 1990, leaving the country was officially an act of treason. Nothing could have prepared Albania and its neighbors for what would happen following the relaxation of these barriers. One of the first indicators that a mass exodus of political refugees from Albania was approaching was the storming of Western embassies in Tirana.

It all began when four hundred people scaled the gates of the Italian and German embassies in Tirana in July 1990. Thousands of others followed. That month, the first of many ships filled with people destined for Italy was seized in the port of Durrës. Would-be emigrants set out on foot to cross the mountainous border to Greece; thousands were captured and returned from Greece, only to try their luck again. Under these circumstances, no one kept count, but a rough estimate puts the number of Albanians who left the country from 1990 to 1992 at between two and three hundred thousand—almost 10 percent of the total population (European Stability Initiative 2008).

Separated from Albania by only forty miles of the Adriatic Sea, Italy's port cities, such as Bari, found themselves unable to cope with the swelling numbers of asylum seekers. Early in 1991 Italy declared a state of emergency and closed its borders to Albanian refugees. In response, many Albanians began paying smugglers to take them to Italy in speedboats and other clandestine vessels. According to the Migration Policy Institute, another two to three hundred thousand people left between 1993 and 1996 (European Stability Initiative 2008).

At first, Italians perceived the Albanians as political migrants who deserved asylum, but the number of Albanian migrants who participated in criminal activities soon cast the entire group in a negative light (Tsaliki 2008).

In Campania—the region of southern Italy that includes Naples and Caserta—local authorities say the Camorra dominates the activities of foreign criminal groups. According to sources, after the fall of Albania's communist regime, Albanian organized crime groups were responsible for providing Camorra soldiers with ammunition (Jamison and Sily 1998). (Whether Albanians continue to provide weaponry to the Camorra remains a matter of debate.) Local and regional law enforcement agencies also noted that Albanian groups have been especially active in prostitution and human trafficking markets within the metropolitan areas of Naples and peripheral cities.

Media reports and interviews with local authorities suggest that the climate of immigrant criminality has shifted within the Campania region in recent years. This change has been motivated by a variety of factors, including the fact that Camorra clan activity has been partially dismantled by local, regional, and federal police forces. Local authorities report that stringent law enforcement action has forced the Camorra to retreat from increasingly clandestine activities in order to evade detection. However, their decision to deal less with products such as drugs, arms, and prostitutes affected some of the Albanian suppliers, since there was less demand for their services.

Another factor stifling the expansion of the Albanian mafia within Campania is the inability to acquire territory already held by the Camorra. In Naples, also known as "Camorra country," a majority of foreign organized crime syndicates are deterred from establishing criminal colonies because of the "service fees" imposed by the native mafia. As reported widely in the national press, when an immigrant group intends to "set up shop" in Naples, it must pay the Camorra a "rental fee" for the *quartiere* (neighborhood) it would like to occupy. Although this payment system generally was respected by Albanian criminals in the early 1990s, when they participated in human trafficking and prostitution, in recent years the Albanians have found it more profitable to seek out criminal opportunities in Western European states that are not under the control of a preexisting native mafia.

In Calabria, the 'Ndrangheta has forged a partnership with Albanian criminal organizations (Jamieson and Sily 1998; Mutschke 2000). According to media reports in 2012, two ethnic Albanians of Montenegrin descent—snipers during the fall of the former Yugoslav Republic—were hired by the Calabrian mafia to perform assassinations.

In Puglia, the Sacra Corona Unita (SCU) is especially active in the region that includes Brindisi, Lecce, and Taranto, port cities that received high numbers of ethnic Albanian migrants during the 1990s. Mass media has reported that the Albanian "mafia" facilitates trafficking of drugs en route from Afghanistan through this region and transports bulk shipments of cocaine and heroin. It was not easy for Albanians to break into the drug trafficking market in Puglia. According to press reports, Albanian criminals who arrived in the port city of Bari attempted to funnel contraband cigarettes and other black market commodities into Italy, but they were sidelined by the SCU and forced to shift their criminal networks further south to Salento, where the local mafia was not as active.

According to police sources, a high concentration of ethnic Albanian migrants resides in and around Florence. In regional newspaper reports, police have described the ease with which Albanian criminals were able to "take command" of Florentine drug markets formerly controlled by Nigerians.

Overall, it is clear that criminal market expansion by Albanian transnational organized crime groups in Italy differs according to the region in question. But it should be noted that the Albanians in this area have not used violence in order to overtake native mafia territories. Generally, they have conformed to Italian mafia traditions, such as payments to the Camorra, or have relocated their criminal groups elsewhere. Despite close cooperation with groups in the Balkans, there is no evidence that the groups operating in Italy were under the control of native Albanian groups.

Criminal Sophistication

Police sources indicate that Albanian organized crime in Western Europe has changed noticeably over the past decade. Since 2003, police in Europe have observed that many transplanted Albanian criminal groups did not survive the move to the new territory, but those that managed to learn lessons from the past have developed somewhat more sophisticated structures and operational methods. Although Albanian organized criminal groups traditionally have been depicted as remarkably violent, hierarchical, and homogeneous, these may no longer be their core characteristics in Western Europe.

Belgium's annual reports on organized crime (2006–2010) support the "rational" view of criminal organizations and offer examples of how criminal organizations have adopted modern management techniques. Some organizations reportedly specialize in a specific part of a criminal network, such as transport. Another specialized crime unit may sell drugs, people, cigarettes, or weapons. This specialization means criminal organizations are behaving like business operators, although it is unclear if there has been indeed a systematic change in the operational methods of Albanian groups over time, or if this description is merely one perspective.

The recent Hollywood-style helicopter escapes of Alket Rizaj, Vassilis Paleokostas, and Nikos Paleokostas from the Korydallos high-security prison in Greece is used as an example of the increased sophistication and heterogeneity of networks involving Albanian criminals. Alket Rizaj, an Albanian immigrant, has been involved in robberies, drug smuggling, and contract killings in Greece since the early years of the twenty-first century. He was convicted for murder in Greece but escaped from Korydallos prison in 2006 with Vassilis Paleokostas, a Greek bank robber who also had been convicted for the kidnapping of businessman Aléxandros Haitoglou (Nellas 2009).

They made their escape by helicopter on June 4, 2006. The operation had been masterminded by Paleokostas's elder brother Nikos, himself a convicted criminal who had escaped from the same prison in 1990 during a mass breakout. (The elder Paleokostas was recaptured and is still in jail, serving time for sixteen bank robberies.)

Rizaj was recaptured in September 2006, and Vassilis Paleokostas was taken into custody in August 2008. While he was on the run, Vassilis Paleokostas is suspected of masterminding the June 2008 kidnapping of a prominent Greek industrialist, Giorgos Mylonas, who was held for thirteen days until his family paid a ransom (Nellas 2009).

Once again, the pair escaped from prison. In February 2009, Rizaj and Vassilis Paleokostas scaled a rope ladder to a hovering helicopter. Rizaj's girlfriend, who was known to have helped with the pair's 2006 escape, tossed them the ladder and fired an automatic rifle at guards on the ground. No injuries were reported.

An elderly couple found the helicopter abandoned near a highway. The pilot was unharmed, bound and gagged with a hood over his head. He told police the helicopter had been chartered by a couple who said they wanted to travel to Athens from the town of Itea, in central Greece. The couple had threatened him with an AK-47 and a grenade, he said, and forced him to fly to the prison (Nellas 2009).

According to Europol, violence and corruption are always part of the criminal market system. Yet some European sources suggest that Albanian offenders today tend to use somewhat less violence in order to reduce the social impact of their crimes. According to Belgian police officer Sartorius, since 2002, "Albanian criminals are active mainly in the fields of organized thefts, drug trafficking, exploitation of prostitution, and facilitation of illegal immigration. Thefts consist mainly of burglaries and [stealing] from trucks in motorway parking areas. In general, the cells active in this type of crime rarely use violence against persons" (interview, Belgium, 2006).

Human trafficking and exploitation of prostitution are still among the predominant activities of Albanian criminals operating in Western Europe. Although they have managed to become involved in sophisticated criminal activities, they still tend to have prostitutes working for them. Janssens noted: "The juridical [older] trials [in Belgium] show that some Albanian prostitution networks are purely ethnic based, but new files are showing a trend of a professionalized multi-ethnic collaboration. Some prostitution cases in Liège and Charleroi show the existence of collaboration between Albanian, Bulgarian, and Italian criminal organizations. The Italians are controlling the prostitution bars while the Albanians and the Bulgarians are delivering the prostitution victims" (interview, Belgium, 2008).

Thus, in parts of Europe, the traditional homogeneous, hierarchical, violent, and impenetrable Albanian organized crime groups seem to be slowly giving way to a more conventional business model. Specialization in the transport industry and decreased use of violence could be regarded as indicators of Albanian criminal advancement in Western Europe. However, once again, although this description may well be true for some Western European countries and for specific criminal groups, we have little evidence to conclude that Albanian groups overall were significantly more homogeneous or hierarchical in the past. Also, available reports do not provide evidence to support the "intentional" migration (or criminal transplantation) hypothesis.

NEW YORK, NEW YORK

The Early Days

Albanians began arriving in New York City in large numbers in the 1960s, settling primarily in Belmont, a mostly Italian neighborhood in the Bronx. Journalist Tom Robbins, writing for New York's *Village Voice,* noted, "Like any other ethnic group, there was a bad bunch among them, and those men quickly developed a reputation for especially nasty brutality and an unwillingness to back down from an argument" (Robbins 2005). By the late 1970s, Albanian organized crime gangs were importing small amounts of heroin from the former Yugoslavia to the Lower

East Side, and Xhevdet Lika, known as "Joey Lika," was the target of investigations by then-assistant US attorney Alan Cohen, DEA agent John "Jack" Delmore, and US district court judge Vincent Broderick.

Lika worked with a seemingly law-abiding Albanian businessman named Skender Fici, who operated a Staten Island–based travel agency called Theresa Worldwide. Using this company as a front, Lika booked trips to Yugoslavia, where many Albanians lived. He gradually became a specialist in handling immigration paperwork, and he strengthened his ties with the community by sponsoring a local ethnic Albanian soccer team. It also appears that Lika used Fici's travel agency to arrange short trips to Yugoslavia and Turkey, where he bought heroin that he then smuggled to the United States.

A prosecutor's memo indicates that Lika had begun distributing heroin in the late 1970s. The drugs were distributed through Chinese clothing stores or sold to other dealers from a social club located in the midst of shops specializing in Judaica. Prior to 1980, Lika's operation appears to have been composed entirely of ethnic Albanians from Staten Island.[10]

There is some evidence that, by the early 1980s, Albanian organized crime groups were no longer operating in strict ethnic isolation. One group formed new allegiances with other ethnic groups, particularly the Italian Americans in the Bronx. It appears as though Albanians were increasingly trusted by Italian American mafiosi to undertake specific criminal tasks. As mentioned earlier, Albanian Zef Mustafa had ties to the Gambino and Gotti crime families and was a crucial player in the Italian mafia.

Albanian criminals in New York imported heroin from the Balkans throughout the 1980s. Although these groups were successful, they were one-dimensional and displayed little diversification. They relied on violence, which began to attract the attention of Italian mafia groups, who soon formed links with them. Albanian criminals in this period were typically older men who had ties with Albania. Little is known about the legitimate businesses they may have operated in the 1980s, or how they laundered money from their criminal enterprises. During this time, there is no evidence that these groups engaged in human trafficking, sexual exploitation, or organized theft, and they appear to have had little awareness of law enforcement techniques.

Albanian Organized Crime after 1991

The volume and variety of ethnic Albanian organized crime grew rapidly in the 1990s. During this time, younger groups of ethnic Albanians emerged on the organized crime scene in New York City. Perhaps as a result of ethnic conflict in the Balkans, combined with weaker social ties to the region than in the 1970s and 1980s, these groups were less involved in importing heroin than their predecessors. Instead, the younger groups concentrated on fraud, violence, extortion, and robbery. During the 1990s, associations and rivalries between Albanian and Italian American crime groups also began to emerge.

The rollout of automated teller machines in New York heralded new opportunities for ethnic Albanians to diversify their criminal enterprises. Groups such as those managed by Nedzad Korac and Iljmija Frljuckic installed cloned ATMs in small supermarkets and convenience stores, along with devices that captured personal bank account information. The groups then used the collected information to make fake ATM cards (Bogdanich 2003).

Such crimes were right up Frljuckic's alley. He had been deported to the former Yugoslavia for bank fraud in 1992, and after completing his prison term in 1994, he returned to the United States and purchased a company that installed cash machines. Nedzad Korac's brother, Fikret, also had been deported because of felony convictions. Fikret Korac was convicted in September 1994 on one count of conspiracy to commit access device fraud and sentenced to one year in prison.[11]

Not all ATM crimes in the 1990s were sophisticated. Dede Gjoni and Gjergi Nika, from south Boston, worked with Albanians from the Bronx to steal cash from more than three hundred ATMs across the country, simply breaking into stores and either stealing or destroying the ATMs to get at the cash.

Ties between Italian American mafiosi and Albanian organized criminals grew stronger throughout the 1990s. The story of ethnic Albanian brothers Afrim and Lulzim Kupa, of Staten Island, provides an example. The brothers were known for their close ties to La Cosa Nostra, and for working with Gambino soldiers Neil Lombardo and Joseph Sclafani, who both had notable criminal records even after they were released from prison (Maddux 2012). Afrim Kupa was known for break-ins at banks and jewelry stores. In October 1995, he was involved in a home invasion robbery where, police claim, he pointed a gun at a four-year-old child. By February 1999 federal indictments accused Afrim and Lulzim Kupa of staging several bank heists across the Midwest. During a seven-month period, the gang allegedly stole more than one million dollars from fifteen different banks (Annese 2010; Owen 2012). In 1998, Luzlim Kupa pleaded guilty in federal court to conspiracy to defraud the United States.

During the mid-1990s, ethnic Albanians became ensconced within Italian mafia circles. As mentioned earlier, between 1996 and 2002 Zef Mustafa earned millions from a telephone and Internet fraud involving sex lines. This operation allegedly made more than 700 million dollars for the Gambino crime family.

By the end of the 1990s, credit card fraud was on the radar of New York–based Albanian organized crime groups. One such group, operated by Faik Musa Istrefi, of Bushkill, involved waiters who stole information from credit cards used in restaurants. The indictment stated that several waiters in New York City and New Jersey restaurants used their positions to glean information from customers' cards.

The DEA, IRS, and Secret Service collaborated on the case, which also charged numerous individuals with immigration offenses.

The Istrefi case represents a watershed in the use of immigration powers, but other problems with border control and migration were becoming apparent. One case from 1999 involved a corrupt public official, Roy Bailey, and ethnic Albanian Antonio Ivezaj, a restaurant owner and construction operator primarily based in Detroit. Bailey was an assistant district director and supervisory deportation officer for the Immigration and Naturalization Service (INS). Payments of more than three hundred dollars were made to this corrupt INS officer, who in turn colluded with the group both to arrange sham weddings and to release detained Albanians who were being held in immigration facilities.

All in all, the 1990s were a dynamic decade for ethnic Albanian organized crime groups in New York. Some groups were solidifying relations with the Italian mafia, while others challenged their dominance. Smaller criminal groups arose to take advantage of new opportunities, such as the expansion of ATMs and credit card payments. Groups acquired the ability to corrupt public officials and thwart immigration controls. Robbery and theft became common, particularly for fledgling groups with fewer connections. Reputations were important, and much of the criminality that occurred was brash and overt. Crime was local, and associations and rivalries were in constant transition.

The New Millennium

In the first decade of the new millennium, Albanian organized criminals in New York moved from high-end burglaries of banks and safe-deposit boxes back to drug trafficking. Various groups were involved in cannabis production, importation, and supply at all levels. They began to import cannabis from Canada, while at the same time installing grow houses in domestic and commercial properties, typically in Staten Island, Brooklyn, and Queens. Many groups also began selling cocaine, typically mixing the drug with other agents to maximize their profits.

In the early years of the new millennium, groups such as those operated by Zia Berisha, or Arben Zenelaj and Astrit Demiri, focused on low-level drug sales. They turned to the cannabis trade, typically finding customers within the Albanian diaspora. But in 2004 and 2005, numerous crime groups emerged on the scene, managed by notables Bruno Krasniqi; Alex Rudaj and Nikola Dedaj; Din Celaj, Moheed Oasman, Xhavit Celaj, and Ali Zherka; and Gjavit Thaqi, Arif Kurti, and Gjevelin Berisha.

The Krasniqi organization was one of the first significant organized crime groups within New York City that was both predominantly ethnic Albanian and able to compete with the Italian American crime families. Bruno Krasniqi, Saimir Krasniqi, Almir Rrapo, Erkliant Sula, and Florian Veshi were the so-called ringleaders of the group, which operated in New York, Michigan, Connecticut, and elsewhere in the northeastern United States. Their criminal enterprise focused on the sale of marijuana, although violence and firearms were used to achieve their ends.

Parid Gjoka, who came to the United States in the 1990s, also supplied marijuana in New York City. In 2002, Gjoka and his small-time group merged with the Krasniqis, and together they imported marijuana from Canada. This appears to be the first instance of what is now a major law enforcement problem: ethnic Albanian groups smuggling marijuana from Canada.

In 2005, however, the alliance between the two groups deteriorated, resulting in a war between the Gjoka and Krasniqi groups. The members of the Krasniqi organization threatened to kill their rivals if they did not disclose the locations of other members of their gangs. But violence was also their downfall.

In 2006, members of the Krasniqi group were found guilty of numerous crimes, including two murders. One victim was a member of Gjoka's group, Erion Shehu, aka Lonka, who was killed in a drive-by-shooting on July 17, 2005. The other victim was Erenick Grezda, shot in the head at point-blank range by Bruno and Saimir Krasniqi on January 14, 2006. After a five-week jury trial, members of the Krasniqi group also were found guilty of racketeering, conspiracy to murder, kidnapping, narcotics trafficking involving more than one hundred kilograms of marijuana, arson, robbery, and extortion.

Albanian authorities extradited Almir Rrapo on charges relating to his association with the Krasniqi organization and his participation in the murder of Erion Shehu, the kidnapping of Neritan Kocareli, and the trafficking of narcotics. On April 11, 2011, Rrapo pleaded guilty pursuant to a cooperation agreement with the government. At the time of his arrest in Albania, Rrapo had been employed as the senior administrative assistant to the deputy prime minister and foreign minister of Albania.

The Krasniqi organization was not the only major ethnic Albanian organized crime group that made its mark in New York around this time. During the first decade of the twenty-first century another group led by an ethnic Albanian, Gjavit "The Doc" Thaqi, was also involved in importing Canadian marijuana, as well as laundering money and committing firearms offenses. Significant deals were made in upper Manhattan, two of which the police intercepted. In one bust, 1.2 million dollars in cash was seized in Manhattan, along with a quarter of a million dollars in cash bound from Long Island to the Bronx. The cash apparently was intended to pay French Canadians for a shipment of marijuana.

The DEA and Immigration and Customs Enforcement ran a joint operation that began in 2009 and resulted in a number of charges against the Thaqi group. Federal investigators found eighteen guns and hundreds of rounds of ammunition, along with 943 pounds of marijuana from Mexico; seventy pounds of marijuana in a tractor-trailer driven from Toronto; and twenty pounds of marijuana during a car stop in Dutchess County, New York.

Imports from Canada were not the only component of the rise in marijuana sales in New York during this period. Between 2008 and 2011, Afrim Kupa became involved in operating cannabis grow houses. The grow houses were sophisticated, and DEA special agents indicated they each could generate approximately 2.5 million dollars per year (Annese 2011). Remarkably, Kupa was arrested in 2011 while wearing an ankle monitor, part of his sentence for burglaries he had committed in 2010. In addition to growing pot commercially, Kupa was part of Gambino's soldier Joseph Sclafani's contemporary Brooklyn-based "re-rocking" operation, where cocaine was diluted with other adulterants to maximize profits. According to a witness, the cocaine was shipped from California to individuals working as doormen in New York City, who were paid to sign for the packages (Annese 2011).

So in August 2011, New York newspapers again were reporting that federal charges had been brought against ethnic Albanian and Italian organized criminals, this time for operating marijuana grow houses. The *Staten Island Advance* claimed that "the arrests read like a Gambino crime family who's who list—Joseph Sclafani, 46, who in 1989 harbored a fugitive mobster who killed a DEA agent in the Charleston section of Staten Island; Neil Lombardo, 55, who shot and wounded an informant's brother; and Afrim Kupa, 38, a professional heist man with ties to Albanian organized crime and the Gambinos" (Maddux 2012).

During this period the Albanian-Italian connection remained visible in more traditional organized crime markets as well. The Rudaj organization, also known as "the Corporation," was a criminal organization whose members engaged in numerous crimes, including murder, extortion, loan-sharking, and illegal gambling. The Corporation was founded in the early 1990s, when Alex Rudaj, of Montenegro, and Nardino Colotti split from the Genovese crime family to form a rival organization. Initially, the Corporation operated in Westchester County and in the Bronx, where it ran illegal gambling operations. Eventually the Corporation became the first Albanian organized crime enterprise to be charged under the US federal racketeering statute known as RICO.[12]

The rise of the Corporation began in 2001 with the organization's expansion into Astoria, Queens, an area traditionally controlled by LCN. Of particular importance was the so-called Soccer Fever gambling monopoly once dominated by the Lucchese crime family, which had been considerably weakened by the FBI's prosecutions of traditional Italian American crime families during the 1990s. In August 2001, several months after Alex Rudaj had ousted the Lucchese family from Queens, the Gambino crime family, represented by Tommy Napoli, established a rival barbout dice game at Soccer Fever; on the second night of the game, Rudaj and his associates beat rival Gambino members. Shortly before this event, members of the Corporation met members of the Gambino family at a gas station in New Jersey, where Rudaj pointed a shotgun at a gas pump and threatened to blow everyone up unless Gambino *capo* Arnold Squitieri's men put down their guns (Fahim and Feuer 2006).[13] The Rudaj organization eventually controlled at least six gambling clubs in Queens, including Athenia, the Saloni Social Club, Sanidisi, Skutarija, and Zeus.

Ultimately, in a RICO indictment in 2004, twenty-two defendants in the Rudaj organization were charged with various crimes, including attempted murder and conspiracy to commit murder, extortion and conspiracy to commit extortion, loan-sharking, extortionate debt collection, and operation of a large-scale gambling business and bookmaking operation.[14]

After a protracted international law enforcement inquiry, Alex Rudaj and Nardino Colotti both were sentenced to twenty-seven years in prison. All were convicted of racketeering. They also were ordered to forfeit 5.75 million dollars and four properties. The assistant US attorneys who prosecuted the case said that Rudaj's group collected at least four million dollars a year from a network of fifty video gambling machines (Preston 2006).

While most Albanian offenders moved on to new endeavors, others remained involved with the same old rackets. For example, Robert Miraglia, son of Gambino soldier "Fat Joe" Miraglia; Nedzad Korac; and Korac's uncle Selin Hakanjian used "information skimmed via ATM fraud to steal nearly $225,000 in a single day" from Chase Bank and Citibank (Morgethau 2010, 112). The three men pleaded guilty to grand larceny in 2004.[15]

During the first decade of the twenty-first century the size of the leading crime groups grew, and on occasion the scale of operations became international. Sophisticated offenses conducted by small crime groups, such as ATM frauds, fell off the radar, with some minor exceptions. Despite this, violence, threats and even murders remained common. According to Gus Xhudo, lecturer at Mercy College, "Today, Albanian criminals in the United States are not afraid to shoot at a police officer. Their evolution in the US is a reversed one, a sort of backward evolution. They are younger, somewhat irrational and hotheaded, and don't care much about consequences. The older generation of criminals was more strategic and cautious. The only thing that may scare this generation is deportation" (interview, New York, 2014).

This decade saw increases in the corruption of local law enforcement officers by Albanian criminal organizations, demonstrating the growing influence of these groups. For example, the case of Din Celaj and Moheed Oasman involved a police officer, Darren Moonan, who joined the New York City Police Department in July 2001 and worked there until his arrest on July 8, 2011. He had a secret life as a one-man security team for the Albanian robbery crew, driving the robbers to and from their crimes, sometimes across state lines and always while carrying a gun and his NYPD badge. The members of the group were charged with drug trafficking, robbery conspiracy, and conspiracy to transport stolen vehicles across state lines, and Moonan was charged with robbery conspiracy.

After the turn of the century, ethnic Albanian criminals went from violent robbers and thieves to marijuana suppliers and facilitators—and incredible profits were made on both sides of the US-Canadian border. Albanian criminals also appear to have forged strong connections with the Gambino crime family. However, many factors associated with Albanian organized crime in other parts of the world are absent in contemporary New York. Apart from strip clubs, there is little evidence that Albanian organized crime groups in the northeastern United States are involved in the sex trade. Money laundering remains unsophisticated, and drug payments are regularly made with other drugs or vast sums of bulky cash.

MEDIA, SOCIAL EXCLUSION, AND THE CULTURE OF "NOW"

Priming

It appears that most ethnic Albanians who become involved in organized crime in the West began their criminal careers outside of their Balkan homeland, or were forced to leave their homeland because of retaliation and prosecution. A significant number of these criminals were raised (or born) in a new territory—that is, their host country. Consequently, one might ask whether, for example, the media's depictions of Albanians, and Western law enforcement's response to Albanian offenders, have led to the social exclusion of Albanian people, which in turn may have led to an increase in criminal activities among members of this ethnic group. If there is no evidence that the organized crime was necessarily transplanted to the new territory, or that the migration of criminal organizations is well planned and strategic, then which factors within the host country might have led segments of this group to become involved in organized crime?

Academic literature demonstrates that a negative depiction of immigrants can serve as a stimulus to the adoption of stereotypes in its observers as messages are funneled to the masses throughout various media spheres.[16] Analyses of news content have shown that minorities and immigrant groups all too often are linked to national security priorities, such as organized crime and terrorism (Schemer 2012; Schwandner-Sievers 2008; Chambliss and Williams 2012). Survey studies conducted by Schemer (2012) found that increased levels of news exposure stimulate negative attitudes toward ethnic minorities, while decreased exposure stimulates positive attitudes.

The influence of news media on stereotypes can also be explicated by a pattern of "priming" (Schemer 2012), the cognitive process undergone by mass media spectators in their formation of biases toward foreigners. Not only is it difficult for individuals to evade priming, since negative portrayals of minorities can be omnipresent within mass media channels, but it is also difficult for individuals to regress and reconstruct their attitudes to include favorable perceptions of ethnic groups after the priming process has been mentally anchored. With this in mind, let us consider whether media attention being directed to Albanian criminality has affected this group's integration experiences within Western societies.

EU, Quid Facis?

In Europe, Albanians are one of the most rejected and stigmatized groups of non-EU citizens within destination state societies (King and Mai 2004; Michilli 2014). Western countries that border Albania by land and sea, such as Greece and Italy, as well as more distant destination states, such as Great Britain and Germany, all have participated in the popular press's polluted portrayal of this ethnic diaspora (Tsaliki 2008; Antonopoulous et al. 2008; King and Mai 2004).

As Albanians began to arrive in Italy, its premier newspaper, *La Reppublica*, released a slew of news articles depicting them as deserving political refugees. However, the tide began to turn in the mid-1990s, when articles began to portray Albanian sojourners as illegal immigrants and greedy economic migrants with leadership roles in the orchestration of transnational crimes (Kosic and Phalet 2006; Michilli 2014).

According to Baldwin-Edwards (2004), Albanians in Greek society were similarly stigmatized as criminals and stereotyped by the state media as dangerous. In the early 1990s, following a massive influx of Albanian immigrants, leading Greek newspapers such as *Ethnos* and *Kathimerini* cast Albanian refugees as released political prisoners who would commit various violent crimes on entering the state. Baldwin-Edwards argued that a "moral panic" emerged from this media stereotyping: "There were repeated claims, such as that reported in a leading newspaper, *Kathimerini*, in January 1996, that 60 percent of all recorded crimes were committed by immigrants, mostly Albanians" (Baldwin-Edwards 2004, 59).

Media stereotyping becomes especially dangerous when cultural in-groups begin to adopt xenophobic attitudes. Through the process of cognitive priming, they begin to endorse the ethnic biases they repeatedly are exposed to through mass media channels. As a result, members of the Albanian diaspora in Western Europe report experiencing difficulty gaining entrance to key social sectors, such as housing and labor markets, because of host country nationals' negative perceptions.[17]

Without opportunities to achieve their ambitions, Albanian émigrés often settled in dilapidated social conditions, residing in poor-quality housing and assuming the lowest-paying options for employment (Paoli and Reuter 2008). Albanian migrants often gravitated toward pursuing the official goals of materialistic consumption by illicit means, since legal conduits were sealed off to most of them.

While an individual's criminal behavior may emerge out of a variety of facilitating sources, once individuals have been defined as deviant in the eyes of society, eroding the negative image and reintegrating into society becomes challenging. Criminology and sociology literature explains how formal institutions such as criminal justice systems and mass media help the criminal label stick.[18] For example, the surging levels of immigrant visibility within national tribunals and other criminal justice forums in host countries may be due to discriminatory arrests by law enforcement officials, which lead to an overrepresentation of foreign nationals in national crime and justice statistics (Asale 2003). Immigrants' criminality, however, may not have been *achieved* but *assigned* by the concentration of programs that allocate resources to target specific "high-risk" immigrant groups.

In Greece, data collected from a series of ethnographic interviews with law enforcement officials show that popular epithets used by detectives to describe Albanians included "worst migrants," "animals," and "worst breed of people." We can infer that deficiencies in police practices may in part account for the fact that Albanians represent 42 percent of all inmates serving sentences in Greek penitentiaries (Antonopolous et al. 2008).

Social labeling is especially corrosive when the stigmatized person embraces the deviant self-concept and consciously subscribes to performing actions and attending to delinquent characteristics that are in direct alignment with this negative, socially attributed label. Recent research demonstrates that individuals belonging to negatively labeled and socioeconomically underprivileged groups refrain from placing themselves in situations where they would be forced to interact with conventional others (Winfree and Abadinsky 2010).

Stereotypes and social exclusion therefore lead to the creation of friend-enemy discourse, isolation, and ethnic homogeneity. Arben Tabaku, a former senior analyst at the EU Police Mission to Albania, PAMECA, explained in 2007 that the hostility toward Albanian communities overseas reinforced ties among them: "Many undocumented young ethnic Albanians who emigrated to the West were unskilled laborers who found no employment. Feeling excluded abroad, they saw crime as the only possible way to emerge" (interview, Albania, 2007). This widespread friend-enemy discourse among ethnic Albanians may have made these close-knit circles difficult for law enforcement officials to infiltrate.

Finally, it is beneficial to understand Albanian criminality from the perspective of social labeling, because the theory suggests that perpetrators may be enticed by the criminal label that society has attributed to the ethnic group to which they belong. Many youth gang members who belong to stereotyped groups of ethnic or racial minorities already may have formed informal deviant identities; being formally labeled by the tribunal system then helps to solidify and make this label official.

The New York Media

The Albanian Bad Boys is a gang that was created by a group of Albanian immigrants who arrived in the Bronx as political refugees and asylum seekers after 1991. Members of this criminal gang were notorious for engaging in violent fights with other ethnic gangs residing in the multicultural neighborhood of Belmont in the Bronx. Rival gangs acknowledged that the Albanians did not start many fights, although they seldom shied away from them, at times showing up in groups of forty to redress a slight to one of their own. The Albanians developed such a reputation for fierce loyalty to their peers that they gained respect within the local schools, as well as on the streets. "They all hate us," said DJ, a seventeen-year-old Albanian from the Herbert H. Lehman High School in the Bronx in 2001. "That's why we hang together" (Filkins 2001).

Some Belmont residents understood that this type of behavior did not reflect the values of all Albanians: "The Albanian Boys . . . are not a representation of the Albanian community, they are just a bunch of knuckleheads" (Gonzalez 1992, 1). Nevertheless, other Albanian migrants expressed personal resentment about the image their ethnic culture appeared to be gaining within the local community (Goodnough 1994).

In the years following these incidents, New York's local newspapers released articles reporting on the criminality of ethnic Albanians. A majority of the press reports circulating in the 1990s concentrated on the Albanians' swift and facile takeover of turf formerly controlled by the Italian mafia, and their determination to control New York City's organized crime scene. Sensationalized press coverage also elaborated on the brutality of these groups: "Poles will deal with 'just about anybody,' Dominicans, Blacks, Italians, Asian street gangs, but they won't go near the Albanian mob. The Albanians are too violent and too unpredictable. . . . They are clannish, secretive, hypersensitive to any kind of insult and too quick to use violence for the sake of vengeance" (McGarvey 2002, 1).

Results collected from a total of 997 articles published between 1985 and 2013 in newspapers such as *The New York Times,* the *New York Post,* and the *Daily News* found phrases such as "ultra-violent threats," "well-armed," and "ruthless thugs" used in stories about Albanians (Michilli 2014). However, these negative connotations stood in contrast to a series of feature stories and news reports that portrayed Albanians and their cultural history in a positive light. Print news media around the turn of the twenty-first century often concentrated on covering the mass exodus of displaced ethnic Albanians refugees, and articles on their criminality took a back seat.

Further analysis of articles published between 1990 and 2014, mainly by London and New York's major newspapers, showed that the largest total counts for articles about Albanians was among the London newspapers, with *The Guardian* totaling 3,890 (2,311 of which focused on negative descriptions, mainly depicting Albanians as criminals and violent mobsters) and the smallest total count was among the New York newspapers, with 769 for the *New York Post* (526 of which were negative). Overall, London newspapers tended to discuss Albanians more than New York newspapers did, despite the fact that the ethnic Albanian diaspora in London is not as significant as the one in New York.

Moreover, the New York–based media did not stigmatize the ethnic Albanian population to the same degree that European press agencies in countries such as

Greece, Italy, and the United Kingdom did. The frequency of European reports on Albanian crime may have been higher because of the geographical proximity of those countries and the greater presence of Albanian criminal activity in them.

Albanian Perceptions: Migration and Organized Crime

How do ethnic Albanians perceive the media, social exclusion, and portrayals of Albanian organized crime in the United States? I conducted approximately sixty in-depth interviews with ethnic Albanian migrants in New York, both documented and undocumented, to determine their views on these topics (see table 3).

The ability of respondents to access social sectors was one of the most important topics surveyed throughout the interviews. Some Albanian immigrants discussed the challenge of securing employment following their arrival in the United States; however, the majority of respondents did not feel excluded from American society. In fact, only four out of sixty respondents (7 percent) felt that Albanians are not treated equally when compared to non-Albanians/"Americans" in New York City. About 78 percent said that they believe they are treated equally. Additionally, more than half the sample noted that it was relatively easy to find employment in the United States.

When respondents were asked if they believed that the US media has portrayed them as criminals, results were divergent, although most did not blame the media for promoting stereotypical attitudes about their culture. Some did argue that the Western media tends to "talk about Albanian crime"; however, many emphasized that the European media focuses on these issues to a greater extent. Few respondents agreed with the idea that the media has depicted Albanians as violent and "crazy" mafia members; others mentioned that if ethnic Albanians were committing crimes, then the public had a right to be informed—and such information, in their eyes, does not constitute ethnic profiling.

Most respondents acknowledged that the rise of an ethnic mob has been a common theme in the movie industry, as seen in the Italian mob films; therefore, this association did not offend most of them. More than half of the respondents in my study (forty-three out of sixty, or 72 percent) referenced the 2009 movie *Taken* as an example of a depiction of Albanian culture as ultra violent and vengeful, although most did not view the media as a root cause of social discrimination or exclusion from institutional spheres in the New York area. On the contrary, respondents mentioned that their ethnic group was not being stigmatized at the same level as it has been in European countries that host members of the Albanian diaspora. Participants noted that if their fellow ethnic nationals were engaging in crime, then media reporting in the United States was not necessarily sensationalized. During one of my interviews, an American Albanian woman in her thirties remarked: "Definitely during the Kosovo war I don't think that we were portrayed

TABLE 3 Responses of sixty ethnic Albanian immigrants interviewed in New York City

	Albanians are treated equally when compared to non-Albanians	It is easy to find housing upon arrival in the United States	It is easy to find employment upon arrival in the United States	People associate Albanians with crime	The Western media presents a negative portrayal of Albanians	People have positive stereotypes of Albanians
Agree	47	47	28	29	20	41
Disagree	4	4	23	24	27	4
Total	51	51	51	53	47	45

Source: NIJ funded study on Albanian migration, 2012–2014.
Note: Neutral positions such as indifferent and missing are not included in this table.

negatively at all; I feel that we were seen as victims. But after . . . there was a recent mob bust and there were a lot of Albanians in Staten Island . . . it's the truth, they were selling and doing drugs. . . . I don't feel like they are portrayed negatively if that is what they are doing" (interview, New York, 2013).

When the topic of negative stereotypes and xenophobia was discussed, survey participants said that they have experienced more positive stereotyping than negative. At work or at school, people often perceived them to be ambitious and hard working—in other words, positive out-group stereotypes.

Based on these sixty interviews, it does not appear that media labeling is affecting the quality of life of members of the ethnic Albanian diaspora in New York City. This conclusion was confirmed by their access to key social sectors, such as housing and labor markets, although it is important to note that in both Europe and the United States Albanian immigrants are predominantly employed as non-specialized laborers in the construction, service, and primary sectors, irrespective of their personal skills (Tsaliki 2008).

Unexplainable Contempt and Immediate Gratification

Media portrayals aside, what other factors encourage ethnic Albanian migrants to commit crimes in Western societies? During interviews, members of the ethnic Albanian diaspora, including offenders, alluded to a variety of factors that lead migrants and first-generation Albanian American nationals to become involved in criminal activity. A number of respondents blamed the discriminatory policies of some European countries. A middle-aged Kosovo Albanian asylum seeker who has been living in New York for the past eight years noted:

I believe that government policies play a major role in immigrants' lives. If immigrants are not provided an opportunity to participate in the labor market, they will most likely turn to illegal means to make a living, considering that most immigrants are at a low socioeconomic status. One relative told me that in Germany, he had a hard time finding a job due to his illegal status and then he, along with some other Albanian friends, turned to organized crime. He told me that they got involved in stealing cigarettes from stores and then sold them to Turkish businessmen.... I wouldn't justify that in New York; if you come here you can legally work, they will give you a tax ID number, so you have a means of making a living and then if you choose to get involved in crime for excitement purposes, that makes you a criminal. (interview, New York, 2013)

Some sources of strain encountered in the host country were linked to the lack of generational longevity, and some respondents cited inequality and financial instability as a stressor leading people to develop criminal coping strategies.

Many interviewees agreed that recent immigrants were driven by the Western world's materialism and became involved in a life of crime because they were impatient and did not want to wait to attain their goals. Some spoke of ethnic Albanians who turned to crime because they were driven by a need for fast cash. One female respondent, now a naturalized American citizen in her late fifties, explained: "The people come from their countries, they want to make easy money, but, I say, you never asked me if I worked twenty or even thirty years for what I have, and some people just want it then and there and they don't want to wait. The new generation is like this; it's the old generation that worked 24/7. The new generation wants everything now" (interview, New York, 2013).

Another younger Albanian respondent from Kosovo similarly observed:

There are people that are trying to achieve the American dream and they are failing, and they give up and look for other avenues. It's a lot about quick, easy money, and it's very appealing. . . . They like people fearing them; it's a power trip but it's hard to get out once you're in. I think it happens when they are adolescents; they get caught by the flurry and they can be swayed; they lure them in, give them gifts, watches and all these things that they buy them. . . . The Albanians take them out and show them the good life to lure them; they know the kids that like good things; they test with a little bit. That's where I understand; I don't agree with it but I understand it. (interview, New York, 2013)

In a *New Yorker* article on the activities of the Pink Panthers (a group of Balkan thieves, including ethnic Albanians), Michel Jugnet, a lawyer who represents a thief named Stojkovic, said, "These are people who were involved in the Balkan wars in one way or another." One of Jugnet's colleagues, Emmanuel Auvergne-Rey, portrayed Stojkovic's actions as born of necessity, not greed. "The war in Yugoslavia, we Europeans saw it from afar. They arrived in Europe, and Europe did not welcome them" (Samuels 2010). This was a generation of young and confused Balkan people who went looking for work outside the Yugoslav borders. Not everyone, however, found the occupation of their dreams.

In 1974, *Gorilla,* a novel inspired by the life of a Serbian thug named Stefan Markovic, was published with great success. Although the story is about Serbian criminality, it speaks to the experience of other ethnic groups from the Balkan region, including Albanians. After immigrating to Paris, Markovic served as a bodyguard for the actor Alain Delon, who starred in the 1967 film *Le Samouraï*, Jean-Pierre Melville's classic gangster noir. In 1968, Markovic's corpse was found in a garbage dump outside Paris. A friend of Delon's, the Corsican gangster François Marcantoni, was indicted, but there was insufficient evidence to convict him of the murder. Delon was questioned but never charged. *Gorilla* is a touchstone for many Balkan criminals who move to the West. As one gang member told *The New Yorker*, "Every mafioso, if they read one book, it's this one" (Samuels 2010).

The story begins with the hero, Stefan Ratarac—Markovic's alter ego—being told by Alain Dupré, a prominent French actor, to beat up a journalist. Ratarac succeeds at this mission, and he soon takes up residence on the ground floor of Dupré's house, where he follows the whims of his master. Ratarac is easily offended and needlessly aggressive.

The narrator explains that Ratarac's "game came out of an unexplainable contempt." The bodyguard "despised small people who earned their everyday bread in a difficult way. . . . Why do they sing in church choirs and light candles? Why didn't they steal, rob, fuck rich Paris ladies, beat, and kill?" (Samuels 2010). Living in the shadow of a rich Frenchman humiliates Ratarac, and he cultivates his resentment: he hates the poor for embodying weakness, and he hates the rich for having what he can't have. The movie star and his friends engage in orgies, and Ratarac secretly films one, in the hope of blackmailing the participants. The actor confronts him, saying, "Why are you doing this? It's stupid." Ratarac responds, "It's stupid to live the way I live! I'm wearing your shirts. Even your underwear. And it's been like that for years" (Samuels 2010).

Gorilla points to the rage that many young Balkan men and women must have felt for the Western world, which teased them with its wealth, yet forbade them legal entry or easy access to jobs and money. The invisible wall erected by the West kept the Balkan criminal elites extremely rich and the rest of the defeated country poor. Although after the wars most of the people started from scratch and worked hard to earn a modest living, some didn't want to accept this harsh reality and felt that the world owed them a better life. They wanted more, now, and they weren't afraid to get it.

· · ·

Ethnic Albanian organized crime figures appear to be active in Western societies, but little is known about their migration patterns. There is not much evidence that Albanian organized crime is a strategically transplanted entity or a rational bureaucracy that has been able to easily move its "businesses" to foreign territories. It does not appear that these criminal groups resemble multinational corporations, or that there is a nationwide Albanian mafia.

Albanian organized crime figures find themselves in new markets not necessarily because they have chosen to leave their land of origin to achieve criminal objectives in the destination society, but because of forced migration, the need to escape legal proceedings and subsequent punishment, or fighting within their own criminal clans. Also, many of these organized crime groups emerged years after the first wave of migration to Western societies, and most ethnic Albanian organized crime figures were, in fact, raised in Western countries. Their criminal mobility appears to be functional and project-based.

Since 2003, police in Europe have observed advancement in some ethnic Albanian criminal groups. According to Western European law enforcement agencies, Albanian groups are developing organizations with fluid structures. Specialization in the transport industry and decreased use of violence also are regarded as indicators of the Albanian criminal advancement in Western Europe. Also, in the United States, there has been a gradual reduction in sporadic violence associated with Albanian criminality, although armed murders do still occur. The size of the leading crime groups has grown, and on occasion, the scale of their operations has become international or better organized.

The new millennium also saw corruption of local law enforcement. While the 1990s witnessed corruption of border agency staff, the ability to corrupt and employ law enforcement officers for the commission of a robbery represents an increase in the capability of Albanian organized crime groups. Ethnic Albanian offenders who were active in the 1980s and 1990s, once violent robbers, became suppliers and distributors of marijuana, cocaine, and heroin. Connections appear particularly strong with the Gambino crime family in the United States and with criminals in Canada.

Finally, in this chapter I have explored the reasons why Albanian migrants become involved in organized crime in Western territories. Without proper integration of new immigrant arrivals, homogenous and closed immigrant communities could become attractive locales for organized crime. Social exclusion, stereotyping, and labels can seriously affect migrants' lives, too. This study agrees with those scholars who highlight the critical need to ensure that job opportunities are accessible to asylum seekers and other migrants without plans of employment or study, but it also acknowledges that, sometimes, even when such opportunities are in place, the seduction of crime and the desire for fast money and instant gratification are stronger than any other structural opportunities.

In the United States, and particularly in New York, media reports do not emphasize Albanian criminality. Nor do members of the Albanian diaspora feel that a criminal label prevents them from accessing key integration opportunities within their current state. In European society, however, it appears that labels and discrimination have been more prominent, and they may have affected the members of some ethnic Albanian communities, leading to the creation of friend-enemy discourse and increases in criminality.

Chapter 4

IRON TIES

In Blood We Trust

The world of organized crime can be described as a kind of jungle, a world in which the stakes are high; yet the rules and the mechanisms which make transactions in the legal world so much easier are absent: entering into contracts, paying via the official banking system and—in the case of disagreement—the availability of mediation or the judiciary. Hence cooperation in the world of organized crime is not so easy, and curbing distrust between offenders is a continuously recurring problem.

—KLEEMANS AND VAN DE BUNT (1999, 19)

One of the most common descriptions of the so-called Albanian mafia is that it is a hierarchically structured, clan-based organization resembling the Sicilian mafia and the American La Cosa Nostra (LCN). The myth has it that the typical structure of the Albanian mafia is that of a family clan, referred to as a *fis* or a *fare.* Several mafia families have an executive committee known as a *bajrak* and select a high-ranking member for each family unit. Each unit is led by a *krye,* or "boss," who selects *kryetar,* or "underbosses," as well as a *miq,* who acts as a liaison to members and is responsible for coordinating unit activities (Xhudo 1996).

According to criminologist Xavier Raufer, the base of the Albanian crime pyramid, in which the ties of blood win out over those of marriage, is a team of men from the same clan or village, often from the same biological family. These men obey their boss—most likely a relative—blindly. "The conditions of access to this criminal clan are strict, codified, ritualized. There is one code, the Kanun, and one biological cadre, an extended family" (Raufer 2003, 64).

One cannot but wonder: Are those who unload contraband cigarettes at the ports of Saranda and Durrës "Albanian mafiosi"? Are those who sell protection to cafés "Albanian mafiosi"? Are those who break into houses whose inhabitants have fled "Albanian mafiosi"? Is the bar owner who cocks an eye, saying, "If you dig hash, let me know" an "Albanian mafioso"? What about those who smuggle barrels of oil across the Shkoder Lake? Who or what is the Albanian mafia, after all?

Analyzing the structure and membership of Albanian organized crime groups is vital for understanding the centrality of Albanian organized crime figures in transnational criminal networks, as well as the impact of social relations on the behavior of Albanian offenders. By studying the social networks of Albanian organized crime figures, it is possible to understand, among other things, the cohesion of the group, the strength and nature of the relations among its members, and the ethnic composition of the group.

Another important aspect of the analysis focuses on whether, over the years, Albanian criminal groups have reorganized in order to avoid detection, accrue political power, and enlarge their profits. For almost a century, LCN has been attacked on all fronts, both in Italy and North America, but it appears that because of its organization and continuing loyalty, the group has managed to survive. Have any Albanian organized crime groups survived after the arrests of major players? Do they have a way to replicate themselves? Will, for example, the Rudaj family or the Kelmendi family be known in twenty years?

THE ALBANIAN MAFIA

I arrived in Prishtina midmorning on July 9, 2008. The road from Skopje had passed through grasslands and fields; now the highway leading into town was empty and lined with gas stations and unfinished buildings. The café where Besmir, described in chapter 2, and I had agreed to meet was on a busy street in the center of town. In the café there were only a few people, all in their twenties. About ten minutes after I arrived, a tall, masculine-looking man, wearing a tight T-shirt, black sweatpants, and a heavy golden chain around his neck, entered the café. It was Besmir.

Besmir, who had been active in Western Europe during the 1990s, spent almost eight years in prison after being convicted of membership in a criminal organization, extortion, kidnapping, numerous fights, and human trafficking, among other offenses. After being released from prison he was deported to Kosovo, like many other ethnic Albanians who were arrested in Western Europe.

I asked him about the concept of an Albanian mafia.

"I don't think there is such a thing," Besmir told me. "That doesn't exist in our context. It is difficult to compare Albanian groups with the Sicilian mafia because it is not in our culture to take orders from others. Albanians don't want to have bosses. . . . We are very loyal when it comes to family and friendship, but we don't want to take orders from others."

"Are you saying that Albanian criminal groups are based on some type of solidarity and mutual respect, and not on hierarchy?" I asked.

"We are a macho culture, and every man's honor is important," Besmir replied. "We make decisions together. Sometimes someone gives orders to others, but in general, Albanians do not like to feel subordinated. When one of us has an idea, he discusses the idea with the entire group, and then we decide whether it makes sense for us to act. We act as a group, and everyone's idea is appreciated."

He continued: "We also help each other, even if a particular problem does not concern us personally. I have gotten myself into so much trouble because of my friends. Trying to help. I even ended up in prison because of them. But I don't care."

Besmir denied police accusations that his family members were involved in his criminal business: "The police always suspected that my father was involved, but he was not. He is not a criminal. My father is a very traditional, old-fashioned man. He is from a different era" (interview, Kosovo, 2006).

Regardless of what Besmir said, evidence showed that, although not all members of his criminal group were related by blood, there were strong family and ethnic ties among them. Besmir's brother was suspected of being involved in the family's illegal business. According to police sources, he was especially engaged in human trafficking or smuggling, and in prostitution. He also was suspected of falsifying documents for illegal immigrants.

Besmir's sister handled some of the group's "administrative work" and finances, along with two Albanian associates and close friends of Besmir, who were known to the police for their numerous criminal offenses. There were indications that Besmir's father, too, was involved in his son's criminal enterprise. The police reported that one of Besmir's girlfriends was collecting extortion money in the restaurant sector and bringing it to Besmir's father.

And Besmir's uncle recorded the names of those Kosovo Albanian migrants who were paying taxes to the Kosovo Liberation Army (KLA). Families who did not pay, or who paid too little, were threatened.

Besides Besmir's family members, many of whom were directly or indirectly involved in his criminal business, Besmir also cooperated with other ethnic Albanians. Some were from Kosovo, others from Albania. Interestingly, Besmir's right-hand man was a man of North African descent.

After Besmir was deported to Kosovo, police sources claimed that his younger brothers took over the family business, but they were not as successful. "They wanted to be like Besmir and used his name to threaten and extort money from nightclubs, but they were not as smart and as organized as their brother," a police officer in charge of Besmir's file said (interview, Belgium, 2007).

Although Besmir claimed that Albanian criminal organizations do not resemble hierarchically structured bureaucracies, their financial support of the KLA bolsters the argument that some Albanian criminal organizations are nevertheless strategic: they seek to use violence not just to enlarge their profits but also to establish political power and long-term influence over state institutions. Because of their political strategy and close ties to ethnic Albanian politicians, some Albanian criminal groups do, perhaps, share certain traits with the traditional Italian mafia.

CLANS AND TRUST
Criminal Ties

Cases, files, field notes, charts . . . hundreds of pages of documents on Albanian organized crime lay on my desk. Yet linking isolated instances of what appear to be "organized crime" and establishing relationships among offenders who may belong to a criminal organization is an extremely difficult task. Is a suspect really connected to organized crime, or is his offense simply an individual violation of the law occurring apart from a larger criminal enterprise? Is a single incident that takes place in country A—a murder, for example, or an act of prostitution or illegal migration—connected to incidents in country B? And are all these seemingly isolated incidents ordered by a "mafia leadership" operating in country C?

Proving that an individual is part of a complex criminal organization is a time-consuming and challenging task for law enforcement officials. Police and court files tend to distort reality, since they represent only a fraction of the effort involved in making that case. Police officers usually discover criminal activity at the street level, mainly in their own territory, long after the planning and conspiracy have taken place in country A, B, or C. Precisely because it is so difficult to tackle a criminal organization in its totality, offenders are charged only for their individual violations of the law, and low-level players sometimes are prosecuted for belonging to criminal organizations. Investigations often result in the arrest of just three to five offenders, rather than the entire criminal network.

As shown in the previous chapter, the use of the term "mafia" itself has further complicated the study of organized crime. Overuse of the term has made it difficult to define a mafia group precisely, and to identify specifically such a group's relationship to organized crime and to crime in general. This is especially true when attempting to garner information from media sources and governments, which have a tendency to dramatize organized crime.

Within the Albanian organized crime scene there are examples of both mafia-type organizations and more entrepreneurial groups that are not interested in influencing politics, or in using strategic violence to obtain political power. In general, criminal cases suggest that blood ties play a fundamental role in cementing the influence of Albanian organized crime groups and act as a major cohesive force within them. In the criminal underworld, it is difficult to identify trustworthy partners. Dealing with information under conditions of uncertainty brings many risks. A well-known Albanian proverb says, "He who trusts all things to chance gambles with his life." The transaction cost of doing business with people who have no reason to trust you increases rapidly. In an unregulated environment, such as in Kosovo during the 1990s, perhaps a six-foot-four, thick-necked man holding a Kalashnikov is needed to ensure that an exchange is honored. Guns, however, attract attention, and attention is not what organized crime groups want.

Therefore, it is not irrational to assume that links between families, clans, or ethnic communities would encourage cooperation among criminals, guarantee that clandestine dealings remain concealed, and ensure secrecy, making it difficult for law enforcement agencies to penetrate these organizations. Closed criminal families, while not entirely immune to betrayals, seem to enjoy lower costs of doing business, and family ties appear to allow greater flexibility and safety for the groups' members. Yet these assumptions require more systematic analysis. They cannot be taken for granted, particularly because close-knit hierarchical criminal structures also have their cost: for example, a lack of expertise in some areas or an inability to grow internationally.

Many scholars have demonstrated the capacity of social network analysis to furnish details about a network's structure, to identify interactions among the actors, and to provide insights into relationships and the control of each subject over others within the network. Scholars also have carried out studies investigating criminal networks, defined as groups of people linked by criminally exploitable ties, and examined their activities and their organization (von Lampe and Johansen 2004). By using social network analysis to study the roles of the actors participating in Albanian-speaking organized crime networks (e.g., connectors, mavens, leaders, bridges, and isolates), I have developed some generic typologies of Albanian criminal organizations in the Balkan and Western contexts that may help to explain how these groups operate, how they are structured, and why they trust the people they trust.

Traditional Clans

While conducting research on organized crime in 2008, I came across an online discussion forum on the Albanian mafia. One blogger, a curious New Yorker, wrote on Streetgangs.com: "All the Albanian people I know are cousins, and I know about twenty. I've been to school with a few and they live in my neighborhood, so whenever I see them at the park, they always introduce me to a new cousin. How weird is this?"

Studying the Albanian clan system might shed some light on this blogger's question. In 2006, Rosario Aitala, criminal justice advisor in the Police Assistance Mission of the European Union to Albania (PAMECA), stated that to understand the complexity of Albanian organized crime one must first investigate the organization of Albanian society. "This defines the nature of the criminal groups operating in the region. Due to the clan-based societal structure, Albanian organized crime is almost exclusively ethnicity-based, divided into geographical areas, highly politicized, hierarchical, and involves strong family ties," he explained.

Scholars, too, have pointed to the clan as an important factor in Albanian society. Writes criminologist Xavier Raufer:

> Our Western European society is individualist. The individual is practically the only motor and actor in social life. Getting involved in a party, acting as a militant in a

union, taking up a religion or joining an association are personal acts relevant to the political, social or religious conscience of an individual. In the Albanophone area of the Balkans this is absolutely not the case. . . . In a society of this type the individual is nothing outside their extended family. (2003, 68–69)

But what do we mean by a "clan-based society"? Simply stated, anthropologists define clans as extended families or associations thereof. Emile Durkheim defined a clan as an organization that has a mixed nature, at once familial and political. In his view, a clan is a family in the sense that all members are considered kin to one another. Although many bonds are consanguineous, the group also may include non-kin. Non-family members can enter a traditional clan by creating a kind of "brotherhood bond." The creation of brotherhood bonds is part of the Albanian tradition, although the incorporation of non-kin into traditional Albanian clans has been rare.

According to article 103 of the Albanian customary law, the Kanun of Lek Dukagjini, "Brotherhood . . . is effected by two men drinking a few drops of each other's blood" (Fox 1989, 144). Article 989 of the Kanun states that "two small glasses are taken and filled halfway with water and raki. Then one of the friends ties together the little fingers of the two parties and pricks them with a needle, causing a drop of blood from each to fall into the two glasses" (Fox 1989, 188). And, according to article 990, after mixing their blood "and stirring it well, the two men exchange glasses and, with arms linked, they hold the glasses to each other's lips, drinking each other's blood. Guns are fired in celebration and they become like new brothers, born of the same mother and father" (Fox 1989, 188). This type of brotherhood causes a permanent prohibition on intermarriage between the brothers, their families, and their descendants.

These are exceptional scenarios, but when one speaks of Albanian clans, blood ties often are implied. The customary Albanian Kanun laws, as shown below, explain the traditional structure of an Albanian family, relationships between families, brotherhoods and clans, and the relationship between blood ties and kinship ties in the ethnic Albanian context.

BOOK TWO OF THE KANUN

Article 19. The family consists of the people of the house; as these increase, they are divided into brotherhoods [vllazni], brotherhoods into kinship groups [gjini], kinship groups into clans [fis], clans into banners [flamur], and all together constitute one widespread family called nation, which has one homeland, common blood, a common language, and common customs

BOOK EIGHT OF THE KANUN

Article 695. For the Albanian of the mountain, the chain of relationships of blood and kinship are endless.

Article 696. Relationships of brotherhood and clan are claimed with all those descended from common ancestors, up to present.

Article 697. Even if the family of the Albanian is divided into four hundred
branches, no intermarriage among its members occurs.

Article 698. Degrees of relationship result from blood and from kinship.

Article 699. Degrees of relationship by blood result from the side of the father;
degrees of relationship by kinship result from the side of the mother.

It is obvious from the Kanun articles that the ties between Albanian clan members in general, and family members in particular, have traditionally been strong.
Clans have lived in the same villages, sharing lifestyle and territories, and extended
families have lived in the same housing units, interacting continually with one
another. During the communist era, however, the societal organization of clans
and tribes was forbidden in Albania. The totalitarian regime also destroyed most
of the non-family associations of civil society, such as corporations, labor unions,
and political parties. The only form of organization permitted to survive was the
basic biological one of kinship.

After the fall of communism, many ethnic Albanians gradually began rebuilding
their networks, starting with the nuclear family and then moving out to the
extended family. In the isolated northern parts of Albania, where the communist
regime was not as influential as in the south, traditional clan structures were more
visible. Similarly, the clan structure was more prominent in Kosovo and Macedonia
than it was in southern Albania. In Macedonia and Kosovo, it remained the basic
social unit for ethnic Albanians during turbulent times, because of their isolation
from the Macedonian and Serbian state system and from other ethnic groups.

As mentioned previously, tradition still plays a prominent role in Albanian life,
and it must be taken into account as we seek to understand not only contemporary
Albanian culture but also Albania's social and political organization. Overall,
despite the philosophy of the totalitarian regimes, the extended family structure
remains significant in the postcommunist Albanian context, and studies about
trust can offer some insight into why this might be the case.

Clans as Trust-Producing Units

Trust is essential for stable relationships, vital for maintaining cooperation, fundamental for any exchange, and necessary for even the most routine, everyday interactions (Misztal 1996). Clans and families are basic trust-producing units founded
on the principles of segregation, familiarity, conformity, and exclusiveness (Durkheim 1965a; Paoli 2003). In hostile environments, such as the Balkan region in the
1990s, people tend to organize themselves into smaller, trust-producing social
units. In order to survive, they socialize with people whom they know well and
trust unconditionally.

German anthropologist Stephanie Schwandner-Sievers observed that strict
group solidarity, enforced with stiff sanctions, correlates to greater disregard

toward all third parties. Within the framework of social and political behavior in postcommunist Albania, this was especially true for foreigners, whom many Albanians felt they could rob with impunity (Waldmann 2001). The secretive and hostile environment fostered by the communist regime, as well as subsequent disappointments with the postcommunist political situation, have added to the overall sense of distrust among Albanians. This distrust, in turn, has strengthened social bonds within Albanian clans. This should not come as a surprise: tight kinship ties most often are found where government is ineffective, illegitimate, or both. In these situations one needs the extended family's muscle to survive, because the police are either predatory or incompetent.

The domestic economic situation in the western Balkan region was dire during the 1990s, but most people adjusted, each in his or her own way. While almost nobody had a "normal" job, since services, factories, and shops were closed down, some businesses thrived. Despite shortages of basic goods, ethnographers and journalists reported that they did not often encounter miserable or starving people in that region during the 1990s. Strong family bonds can provide, and even impose, mutual aid. For example, an Albanian who meets a distant cousin on a bus will give him his money. Also, despite the Balkan conflict, ethnic Albanian families were not reluctant to expand, as often is the case in a postwar period.

The isolation of Albanians has led to an expansion of the friend-enemy discourse in Albanian settlements. The distrust that Albanians generally feel toward "foreigners" is an outcome of a turbulent past, a violent present, and an uncertain future. During interviews, Albanian offenders from Kosovo openly stated that "committing crimes in the West" meant little to them, but hurting their "own kind" was a different thing.

Here, the key idea that frames the assumption about selective social bonding is the concept of *homophily*. According to McPherson, Smith-Loving, and Cook (2001, 416), "homophily is the principle that contact between similar people occurs at a higher rate than among dissimilar people." The more commonalities the actors share, the stronger the bonds among them. A number of conditions increase the opportunities for bonding and facilitate the formation of bonds among people and groups. Geographical proximity facilitates the establishment of social ties. Similarities in language, culture, and religion, along with shared history and political ideas, increase the likelihood that people will form a social bond. Participating in the same social group and sharing the same economic or other motives also facilitate cooperation among individuals (McPherson, Smith-Loving, and Cook 2001).

For these reasons, clans have much closer internal relationships than, for example, interest groups or ad hoc coalitions. Clan members are related through kinship, culture, religion, race, language, or political interests. They socialize among themselves and live in close proximity, and they tend to behave alike, entertaining similar views of world affairs. Their common interests and heritage make the ties among them strong. Such exclusive social organization helps the group function normally, producing a feeling of security and reducing the fear of being attacked by outsiders.

The relationship between individual members and their intimate personal groups is also a reciprocal one, particularly in regard to decision-making processes. On one hand, people associate themselves with a specific group because they consider themselves similar in nature to its other members. On the other hand, an individual's intimate group greatly influences his or her decisions, motives, and behavior, as well as his or her perceptions of the risks, efforts, and rewards involved in violating or obeying formal laws.

Therefore, isolated groups such as kinship-based clans are relatively durable and stable social units, with nonshifting boundaries and a high level of solidarity. This is true of nuclear families as well, which have even higher levels of solidarity than clans, despite the fact that certain individuals in the household may act as leaders. Individual identities are firmly embedded in the group identity. In clans, every person sticks with the group and has little opportunity to acquire an individual reputation (or to trade on such a reputation in making deals with possible allies). This intra-group solidarity is a characteristic of survival, not of development.

THE CRIME "FAMILIES"

Clan-Based Criminal Groups in the Balkans

The importance of kinship ties in ethnic Albanian organized crime groups has been emphasized in Europol and INTERPOL threat assessments for years. It has been recorded in the scholarly literature, too (Raufer 2003; Michaletos 2006).[1] Marko Nicovic, vice president of the International Narcotics Enforcement Agency (INEA), told the *National Post* of Toronto that "Kosovo Albanians make the perfect mafia—even better than the Sicilians. They are a small ethnic group made up of clans or families that have very close to family relations. The brotherhood, or *fis*, is impenetrable by outsiders. It is difficult to find translators to work with police and impossible to get an informer or agent inside the organizations" (Graham 2000). Likewise, Ioannis Michaletos, coordinator of the World Security Network Foundation for Southeast Europe, argued that, because clans are based on blood ties, the bonds between them are very strong, which makes infiltration almost impossible. Members of other ethnic groups, according to him, are accepted only to execute certain one-time or secondary jobs.

Olsjan Cela, head prosecutor in Tirana, and Vladimir Sharovic, former head of the Sector for Violent and Serious Crimes in Macedonia, share this view to a certain extent; they agree that "iron family ties" lie at the heart of Albanian criminality. According to Sharovic, "Blood is not water; it plays a role in understanding

Albanian organized crime. The blood ties are not only typical of the Albanian society as such, but also of its criminal organizations."[2]

However, my own research points to the conclusion that ethnic Albanian criminals tend to trust people with whom they have continual interaction above all, irrespective of their qualifications. According to Von Lampe and Johansen (2004), this type of trust is known as individualized trust: the expectations of agreeable behavior relate specifically to the trustee as an individual. The basis for this individual trust may lie in previous observations of the trustee's behavior, characteristics, and disposition. The motivation to trust a particular individual may be rational, based on expectations of the trustee's qualities, or irrational (emotional), the result of affections the trustor feels for the trustee (Gambetta 1993; Misztal 1996). Due to the clan-based structure of Albanian society, relationships based on individualized and emotional (or "irrational") trust that involve family members are indeed common among ethnic Albanians.

Kleemans and van de Bunt's concept of "social embeddedness" helps to explain why networks, social ties, and families are so important for understanding the decision-making process of offenders. They argue that close personal relations lessen the problem of distrust because these relations are "socially embedded." The rule of homophily, discussed previously, applies to criminal relations. Like social relations, criminal relations follow the laws of social and geographical distance: the more grounded people's activities are, the greater the probability that ties will emerge among them. Criminal trust in family and clan members rests above all on familiarity, conformity, and individualized trust that grows out of continual interaction among members. If Albanian criminals stay in close contact with clan members and distrust foreigners, it is logical to assume that most clan members are aware of the activities conducted by their kin. As Edwin Sutherland (1939), the father of differential association theory, wrote, crime is culturally transmitted: criminal behavior is learned through social interaction in intimate personal groups.

Of course, depending on clan dynamics, a clan can either support the behavior of its deviant kinspeople and become a deviant subculture, or resist the criminal temptation and ostracize deviant members from the clan. Certain clans may never acquire the "right opportunities" to become criminal clans, or their members might be satisfied with the prospect of working-class jobs. Which path a clan takes often depends on the power of the traditional role models in the group, such as the fathers, and their beliefs and values. If these social units give way to economic pressures and the fathers lose their traditionally powerful roles within their families, one might expect a clan to become a deviant subculture. Clans or households that are unable to resist the temptation to get rich quickly may turn to criminal innovation in order to obtain material gains, an enhanced reputation, or other benefits.

Alternatively, a clan may be driven into crime because some of its more influential members are profiting from illicit activities and the other clan members are

FIGURE 14. A clan-based criminal group (the gang of Nehat Koulla) (Tirana, Albania, 1997). Copyright © Laurent Piolanti.

enticed by the temporary benefits of such crimes (see figure 14). These deviant "role models" are crucial in understanding clan dynamics, because they not only provide the clan with criminal opportunities but also teach the other members how to commit the crime. This criminal learning process also includes specific direction in terms of motives, drives, rationalizations, and attitudes. This could be seen in Besmir's criminal group, discussed earlier in this chapter, and the various ways that his family was involved in his criminal business.

Of course, this is not the only case in which family members heavily involved in organized crime have served as role models for the rest of their family or clan. The core of the drug trafficking criminal group led by Kosovo Albanian Naser Kelmendi, discussed in chapter 2, allegedly is composed of members of his family. Sarajevo Cantonal Police have filed at least thirteen criminal complaints in the past several years against Kelmendi and his sons Elvis, Liridon, and Besnik. Kelmendi, his sons, and his half brother run a number of firms in Bosnia, Montenegro, Serbia, and Kosovo.

Finally, the behavioral patterns of isolated groups are difficult to change or uproot when external influences are lacking. There is a chicken-and-egg issue here: the close ties of kinship that can create effective rebels, mobsters, and fanatics often flourish because of ineffective states, lack of clear norms, and weak social control—but just and effective governments are hard to establish and maintain among populations whose extended family structures are conducive to criminal activities. In particular, close family ties among criminals have been observed in the prostitution and human trafficking market run by clans from northern Albania, Macedonia, and parts of Kosovo.

One also may argue that the "Kanun mentality" has been more prominent in northern Albania, particularly among the Gheg population, which makes the clan structure vital to the survival of this group. Northern Albania and parts of Macedonia have been beyond the reach of the law for years, and sticking to one's clan has been an essential survival tool for people from these areas. Numerous court cases support this contention. For example, the Belgian court case Lleshi, from 2000, involved Albanian family-based "lover-boy" criminality, in which trafficking victims were seduced and then sold by the Lleshi clan in Albania.[3] The clan controlled part of a region in northern Albania where it monopolized the trafficking of women to the West for sexual exploitation. The Lleshi brothers operated internationally, but they came back to this region regularly to check the quality of the "merchandise" before they paid the recruiters, who were, in fact, their relatives and members of the same clan in Albania. These clan members supplied the Leshi brothers with girls from Albania, Moldova, and other places.[4] One of the victims, called Tanja, described the situation: "The Lleshi family originates from the same region in Albania as the Kaloshi family [another criminal clan involved in the same business]. The two families are forming a real mafia in Albania, and they organize human trafficking and exploitation of young girls, not only in Belgium but also in Italy, Luxembourg, and the UK."[5]

Similarly, the Sokol case tells of three ethnic Albanian brothers active as "lover boys" in Belgium during the 1990s. These ethnic Albanians, born in Skopje, Macedonia, were prostituting Eastern European girls. They perceived their activities as a kind of family business. The brothers operated mainly in Belgium, but when it came to the recruitment of girls, they were supported and assisted by their entire family back home. Kati, one of the brutally abused victims, claimed that the Sokol brothers and their extended family were well known in Macedonia. In Belgium, the victims were prostituting themselves in a bar owned by friends of one of the brothers. The three brothers were prosecuted and convicted in Belgium in 2001.

In terms of blood ties, it is difficult to make any clear distinction between the structure of criminal groups from Albania's south (Tosks) and north (Ghegs). There have been cases where Albanian family and clan members from both regions have been involved in everything from marijuana and heroin trafficking to extortion, murder, trafficking of human beings, and arms dealing. The numerous aliases and fake identities used by the offenders make it extremely difficult to establish accurately the kinship relations among them. According to INTERPOL documents from 2009, some of these people have more than thirty aliases. And as

Belgian police officer Francois Farcy explained, "Even when Zakim and Sami [Albanian organized crime members in Verviers] were confronted with DNA evidence, they still denied that they were brothers" (interview, Belgium, 2007).

According to Albanian law enforcement estimates, around the turn of the century, more than twenty large and well-organized criminal clans or families were operating across Albania, and a number of criminal clans or families also were operating in Kosovo and Macedonia (see table 4). Police estimates show that in the late 1990s, there were about one hundred kinship-based or interest-driven criminal groups in Albania, with about two thousand total members.[6] According to Prime Minister Sali Berisha, between 2005 and 2006 alone, "we have destroyed in Albania 141 criminal groups [elsewhere, 206]; 1,170 members and leaders of these groups were arrested and brought to justice."[7] However, although reference often is made to "criminal clans," this does not necessarily imply that all criminal groups are kinship-based.

The situation in Kosovo has been similar to that in Albania. In Kosovo, a 2007 report by the Berlin Institute for European Policy argues that the real power lies with fifteen to twenty family clans that control "almost all substantial key social positions" and are "closely linked to prominent political decision makers" (Schwarz 2008) Hashim Thaçi, prime minister since 2008, has been specifically incriminated for allowing these clan-based organized crime groups to take over the country (Schwarz 2008).

Similarly, a report from 2005 written by the German secret police, BND, reports: "The structures around Ramush Haradinaj [leader of the KLA and the former prime minister of Kosovo], based on family clans in the area of Decani, are engaged in the entire spectrum of criminal, political and military activities, which substantially influence security conditions throughout Kosovo. The group consists of approximately 100 members and is active in smuggling arms and drugs and in the illegal trade of goods liable to customs duty" (Schwarz 2008).

For years the "clannish" organized crime groups in the Western Balkans were usually composed of about fifteen to thirty members; reports note that some groups had as many as one hundred members. The number of members within a specific group depends on the criminal activity in question, but during the turbulent conflict era in the Balkans, numbers represented power. Former public prosecutor Ardian Visha said, "In the past, the greater the group, the more fear it evoked in the eyes of its victims, enemies, and competitors" (interview, Albania, 2006). This is called the "audience effect": large fighting or criminal groups create their own emotional zone, pump one another up with enthusiasm while reducing their own fear and tension, and instill fear in observers. In this manner larger groups become capable of more serious violence and crime than smaller groups or individuals (Collins 2008).

Kinship ties between criminals are not typical of ethnic Albanians only. According to scholars, criminal relations in general tend to be embedded in kinship ties. Antony Giddens (1971) suggested that kinspeople usually could be relied on to

TABLE 4   Some clan-based organized crime groups in Albania (1991–2007)

Town	Group(s)	Town	Group(s)
Berat	Caka	Gjirokastër	Lazarat
	Cala	Korçë	Cobenjte
	Cobo		Kapurani
	Hasani	Kurcaj	Allushi
	Dardës (Banda e	Lac	Fufi
	Altin Dardës)		Trokthi
	Koxhaj		
	Mahmutaj	Lushnje	Bare (Banda e Lushnjës)
	Tot	Shkodër	Cafi
Diber	Rasim Shira		Cela
	Reci		Gjoka
	Ymer Lala	Tirana	Gina
Durrës	Berisha (Banda e		Rexhina
	Lul Berishes)		Shullazi
	Dokle	Tropoje	Haklaj
	Gjoka		Haxhia
	Hasanbelliu		Hoxha
	Koka		Mulosmani
	Salillari	Vlorë	Caushaj (Banda e
	Xhakja		Çoles)
Fier	Baca		Gaxhi (Banda e
	Borici		Gaxhait)
	Hamiti		Ramadani
	Isufaj		Tozaj
	Kajolli		
	Nazeraj		
	Pusi i Mezinit		
	(Banda e Pusit		
	të Mezinit)		
	Saliaj		
	Shanaj		

SOURCE: Arsovska and Sartorius (2008). The original document has been updated and modified to include additional groups identified through document analysis. This list is not exhaustive and not all of these clans/territorial groups are defined as criminal organizations according to the UN Palermo Convention 2000.

meet a range of obligations, regardless of whether they felt personally sympathetic toward the specific individuals involved.

Regional Cooperation

Despite the existence of many Albanian family-based criminal structures in the Balkans, it is apparent that at least some "business-oriented" ethnic Albanian offenders have learned to overcome socially constructed differences between themselves and "other" groups. Cooperation between somewhat "different" groups has been observed on local, regional, and international levels.

My research from the Balkans and the United States indicates that in the past, for example, Albanians from Albania (in particular Tosks from southern Albania) often avoided cooperation with Kosovars because of the latter group's reputation as dishonest traders. At the same time, Kosovo Albanians stated in interviews that Albanians from Albania, as a result of their communist past and total isolation, tend to be "crazy," irrational, and unconcerned about the consequences of their actions. Consequently, Tosks often cooperated with people from their own cities or neighbourhoods, or with Greeks and Italians. Conversely, Ghegs from northern Albania worked with Ghegs from the same region, and sometimes with Ghegs from Kosovo.

Throughout the years, however, emerging opportunities for profitable business enterprises have led to project-based cooperation between Ghegs and Tosks. According to intelligence reports, even during the UN embargo of Yugoslavia from 1991 to 1996, Albanians from the north frequently engaged in oil smuggling, which also was also a profitable business for Albanians in the south. Crime groups from southern Albania were in contact with criminals in Greece, and they smuggled oil from there into northern Albania. To accomplish this, the southern Albanian offenders often cooperated with northern Albanian clans. Although in principle Albanians from the south and the north were long-standing "enemies," groups from these regions cooperated efficiently. To coordinate the oil transport from Kakavia, on the Greek border, to Hani I Hotit, on Albania's border with Serbia, required a synergy between clans from the south and the north.[8]

Information gathered from investigative files shows that in strategically important cities, such as Tirana, Durres, and Vlore, criminal groups generally were composed of fifteen to thirty like-minded individuals (e.g., gangsters, ex-security agents, former policemen, common people, and others) who came from the same locality and had same political affiliation but were not necessarily related by blood. Because of their locations, some of these criminal groups had opportunities for regular contact with offenders of other ethnicities (and nationalities), such as Italians, Greeks, and Turks. Likewise, in the more diverse southern areas of Albania, blood relations were not always a prerequisite for belonging to a criminal group, and the groups were rarely organized around clans. According to criminal analyst Arben Tabaku, they were, however, often organized around nuclear families, since the family structure—as understood in a Western context—was more typical for this region (interview, Albania, 2007).

Thus, major organized crime groups were mainly territorial and very political. Aldo Bare, Zani Çaushi, Gaxhai, Pusi I Mezinit, and the Banda e Lul Berishes all share similar stories. "They were all friends from the same neighborhood and the same village, although not necessarily blood-related. They did, however, support the same political parties," a source reported. "Some were imprisoned during the communist regime, and then formed groups after they were released from prison. In the case of Pusi I Mezinit, members, mainly ex-prisoners, came from across South Albania. They were called 'the strongest of the South,' and now most are dead. They were supporters of the Democratic Party. The gang of Zani Çaushi, who supported the Socialist Party, was their main rival" (interview, Albania, 2008).

Since 2003, territorial cooperation among different families and clans has become even more significant for ethnic Albanian organized crime groups. In the past, larger groups from Albania, Macedonia, and Kosovo violently imposed their control over well-defined territories within their respective countries. If opposing groups operated in the same territory, shootings and killings were likely, as in the case of the assassinations linked to Lulzim Berisha's criminal group in Durres, or those linked to Zani Çaushi in Vlore. But in more recent years, it is more common to find multiple criminal groups operating in the same territory. These groups maintain contact with one another, often showing respect for each other's businesses. They also cooperate, engaging in project-based exchanges of "qualified workers." Thus, they have established decentralized structures, where various groups are loosely connected.

For example, Altin (pseudonym) from Skopje, Macedonia, is the alleged leader of an ethnic Albanian criminal group involved in organizing the transportation of heroin from Turkey, Bulgaria, Macedonia, Kosovo, Serbia, and Croatia to Slovenia, Austria, and Germany. The group also allegedly prepares and traffics weapons and explosive materials, and both Altin and his son Besim (pseudonym) sell cocaine, heroin, and marijuana. Altin has criminal contacts with the group led by Ekrem (pseudonym), which actively traffics drugs in the same region of Macedonia. Altin's son Besim is involved in organizing the transportation of marijuana from Macedonia to Greece for Ekrem, whose family-based organized criminal group is known as "the Colombians." Residing in the village Aracinovo, the Colombians are involved in illegal trafficking of heroin, cocaine, weapons, and explosive materials. There is intelligence suggesting their involvement in violent crime, blackmail, and extortion. In addition, Ekrem and his brother own a construction company in Germany that is used as a cover for transporting drugs to Germany, Croatia, and Spain.

In addition to his contacts with Altin, Ekrem closely cooperates with the criminal group led by Dimal (pseudonym), a Macedonian Albanian from Kumanovo. Dimal is involved in trafficking illegal drugs, mainly heroin, and smuggling cigarettes. Law enforcement agencies in Switzerland have been interested in Dimal because of his alleged involvement in trafficking large amounts of heroin from Turkey to Switzerland and in producing cigarettes illegally. During one police operation in Macedonia, authorities seized approximately twenty-five tons of illegally produced cigarettes. The group's members put pressure on the local courts, setting themselves up as the only buyers of several commercial facilities in Kumanovo whose owners had filed for bankruptcy or liquidated their businesses.[9]

Stronger territorial cooperation shows that ethnic Albanian society has become more stable, allowing people to expand their bonds of trust beyond family ties and even beyond their own cities.

The Case of Kelmendi

The structure of the criminal group led by Naser Kelmendi vividly demonstrates the family-regional dynamics and cooperation of Albanian organized crime groups in the Balkans. As noted above, the core of Kelmendi's group is composed of members of his family, mainly his three sons. Throughout the years, however, they also have built strong connections with members of other criminal groups composed of Serbians, Montenegrins, Turks, Macedonians, and people of other ethnicities and nationalities. Additionally, they have remained in close contact with ethnic Albanians from Germany, Switzerland, Spain, and the United States. Today, Kelmendi's group comprises more than forty individuals, most of whom are still active in the Balkan region. According to confidential police report from 2009, Kelmendi's group stays in contact with members of the Dacic family that have been operating largely on the territory of Montenegro, Bosnia, and Sandzak, Serbia.

Born in Montenegro, the Dacic brothers, Hamdija and Ljutvia, have a history of drug-related arrests that dates to the 1990s. Another close associate of Kelmendi, Acik Can, was born in Germany but has Turkish citizenship and has been living in Bosnia on a permanent residence permit. He is suspected of being involved in the transportation of heroin from Turkey to Spain, via Kosovo, Serbia, Montenegro, and Bosnia-Herzegovina, and of moving cocaine from Spain to the Balkan countries.

Serbian intelligence reports allege that Kelmendi controls Kosovo together with the Osmani brothers and Ekrem Luka's group. Although many Albanians deny it, Serbian authorities confirm that these groups funnel money to the former KLA commander Ramush Haradinaj and Kosovo's current prime minister, Hashim Thaçi.Interestingly, Kelmendi also seems to have worked closely with Darko Šarić, a Serb who led a powerful Balkan criminal organization that for years trafficked cocaine from South America through the Balkans, Italy, and Slovenia to Western Europe. Business records show that Šarić laundered those profits by investing in hotels in Serbia and buying companies from people who were charged or convicted of being involved in organized crime, mostly cigarette smuggling.

Šarić was unknown to the public until October 2009, when more than two tons of cocaine was seized near the Uruguayan coast in an international police action code named "Balkan Warrior." According to Slobodan Homen, secretary in the Ministry of Justice of Serbia, Šaric and his group had yearly profits of one billion euros. Šarić fled before he was arrested; however, four years later and despite a few plastic surgeries, he finally was found and arrested in March 2014. It is interesting, although not surprising, that Kelmendi may have worked closely with one of his "enemies"—a Serb.

Kosovo police arrested Kelmendi in 2013 pursuant to an INTERPOL Red Notice, and he was detained by EULEX (European Union Rule of Law Mission in Kosovo) after police in Kosovo released him. One year earlier, Elvis Kelmendi, his son, was sentenced to four years in prison.

ETHNIC HOMOGENEITY IN THE WEST

Sami and Zakim

How important are clans and families among Albanians operating in a Western context? Belgian law enforcement agent François Farcy provided information about the importance of clans and families among Albanians operating outside of Eastern Europe. Farcy has worked on several Albanian cases, including the case of brothers Sami and Zakim. "With little hierarchy and a horizontal system, the structure [of Albanian criminal groups] seemed to function with easy efficacy according to its needs and activities," Farcy said (interview, Belgium, 2008). Bosses arose, but the police could not determine whether they had always been in charge or had been designated as leaders by their friends—or even by themselves.

Sami and Zakim were the alleged bosses of an Albanian criminal group in Verviers and Mons, Belgium. The group led by Sami and Zakim was active in multiple criminal activities in this region, including organized thefts, robberies, trafficking and smuggling of people, and prostitution. Eventually, Sami, who was described as a charismatic leader, became dominant among the criminal element in Verviers, and Zakim settled in the Mons region. Some members of Zakim's organization became accomplices to Sami.

While benefiting from the organization's activities, some of the organization's members, such as bodyguards, were considered peripheral and not necessarily central players. "Other members, from the 'second circle,' were used as cover for addresses, payments, and buying or licensing of vehicles," Farcy explained. "Often, as in most criminal organizations, [there were] concubine girls covering for numerous deals. Let me tell you, these girls were 'in love' with the 'charming' Sami. He was so generous with them, buying them whatever they wanted" (interview, Belgium, 2008).

The burglaries committed by Sami's criminal group required many hands. In addition to providing addresses, criminals from the "second circle" were used as soldiers. Many of them were candidate refugees who recently had arrived in Belgium, and they participated in the burglaries in order to repay the organization for its assistance in their clandestine immigration. Almost all were between twenty-five and thirty, and they all had an impressive list of false identities, which complicated the inquiries. As an example, in order to identify Sami and Zakim, investigators had to retrace their itineraries from the time of their arrival in Belgium. The two brothers had arrived at the Foreigners' Office on the same day, but they were registered under two different family names. Because of the decay of the administrative structure in their state of origin, and the nonexistent national register in Albania and Kosovo, any formal verification of their identities was impossible. Even their family bonds or clan membership was difficult to ascertain.

"First the brothers came to Belgium as Kosovars, but then we had information that they were coming from Tropoje [in northern Albania], which is close to the Kosovo border," Farcy explained. "As far as the two brothers in the Verviers case are concerned, until the very last moment, and even when confronted with DNA evidence, they denied that they were brothers" (interview, Belgium, 2008).

Sami worked not only with Albanians coming from Tropoje, but also with some from Durres and Kosovo. Although it was not common practice among criminal groups in the 1990s, he occasionally would accept or at least collaborate with non-Albanians, mostly for activities related to housing, the transfer of prostitutes, drug trafficking, illegal gambling, and the management of local bars.

"In some cases there were local partnerships," Farcy said. "They were [working] with the mafias of Maghreb or Greece, and were linked to drug trafficking, human trafficking, and the comanagement of establishments" (interview, Belgium, 2008).

Western Europe

While family and clan ties remain significant among ethnic Albanian criminals operating abroad—as illustrated in the cases of Sami and Zakim—another, even more relevant "binding" factor is the ethnic background of the offender. In addition to trust based on close personal contacts, there is also trust based on generalizations, which is built mainly on a sense of similarity and shared norms and values. Here, trust is linked to social groups rather than to a particular individual. The trustor places trust in the trustee based on the presumption that the trustee conforms to some more general norms or patterns of behavior. As von Lampe and Johansen (2004) illustrate, under conditions of illegality, such generalizations could be attached to members of delinquent subcultures, or of a mafia-like fraternal association, based on the assumption that they adhere to certain codes of conduct. Local and ethnic communities also could produce generalized trust through familiarity and conformity.

One ethnic Albanian criminal group was involved in the smuggling of illegal drugs from Turkey to the Scandinavian countries. The alleged leader was Marko (pseudonym), an ethnic Albanian from Tetovo, Macedonia. For years, Marko organized the smuggling of drugs to Denmark with his brother and his cousin. Marko was imprisoned in Denmark, but he escaped and went back to Macedonia, where he allegedly continued his illegal business. He made use of drug couriers from Tetovo who delivered heroin, mainly to Denmark. These couriers were all ethnic Albanians from Macedonia who had been living for years in Denmark and Germany, as well as throughout the former Yugoslavia. The group made extensive use of another family from Tetovo. All children in this family—eight in all—were used as drug couriers.[10]

Trust based on generalization has been common among ethnic Albanian criminals, particularly those living in foreign countries, as they have often relied on the Albanian diaspora for assistance. "When the new immigrants arrived in Belgium in the 1990s," Sartorius, the police agent from the Belgian federal police, said, "they had the support of segments of the old diaspora and settled in communities where the older diaspora was living: Antwerp, Liege, and Brussels" (interview, Belgium, 2006). But why was this the case? The link between ethnicity and trust can be fairly easily established where close-knit ethnic communities exist. Ethnicity must be considered a trust variable, especially when the marginalization of ethnic minority groups is taken into account.

Some segments of the ethnic Albanian communities in the West—founded on the principles of segregation and exclusiveness—felt it was their duty to help their compatriots, criminals or not. After all, they were of "the same flesh and blood." At first, Albanian criminals did not cooperate with or have significant links to other ethnic criminal groups. Police and court files indicate that the social network of the ethnic Albanians was closely linked to the cafés where Albanians met daily and established connections. In numerous files it was evident that these cafés, or coffee bars, also were important in connecting Albanian criminals. In Belgium there are many Albanian social clubs where Albanian men get together to drink *rakija*. This is part of their networking strategy. The ethnic cafés usually are located in cities where the old diaspora lives.

One Albanian émigré who was forced to leave Kosovo described these coffee bars as a place to obtain false travel documents and help with illegal migration.

> In 1999, my family went to a Macedonian refugee camp. I escaped earlier, in March 1999, right before the bombings. I either had to join the KLA or leave, because with the KLA it would have been safer because I would have arms. . . . I left for Albania and then illegally went to the United Kingdom. I went to Tirana with a cousin of mine and we were looking for people who gave you fake documents and forged visas. . . . I went in the public square, where there are these cafés, and asked around. . . . I wanted to go to London because I had my cousins there. One guy told me that he could get me a German residency visa. . . . He also bought the border police. . . . We made it to Italy, and from Italy we took a train to Torino, from Torino to Paris, from Paris to Belgium. Then [in] Belgium, I met a cousin . . . and he helped me find someone who smuggles people; we went to the Albanian community, in the coffee shops, and we would ask people and we found this Albanian guy married to this Belgian woman. He took us to this safe house, where there were twenty-thirty people . . . mainly Albanians. (interview New York, 2013)

Ethnic cafés have played a direct role in illegal immigration and in prostitution. One of the defendants in the Dendermonde case (2001–2003) from Belgium was the Albanian owner of Luma, a coffee bar in Brussels that served as the central meeting place for the transportation of illegal immigrants from Belgium to the United Kingdom. An Albanian victim declared that an Albanian trafficker in Tirana told him to go to this particular ethnic coffee bar in Brussels. In the Dendermonde case, it appears that the "bosses" never came directly to the coffee bar, but instead sent trafficking victims there to meet with the drivers. This case identified five coffee bars that served as meeting places for illegal immigrants and trafficking victims.

In the Sami and Zakim case, the criminal headquarters were ethnic Albanian coffee bars in the city of Verviers. The coffee bar where the criminals most frequently met was owned by a friend of the two brothers who led the criminal group. The café owner, who was from Albania, also worked for Sami.

Sartorius also explained that, although Albanian men usually prefer to marry Albanian women, the criminals who arrived after the 1990s often married Belgian women so they could become Belgian citizens. "Of course, if there were a possibility of marrying a Belgian woman of ethnic Albanian origin, this would be ideal," he said. "But frequently the Belgian women that married the Albanians ended up in brothels" (interview, Belgium, 2006).

In any discussion of the role of ethnicity as a trust-producing factor under conditions of illegality, it should be emphasized that in many instances where bonds of trust are attributed to ethnic cohesion, the actual foundation ultimately may lie in social relations such as kinship, friendship, or community ties.[11] Before 1998, it appears that ethnic Albanian offenders in the West sometimes refused, or were somewhat reluctant, to cooperate openly with ethnic Albanians who came from a locality other than their own, or with those of a different subethnicity (e.g., Ghegs or Tosks). Most commonly, extended families with the same cultural and political orientation, and roots in the same city or village in Albania or Kosovo, worked together.

Belgian police investigations from the 1990s show that Albanian Ghegs from northern Albania were cooperating almost exclusively with Ghegs from the same locality, and occasionally with Ghegs from Kosovo, whereas Tosks from the south of Albania were working mainly with other Tosks. This cooperation among people from the same locality or among members of extended or loosely connected criminal families (clan-based structure) has been especially common in smuggling cases and cases of organized theft, which are more typical of people from the north of Albania and Kosovo. In prostitution cases, particularly those before 2002, the offenders were most often brothers (nuclear family structure) who usually came from southern Albania or Macedonia. However, almost all of these groups occasionally found themselves in a need of a few "external contacts" from regions or even countries other than their own.

In the Belgian Dendermonde smuggling case discussed above, approximately thirty people were arrested in 2003 for smuggling illegal immigrants—mainly

Albanian, but also Asian—from Belgium to the United Kingdom. Twenty-three of those tried were Albanian criminals originally from Albania. Almost all Albanian offenders in this case were Ghegs from northern Albania, including the cities of Shkoder, Kukes, Kruje, and Lac. Only four offenders came from Tirana, Fier, or Kosovo. Although not all the offenders were related, there were many kinship ties among them. Police established that several of the offenders came from the same nuclear family, while some were cousins and more distant relatives from the same region of Albania. It was, however, quite difficult to identify each offender's exact city of origin and family ties, because the men often had several false identity cards and used many aliases. All the offenders arrested in this case were prosecuted and convicted in Belgium.[12]

Because so many Albanians isolate themselves to their families, clans, and ethnic communities, Western Europeans may view them as secluded and untouchable—something unknown, mysterious, and foreign. Ethnic Albanian organized criminal groups consequently came to be understood in Western Europe and beyond as homogeneous, ethnic- or clan-based, and dangerous.

US-Based Ethnic Albanian Criminal Groups

Ethnic Albanian organized crime groups in the United States appear less structured along strict clan or family lines than those in Europe, and they do not necessarily identify themselves with specific clans in Europe or the Balkans. Officials claim that clans are not as important in the United States as they are overseas, but this is not to say that familial relationships are insignificant to US-based Albanian criminal groups.

Ethnicity, however, remains one of the most important "binding" factors among ethnic Albanians in the United States. In June 2010 seventeen men were arrested in a joint operation conducted by the FBI and New York Police Department. The names of the defendants, part of the Krasniqi organization mentioned in the previous chapter, indicate that they were almost all ethnic Albanians, most reportedly from Albania.[13] The Krasniqi organization was run by two young Albanian brothers, Bruno and Saimir Krasniqi, who led a crew of hustlers that operated in New York, Michigan, and Connecticut between 2003 and 2010. The Krasniqi group had ties with ethnic Albanian groups in Albania and Macedonia. One of its members, Almir Rrapo, committed heinous crimes with the Krasniqis' Staten Island–based group before becoming a top aide to Albania's deputy prime minister. Rrapo had been extradited to the United States to face charges for a deadly 2005 drive-by shooting in Queens, a violent kidnapping, and other offenses. The leaders of his former criminal group, the brothers Krasniqi, were both sentenced to life behind bars after Rrapo's testimony helped convict them.

In 2009, the FBI operation Black Eagles targeted the criminal organization led by Albanians Kujtim Lika and Myfit Dika. Their organization was accused of transporting heroin, primarily from Afghanistan, through Turkey and into Albania. From there it was sent to Europe or shipped though a front company into the United States. According to Special Agent Jim Farley, "The whole organization was about twenty-four strong. But these two, Lika and Dika, were basically the leaders of the organization, or at least one facet of it" (FBI 2009). The group's US territory was mostly in northern New Jersey and New York, but it had ties to Chicago, Detroit, and cities in Texas, as well as international ties back home in Macedonia and Albania.

In 2013 an Albanian national who migrated illegally to the United States in the early 1990s and who allegedly took some part in the activities of Lika and Dika's group claimed that ethnic Albanian offenders in New York cooperate along ethnic lines and maintain close ties with Albanians from Macedonia, Albania, Kosovo, Italy, and Venezuela. They depend on their trans-Atlantic ties both for trafficking heroin and for smuggling people. The male respondent, in his early thirties, noted:

> All contact points for the activities of our group were ethnic Albanians. We were bringing heroin from Macedonia, and we cooperated with ethnic Albanians there. For smuggling of people and production of fake passports we cooperated with Albanians from Italy. We would ask them to find Italians who wanted to sell their passport. We asked those peasants not to report to the police that the passport was stolen until we told them to do so. We then sent the immigrants to Venezuela and then to Mexico. We have our own people down there and also people at the customs [office] who for a fee let the immigrants pass. Then they pass illegally to the United States, and only then is the passport reported as stolen. Only sometimes we had to cooperate with other criminal groups and individuals from other ethnicities, but all main positions were held by ethnic Albanians. (interview, New York, 2013)

Similarly, the FBI (2009) reports that many of the leaders of Alex Rudaj's organization, discussed in chapter 3, were ethnic Albanians who previously had worked with established Italian crime families in the area. These leaders included Nikola Dedaj, the group's alleged enforcer; Nardino Colotti, an Italian American protégé of the late Gambino soldier Phil ("Skinny Phil") Loscalzo; and Ljusa "Louie" Nuculovic, an Albanian mobster from the village of Koja e Kucit, in Montenegro. In 2004 more than twenty members of the Rudaj organization, most of whom were either ethnic Albanians or first-generation Albanian Americans, but several of whom were Greeks or Italians, were charged with various crimes.

Another important case from the New York City area that points to the ethnic composition of Albanian crime groups in the United States is that of the Thaqi organized crime group. The syndicate was responsible for organizing the importation and distribution of large quantities of hydroponically grown marijuana from Canada and Mexico; MDMA from the Netherlands and Canada; cocaine from Mexico, Colombia, Venezuela, and Peru; and prescription pills, diverted to illegal channels. The group also allegedly obtained cocaine from sources in the United

States for export to Albania and Europe; the drugs were concealed in hidden compartments inside luxury automobiles and shipped under the auspices of ostensibly legitimate car dealerships that actually were controlled by Albanian criminal members.

Court papers allege that the criminal group consisted of interrelated ethnic Albanian family clans, with hundreds of associated members, workers, and customers. Thaqi operated his criminal business with his cousin Arif "The Bear" Kurti. At the close of 2013, Kurti apparently was in an Albanian prison, convicted of heroin trafficking. Thaqi had previously been married to a woman named Lauretta Lokaj, who was one of two women tasked with the money-laundering aspects of the operation. Elsewhere, the group used non-Albanian members to carry out more menial tasks, such as operating marijuana grow houses. The group allegedly also was linked to Albanian mobster Bajram "Van Damme" Lajqi, a hit man who was arrested after killing an associate involved with the Canadian drug smuggling operation.

The three leaders of the Thaqi organization—Gjavit Thaqi, Arif Kurti, and Gjevelin Berisha—have been identified as ethnic Albanians from Albania. One of the alleged ringleaders was arrested by law enforcement agents in Albania and was extradited to the United States. To date, forty-nine suspects have been arrested, and they all entered guilty pleas in August 2013.

These and many similar cases demonstrate that ethnic ties remain very important to Albanian organized crime groups abroad, though such groups do sometimes cooperate with other ethnic groups or nationalities as well.

INTERNATIONAL COOPERATION

Reputation and Functional Ties

A police file on the ethnic Albanian criminal group of Qamil, dealing with trafficking of narcotic drugs in the first decade of the twenty-first century, illustrated that the group's family and clan ties were always strong at the leadership level, even if they were looser elsewhere within the organization. In the group's middle and lower levels, the number of family members decreased rapidly. Second- and third-generation Albanians were taking over the lower and mid-level positions, but there were several bridge builders of different ethnic backgrounds and nationalities (e.g., Turkish, Greek, Italian, and Belgian) contributing to the group's international dimension. Despite Michaeletos's claim, mentioned earlier, that members of other ethnic groups have been accepted into Albanian criminal organizations only to execute certain one-time or secondary jobs, a number of cases indicate that Albanians have been working closely with other ethnic groups in various capacities.

"Weak" and "functional" ties are in fact necessary for the functioning of any business, particularly an international one. So although kinship bonds have no doubt been strong among members of Albanian groups, so-called weak bonds also appear to be necessary for their survival, and particularly for expanding their criminal opportunities. Albanian criminals cannot afford to trust family members alone. As a 2009 INTERPOL report concludes, sharing a family name does not necessarily mean that two people are related by blood or have the same ethnic background.

In 2006 former inmate Jimmy (pseudonym) a Kosovo Albanian involved in prostitution and human trafficking, among other offenses, jokingly told me: "I'll pretend to trust you if you pretend to trust me. No matter how risky trusting someone may seem, without trust there is no business. Who doesn't trust cannot be trusted" (interview, Kosovo, 2008).

He then continued, with a degree of enthusiasm: "You have to understand that there is a big difference between Albanians from Albania and Albanians from Kosovo. Albanians from the north are crazy; they always get me in trouble. We are more rational. This doesn't mean we don't cooperate. My closest friends are Albanians from the north of Albania. If you want to make money, you have to work with others, too. I also work with guys from Belgium, Chechnya, the Netherlands, Macedonia. "I personally don't trust the Turks," he added, laughing. "Only a dead Turk is a good Turk."

He continued: "I had a few close Albanian friends on board, but I also had friends from the discotheques in which I worked that were other ethnicities. At that time, the coolest guys were the blacks, Moroccans, Turkish. . . . These groups came first, and the Albanians were not so prominent back then. We took over later, but we tried to work together with some other groups. I also needed Belgian and Dutch girls to help me infiltrate some local discotheques. Sometimes relationships were built out of necessity" (interview, Kosovo, 2008).

In the drug trafficking group of Vulnet, new members were recruited first from members of the family and clan, regardless of their country or city of residence. Trustworthy outsiders were recruited only when the criminal group was testing new channels. Recruiting new members, especially as drug couriers, among ethnic Albanians living in foreign countries—most often but not exclusively second- or third-generation ethnic Albanians—started becoming common only in recent years. Albanians often have become citizens of their new countries, which makes it difficult to trace the origins and ancestry of crime group members.

From their new countries of residence, the Albanian couriers would travel to their country of origin to collect the drugs. The advantage of this approach is that the couriers have legitimate travel documents that allow them to return to the European Union or the United States, and usually they are unknown to law enforcements agencies in their country of origin. In order to avoid suspicion, new members of criminal groups sometimes are recruited in the villages or cities of origin of the group's leaders. But someone must recommend the new member, vouching for the recruit's trustworthiness based on friendship or prior business relations.[14]

Albanian criminals are also well aware that EU and US-based law enforcement agencies are seeking to control their activities, and this fosters cooperation with individuals from other ethnic groups as well, in order to avoid detection. In the drug smuggling business, for instance, Albanian traffickers often use Belgian and Dutch women as drug couriers. Some of these women are former sex workers or "madams," or girlfriends of the traffickers. They are seemingly "less noticeable," particularly when compared to Albanian male offenders who often attract police attention. The US-based Albanian drug trafficking group of Taulant Hysko also relied on young female couriers who made international flights between New York and Italy to smuggle cocaine to Europe and heroin and ecstasy to the United States.

Moreover, external players usually are brought into the picture as "partners" when they contribute to the growth of the criminal organization or have been recommended by other close associates. As mentioned earlier, this trust relationship is often built on reputation. The trustor in this case relies on publicly formed and held opinions about the trustee. This type of trust hinges on the flow of information. In terms of content, various personal characteristics can be expected to form the reference point for a criminally relevant reputation, including reliability in keeping deadlines, providing support, and maintaining self-control under stress (von Lampe and Johansen 2004).

Reputation is extremely important in criminal circles and ensures the longevity of a criminal organization. Kleemans and van de Bunt (1999) argue that because of "network embeddedness," cooperating partners may use information from network contacts about one another and establish relations beyond kinship. This has a stabilizing effect, because the criminal's own reputation within this wider social network must be maintained.

Criminals in this case form a type of "brotherhood" or enter into what Paoli (2003) calls "contracts of fraternizations."[15] According to Paoli (2003), in traditional societies, where kinship remains the primary basis of solidarity relations, fraternal association is effective because it uses quasi-kinship relations to extend bonds of loyalty and obligation beyond the family, to incorporate people into kin networks, and to create new relations with a sense of kinship.

In the turbulent 1990s it was relatively difficult for Albanians, particularly Albanian criminals, to trust "outsiders" and build strong partnerships with nonfamily members on the merits of their "good" reputation or professional specializations. Although trust based on reputation was initially uncommon among Albanians, that does not mean it did not exist. With time, police files indicate, reputation-based trust became inevitable for criminal groups, because isolated, like-minded groups cannot have expertise in everything. Instead, they must rely on the expertise of other criminal groups or common people.

Court cases and media accounts illustrate that even in the 1990s, more advanced Albanian criminal groups from the Balkans cooperated with foreign groups—most often Italian and Greek—in order to expand their criminal empires.[16] In such cases, bonds based on reputation were regarded as crucial for the transnational dimension of the business, although at the leadership level, the group frequently remained ethnic Albanian.

In 1999, the Albanian daily newspapers *Koha Jone* and *Gazeta Shquiptare* reported that Italian Guiseppe Muolo, leader of Sacra Corona Unita (United Holy Crown), had been arrested in Tirana. Muolo had been traced to Tirana after first being spotted at the villa of an Albanian crime boss in Albania's main port of Durrës.[17] In the early 1990s, contraband cigarettes had been stored in Durrës for illegal transport to Italy, especially to Apulia. In fact, transporting contraband cigarettes became the principal activity of the Apulian organized crime group UHC in the Brindisi area of southern Italy, and consequently, some functional ties between Albanian and Italian criminals were established. Interestingly, police reports also show a history of cooperation between ethnic Albanian offenders, including Kosovars, and people whom they allegedly considered their "enemies," the Serbs.[18]

Multinational cooperation involving Albanian crime groups has grown stronger in recent years, as human trafficking and smuggling cases from the Balkans make plain. In May 2005, for instance, Albanian police uncovered a smuggling channel involving Turks, Albanians, and Macedonians that was attempting to transfer a group of Kurds illegally from Turkey into Western Europe. A five-member group composed of one Macedonian, two Albanian, and two Turkish citizens set up the illegal transfer from Turkey to Italy via Albania.

In 2006, Greek journalist Ioannis Michaletos of the Research Institute for European and American Studies (RIEAS) reported: "In order to thrive, the Albanian criminal syndicates involved in the Balkans narcotics trade need friends in high places. Smuggling rings with alleged links to the 'Turkish deep State' are said to control the trafficking of heroin through the Balkans, cooperating closely with other groups with which they have political or religious ties" (Michaletos 2006).

In November 2006, the Macedonian criminal court closed one of its most significant organized crime cases, South 1, which dated to November 2005. The court sentenced 28 people to a total of 114 years in prison for smuggling 44 Albanian immigrants, as well as luxury cars, from Macedonia to Greece. The criminal group was composed mainly of Albanian, Macedonian, and Bulgarian nationals. Among the convicted Bulgarian nationals were a corrupt police officer and the head of the border police station. Although interethnic cooperation traditionally has not been a key characteristic of Albanian organized crime in the Balkans, that seems to be changing.

Today, when necessary for the business, it appears that members of ethnic Albanian criminal groups based in the Balkans, the European Union, and the

United States all cooperate with foreign groups as well as female accomplices on different levels, in order to achieve their criminal aims.

The Belgian Experience

Several case studies from Belgium illustrate the importance of international ties in the human trafficking and people-smuggling business. One that attracted a lot of attention was the Wexford case. On December 8, 2001, in an industrial park in Wexford, Ireland, thirteen clandestine passengers, all Turkish, were discovered in a compartment of a truck that was transporting furniture. The driver of the truck was not charged, because he was unaware of the whole operation. The illegal immigrants, who were traveling from Turkey to Italy, had been placed in a container that was sealed in Italy. During the long journey, eight of the illegal immigrants died from lack of oxygen, and the other five were in critical condition when they were found.

Law enforcement officials from Belgium, Turkey, Germany, France, the United Kingdom, and the Netherlands, along with Europol and INTERPOL, started a joint investigation on December 9, 2001, when a Turkish man who lived in Belgium called the Belgian police and reported that some of the immigrants found dead in Ireland were his relatives. He gave the police telephone numbers of some Turkish and Albanian traffickers who were involved in the case. He explained that the illegal transport had been organized by Dogan, a Turk who lived in the United Kingdom; Mehmet, a Turk who lived in France; and an unknown Albanian who lived in Brussels. The British authorities also linked Dogan with the infamous Dover case, in which fifty-eight Chinese immigrants were found suffocated in a tomato truck heading for Dover, England, from the Netherlands in June 2000.

The criminal network that smuggled the Turkish immigrants in the furniture truck was composed mainly of ethnic Turkish criminals living in Western Europe. Several ethnic Albanian criminals from Kosovo also were involved in the transport from Belgium to the United Kingdom. The Albanians in Belgium used a Pakistani hotel in Brussels—a location linked to prostitution—as a safe house for the immigrants. All suspects in this case were condemned to prison sentences of two to ten years. In Belgium, eight people were charged—one Turk, six Kosovo Albanians, and one Belgian national. Seven people ultimately were convicted in 2003.

The recent heterogeneity of Albanian organized crime groups also is evident in an Antwerp smuggling case known as Suku (2002–2003), in which Albanian smugglers were found to be cooperating openly with the Chinese Triads in Belgium. And in the Staka smuggling case (2005–2006), Albanians were found to be working as specialized subcontractors for Indians. There was no hierarchy within this criminal network, which had contacts in Albania, the Netherlands, Switzerland, Germany, the United Kingdom, Italy, Spain, Romania, Norway, Greece, China, and Austria.

In Bar Ritz, a Belgian prostitution case (2004–2006), an Albanian-Romanian supply group delivered girls from Romania and Bulgaria for prostitution in a bar in Antwerp that was under the control of Dutch and Surinamese exploiters. The Dutch exploiter owned four entertainment firms—three in Belgium and one in the Netherlands—that were connected with his prostitution business. A Belgian accomplice also created a website for recruiting Polish girls.

Another prostitution case, from Liege and Charleroi in Belgium, involved collaboration between Albanian, Bulgarian, and Italian criminals in one criminal network. The Italians were active in money laundering and owned the bars where the girls met their clients. The Bulgarians specialized in the delivery and sale of false documents. The Albanians (and some Bulgarians) supplied the prostitution victims. The pimps were both Albanians and Bulgarians.

The Asslan-D'Angelis case (2002–2004) revealed a partnership between Albanian and Italian pimps. Asslan, a Belgian of Albanian origin, and D'Angelis, an Italian, were identified as leaders of this network. Both were powerful actors with links to politicians, well-known Albanian offenders, and mafia bosses in Sicily. They were mainly involved in prostitution and money laundering, but they also had strong links to Bulgarian traffickers and Albanian smugglers of illegal immigrants. Both pimps owned their own bars and elite restaurants, and they ran a highly professional prostitution network with Bulgarian women. Because they were paid quite well, the women never perceived themselves as victims. They often came to the exploiters of their own accord.

The Bulgarian girls arrived as tourists in Belgium, where they had the legal right to remain for three months. After their three-month stay, they went back to Bulgaria, and then returned to Belgium. They worked in "window prostitution," soliciting passersby, and each prostitute had to pay one hundred euros per shift for her streetside cubicle. They often were supervised by *dames de compagnie,* who were former Bulgarian prostitutes. These women protected the girls, but at the same time they gathered the money and compelled the girls to be productive. By Bulgarian standards, the girls were very well paid. In one bar, one girl had an average gross profit of seven thousand euros per day. At another bar, where ten girls worked, the average gross income for thirty days was more than two million euros. From this money the girls had to pay their rent, pay the pimps, and cover some other minor expenses. The rest of the money they kept for themselves.

Finally, the Gengo-Valkanov case (2002) illustrates the role of Albanian traffickers in a sophisticated, multinational business network. This interethnic network was divided into sectors, with Italian, Bulgarian, Albanian, and Greek human traffickers all working together. A Bulgarian and a number of Albanian accomplices supplied the prostitution victims and specialized in creating false documents. A Calabrian Italian was accused of controlling the bars and money-laundering activities. The girls were bought in the Netherlands and from

TABLE 5 Hierarchical model of organized crime

Structure (that forms the basis of criminal activities)
1. Family structure with graded ranks of authority from boss down to soldiers
2. Bosses oversee the activities of family members
3. A "commission" of bosses handles interfamily relations and disputes

SOURCE: Albanese (1994).

areas on the Greek-Albanian border from other criminal networks that delivered girls from Albania and Bulgaria (Arsovska and Janssens 2009).

Today, ethnic Albanian organized crime activities are conducted either by informal networks that still exist in the form of small groups of individuals with strong family ties, or by formal organized crime organizations with links to other international organized criminal groups and to legal businesses. Their growing ties to legitimate businesses make these groups even harder to track, uncover, and prosecute. The international media has often labeled these groups as criminal clans, but this doesn't mean that the membership is based exclusively on kinship ties.

HIERARCHIES AND SOLIDARITY BROTHERHOODS

The Hierarchical Model

The importance of rigid hierarchies within Albanian crime groups, like that of ethnic and kinship ties, requires further analysis.

As noted in chapter 3, in the 1960s, Joseph Valachi was the first insider to describe the organizational structure of La Cosa Nostra as consisting of the individual bosses of the member families, each with an underboss, a *caporegime* (lieutenant), and soldiers. Territory and criminal enterprises were divided among these families, all headed by men of Italian descent. This model came to be characterized as having a government-like structure, in which activities are conducted with the approval of superiors. Various scholars over the years have termed this the "bureaucratic" or "corporate" model of organized crime (see table 5).

Criminologist Donald Cressey (1969) claimed that mafia families in the United States also were hierarchically structured, with bosses, captains, "buffers," "soldiers," and "buttonmen," and that they formed a well-defined criminal organization. But, as illustrated earlier, Albanian organized crime groups shouldn't be regarded as rigid hierarchies, despite the fact that Albanian society is known to be clan-based. Clans are recognized not only for the strong kinship ties among their members, but also for the fact that they are political units with a degree of hierarchy. According to Durkheim (1965a), in simple societies the clan is at the same time the fundamental political unit: the heads of clans (or the heads of households) are the only social authority. In the traditional Albanian

Kanun, the rights, obligations, and duties of the head of the house are very clearly defined.

According to article 20 of the Kanun, "the control of the house belongs to the eldest living under the roof of the house or to his first brother" (Fox 1989, 15). Among the list specified herein, the head of the house is said to have the following rights (see Fox 1989, 15–16):

(1) To occupy the chief place of the house . . . ;
(2) To possess his own weapons, even at the cost of a hundred purses . . . ;
(3) [To have control] over the earnings of those who live in the house, their salaries, and their recompense;
(4) To buy, sell and alter the land . . . ;
(5) To punish those who live in the house. . . .[19]

Similar rules apply to the chief of the clan, according to the Kanun (Book 11):

Article 1146: The Chiefs are the heads of the clans.

Article 1147: Chieftainship is a hereditary position.

Article 1148: Every Chief has authority over his own clan. . . .

Article 1149: In trials and judgments within the district of a Chief, there may be no interference by the Chiefs of other clans.

Article 1150: The Chief of a clan, together with the Elders and the people of the brotherhoods, has the right to call assemblies, to contract alliances, to make judgments, to levy fines, and to place under ban.

Article 1157: The Chief of a clan, like any other man, may be fined, may have his house burned, may be placed under ban, may have his property destroyed, and may be expelled from the country.

This conferring of power to elderly males in the family is one reason why Albanian organized crime groups are often depicted as hierarchies, but this fails to take into consideration the fact that culture and societal organization are not static phenomena; they are subject to adaptation and change. Let's explore this further.

Albanian Fathers: Not "Godfathers" but Mediators

Police cases illustrate that ethnic Albanian fathers often appear to play a role in the criminal businesses of their sons. Sometimes they are presented as key players, and at other times as peripheral actors. This is not surprising, given the kinship ties of Albanian criminal groups. When it comes to organized crime, however, the role of the father in an Albanian family is not always clear.

Conventionally in Albania and Kosovo, the main representatives of the classical Kanun, and thus the leaders of the clans, were highly respected older men. Fathers and older clan members have always had a significant say within their own clans. Because clans are based on family ties and mutual solidarity, older figures traditionally have had great social authority within the clan and the household. Many emergent criminal clan-based groups, nevertheless, seem to be created by younger and often more aggressive—or more "socially confused"—men who have replicated the cultural model with the addition of an inflated sense of honor.

This is not to say that fathers have completely lost their traditional power within Albanian families or clans. Patsy Sorensen, a former member of the European Parliament, an expert on the trafficking of women, and director of the victim shelter Payoke in Belgium, stated:

> When a gang is broken up and the ringleaders are jailed, business continues as usual. . . . The junior members start carrying out the work, while the elderly father, although he may present himself as poor and innocent, is the man entitled, according to the Kanun, to take over control of the operation. Albanian traffickers who have served their time leave jail as wealthy men, and even heroes of sorts, who have done well by their families and fathers. (interview, Belgium, 2007)

The role of the father, or of other older members in a family or clan, has been stronger among criminal groups coming from or operating in Kosovo and northern Albania, where the Kanun has been practiced to a greater extent than in Albania's southern region. The Kosovo Albanian offender Haki (pseudonym) appeared to have a close connection with his family in Belgium. He was also close with his extended family in Kosovo, with whom he lived after being deported to Kosovo from Belgium. During one of our meetings he received a telephone call from his uncle in Kosovo, who asked him to bring some bricks for the new house they were building and to help him with the work. This was not a problem for the so-called "mafia boss."

Haki, two hundred–plus pounds and six feet tall, with a shaved head and a Viking beard, quickly morphed from a "tough guy" to an obedient son, grandson, and nephew. He excused himself and explained that we had to continue the interview at his house. He bought the requested bricks, placed them in his car, and then worked for a bit in the yard with his uncle and grandfather. It appeared that the word of the older family members came before everything else. During a later conversation, Haki said, "The father is most important in the Albanian context. He doesn't care what I do, and whether I am a big, tough criminal. I need to respect everything he says. He is the law in the house. Also the mother is very important, and her word is highly respected in our context" (interview, Kosovo, 2007).

Although the fathers might not be the leaders of criminal families and clans, younger men within a clan will not engage in organized crime if their actions are not supported in some way by influential members of their families, particularly the respected fathers. Because of these strong family ties, and the high level of solidarity within clans, younger members are unable to gain individual reputations without the direct or indirect approval of other family members. Even if these family members have not explicitly condoned the behavior of the young delinquents, they probably have not denounced it, nor have they taken measures to counter it. Albanian prosecutor Olsjan Cela explained it like this:

> I don't believe that older Albanian fathers and grandfathers are themselves involved in organized crime. People who lived most of their lives during communist times don't know much about organized crime. It is naïve to think that they are some kind of group leaders or "bosses." These people are simple people, and they have been brought up in a completely different environment. However, they might be very well aware of what their children are doing, since these are often poor men unable to provide for their children. . . . They cannot offer any better alternatives to them. Now, the "new generation" of fathers are those that are the most dangerous ones. Criminals who were ten or fifteen years old when the communist regime collapsed are now fathers themselves. They might transmit their criminal values to their own children, creating real criminal families where the father is indeed the leader. (interview, Brussels, 2008)

An Albanian offender operating in New York told me in an interview in 2013:

> I arrived illegally from Albania to New York in the 1990s. In Albania I was a criminal, so I wanted to escape that lifestyle and search for a better life in New York, where my family lived. However, only my father was working—[at a] very low-paid, blue-collar job. I couldn't find a job. We hardly had any money to survive. My mother got sick at that time, and I said, 'I will do what I have to do to make some money.' But my father didn't do these kinds of things. He is an honest, hardworking man. Unfortunately, he could hardly make any money. I could have been a lawyer under different circumstances, but I continued committing crimes because we all needed the money. (interview, New York, 2013)

Because of the dysfunctional nature of many Albanian families, clan members who bring money to the family—apparently without regard for how they do so—are highly respected within the clan and commonly serve as role models for the younger members, such as brothers or cousins. It appears from investigated cases that many clan members have been seduced by the monetary success of their older brothers and cousins, whose criminal behavior often has been rewarded instead of punished by the family. If the father does not strictly forbid the actions of the criminal members of the family, other members tend to engage in crime without too much thought. Everyday, cultural reinforcement of deviant behavior, and opportunities for social interaction with role models who themselves have assimilated criminogenic values, affect one's individual mind-set.

In many cases, fathers have been indirectly involved in the criminal businesses of their sons; they have not prevented the crimes committed by their children, and they have even provided assistance and "words of wisdom" when required. More specifically, police files on Albanian-speaking criminal organizations point out that the fathers in Albanian families play important roles as mediators between criminal groups. Criminal actors carry out their illicit activities in an unregulated and hostile environment, without the assistance of the criminal justice system; therefore, they are obliged to develop their own ways of "doing justice" and making settlements. The role of fathers, in this respect, is significant.

For example, after a shooting in a bar in Antwerp in the late 1990s, it was the fathers of the Albanian criminal "families" involved who decided whether there would be peace between them, or war.

One night, Asprim, the brother of a notorious Albanian criminal boss from Antwerp called Viktor, had an argument with some other Albanians, which subsequently led to a fight. This group had insulted Asprim, who was not used to being insulted, because he is the brother of the powerful Viktor. So Asprim then called on several of his associates, including Baftir and Bekiri.

Asprim and his supporters went to a coffee bar in Antwerp where the other rival Albanians were rumored to be, and waited for them to arrive. Bekiri took out his gun and started shooting; one of the Albanians ran to his car and attempted to run Asprim over. The offenders quickly got rid of their weapons, throwing them into a nearby canal. Someone called Bekiri's father and told him about the fight, and Bekiri's father drove his son to Germany.

A day later, after speaking with their sons, the fathers of the families involved held a meeting. They were all part of the same social club, and they knew one another well. Soon, word spread throughout Antwerp that the fathers had decided for war—revenge had to take place.

The group that originally had insulted Asprim contacted some Kurds from Holland, and offered five thousand euros for the murder of some members of Asprim's group. However, they didn't go through with the plan, allegedly because becoming linked to the Kurds in Holland would cause further problems.

In summary, although older Albanian fathers do not remain at the top of the hierarchy within criminal clans, they could be involved when it comes to providing mediation and occasional assistance to their sons. Fathers appear to be peripheral actors within many criminal clans. If Albanian criminals are arrested, however, they often will deny that their brothers, cousins, or fathers are involved in the criminal business on any level to protect them, even when they are presented with hard evidence (e.g., DNA tests, phone taps, birth certificates, and so on), as in the case of Sami and Zakim discussed earlier.[20] The fathers, in particular, are always protected; thus, it is difficult to assess their precise involvement in organized crime.

Reciprocal Solidarity and Horizontal Structures

Ethnic Albanian organized crime groups are not as strictly hierarchical as some may believe, nor is there a clear division of labor among their members. According to a Belgian law enforcement official: "The feeling is that there are no particular organized groups (*cupola*) that are gathering together regularly to have meetings and discuss activities. We do not have evidence about some highly organized structures operating in Albania" (interview, Belgium, 2006). US intelligence reports state that there is no evidence of a central figure directing Albanian organized crime activities in the United States, either. These reports point out that no national-level hierarchical structure exists in US-based Albanian organized crime. Although several prominent individuals in various regions across the United States act as leaders, there are no prominent families in national leadership roles.

Ethnic Albanian organized crime groups tend to work on the principle of reciprocal solidarity. On a societal level, even though the Albanian Kanun implies that each household or clan has a leader, the members of the household or the clan can easily replace the leader if he (the leaders are usually men) does not perform his "household duties" properly. Similarly, members of a criminal organization have their status within the group, and there are often charismatic leaders, but there are not clearly identifiable bosses and underbosses who hold permanent positions. Even though certain members (often two or three) may act as the masterminds of the organization, this should not lead to the conclusion that Albanian organized crime groups are hierarchically structured enterprises.

Members of many Albanian organized crime groups divide their tasks and responsibilities according to their mutual needs. Roles within the organizations sometimes shift depending on job requirements and skills. Therefore, these groups are somewhat flexible. Offenders arrested in Western Europe have sometimes fled to the Balkans, a safe haven, in order to avoid prosecution, but this does not mean there is a body of well-organized Albanian mafia bosses living in Albania or Kosovo and controlling the Albanian criminal scene in the European Union or the United States.

During an expert workshop at the Belgian Federal Police, in October 2008, Albanian prosecutor Olsjan Cela stated: "People who do not understand our culture create images of hierarchies and strict division of labor. This is pure imagination. Albanian criminals do not work like that. The relationships in the groups are reciprocal, based on family and friendship ties" (interview, Brussels, 2008).

Even offenders themselves have acknowledged a problem with the widespread image of the Albanian mafia. The concept of a "mafia" should be used carefully, or at least defined more accurately, lest it obscure serious research. The term may cloud the truth even in the case of the Sicilian mafia. Although for years it has been portrayed as a hierarchical and bureaucratic organization, one of its members, the defector Tomasso Buscetta, testified that "belonging to the Cosa Nostra implied being men of honor: this was the heart of everything. One could then invent hierarchies, positions, commissions, but within each family you breathed an air of equality because we all felt that we belonged to a very special elite" (Arlacchi, cited in Paoli 2003, 80).

Numerous personal interviews and court files indicate that members of ethnic Albanian criminal groups cooperate on various levels and often perform different

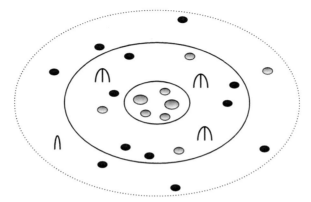

FIGURE 15. "Core group" organization. Source: UNODC (2002)

tasks, making it relatively difficult to pinpoint an actual boss of the organization. The most common structure identified by European law enforcement officials is that of a "core group," which constitutes part of a larger network (figure 15). These semi-flexible solidarity groups, often led by two or three individuals simultaneously, also have been labeled as "oriented clusters," "solidarity cells," or "crews."

The "core group organization" is often structured around a core group of four to ten ethnic Albanian criminals who stay in close contact with one another, but cooperate and maintain occasional contact with ethnic Albanians from other countries and other criminal groups, or with *brokes* ("bridge builders") of other ethnicities. However, no single organizational structure is applicable to all ethnic Albanian crime groups.

US officials also support the view that the organizational structure of ethnic Albanian criminal groups in the United States is mostly horizontal and organized into several levels, depending on how large the family or clan is. The leader (again, more a charismatic leader than a mafia boss) in a given region directs the criminal activities of lower-level associates. The regional leader generally serves more as a point of contact for the region than as a director of regional activities. Regional leaders maintain communication with Albanian criminal leaders and members in other areas, although individual members also often maintain their own personal contacts throughout the country. Networks of familial relationships connect these individuals, and Albanian groups rely heavily on one another to further their operations.

In 2009, FBI official John Farley, discussing the case of Dika and Lika from New York, stated:

With Albanian organized crime, it's different than the LCN. There is no true hierarchy. It's hard to determine exactly where the leadership is, and where the organization
ends and where it begins. It's mostly a loose-knit group where whoever has the goods
at the time, whoever has the connections at the time, moves up in the chain and takes
control of that, and then it can switch. They go to each other for whoever has an 'in' to
whatever criminal activity is being pursued. It's very difficult to counter, because we
can't determine the hierarchy because it is fluid, so it's a different way; it's an emerging
problem. Albanian organized crime is becoming more of a difficult task for us. (FBI
2009)

. . .

As this chapter has demonstrated, there is not one common structure that fits all
ethnic Albanian crime groups, although there are some bases for comparison: ethnic Albanian organized crime groups are often structured around their families,
clans, and most importantly, ethnic groups. Kinship and common territory have
served as powerful bonding and trust-producing elements for both ordinary Albanians and criminal segments alike. Such strong ties have enabled many Albanian
groups to flourish in hostile environments.

During the 1990s, many ethnic Albanian criminal groups survived through
turbulent times because of their similarities, their mutual respect, and close ties
built on personal trust. Common territory, homogeneity, kinship and political ties,
absence of hierarchy, and overall group solidarity were some of the key attributes
of Albanian organized crime groups in the 1990s. In addition, although ethnic
Albanians at this time did not maintain many weak ties because of their distrust of
"foreigners," some such ties did, in fact, exist, and these ties were important for the
growth of Albanian organized crime groups. As this chapter has demonstrated, if
language and cultural differences did not pose a communication obstacle, then
personal trust built on frequent interaction remained even more important for
Albanian criminal organizations than trust based on ethnic similarities.

Today, organized crime activities involving ethnic Albanian offenders are conducted either by informal networks, which traditionally exist in the form of small
groups of individuals with strong family ties, or by more formal organized crime
groups that have links to other international organized criminal groups. The latter
represent the new generation of ethnic Albanian organized crime. Particularly
after 2003, some Albanian criminal groups have visibly strengthened their international dimension, despite the fact that the "core group" often remains Albanian.

Chapter 5

VIOLENCE, HONOR, AND SECRECY

"Have you heard? Gjorg Berisha has killed Zef Kryeqyqe."
"Gjorg Berisha has taken back his brother's blood."
"Are the Berishas going to ask for the twenty-four hour besa?"
"Yes, of course."
". . . Besa has been granted by the Kryeqyqes."
". . . At least we'll have twenty-four hours without bloodshed."
—ISMAIL KADARE, *BROKEN APRIL* (1998, 13–14)

Ethnic Albanian organized crime groups are known to be ruthless and unpredictable.[1] Since the early 1990s, violent home invasions, witness intimidation, assaults, kidnappings, decapitations, drive-by shootings, contract killings, and threats to law enforcement agents and prosecutors have been integral parts of the ethnic Albanian modus operandi. Albanian organized crime groups became infamous not only for their disregard for human life, but also for their "code of silence" and alleged loyalty to the members of their criminal organizations. An experienced FBI agent described Albanian criminals as "hot-headed individuals" who will do anything to achieve their ends. "However," he said, "if an Albanian crew member is arrested, he will serve the time as opposed to providing information to officials" (US Department of Justice 2005).

Especially after 1997, it became commonplace for journalists to refer to Albanian criminal groups as the "new Sicilian mafia" because of their ruthlessness and secrecy (Fahim and Feuer 2006; Hartocollis 2005). As previously mentioned, some went so far as to label New York's ethnic Albanian Rudaj organization the "sixth crime family" because of the group's alleged respect for codes of conduct resembling those of the five families of La Cosa Nostra.

However, some scholars have argued that the Sicilian mafia is more than just a group of criminals working together to make money; it entails a cultural and political attitude. Members who share this collective identity have killed to enforce the group's beliefs about "honor." But is this the case with Albanian organized crime groups? What are the drives and rationalizations that enable Albanian offenders to commit brutal crimes and remain silent about them? Do they use violence to terrorize their victims into silence, gain political power or reputation in criminal circles, defend their "honor," or simply project masculinity? What can culture, both traditional and popular, tell us about the codes of conduct of Albanian organized crime groups? Are the conditions of access to these groups strict and ritualized, as some have argued? Do Albanian organized crime figures respect the Kanun laws, and is this ancient code what makes these groups vengeful and secretive?

VIOLENT LIFESTYLE, BRUTAL EXECUTIONS

Dajti's Gun and Daja's Head

Dritan Dajti, a dangerous Albanian offender, killed four police officers who tried to arrest him in the seaside town of Durrës on a mid-August day in 2009. Dajti had been wanted for ten years for allegedly killing the president of construction company Besa Konstruksion, Agim Beqari, in 1999; he had escaped from custody while being escorted to Tirana's district court and was sentenced in absentia to twenty years in prison. When the police finally confronted him, Dajti shot four of them dead and wounded six other people, including bystanders. It was the highest number of Albanian policemen killed in a single day since 1997.[2]

For four years no defense lawyer wanted to defend Dajti, and the Serious Crimes Court had to postpone his trial several times. The court requested a disciplinary measure for the twenty-five lawyers who refused to defend the accused.

Datji's trial finally began in 2013. In June, during the 228th session of the proceedings, the defendant spoke directly to the judges. After police brought one of Dajti's relatives into the courtroom, the accused killer threatened them: "You threatened my family by bringing a relative of mine against his will, so I will do the same with you and your relatives." Judge Idriz Mulkurti tried to remind the defendant that the proceedings were not personal, and that his relative hadn't been forced to appear. But Datji continued: "I have it personal with you now. I know the laws. Don't forget that you are talking with Dritan Dajti. . . . I still haven't found out which one of the court members gave the order to detain one of my relatives and to exert pressure on him, but I'm letting you know that if you continue to act in this way, by exerting pressure on my relatives, I will do the same thing with your relatives" (Kasapi 2013).

In 2011, the Serious Crimes Court dealt with another Albanian criminal, Aldo Bare, the "vengeful professor" described in chapter 2 who led the notorious Lushnje gang (see figure 16). Bare's trial was as intimidating and disturbing as Dritan Dajti's.

"In the summer of 2002, I returned from Italy and had a BMW car." Standing on the witness stand, Niko Qevjani started his testimony about being extorted by the Lushnje gang and the torture he had endured in Aldo Bare's Station No. 2. "I drove down to the city to wash my car. Across [from] the Blerimi store, a vehicle

FIGURE 16. Aldo Bare in the High Court for Serious Crimes in Tirana. Source: Top Channel TV (2011).

was parked. It belonged to the Public Sewage director, but it usually was driven by his son. Sajmir Alicko, Arjan Alicko's brother, got out and told me that I'd scratched their van and had to pay for it. I told them that I was not aware of such damage, but if I did it, I was offering to pay."

After a short break, the witness continued:

> I was ordered to follow them in my car. We stopped close to Station No. 2. I was dumbstruck, because I had heard that if you entered those premises, you do not come out alive. They kill you and bury you in Divjake. Arjan Alicko violently dragged me out of the car and forced me to walk to Station No. 2. There he made me kneel down and asked me to pay him thirteen million *lekë* [approximately $120,000] for the damage to their van. I told him that I don't have that money.
>
> Arjan Alicko and his friend Bledar Flamuri began hitting me with hard objects. Several times I became unconscious from pain. They hit me even harder just because my blood spilled and stained Arjan's shirt. Then they told me I had to pay them two million *lekë* [approximately $18,000]. With blood on my face, we went to a Western Union in Lushnje, and I asked the owner to lend me the money so they would not kill me.
>
> On the way to Western Union, we were stopped by a police patrol. As I was afraid for my life, I told police I had been in an accident. I also figured police would not do anything to them anyway. I took the money and handed it over to Arjan Alicko, who later released me.
>
> Alicko would go in and out of the local police station as if he was the police chief, and no one would ever question him, even though I reported him three times.[3]

The Lushnje gang became particularly notorious in 1997, when Bare's brother Ramadan was killed by Artur Daja and Bare launched retaliatory actions against Daja's group, as discussed in chapter 2. The first target was Xhevat "the Kosovar" Demiri, one of Daja's close friends. On the day of the execution, Bare's group waited for Demiri and shot him dead in the presence of his wife and two children.

When Bare finally decapitated his brother's alleged killer in October 1998, he paraded Daja's head through his hometown of Lushnje, in order to broadcast that his brother's death had been avenged and his honor restored, and Banda e Lushnjës members played with Daja's head in the town center. Daja's headless body was blown to pieces with explosives in a public display of violence that raised Banda e Lushnjës's reputation for violence to a new level (*Gazeta Shqiptare Online* 2009; *Shekulli* 2009).

Finally in July 2012, Bare was sentenced to life in prison by a judicial panel delegated by the High Council of Justice.

The acts of Dritan Dajti and Aldo Bare helped cement the reputation many Albanian organized crime groups operating across the Balkan region received for being ruthless, cold-blooded, and vengeful.

Violence across the Atlantic

Across the Atlantic, revenge killings and brutal executions coordinated by Albanian organized crime groups—although not as dramatic or as frequent as those in the Balkans—also occurred. Kosovo Albanian organized crime figure Xhevdet Lika (aka Joey Lika) was the so-called leader of an ethnic Albanian criminal group involved in trafficking heroin from Afghanistan and Turkey into the United States, as described in chapter 3. According to Hoffman and Headley (1993) Lika didn't like Italians, and they left him alone because he was so violent.

In 1981, restaurant owner Duja Saljanin agreed to import several kilograms of heroin for Lika, but he short-weighted the delivery by a kilogram. The solution was simple: In January 1981 a meeting was held in a Park Avenue South restaurant that Saljanin operated. Lika, Mehmet Bici, and Vuksan Vulaj attended, and Saljanin was shot. Bici later testified in federal court that Vulaj pulled a gun and shot Saljanin. "Lika had a gun, and he shot him too. I was there, and I shot him too. And then we just left, crossed the street" (DeStefano 1985). Even with thirteen bullet wounds, Saljanin lived for a short while—long enough to talk. Vulaj later was shotgunned to death. The series of incidents sparked protracted inquiries that in 1984 led to Bici, who was then serving a sentence in a New York state prison for the attempted manslaughter of his wife.

According to the testimony of Rudolph W. Giuliani, then US attorney of New York, Lika offered four hundred thousand dollars for the assassination of Alan Cohen, an assistant prosecutor; Jack Delmore, a DEA agent; and US district court judge Vincent Broderick. Giuliani and his chief assistant, William Tendy, evaluated the threat, which was reported to them by a member of a New York–based drug organization. Five other informants later corroborated it, and reporter Anthony M. DeStefano published the story in *The Wall Street Journal* on September 9, 1985.

More information about the threat came from Donald "Tony the Greek" Frankos, a suspected Lucchese crime family member and contract killer who once claimed he took part in the murder of Jimmy Hoffa (Hoffman and Headley 1993). Frankos was in prison and a federally protected witness in 1985 when he had a conversation with Xhevdet Lika in which the pair discussed their assassination plans.

Judge Broderick remarked during the trial that the case involved the most reckless disregard for human life that he had ever seen. Giuliani also noted that the threat against Cohen "was the most serious threat" to an assistant US attorney that he had encountered (DeStefano 1985). For three months, from late 1984 to early 1985, federal agents provided around-the-clock protection for Cohen, Delmore, and their wives. "You can't believe what it is like," said Cohen, who was guarded in court, even when he went to the men's room (DeStefano 1985).

When a jury convicted Lika and his partner, Fici, on charges of racketeering conspiracy and running a criminal enterprise, Giuliani appeared in court for the sentencing. As the sentence was about to be rendered, Lika denied that he had wanted anyone to be killed, but he nevertheless was sentenced to life in prison, and Fici to eighty years. Mehmet Bici pleaded guilty to heroin trafficking and racketeering and was sentenced to eight years in prison.

Giuliani later reported that there had been an effort to fulfill the assassination contract. "After you have been convicted," he noted, "there is no rational reason to kill a prosecutor, except revenge" (DeStefano 1985).

Almost two decades after Lika's prosecution, the Albanian American crime scene had not changed significantly. The Krasniqi organization, discussed in previous chapters, used firearms and violence to protect its power and territory, as well as to instill fear among rival drug dealers and victims.

Albanian teenager Parid Gjoka, introduced in chapter 3, formed a criminal group to deal marijuana in New York City. After 2002 he hooked up with the Krasniqis, and the two groups worked together to distribute marijuana that had been smuggled from Canada. In 2005 a fight broke out between the groups. Someone pulled a knife on Gjoka in a bar, and he allegedly did not fight back. Later that year the Krasniqis refused to pay for a shipment of marijuana they got from Gjoka, because they "sensed a weakness and lost respect for Gjoka" (Heldman 2011a). Gjoka and another member of his group, Cela, went to discuss this with the Krasniqis, and Samir Krasniqi pulled a gun on them (Heldman 2011a).

According to legal documents, the Krasniqi crew kidnapped and beat one of Gjoka's associates, identified only as "T.K. (Victim No. 1)," around June 2005. Bruno and Samir Krasniqi, Almir Rrapo, and other members of the Krasniqi organization kidnapped T.K. at gunpoint, pistol-whipped him, and placed the muzzle of a firearm in his mouth, threatening to kill him if he did not disclose the locations of other members of his narcotics crew.

The violence did not end there. Another member of Gjoka's group, Erion Shehu, was shot and killed in a drive-by shooting outside a Queens café on July 17, 2005.

Approximately six months later, Bruno and Samir Krasniqi shot yet another member of Gjoka's group), Erenick Grezda, twice in the head at point-blank range while they were driving on the Brooklyn-Queens Expressway. They dumped Grezda's body on the side of the highway. The brothers believed that Grezda had set up Bruno Krasniqi to be kidnapped by a group of Albanian marijuana dealers from whom the Krasniqi organization had stolen approximately $250,000 worth of drugs. After Grezda's murder, Florian Veshi and Erkliant Sula drove the SUV in which he'd been killed to New Jersey, where they set fire to it. Allegedly, some members of Gjoka's group switched allegiance when they sensed Gjoka was no longer "tough enough."

Court cases illustrate that during the 1980s and 1990s Albanian expatriates in the United States were actively recruited as couriers, transporters, or hit men for the Italian mafia. The brutality with which they completed their criminal assignments allowed them to advance within the mafia network—so much so that by 1996, the top hit men for the Gambino crime family were ethnic Albanians. Although many interviewed Albanian organized crime figures disagree with this version of the truth, claiming that it is sensationalized and twisted, this nevertheless remains the official version as presented in court and police files.

THE MEANING OF CRIME

Sources of Delinquent Ideas

Violence among Albanians is not restricted to criminal organizations. Legal cases and expert interviews illustrate that segments of the Albanian community can be particularly brutal, whether or not organized crime is involved. In Hamtramck, Michigan, for example, an Albanian man who reportedly was enraged by his wife's contraction of a venereal disease shot three people at a clinic and then killed himself. In other attacks, women have been slashed with knives, and crowded restaurants and bars have been raked with gunfire. During an investigation of Albanian crime in Shelby Township, Michigan, a bomb exploded next to the police station. "They're a wild bunch of people," said Glen McAlpine, of the Michigan state police (DeStefano 1985).

INTERPOL, the US Department of Justice, the FBI, and Europol officials have argued on numerous occasions that violence, torture, extortion, and murder are often part of the ethnic Albanian modus operandi. Violence can be directed at ethnic Albanians and non-Albanians, ordinary people and law enforcement officials. Albanian criminal groups have been known to use violence to extort money from members of their own community. Most commonly, however, ethnic Albanian offenders have used violence against rival criminal groups, usually in turf battles or to demonstrate dominance over others.

Investigations indicate that Albanian-speaking criminal organizations in Belgium, for instance, focus less on the commercial structures of their organizations and more on the use of violence in order to achieve their aims. As a result, at least until 2005, Albanian organized crime figures were regarded as violent thugs (see chapter 3). Analysis of organized crime cases from 2003 reveals that criminal organizations in Belgium, on average, achieved their criminal aims using commercial structures 70 percent of the time, violence 50 percent of the time, and corruption 20 percent of the time. In cases involving Albanians, however, the level of violence rose to 81 percent, which is much higher than the overall average. The police also reported that Albanians received much stiffer sentences than the typical Belgian criminal: on average, Albanians were sentenced to fifty months' imprisonment, while the Belgian average was twenty-five months. In Belgium, the average prison sentence for purely economic crime is around fifteen months. It rises to between ninety months and a life sentence for murder or an extremely violent crime. If one examines the average sentences that the Albanian offenders received, it appears that Albanian criminals are involved in violent crimes more than any other ethnic group.

Although ethnic Albanian criminals often flaunt materialistic emblems of success in front of ordinary citizens, they also have been described by some law enforcement agencies as secretive and adhering to codes of silence. But why are violence and secrecy typical of ethnic Albanian criminal groups? There must be a more reasonable explanation than that "they're a wild bunch of people." As anthropologist Prato (2004, 69) wrote, "The devil is not as wicked as people believe, neither is the Albanian."

Earlier chapters presented the view that factors including sociocultural confusion, and not traditional Albanian culture per se, led to violent and organized crime. It appears from the cases presented above, however, that some prominent cultural themes, originating in the wider cultural context, have been selectively utilized by Albanian organized crime groups to justify criminal behavior, derive excitement from committing crimes, and bring order to the criminal organization. By invoking commonly available extenuating accounts, members of criminal subcultures have been able to neutralize moral proscriptions, and thus to act.

The values and norms implicit in organized crime groups are clearly related to delinquency. Such values and norms depart in some manner from conventional traditions. However, the relationship between a subculture of delinquency and the wider cultural context cannot, and should not, be summarized in terms of opposition. The relationship is subtle, complex, and sometimes devious. Renowned sociologist David Matza wrote that "a subculture is almost always not simply oppositional precisely because it exists within a wider cultural milieu which affects it and which it, in turn, affects" (Matza 1990, 37). Likewise, criminologist Paul Rock (2012, 68) argues that subcultures themselves are taken to exaggerate, accentuate, or otherwise edit cultural themes prevalent in the wider society. According to him, "a subculture was not conceived to be utterly distinct from the beliefs held by people at large."

Marvin E. Wolfgang and Franco Ferracuti, leaders in quantitative and theoretical criminology, argue that all deviant acts have an unfolding personal logic that draws on accepted practices within a society. Meanings and motives are established not in a social vacuum, but in a socially conditioned environment. The appearance of a weapon in the hands of an adversary is a stimulus perceived and interpreted differently by various categories of people. Social expectations of response, in particular types of social interaction, result in differential definitions of the situation. So, understanding how different categories of people define certain situations, and why some people act in certain ways, must be viewed in terms of the historical, social, and cultural context from which these people spring (Wolfgang and Ferracuti 1967).

An individual's environment and culture have a significant impact on that person's preferences—especially on norms, but also on wants. Human behavior is determined either by bounded rationality, in which an individual's behavior and decisions are affected by history, culture, and social relations, or by expressive rationality, in which an individual, through symbolic acts, demonstrates self-conception and worth. With this in mind, we will explore the extent to which codes of conduct, from both traditional and popular culture, can be considered a source of delinquent ideas in Albanian criminal subcultures. The following text is an extract, presented verbatim, from a 2008 online discussion between two individuals from different cultures who are both interested in organized crime.

> Individual X: Cosa Nostra has been bombarded on all fronts—in Italy and America because of their strength, organization and continuing loyalty to an idea. Although you said that Italians are rats you got to understand that there has been thousands of Mafioso who did not snitch. Anyone facing a life sentence will presumably think about snitching, Italians have been hit harder than anyone else in this country [USA]. And they are still here. . . . What is Albanian culture anyway? Name one self-recuperating Albanian crime group. Don't tell me about Alex Rudaj, because there is no Rudaj cartel or organization today. But there is a Nuestra Familia Eme, and Italian Cosa Nostra. You paint Albanians as organized crime groups when they have no cohesiveness, no structure and . . . who with one blow from law enforcement are finished, they have no way to self-replicate—and don't follow the ideas of omerta. . . . Albanian criminal groups have some type of political aspiration, Islam or whatever.
>
> Individual Y: It's funny how you think the Mexicans have more honor and loyalty then [sic] the Albanians. The Albanian mafia is known to be incomparably violent and air tight when it comes to infiltration. The Mexicans are significant gangsters only because in America they amount to like 10 percent of the population. Not because of honor. If the Albanians numbered even 2 percent of America, they would surpass everyone. . . . Albanians don't have to set any omerta code. Our national code the Kanun of Lek Dukagjini already stressed those codes among many other codes of

conduct throughout life. If you knew anything about Albanians, you would know that most Albanians are irreligious. I'm Catholic myself but I could care less about the bible. . . . Albanians believe in their nationality.[4]

Let's explore two rather different postulations made in the discussion quoted above. The first point is that Albanian organized crime groups are not self-reinforcing (that is, they lack continuity), and that they fall apart once law enforcement makes some arrests. On the contrary, mafia-type organizations do not cease to exist when members are imprisoned or dead. They are known to be able to endure institutional attacks through a perpetuating structure. The second argument is that Albanians do not adhere to cultural codes of conduct and that they are unable to survive in the context of a persistent subculture that has its own boundaries.

Criminal Subcultures, Symbols, and Style

Although the relationship between a subculture of delinquency and the wider cultural context is not necessarily oppositional, criminal identities are often generated within the boundaries of criminal subcultures.[5] While their boundaries might be ill defined and membership may shift in both numbers and level of commitment, these subcultures constitute definitive human associations for those who participate in them (Ferrell 1998; Anderson and Howard 1998).

Criminologist Ferrell (1998, 2) points out that "biker, hustler, Blood and Crip, pimp and prostitute—all name subcultural networks as much as individual identities." Wolfgang and Ferracuti (1967, 155–156) also argue that the more a person is integrated into a specific subculture, the more intensely he or she embraces its prescriptions of behavior and its conduct norms, and integrates them into his or her personality. In fact, as obedience to external rationalized rules comes to define success, sameness becomes a virtue and independence of mind a problem; certain subcultures emerge to signify independence of mind. Belonging to a criminal subculture may mean that you are a brave risk taker and, above all, a free spirit. However, this doesn't mean that subcultures do not have rules that members must follow. And just as the dominant society punishes those who deviate from its norms, deviance by the nonviolent or nondelinquent individual from the norms of the violent and criminal subculture also may be punished: the nondelinquent may be ostracized or treated with disdain.

To speak of a criminal subculture is to recognize not only an association of people but also a network of symbols, meanings, and knowledge. Members of a criminal subculture learn and negotiate motives, rationalizations, and attitudes. They develop elaborate conventions of language, appearance, and presentation of self. In doing so, they participate in a subculture: a collective way of life (Ferrell 1998).

When describing the Sicilian Cosa Nostra, Letizia Paoli (2003) argued that the members of this mafia group undergo a ceremony of affiliation. The ceremony starts with a rite of "separation," by which the individual is separated from his or her initial state and starts the "transition." The final ritual, termed "incorporation," ends the ceremony and emphasizes the individual's integration into his new state. According to Paoli (2003, 72), the rite of mafia initiation establishes a ritual kinship between the novice and the rest of the group. Upon affiliation with a mafia family, the new member enters into an almost religious communion with the other members of the mafia community, who share a collective identity. That is, the new member becomes part of a common body, losing an individual identity of belonging to a blood family, and instead subjugating the individual to the norms and interests of the association.

Many former Sicilian mafiosi have stated that on the day when they became members of La Cosa Nostra they also grew in stature, starting a new life with new rules.[6] According to their testimonies, at that point they became people who had to respect the law of honor and ensure that others also respected it.

Some scholars, however, have argued that it was in the interest of mafia families to use symbols and rites extensively, because it enabled them to exercise unconditional claims on their associates and to create brotherhood ties among them. Others have claimed that brotherhood bonds, rites of passage, fraternization contracts, archaic codes, and ritualized affiliations are just sensational interpretations of the mafia (Gambetta 1993).

In practice, the boundaries of ethnic Albanian organized crime groups are not clearly defined, and their membership tends to shift (see chapter 4). Members of ethnic Albanian criminal subcultures neither undergo ritual ceremonies nor sign contracts in order to join. It appears that these groups are more spontaneously formed than, for example, the Sicilian Cosa Nostra. Although some have argued that the conditions of access to Albanian criminal organizations are "strict, codified, ritualized" (Raufer 2003), there is no evidence to support this claim.

Nevertheless, the term "subculture" still applies when referring to Albanian organized crime groups. Members of these groups often share similar values, interests, and worldviews, as well as strong—but not exclusive—ethnic bonds. Although it is uncommon in the contemporary Albanian criminal context to share ritual affiliations or ceremonial rites of passage, these groups are no less resilient for it. The strong ethnic and kinship ties, combined with support for similar cultural values and social codes (e.g., mutual aid, solidarity, secrecy, honor, vengeance, machismo, materialism, subordination of women, and fascination with firearms), have made many Albanian criminal groups hard to break or infiltrate. Although in a less structured way than in the Sicilian mafia, members of Albanian organized crime groups share a collective identity and subject themselves to the norms and interests of the association.

Before analyzing some common codes of conduct applied by Albanian organized crime groups, it is important to examine whether these groups make use of unique symbols that help them in building their criminal identity. As earlier research has found, subtleties of collective style define the meaning of crime and deviance for subcultural participants, agents of legal control, consumers of mediated crime images, and others (Ferrell 1998). For example, by paying attention to dark sunglasses and white undershirts, and to precise styles of walking and talking, Katz (1990) sketches the deviant subculture in which so-called badasses, *cholos,* punks, youth gang members, and others participate. If we are to understand both the terror and the appeal of organized crime groups, we must be able to make sense not only of their criminal activities, but of their collective aesthetics as well.

Although Albanian organized crime groups do not necessarily use exclusive symbols, names, or objects in making their criminal organization distinctive, they nevertheless inhabit a particular lifestyle that allows them to act out certain roles. Gold chains, guns, a shaved head, a fringed beard, luxury cars, black suits, and dark sunglasses—these emblems of "success" or "toughness" are not necessarily unique to the Albanian criminal subculture, but they can be considered informal symbols of recognition that give offenders esteem and status among their peers (see figures 17 and 18).

There are significant differences with regard to styles maintained by different Albanian organized crime groups, however. For example, members of more sophisticated groups—often those dealing with large-scale drug trafficking, cigarette smuggling, white-collar crimes, illegal gambling, and so on—present themselves as legitimate businessmen and not necessarily as violent, macho thugs. These groups often are run by middle-aged businessmen in black suits, such as Bajrush Sejdiu, Naser Kelmendi, Alex Rudaj, and Dhimiter Harizaj. They tend to keep a lower profile than other criminal groups. One could even label these groups as more "rational" and money-driven than their thuggish colleagues in crime.

On the other hand, smaller groups that deal in extortion, prostitution, theft, robberies, home invasions, or other similar activities often prefer a more vulgar style that reflects a tough personality. Often composed of younger individuals, these groups tend to expose themselves to a greater extent, trying to impress their observers and to impose fear and respect in the eyes of their audience. They have been regarded as driven by emotion, a need for respect, and peer recognition.

The latter criminal groups want to show off, and in most cases they do not hide their accumulated wealth. Particularly in the Balkan context, they publicly flaunt their emblems of success. As Klaus Shmidt, the head of the Police Assistance Mission of the European Community to Albania (PAMECA), and Arben Tabaku, a senior analyst within the same organization, rightly observed, shaved-headed young men are frequently seen in Albania and Kosovo driving high-performance vehicles while talking on cell phones. They spend all the money they make from their illegal activities on cars, clothes, women, and restaurant meals.

FIGURE 17. Tough macho with charisma (Prishtina, Kosovo, 2006). Copyright © Jana Arsovska.

The Krasniqis and the Hoxhas are examples of this. Similarly, Parid Gjoka allegedly made a lot of money, but he was always broke because every week he bought clothes and jewelry and took his friends and associates to expensive restaurants (Heldman 2011b).

It is also important to note that ethnic Albanian offenders, particularly young men, appear to fill the vacuum left by societal neglect by congregating in places that allow them to show off their style and act out roles that afford them esteem and status. Members of more street-oriented organized crime groups often use staging areas in their search for identity (Anderson 1999). The staging area or hangout may be a public place where activities occur that set the stage for other activities. Those activities may be played out either on the spot, in front of all who have congregated there, or in a less conspicuous location.

Ethnic Albanian criminals often use ethnic cafés, infamous bars, nightclubs, and other locations as hangouts and meeting places. Social media, including Facebook and YouTube, also can serve as virtual meeting places where one can "show off." People gather in real or virtual space to project the image by which they wish to be known. They try to present the most valuable notion of who they are and

FIGURE 18. Golden chain with KLA initials (Prishtina, Albania, 2006). Copyright © Jana Arsovska.

how they stand in relation to others. In such settings, public displays of decency get little respect, while looking "hard" and dominant is often what counts. In a four-minute YouTube clip, for example, members of the Albanian Bromley gang (not necessarily an organized crime group), pose with AK-47 assault rifles and handguns (see figure 19). The sound of gunshots can be heard in the background (*Daily Mail* 2010).

Albanian criminal groups also sometimes make use of the eagle found on the Albanian flag as an informal symbol, believing it demonstrates patriotism, courage, and respect for their origins. Various police files reveal that many Albanian criminals use the eagle symbol as a flag in their car, a tattoo on their body, or even a logo on membership cards. Of course, such patriotic symbols are not associated only with members of Albanian organized crime groups. Law-abiding people, too, tend to make use of patriotic symbols to provide a sense of belonging and shared identity.

In some organized crime groups, youths also bond through rap music, posing in parking lots in the Bronx or Yonkers or Staten Island in New York, or on 15 Mile Road outside Detroit. Wearing double-eagle bandannas, stick-up style; brandish-

FIGURE 19. Members of an Albanian gang brandishing automatic weapons in images posted on the video-sharing website YouTube. Source: YouTube, 2010.

ing automatic weapons, or pretending to; or smoking marijuana, they call out real and fake Shqiptar (Albanian). Groups such as the Albanian Bad Boys, the Bloody Alboz, TBA, Unikkatil, Uptown Affiliates, and others hang out in clubs and identify with lyrics such as these, to the rap song "If I Die, You Die," by Rebel, aka UniKKatiL:

> It's the two-headed eagle, better watch your back,
> I'm about to attack, dressed red and black . . .
> I got a lotta brothas, terrorists, killaz, mafiaz, drug dealaz
> And most of them soldiers, they used to be rebels,
> Living by the mothafuckin gun,
> So if you ever even think about fuckin with Albanians,
> I swear to god you gotta' run . . .

Not all ethnic Albanian organized crime groups, gangs, or criminal subcultures use symbols and attention-seeking styles. As previously mentioned, more sophisticated, money-driven groups tend to avoid too much public exposure because of the attention it brings. They often prefer to blend in with ordinary citizens or those involved in business. Even some street-oriented and power-driven organized crime groups, particularly those operating in Western Europe, have learned in recent years that public displays do not always serve the best interests of their criminal organizations. The need to show off and impress people, as discussed in chapter 2, may be considered an outcome of the pathological materialism present in Albanian society and the social pressure to be rich, famous, and tough.

The Kanun and Popular Culture

Ethnic Albanian criminal groups make use of distinctive subcultural codes, which are not entirely different from, or in conflict with, those of mainstream society. It should be acknowledged that organized crime groups in general, and ethnic Albanian organized crime groups in particular, share some basic, common value systems. However, these value systems are often linked to the specific sociocultural context from which they emerge.

As outlined in chapter 2, the Kanun of Lek Dukagjini contains the rules on which traditional Albanian culture is based. Martin Camaj, a professor of Albanian studies, explains that particularly for the clans of northern Albania, the maxims of the Kanun took precedence over all laws in the country (1989). In terms of content, the Kanun is a formal expression of the Albanian people's deeply felt concept of honor (*ndera*). According to the Kanun laws, "the foundation of it all is the principle of personal honour. Next comes the equality of persons. From these flows a third principle, the freedom of each to act in accordance with his own honour, within the limits of the law, without being subject to another's command. And the fourth principle is the word of honour, the besë (def.: besa), which creates a situation of inviolable trust" (Malcolm 1998, 18).

The Kanun details the laws according to which a person can protect his community against the attacks of third parties. This protection includes the moral obligation to apply retaliatory attacks until the honor of one's own group has been reestablished (*gjakmarria*).

Toughness and masculinity also appear to be very important to Albanian men. Traditionally, Albanian men have been socialized into a rigid and limiting definition of masculinity. They have been raised to be "real men" and fighters, and they fear being ridiculed as "too feminine" by other men. Over the years, this fear has perpetuated homophobic and exclusionary masculinity.

Data released by the European Social Survey in March 2013 reveal that a majority of Albanians are conservative and disapprove of same-sex relationships. According to the survey data, 53 percent of Albanians believe that "gays and lesbians should not be free to live life as they wish" (Likmeta 2013a). In fact, Albania has a higher percentage of respondents holding that view than any other nation polled for the survey (Likmeta 2013a). Results of previous polling by Gallup's Balkan Monitor, taken in 2010, show that 54 percent of Albanians consider homosexual relations wrong, while 23 percent do not.

During the 1990s, Albania, Kosovo, and Macedonia seem to have experienced a sociopolitical and cultural shock while various segments of the so-called "Kanun morality" experienced an upward revaluation. Criminologist Xavier Raufer goes so far as to argue that in Albania, and especially in the country's mountainous north, the Kanun has survived in an almost "chemically pure form": "For most of the mafias these rules and laws are implicit, passed down by word of mouth. But in Albania the code of honor or Kanun is written down and the brochure that contains it is on sale in newspaper kiosks" (Raufer 2003, 65). Scholars, or even common people, may disagree about whether the Kanun codifies "mafia" rules, but there is evidence that personal interpretations of this code have been used to justify criminal behavior.

In their search for identity, some socially confused Albanians were influenced not only by ancient cultural codes but also by popular culture and the media, as mentioned in chapter 2. Albanian organized crime figure Ketjol Manoku commented, "The Krasniqis watched too many movies" (Heldman 2011b). The members of the Krasniqi crew in fact loved *Scarface, Donnie Brasco,* and *Goodfellas.* One even nicknamed himself "Tony Montana," after the protagonist of *Scarface.* And Kosovo Albanian organized crime figure Viktor Hoxha was fascinated by the TV crime series *24.*

Focusing on the deregulation and privatization of desire within contemporary consumerism, Zygmunt Bauman coined the phrase "sensation-gatherers" to characterize a peculiarly late-modern form of subjectivity (Bauman 1997, 146). He describes how the "soldier-producer" of industrial capitalism has been supplanted by a different type of subject, one who constantly craves new experiences. Bauman describes a series of emotions that might be seen as characterizing the sensation-gatherer: dissatisfaction, narcissism, impulsivity, and spontaneity—frequently the very emotions behind a host of risk-laden criminal acts. These illegal forms of excitement represent a break with the banalities of everyday life and mark an entry into a new world of possibility and pleasure. The seductiveness of crime thus may derive, in large part, from the new kinds of sensations it offers. Not only are we constantly on the lookout for new and ever-more-thrilling experiences, but we inhabit a world where old normative systems cease to matter.

Today, emotions have transgressed the rules of rationality on various levels, and consumer culture has cultivated a desire for immediate, rather than delayed, gratification (Hayward 2007; Presdee 2000). In the course of their daily lives, many people seek out the excitement inherent in the act of doing wrong and of living on the edge of law and order. The influence of the sensational media no doubt has been particularly strong among young and deprived Albanians, who lack access to legal opportunities to make money fast, and who feel they have very little to lose.

Sensational media and self-interpretations of the customary code have been important sources of criminal stimulation for Albanian criminal subcultures. Albanian criminals have invoked commonly available extenuating accounts, linked to traditional and popular culture, to neutralize moral proscriptions.

Understanding Albanian criminal subcultures and their codes of conduct has become important for law enforcement officials. In the offices of the Balkan organized crime units of the FBI and the Belgian Federal Police, one can observe the Albanian double-eagle flag hanging on the wall, as well as a copy of the Kanun.

BLOOD IS PAID FOR WITH BLOOD

Violence in the Name of Honor

Explaining the sometimes irrational use of violence in some Albanian criminal organizations requires a closer look at the Kanun laws. According to these laws, "there is no fine for an offence to honor. An offence to honor is never forgiven. The person dishonored has every right to avenge his honor; no pledge is given, no appeal is made to the Elders, no judgment is needed, no fine is taken. The strong man collects the fine himself" (Fox 1989, 130). One who meets the revenge obligations outlined in the Kanun is purified, whereas one who does not fulfill them is labeled unclean and will be humiliated in front of the village community (Waldmann 2001; Schwandner-Sievers 1999).

The following articles from the Kanun illustrate the importance of revenge in traditional Albanian society:

> Article 901. If two men kill each other in the course of an argument, the law that states "a head for a head or blood for a blood" has been fulfilled, since both are dead.
>
> Article 903. If one is killed and the other is wounded, then the wounded man must pay the balance of the blood-money for the murdered man.
>
> Article 904. If someone kills my brother and I track down a member of the murderer's family, wounding him once or up to twenty times, and then I turn my gun and kill his brother, who is the murderer of my brother, all the wounds must be evaluated and paid for, but the murder is in accordance with the rule of "a head for a head" and avenges my brother's death.
>
> Article 905. Even if the murdered man was wounded twenty times, no compensation is paid for the wounds: the first victim has been avenged by "blood for blood."
>
> Article 906. If I fire at someone and only graze his head, I must still pay for the wound.
>
> Article 907. If I hit his foot, I must pay 750 grosh.
>
> Article 908. A wound above the belt is evaluated at 3 purses; below the belt, at 750 grosh. (Fox 1989, 172)

According to article 601 the Kanun, some of the situations in which a man is considered dishonored are the following (see Fox 1989, 131–132):

> (1) If someone calls him a liar in front of a group of men;
> (2) If someone spits at him, threatens him, pushes him, or strikes him;
> (3) If he reneges on his promise of mediation or on his pledged word;
> (4) If his wife is insulted or if she runs off with someone;
> (5) If someone takes the weapons he carries;
> (6) If someone violates his hospitality, insulting his friend or his worker;
> (7) If someone breaks into his house;
> (8) If someone does not repay a debt or obligation.

In all these situations a man has the right to defend his honor. The original Kanun includes specific clarifications concerning the accepted manner of retaliatory killings, for restoring honor to the offended when the laws are disobeyed.

Article 600 of the Kanun states that "an offence to honor is not paid with property, but by the spilling of blood . . . [A] man who has been dishonored is considered dead according to the Kanun" (Fox 1989, 130). The Kanun stipulates that, in some cases, an offense to honor can be "paid off" by a magnanimous pardon (through the mediation of good friends). If a person's honor is offended, there is no legal recourse for such an offense; the Kanun says, "Forgive, if you see fit; but if you prefer, wash your dirty face" (Fox 1989, 130).

This "eye for an eye" philosophy is closely linked to the phenomenon of blood feuds in Albania and the surrounding region. A blood feud generally begins with an argument, usually between two men. The argument could have any cause—an accident, a perceived insult, a property ownership disagreement, or a conflict over access to electricity, water, or fuel. The argument escalates into a physical fight, and one man kills the other. The victim's family then feels that it is "owed blood" by the killer's family.

Generally, it is not permitted by the Kanun to kill a family member in his own home, or to kill a woman or child. Thus, when a killing occurs, the male members of the killer's family immediately "self-isolate" and do not leave their home. The isolated family presumes that an attack is possible, unless the other family offers them a *besa* (an often limited or temporary reprieve from the threat of revenge). They often also feel that, in the absence of a *besa,* honor requires them to remain isolated, even where there has been no concrete threat. The blood feud continues until the lost blood is avenged, or until the family of the deceased man forgives the killer's family.

Today, for ordinary Albanians, the Kanun statement "blood must be taken" still has great significance. In a survey of 864 ethnic Albanians from Kosovo, Albania, and Macedonia, 35 percent of the Albanian respondents agreed with this statement, and 22 percent did not provide an answer. This indicates that although actual knowledge of the Kanun laws is weak, a significant percentage of people support the idea behind the blood feud. Nevertheless, there are deep discrepancies in the statistics concerning blood feuds and related revenge killings in contemporary Albania. At one extreme, media reports have referred to hundreds of blood feud killings per year and thousands of children living in isolation. At the other extreme, according to government statistics, such killings fell steadily from forty-five in 1998 to one in 2009, while the number of isolated children ranges from thirty-six to fifty-seven countrywide, of which between twenty-nine and forty-five are in Shkodra. The number of families in isolation was estimated to be between 124 and 133 countrywide (Alston 2010).

The figures used by civil society groups also vary widely. One organization with extensive field operations notes significant reductions in blood feud killings over the last five years and reports that there now are only a few blood feud killings annually. They estimate that no more than 350 families and 80 to 100 children are in isolation nationally. However, another prominent organization estimates some 9,800 blood feud killings since 1991, dropping to a figure still in excess of 30 in 2009. By their calculations, there are 1,450 families and 800 children in isolation (Alston 2010).

Revenge, blood feuds, and honor are topics that often emerge in discussions of Albanian organized crime. Law enforcement officials often link the use of violence among Albanian organized crime groups to the "Albanian culture of violence" and the values promoted by the Kanun laws. "Albanian criminals act irrationally, and they attract too much attention," explained Laurent Sartorius, a Belgian law enforcement officer. "For example, person A asks person B to do something; person B says he will do it, but he doesn't. This can result in a killing. Albanians will never step aside and lose face in front of the others. They will not say, 'OK, you are right.' Culture might provide some answers for explaining such behavior" (interview, Belgium, 2008).

The 1996 murders of twenty-five-year-old waiter Jonathon Segal and twenty-two-year-old bouncer Michael Greco in New York City's Scores nightclub illustrate the indifference and haste with which Albanians often kill. In 1996, brothers Simon and Viktor Dedaj were tried for the double murder outside the strip club on East 60th Street. Those attending the trial heard how the club attracted celebrities, executives, and Gambino family crime figures. Prosecutors claimed that the Gambinos extorted millions of dollars from the club and its employees, including the strippers and hat-check personnel (McFadden 1999).

In 1999, *The New York Times* reported: "Law-enforcement officials said the trouble began at an after-hours birthday celebration when the Dedaj brothers began to make advances to the girlfriend of a Gambino crime boss. Willie Marshall, a self-described 'leg-breaker' for the Gambino family, along with Mr. Segal and Mr. Greco, told the brothers to leave. Michelle Romano, a topless dancer whose stage name is Pebbles, testified that Simon Dedaj put Mr. Segal in a headlock" (McFadden 1999). The defense argued that the headlock began as a playful gesture between two former wrestlers. But the struggle then turned deadly. Simon Dedaj shot Greco in the forehead, while Viktor Dedaj attacked Segal with a knife.

After the shooting, the Dedaj brothers went on the run, but within the next two years they were arrested and brought to trial. Little is known about the Dedaj brothers until this event, so it remains unclear what types of crime they may have been involved in before the murders and what their relationship with the Gambinos may have been. The murders made headlines in New York, but in the Balkan region such assassinations over issues of apparently minor importance (quality of service, or women) occur frequently, so they did not draw as much attention there.

The use of violence serves simultaneously as one of the most advantageous and disadvantageous characteristics of ethnic Albanian organized crime groups. On one hand, it has helped many Albanian criminal groups to gain a reputation in criminal circles, where competition can be fierce, and it has kept their victims silent and their members "loyal." On the other hand, the open use of violence has made law enforcement officials more aware of the Albanian presence in certain cities. By using violence, ethnic Albanian organized crime groups have attracted enormous international attention.

Revenge and Driving Out Competition

Different types of violence are practiced by organized crime groups: internal violence; violence against rival groups and competitors; violence against magistrates, police, and judges; and violence against victims. Police files show that ethnic Albanian criminal figures appear more willing to kill Albanian men who want to take over their business than police officers or victims. Violence against members of rival groups also remains at high levels.

Some years ago Albanians had to establish themselves as prominent organized crime players; if they hoped to compete on the international crime scene, they needed to show their readiness and willingness to use violence. They gained control over prostitution markets in some parts of London, Milan, Brussels, and Berlin (CEOOR 2006; Barron 2000). They also shouldered aside the Turks who had controlled the heroin trafficking business in Switzerland and some Scandinavian countries (BBC 2008c; Europol 2011).

The situation in the United States appears to be similar. Although in the case of Zef Mustafa (see chapter 3) his defense lawyers argued that Mustafa's "bat man" moniker is the vague product of multiple levels of hearsay, the reputation nevertheless remained. According to one Arthur Avenue regular who watched Mustafa's career evolve, Mustafa was "all violence, no brains. A truly bad kid" (Robbins 2005). And during Mustafa's trial, a captain in the Genovese crime family noted, "I hate these fuckin' Albanians. . . . If you have a beef with them you have to kill them right away. There's no talking to them" (Robbins 2005).

Media reports cite a court statement from assistant US attorney Timothy Treanor, who worked on the 2004 case against Alex Rudaj and "the Corporation." He reported that the Albanians "were incredibly violent and incredibly feared on the street. They beat up made men and mafia associates. One man was shot five times in the back of his neck, but survived."[7] According to one anonymous investigator, "They're like the old Sicilians. They don't roll, and they don't cooperate" (Fahim and Feuer 2006).

According to federal prosecutors, in addition to the violence against the Lucchese and Gambino crime families described in chapter 3, Rudaj was the triggerman in a 1993 shooting of another organized crime figure after a high-speed chase in the Bronx. Rudaj hung out the sunroof of a car and fired at Guy Peduto as he fled. Prosecutors also described an incident in which Rudaj showed up with twenty thugs to take over late mob boss John Gotti's table at Rao's, an exclusive Italian restaurant in East Harlem.

Later, Prenka Ivezaj, one of Rudaj's associates, was recorded, in a tape played for the jury during the trial, saying that if the Italians had pulled their guns, "Everybody dies. Guaranteed. Nobody walks out of there alive. Either them or us" (Hartocollis 2005). However, Rudaj, who attended Gotti's funeral, firmly denies many of these allegations. Ron Rubinstein, the lawyer for Prenka Ivezaj, noted, "As we used to say in the schoolyard, they made a federal case out of a little gambling" (Hartocollis 2005). According to Rubinstein, there was no corroboration of an accused mobster's boast that the Albanian group had taken over John Gotti's table. He said that the defendants had attended Gotti's funeral, but they were just "wannabes" who were "hoping to be noticed" (Hartocollis 2005).

Nevertheless, the activities of other Albanian organized crime figures continued to shock the American public. In 2008, ethnic Albanian Marash Gojcaj was charged with the murder of a popular restaurateur—his uncle and business partner, Zef Vulevic, the owner of Gusto Ristorante in Danbury, Connecticut. Circumstantial evidence indicated that the Albanian mob was involved in Vulevic's murder as well. News media reported that Vulevic was having significant financial problems at the time of his murder and had borrowed from a mob loan shark. Vulevic, married and the father of two, was in debt when he died (New York Post 2008).

Vulevic's murder was brutal. His chopped-up body was discovered in several plastic bags in a wooded area of Bedford, New York, during an Earth Day cleanup three weeks after he disappeared. Perhaps to send a message, there was no serious attempt to hide the body. Police then determined that Vulevic was shot twice in the back of the head before someone cut his body into seven pieces. News media reported that in the Vulevic case, the ethnic Albanian code of silence seemed to be in effect, but on September 4, 2008, in Danbury Superior Court, a fifty-seven-page arrest warrant charging Marash Gojcaj with the murder of his uncle was made public. The warrant was based on testimony from several anonymous witnesses, including restaurant employees and an alleged organized crime informant. Finally, in 2010, a jury found Marash Gojcaj guilty (Miller 2010).

Competition came into play in the case of Ketjol Manoku, who ended up in prison because of friction between two groups of young Albanians in Michigan. "It was about north versus south Albanians, or perceived disrespect, or something to do with a woman, or a physical fight, or all of the above," journalist Kevin Heldman (2011b) wrote. Manoku said he called for a peace meeting after an altercation; handshakes were exchanged and the dispute supposedly was resolved. But a week later, two northern Albanian boys jumped members of Manoku's crew.

Two nights later, on July 17, 2004, Manoku was hanging out with some friends in the parking lot of an apartment complex. A van rolled into the parking lot with five young men inside. Someone pointed an AK-47 out the vehicle's window. Manoku dived under a bush where his nine millimeter was stashed. He pulled it out before shouting, "Put the gun down!" (Heldman 2011a).

Manoku said the van accelerated toward him and he fired, hitting four of the five passengers. One of them died and the others were injured. The state charged Manoku and his group with conspiracy and premeditated murder, asserting that they had plotted to kill the north Albanian boys.

The methods used by ethnic Albanian groups in the Balkans, particularly during the 1990s, were even more violent than those practiced in the West. In the Balkans, using violence meant gaining a reputation; one might be required to fight in public, an effort that inevitably would reflect on one's name. As described earlier, Aldo Bare paraded through his hometown with the head of his rival, Artur Daja. And in Macedonia, the ethnic Albanian group led by Sejdiu Bajrush drove out competitors by resorting to violence, threats, and corruption.

Zani Myrteza Çaushi's criminal group in Albania also gained power and reputation quickly through the use of brutal violence and threats (Raufer and Quéré 2006). Çaushi and Petrit Gerdhuqi, followed by fifteen or sixteen armed men, went to the village of Mifol in Albania to avenge the killings of the three Gerduhi brothers. For at least an hour the armed gang terrorized the village, beating and threatening its residents. They demanded to be told where the killers were hiding. Two village residents were seriously wounded.

While the criminal group was terrorizing the villagers, police in Vlore learned of the abuse and officers were sent to the village. Çaushi's gang did not surrender. In fact, they fired on police with Kalashnikovs. The police closed in, and the last five minutes of the violent clash were especially fierce. All routes leading out of the village were closed, yet only five offenders were arrested.

The city of Vlore has been the site of other episodes of brutal violence between criminal groups as well. In 2014, the police arrested members of a criminal group, suspected to be the main organizer of at least a dozen remote-detonation murders. Among other activities, the group carried out assassinations-for-hire. One of the suspected contract killers, Julian Sinanaj, was arrested in 2014, and his trial is ongoing. The police suspect that he might be responsible for at least twenty murders outside of Albanian borders, mainly in Greece and Italy, and of several crimes in Albania.

In fact, Sinanaj implicated two Albanian cousins, local businessmen, in several crimes committed between 2011 and 2013, including an attempt to place explosives in the apartment building of businessman and Democratic Party member of Parliament Ardian Kollozi. The goal was to spread panic among the families and residents, and to damage Kollozi's building. Sinanaj claimed that he was hired by these cousins to kill another several other victims, including Sokol Veizi, Agron Cela, and Pirro Bare. He was usually paid between fifty and one hundred thousand euros per assassination.

In Macedonia, the group led by Dzhelal Ajeti (aka Dzheljo), from the village of Arachinovo near Skopje, appears to have grown strong over the years. Ajeti has a long criminal record, going back to 1996. Eighteen charges have been pressed against him, for murder, extortion, fights, possession of weapons, and other crimes. Unofficially, according to investigative journalists, Ajeti's key activity was loaning huge sums of money at an interest rate of as high as 10 percent a day. Some allege that Ajeti also was involved in the regional drug trade.

Until his assassination in 2009, the ethnic Albanian Agim Sherifi was Ajeti's righthand man. Sherifi was kidnapped before he was killed, and this was kept secret until his corpse was found—with a bullet in his forehead and several other gunshot wounds to his head and body—at an old dump on the road between Kumanovo and Arachinovo. According to the media, Sherifi's murder was proof that there was a war in the Macedonian criminal underworld.

Then, in 2010, a group of armed men attacked Ajeti's café in Skopje and mistakenly killed his fifteen-year-old nephew, who was at the wrong place at the wrong time. Three years later, in November 2013, a man wearing a black mask and carrying a fully loaded Kalashnikov shot Ajeti to death in his own café. After the assassin fired about thirty bullets, he reloaded his Kalashnikov and left the café.

Ethnic Albanians do not use violence only against their rivals and competitors. Sometimes violent clashes break out between members of the same group or the same criminal network. The groups led by the Krasniqis and Gjoka, for instance, went to war over the marijuana market in New York after years of working together. In Belgium in the 1990s, a conflict erupted among ethnic Albanians in Antwerp, resulting in numerous shootings in the city streets and in café bars, even in a broad daylight. This type of unnecessary violence, committed for revenge or honor, may appear irrational to those in the West.

Violence against Judges, Police, and Politicians

Violence against law enforcement officials is uncommon, particularly in Western Europe, although it does occur. In Belgium, for instance, Albanians have intimidated police officers, although they have not used real violence against them. But police officials in the Balkans and in the United States have reported that ethnic Albanians do not hesitate to use violence, or at least threats, against law enforcement officials. As mentioned earlier, drug trafficker Xhevdet Lika offered four hundred thousand dollars to anyone who would kill a certain assistant US attorney and federal drug enforcement agent.

In Albania, Aldo Bare's group was accused of ordering the murder of local police officer Klejdi Bano in 2001 and bombing the houses of various police chiefs who were investigating the group's criminal activity. Bare also was charged with murdering the deputy of the secret services for the region, Lushnje Bashkim Shkurti, and Deputy Mayor Drago Voshtima in 1998. Zani Çaushi's group in Vlore also resorted to shooting at police, as mentioned in the previous section.

Remote-controlled bombs also have appeared in Albania, with businessmen, judges, prosecutors, and politicians as the most frequent targets. In 2011, Judge Skerdilaid Konomi was killed when a blast hit his car as he drove to work at the Vlore District Court. The former head of the Vlore Prosecution Office, Dorian Tafili, was injured in a car bomb attack in January 2012. In addition, numerous businesspeople and politicians have been killed or seriously injured when remote-controlled bombs detonated in their cars.

Other victims of violence include Mirela Mishgjoni, a criminal judge in Vlore, who was injured in 2013 when an unknown assailant threw medical acid in her face. The Supreme Court and the High Council of Justice emphasized that authorities needed to do more to protect judges, who have become increasingly frequent victims of brutal mafia-type attacks.

In the long run, it seems that the use of extreme violence and violence against law enforcement officials does not work to the advantage of Albanian criminal organizations. As a result of such violence, law enforcement agencies have labeled some of these groups as irrational, impulsive, and emotion-driven, and many of their members have received unusually long prison sentences. According to Gus Xhudo, the younger generation of Albanian offenders in the United States in particular is not afraid of going against law enforcement officials. "They don't care about consequences," he said. "Nothing scares them" (interview, New York, 2014).

This behavior, however, may not be as irrational as it seems. In some twisted way, it is partially rooted in history and tradition, as well as in popular culture.

Violence against Victims

Much of the brutal violence meted out by ethnic Albanian organized crime groups is directed against victims who are not organized criminals themselves. In particular, women and children are exploited for prostitution. Non-governmental organizations that work with sex workers have reported that Albanian pimps have the worst reputation for violence and exploitation in Europe (Renton 2003; CEOOR 2005).

The Ali case involved an international group composed of Albanian, Belgian, Dutch, Moroccan, and French criminals. The actors in this case were suspected of human trafficking, rape, prostitution, violence, use of arms, falsification of documents, and other offenses. A Belgian man called Luli recruited psychologically vulnerable Belgian girls for prostitution. Typically, the girls were told they would work as escorts in the Netherlands and earn "big bucks." The girls needed a place to stay, so Luli would bring them to his house. He then exploited them sexually before sending them to two Albanian friends, the Ali brothers, for prostitution in a legal prostitution bar in Rotterdam.[8]

The girls were told that they only had to entice customers to drink more in the Rotterdam bar, but this was not always the case. And the big bucks never materialized. Half of the money the girls earned went to the bar owners in Rotterdam, one-fourth went to Luli and the Albanians, and the girls had to pay expenses for taxis and rent from what remained. In a period of three weeks, each girl generated about 5,000 euros, of which she personally received only 250 to 300 euros. The role of the Albanians in this case was to control the girls and to ensure that they could not escape. If a girl was disobedient or refused a client, the Ali brothers beat her severely.

One of Luli's girls was sent to work as a prostitute in Antwerp. The first day she earned five hundred euros, yet she received only twenty euros. Later, she decided to take on fewer clients. Luli was not happy about this, so he called the Albanians, who brutally abused the girl. She escaped and sought refuge with a Moroccan drug dealer, who also knew the Albanians. The girl said that she'd run away from Luli because she heard that he was arranging a fake marriage between her and a nephew of the Ali brothers. The Albanians were getting five thousand euros for this deal.

When the Albanian brothers found the escaped girl, they locked her in a truck, where they raped and abused her. Her face was seriously disfigured as a result of her ordeal. The girl, who was pregnant, begged for the life of her unborn child, but the Albanians were merciless. During the subsequent trial, the Albanian brothers claimed that the girl was lying and stated that it is not a part of their culture to beat and abuse women. However, these same Albanian brothers were known to the police because of several previous acts of violence. Ultimately, they were convicted in France for rape, kidnapping, and the use of violence. An Albanian organized crime figure involved in more traditional organized crime activities, including extortion and illegal gambling, noted: "I don't understand human trafficking and prostitution. These men don't have kids of their own so they don't care about children and women. Those are dishonorable crimes. Prostitution and drugs. I imagine someone doing that to my own kids, and it drives me crazy" (interview, New Jersey, 2014).

Ethnic Albanian victims of extortion and kidnapping, however, also have had terrifying experiences. During Aldo Bare's court case, witness Mimoza Haxhiu told of how, in August 1998, Lushnje gang members arrived at her home while her husband was away. They demanded to know where her husband was, and they threatened to burn her alive if she did not reveal his whereabouts. Within days, the criminal group burned down her brother-in-law's house. Mimoza Haxhiu received many threats and eventually was forced to flee with her family, first to Greece and later to Turkey and then Germany.

Pranvera Haxhiu, another witness in this case, was held hostage by members of Bare's group for several hours. They told her that they were police officers and grabbed her husband, Karafili, and her. They forced them into a camouflaged van.

Some scholars have argued that the culture of machismo, of "tough guys," is more about staging an impression of violence than about violence itself (Collins

2008). This staging sets up a distinction between insiders and outsiders, those who understand that the staging is being done and those who are taken in by it. Collins argues that confrontation between equals tends to stabilize at the level of bluster—but as we have seen, this has not been the case with ethnic Albanian offenders. Ethnic Albanian offenders have used violence against their associates, competitors, and police—all tough and masculine opponents—but also against weaker parties, such as their victims, including women and children.

Although their use of violence may appear to be unnecessary or irrational, these groups have found a way to justify their acts. On occasion, cultural themes relating to honor and revenge have been exploited in order to neutralize moral proscriptions or to avoid punishment. An Albanian organized crime figure in his late forties, currently serving a prison sentence for leading a criminal organization, noted: "Albanians fight and kill because they are scared, they don't go looking for trouble. It is not because they want fun, or a thrill. Only teenagers and younger criminals do it for that reason. In general, nobody likes violence. It is fear, and maybe sometimes pride, that makes them act in certain ways" (interview, New Jersey, 2014).

BESA, MUTUAL AID, AND SECRECY

The previously mentioned concept of *besa* is a highly valued cultural element associated with the Kanun laws. It has been argued that the "fundamental rule of the Kanun laws of Albanian clansman organization is Besa—a concept that simultaneously converges loyalty, fidelity, dignity and honor of one's word" (Bozinovich 2007). *Besa* is a sacred promise and an obligation to keep one's word. It also appears in the "rhapsodies" of the Albanians who migrated to southern Italy. In the famous song "Kostantini e Gerendina," the mother reminds her son of his *besa*: "Konstantin, my son, where is the *besa* you gave me, that you will bring Carendina back to me, Carendina, your sister? Your *besa* is under earth!" In the course of this rhapsody, Konstantin rises from the dead, fulfills his promise, and returns to his grave (Camaj 1989, xv).

Originally, the Albanian Kanun laws (and other canons) were not written down. Hence, there was no written contract of obligation. Albanians replaced the signature with a handshake, a gesture that took the place of the formal contract and became known as *besa*. To an Albanian, saying "I gave my *besa*" is the same as saying "I signed a contract." In addition, the obligation of *besa* is more than a material transaction; it is bound by honor. As an old Albanian saying goes, when an Albanian gives his word, or *besa,* he would sooner lose his son than break that *besa.* A of number Kanun articles focus on the concept of *besa* and the significance of giving an oath (a sacred promise) to an Albanian.

> Article 529. The oath is a religious utterance, by means of which a man, wishing to exculpate himself from a shameful accusation, must touch with his hand a token of faith while calling upon the name of God in testimony of the truth.

Article 530. This sort of oath is acceptable by the law of the mountains of Albania in order both to clear oneself of accusations and to make pacts binding.

Article 531. A spoken oath is not acceptable to the law or approved by it. In order to exculpate oneself from accusations it is absolutely necessary to take the oath upon a token of faith and to touch it with one's hand.

Article 532. The oath of the Albanians involves two aspects: a) To call upon God in testimony of the truth; b) To submit oneself to the weight of eternal punishment and to the temporal penalties prescribed by the Kanun. (Fox 1989, 120)

In a survey of 864 ethnic Albanians, respondents were asked to assess, on a seven-point scale, the behavior of a person who had committed revenge killing. Was this killing justified? The respondents were presented with the following true story:

A man was killed in broad daylight in Shkoder. The victim's brother went immediately to search for the killer. Fearing that he might be discovered, the killer knocked at the first door he found, asking for *besa* (protection). The head of the house, who was in fact the father of the victim (but did not recognize the killer of his son), welcomed the visitor. When the victim's brother returned, he recognized the killer. The victim's brother immediately shot their guest—the killer. After this incident, the victim's brother was arrested. He explained that he was just avenging the murder of his younger brother, according to the customary laws of his country. None of the parties had any previous criminal record.

This "revenge story" includes three important cultural elements: *besa*, hospitality, and revenge. Culturally speaking, the murder of the "guest" in this story is not justified. In Albanian culture, *besa* and hospitality are of the highest value, and they create a situation of inviolable trust. Consequently, if *besa* has been given, revenge cannot be taken. The guest should be treated well under any circumstances, because the Kanun stipulates that the life of a guest comes before the life of a brother. According to the Kanun, the murder could only have been justified if it had happened outside the house, before the killer was granted *besa*.

Most of the survey respondents (84 percent) stated that *besa* has a very significant meaning for them. Only 9 percent stated that *besa* is not important for them. However, the survey results showed no significant difference in the level of justification between people who said that *besa* is significant for them and those who said it is not. It seems that Albanians say they believe the word of honor is important, but it is not always valued in practice. Approximately 18 percent of the 864 respondents found the offender's behavior totally justified, while 14 percent remained undecided.

Interestingly, respondents' support for revenge killing was not related to their reading of the Kanun, but it was closely linked to the importance of cultural norms. Respondents who said that cultural norms were very important to them were more supportive of the brother than those who said that traditional culture was not important to them. Although this story goes against some core traditional values, such as breaking a *besa* and harming a guest, it simultaneously supports other values, such as avenging a murder and defending the family's honor. It is obvious that a significant part of the Albanian population believes in some traditional norms, but they do not know these norms well. When asked to identify the main motivation for the offender to kill the man who murdered his brother, 38 percent stated that he had to respect the Kanun laws. Most of the other respondents (44 percent) said the act was based solely on personal emotional drive.

One further observation could be noted in respect to the question of how justifiable the behavior of the offender would have been if the murder had happened outside the house, before *besa* was granted to the guest/killer: this revenge killing would have been committed in accordance with the Kanun. Respondents' support for the offender in this version rose by about 10 percent, with 26 percent stating that the gunman's behavior was (totally) justifiable, while 21 percent remained undecided.

The Word of Honor and Secrecy

In the traditional Albanian context, *besa*—the word of honor and a sacred promise—has been exceptionally well respected, and it represents one of the core elements promoted by the Kanun. Traditionally, once a word of honor has been given and an oath has been taken, an Albanian man cannot break his word, because it is believed that he will suffer eternal punishment if he does (Fox 1989, 120). Today, according to media and law enforcement officials, the concept of *besa*—although not in its pure form—appears to be used by ethnic Albanian organized crime groups to keep their members loyal and, above all, silent. Official and unofficial sources point out that *besa,* in the criminal context, may promote an extreme form of loyalty and solidarity in the face of authority. One of its tenets holds that it is deeply shameful to expose even one's deadliest enemy to the authorities.

Although some may disagree, law enforcement officials from Western countries have argued that crew members' loyalty, solidarity, and adherence to the so-called code of silence make infiltrating Albanian criminal groups almost impossible. According to a 2005 US Intelligence Report, "[Albanian crew] members are bound by a sense of secrecy and loyalty, coined *besa*. This informal oath causes members of criminal groups to be reluctant to cooperate with law enforcement personnel, thus making it extremely difficult and frustrating for authorities to dismantle the groups" (US Department of Justice 2005). Belgian law enforcement officials have reported similar problems regarding the Albanian code of silence. They claim that even when faced with real evidence about their identity in relation to the committed offenses or other members of the organization, Albanians continue to deny all accusations. The media, too, has made note of the concept of *besa:* "One of the problems facing law enforcement agencies is that Albanian criminals are governed by a code of honor that makes the Mafia's *omerta* resemble little more than a casual word of warning. The *Kanun* . . . covered . . . matters of honor, under which a *besa,* or pledge, must never be broken" (Cobain 2002).

This steadfast denial of all accusations was evident in a 2003–2004 Brussels smuggling case. One of the Albanian defendants, when confronted with wiretap evidence presented to the court, said he did not recognize his own voice and was unfamiliar with the content of the telephone calls that had been taped. Defendants in the Belgian Verviers case, when presented with indisputable DNA evidence about their blood relations, claimed they did not believe in DNA. And the Albanian organized crime figure Alex Rudaj remains silent in prison. Journalist Heldman reported in 2011 that Rudaj "never said a word" about the illegal activities of the so-called sixth crime family in New York, the Corporation (Heldman 2011a). In the case of Thaqi, Kurti, and Berisha in the United States, one of the interviewed offenders noted, "They arrested forty-nine members of our group but no one said a word. We all accepted guilty pleas because that is the manly thing to do. *Besa* means a lot. I am so proud of my group" (interview, New York, 2014).

Members of a criminal group who remain silent about their own crimes, as well as those of their associates, are considered honorable and trustworthy, at least within criminal circles, where such behavior earns them both status and respect. Although *besa* is not given during any formal ceremony, nor mentioned in written contracts, Albanian offenders often make use of it in an informal way when they want to join a group or make a deal.

Besa also creates a debt of honor, as illustrated in the 2003 Belgian "Hyseni" case, which involved an Albanian family-based organized crime group that had been trafficking drugs on the Columbia–Belgium–Italy route since 1996. In 2003 the group got involved in the prostitution market, buying Bulgarian and Romanian prostitution victims in Italy. The case file shows that one of the Albanian traffickers declared that he was obliged to collaborate with this Albanian criminal group because of a debt of honor to the criminal family that he had to fulfill.[9] His motivation was not profit per se.

A debt of honor also creates debt bondage. This often is used to entrap smuggling or trafficking victims who are obliged to give *besa* to criminals before they are transported abroad. Victims promise to pay off the cost of the smuggling trip by working free of charge for the criminals. Albanian trafficking networks also silence their victims by making them give *besa,* promising that they will not cooperate with authorities. Although the concept of *besa* has been an important traditional virtue, ethnic Albanian organized crime groups today manipulate it for their own purposes.[10]

The use of cultural tradition is an effective way of controlling both victims and members of criminal groups. The use of *besa* by Albanian crime groups has led those groups to be compared with the Sicilian mafia, since many scholars consider the obligation to maintain secrecy one of the most important duties associated with Sicilian "men of honor." In the Italian context, the cultural code that symbol-izes the obligation of secrecy is *omertà*, a code of honor common in areas of southern Italy where criminal organizations such as the Sicilian mafia, 'Ndrang-heta, and Camorra are strong. According to some scholars, it is a common mis-conception that the Sicilian mafia created or instituted *omertà*. Like the Albanian *besa*, *omertà* is a long-established code that appears to have been adopted by Sicil-ians long before the emergence of La Cosa Nostra. It is also deeply rooted in rural Crete, other areas of Greece, and many other places around the Mediterranean.

At the core of *omertà* lies the prohibition of cooperation with state authorities or reliance on their services. This applies even when one has been the victim of a crime. Such is the force of this prohibition that even when members are condemned for crimes they have not committed, they are supposed to serve their sentence with-out giving the police any information about the real criminals (Paoli 2003, 119).

According to one researcher on the Sicilian mafia, former public security officer Antonio Cutrera, *omertà* seals the lips of men even in their own defense and even when the accused is innocent of the crimes with which he has been charged. Cutrera quoted a Sicilian saying first uttered by a wounded man to his assailant: "If I live, I'll kill you. If I die, I forgive you" (Nelli 1981, 13). In Sicily, as in Albania, the suspicion of being an informant constitutes the blackest mark against manliness, according to Cutrera. Under *omertà*, each individual is obligated to look out for his own interests, and to prove his manliness by not appealing to legally consti-tuted authority for redress of personal grievances. A wronged person is expected to avenge himself, or to find a patron who will see to it that the job is done. Similar attitudes can be observed among some Albanian offenders, but certainly not all.

Although Albanian organized crime figures appear to have adopted the idea that one cannot break *besa*, this does not mean that *besa*, in its traditional form, is always respected in criminal circles. In court cases involving Albanian offenders, it is not uncommon for defectors to accept plea deals and join witness protection programs.

Some scholars argue that the Kanun laws cannot be used to benefit Albanian organized crime any more than the US Penal Code can be used to benefit US-based organized crime. An Albanian offender involved in extortion and gambling noted:

> I am serving more than a twenty years prison sentence because of jealous Albanians that like to talk. Let me tell you a joke. All sorts of ethnic groups are kept in purgatory in locked cages to keep them from getting up to Heaven, but Albanians don't need to be kept in locked cages, because they will do whatever it takes to prevent each other from getting up to Heaven. If an Albanian tries to escape the other Albanians will pull him right back into the cage. Albanians burn inside when they see someone doing well. Only some are good and want good for you. So if there is something in it for them they will talk. If they don't talk, it is not because of the Kanun. (interview, New Jersey, 2014)

Despite this, the notion of *besa* should not be disregarded entirely. Although *besa* traditionally meant only a sacred pledge, criminals groups have imbued it with an importance beyond its original meaning in order to achieve their goals.

Distrust and Silence

Of course, the word of honor, *besa,* is not the only reason why ethnic Albanian criminals and their victims stay quiet about crime. Another reason is a general disrespect for law enforcement agencies and institutionalized forms of justice—an outcome of a difficult history that embraced communist values and dislike of state authorities. Research findings indicate that many Albanian criminals do not care about ending up in prison; consequently, their behavior sometimes appears irrational to outsiders. For them, earning respect within their own criminal groups, clans, and families appears to be much more important than whether or not they serve a prison sentence.

According to US officials, if members of Albanian criminal organizations are arrested, they will serve their time rather than providing any information regarding their criminal cell and its members (US Department of Justice 2005). American officials argue that, culturally, law enforcement should be aware that Albanians have little trust and respect for authorities: "Some of these criminals have no problem with killing law enforcement officials" (US Department of Justice 2005). Offenders themselves also point out that they do not want to be associated with the police in any way, even when their lives are in serious danger. "Going to the police? Why? I can take care of myself. I don't want to be perceived as a traitor, a spy, a collaborator with [the] police," an Albanian organized crime figure told me (interview, Kosovo, 2007). Another offender serving in a New Jersey prison noted:

> No one will talk to you because they all think you are an FBI [agent]. You need to explain better. The government is a little bit racist and hard on immigrants. The FBI came busting into my house when I was in my boxers, and pointed a gun at my son's head. He was six years old then. The kid tried to run away because he was frightened. Why did they have to do that? I have no respect for them. No respect for the FBI or the media. They all twisted my words, and I don't trust them. (interview, New Jersey, 2014)

Even entire communities sometimes stay silent about the criminals in their midst. During one interview, Vladimir Sharovic of the Macedonian Ministry of Interior, reported that ethnic Albanian criminals in Macedonia often get support from their ethnic communities. This makes infiltration into these groups almost impossible. The communities often provide support to the criminals because they are related, or because they receive various other benefits. For example, criminals may provide community members with protection or financial support, paying for the construction of local roads, supplying local villages with water and electricity, or loaning them money.[11] In this way the criminals gain the trust of the local

population, and they create a form of social dependency that discourages cooperation with law enforcement agencies. If people cooperate with the police, the
community might perceive them as traitorous, dishonorable, or cowardly.

Crime victims, meanwhile, often distrust law enforcement authorities, and fail
to cooperate with them, because so many are involved in criminal activities themselves. For example, despite setting up a special antitrafficking police unit, the
Albanian Ministry of Public Order failed to follow up on high-profile trafficking
and corruption investigations. According to a UK Home Office Report on Albania, "Local police often tipped off traffickers when raids were scheduled. On one
occasion, a police supervisor checking on his men found them helping traffickers
with their boats" (UK Home Office 2004). An Albanian immigrant and former
police officer currently residing in New York noted: "There is crime everywhere
and that is normal, but what is disturbing about Albania is that many criminals
either get government jobs and are never prosecuted, or they simply 'disappear.' So
how can one trust the system?" (interview, New York, 2014).

And in 2014, in the United States, a thirty-four-year-old NYPD officer of Albanian origin, Besnik Llakatura, was indicted, along with two other men, in an
alleged extortion scheme that saw them threaten at least one Queens restaurant
owner. Shortly after opening his new business in Astoria, an unidentified Albanian
restaurant owner allegedly was approached by Albanian Redinel Dervishaj. Dervishaj told the restaurant owner he had to pay to "operate in our neighborhood."
Llakatura, reportedly a friend of the restaurant owner, insisted he had to pay
because "these people run Astoria" (Goldstein and Secret 2013).

Surprisingly, the restaurant owner and co-owner then went to the FBI. The
agency gave them marked bills to pay off Llakatura and the others. They paid the
alleged mobsters twenty-four thousand dollars over the course of five months,
with six thousand dollars of the collected cash going to Llakatura himself. "The
defendants told their victims they offered 'protection,' but in reality, they peddled
fear and intimidation through the Albanian community—their community—of
Queens," said US Attorney Loretta Lynch in an FBI press release. "When one victim turned to law enforcement for help, he was betrayed again by a corrupt officer
on the take, who turned his back on his badge, his oath, and his friend in exchange
for extortion money in his pocket" (FBI 2013).

Much of the success of organized crime groups in the Balkans and elsewhere
results from the many partnerships they have struck with police, customs agency,
and border guards, along with the political class. Meanwhile, general distrust of
authorities increases the likelihood that crime victims will remain silent.

Fear and Shame

Often, however, investigative files and interviews indicate that being silent about
crime has nothing to do with honor, reputation, or (dis)respect. Instead, it is sim-

ply fear that keeps members of criminal groups, communities, and individual victims silent. Scholars who study the Italian mafia have debated for years whether *omertà* should be understood as an expression of social consensus surrounding the mafia or whether it is instead a pragmatic response based primarily on fear. The point is made in a popular Sicilian proverb: *Cu è surdu, orbu e taci, campa cent'anni 'mpaci* ("He who is deaf, blind, and silent will live a hundred years in peace"). In the Italian context, many have linked the notion of secrecy to that of violence. In mafia consortia, Paoli (2003) argues, the link between secrecy and violence is indissoluble; violence leads to secrecy and this, in turn, compels the use of violence. Similar questions surround the Albanian organized crime phenomenon: is it fear or honor and *besa* that keep Albanian criminals and their victims silent?

The traditional *besa* appears to be one of the tools misrepresented by criminals to strengthen the level of secrecy within their criminal groups, although it is actually violence and the fear of revenge that keeps criminal members and victims silent and cooperative.[12] In the Krasniqi case in the United States, for example, the FBI agent in charge tried to enlist Franc Shestani to trap the Canadians who had kidnapped one of the Krasniqi brothers. Shestani agreed, but when the kidnappers later called him to see what was going on, Shestani just kept on repeating, in Albanian, "Hello! Hello! Hello!" He was reportedly hysterical and scared that the Krasniqis would think he had cooperated with the police. According to investigative journalist Heldman, Shestani told the FBI: "Kill me, just kill me now. You have to understand, I have family. You don't know what they can do to my family. They'll kill me if I cooperate" (Heldman 2011a).

Similarly, in a smuggling case (2001–2003), an Albanian trafficker told the Belgian police that he was afraid for his and his family's lives. For this reason, he would not dare to reveal any names. He believed that his brother-in-law had been murdered because "he said too much," and he did not want the same thing to happen to him and his family.

Moreover, police described a brutal 2005 murder in Macedonia as possible blood revenge. Mile Petkovic, the owner of a bar called Brus, was shot fifty times with Kalashnikovs. The attack took place in the middle of the day in front of about two hundred people. Petkovic previously had filed complaints, and it appears that his murder was revenge for the death of one of the killers' relatives, Nedzmedin Ajeti, who had been wounded a few months earlier in Petkovic's bar and died as a result of those injuries.[13] Among the two hundred witnesses, not one dared to identify Petkovic's killers, most likely out of fear. The witnesses were immediately terrorized into a code of silence (*Vest* 2005). Less than two months before Petkovic's murder, two people had shot at his house with automatic weapons and thrown grenades while only women were present. Although, as mentioned earlier, it is not permitted to kill a family member in his own home, or to kill women or children, the would-be killers did not appear to care about the specifics of Kanun rules in this case.

The Petkovic family relied on the authorities for protection, but the police never officially charged the suspect, Dzelal (Dzeljo) Ajeti, and the murderer was never arrested. The Petkovic family notified the press that Ajeti's family had given *besa* that for one of their heads (the murder of Nedzmedin Ajeti) they would take two lives— that is, two males from Petkovic's family would be killed (Chancharevic 2009).

Ethnic Albanian offenders do not hesitate to use threats and extreme violence to keep even their own members, people from their own communities, or victims absolutely silent. Throughout the years they have gained a reputation for being fearless and vengeful, so it is no wonder that it is difficult for law enforcement officials to obtain information about their criminal network or its alleged leaders.

Fear also keeps the victims of Albanian offenders silent. Trafficked women, for example, are threatened by their Albanian exploiters and dare not say anything to the police. Their families are afraid to report traffickers, because such action might result in revenge killings. Threats of reprisal against victims' families are a serious issue, because they keep victims' families from seeking revenge.

In the Skenderi case, the Romanian victim had two children. The criminals threatened to kill the victim's children if she spoke out. Ultimately, the Romanian victim's throat was cut, allegedly because "she couldn't be trusted." According to medical files, she was beaten on her back, arms, and face, where she had numerous wounds. Ruth Hopkins, an independent researcher from the Netherlands, explains that trafficking victims themselves will never say anything about their traffickers. She claims that organized crime groups use fear, respect, and moral justification, often associated with the Kanun, to terrorize victims into upholding a code of a silence (Hopkins 2004).

In the "Ali" case (1997–2002), the Albanian victim, Bruna, was married to an Albanian pimp, Ali. Bruna lived in Ali's village in Albania, and she met Ali when she was a minor, and then became his girlfriend. In 1997, Ali and Bruna left Albania for Belgium. He asked her to prostitute herself in Antwerp. Belgian police intervened, and Bruna was repatriated to Albania. But she did not return to her parents; instead, she went to live with Ali's parents. After some time, Ali and his family in Albania arranged for Bruna to obtain a Greek passport. One of Ali's "friends" then put her to work in a prostitution bar, this time in Holland. Again, after police intervention, she was repatriated to Albania. At this point Ali came to Albania to marry her. The couple once again relocated to Belgium, and soon Ali forced his wife back into prostitution, this time in Brussels. He became increasingly violent with her, cutting her with a knife, threatening her with a pistol, and burning her arms. Despite all this, Bruna confirmed that she had sent eighteen million *lekë* (138,000 euros) from the prostitution business to Ali's family in Albania.

During questioning, the Belgian police were struck by Bruna's nervousness. "I am the reason why the people you have arrested are in prison right now," she told them. "They come from the same village as me in Albania. I really don't want my family to have problems because of me." Bruna wrote a letter to the judge in which she claimed that her husband had never forced her into prostitution. However, the police knew where the money had been sent. Ali was charged with human trafficking for the purpose of prostitution, as well as for being part of a criminal organization.

Gender issues also can silence crime victims, contributing to the overall secrecy of Albanian criminal groups. Men, particularly those from a culture with a traditional view of masculinity, do not want to admit they have been victimized. They fear that such a disclosure may lead to perceptions of diminished masculinity. Trafficked women who suffer sexual abuse also are reluctant to seek assistance, because of the shame they feel and the way that society may stigmatize them. They are afraid that their experiences will bring shame on their families back home, and that their families will renounce them. These sociocultural elements contribute to the level of secrecy within and around an Albanian criminal organization, allowing the group to operate without hindrance.

Valor and Loyalty

The relationships between members of ethnic Albanian criminal groups are often constructed on the principle of "generalized reciprocity." This principle, emerging from traditional culture, presupposes altruistic attitudes, often with no prospect of short-term rewards. It is built on heroic themes of honor, valor, solidarity, and loyalty. As such, it strengthens mutual aid within criminal and other subcultures. Valor and loyalty are, in fact, among the most traditional of manly virtues—not only in Albania and Kosovo but also in other traditional societies, such as those across the Mediterranean. In 1885, Tommaso Colacino (cited in Paoli 2003, 81), discussing the Fratellanza of Favara (the Brotherhood of Favara, a mafia-type group), stated that by turning upside down all moral meaning, "mutual aid was a very important law in the association, because its statute affirmed that all the affiliates were to help and protect each other in case of damage or injury, without hesitation, without dislike for anyone, *sicut cadaver.*"

Valor is emphasized within organized crime groups even more than among ordinary citizens, and it is usually connected with a high regard for loyalty. According to criminologist David Matza (1999, 157), valor and loyalty "are among the traditional martial virtues. They are bound together by a conception of reputation. Reputation reveals a concern with how one appears before others, and the urgency of maintaining it depends on the depth of belief in group solidarity. Thus, valour is most assiduously pursued in groups that celebrate the precepts of loyalty." This certainly is true of ethnic Albanian organized crime groups.

Ritualized or contractual agreements with regard to mutual aid and loyalty are uncommon within Albanian organized crime groups, yet the principle of generalized reciprocity remains at the heart of Albanian criminality. The manly virtue of helping compatriots in need has been part of Albanian culture for centuries, and it apparently has remained in the mind-set of many Albanians as a highly valued social rule. The Kanun, for example, openly promotes solidarity and loyalty among family and clan members, as well as among ethnic Albanians in general. Article 609 of the Kanun states, "At any time of the day or night, one must be ready to receive a guest with bread and salt and an open heart" (Fox 1989, 132).

Besmir, the Kosovo Albanian organized crime figure who served a lengthy prison sentence in Western Europe, described a situation in which he "ended up in prison because of a friend."

> My Albanian friend was dating this girl, and he was falling in love. But after some time she ran away with some Moroccan guy. My friend went crazy. I told him, it is not worth it to run after her. She is a prostitute. Yet he was so stubborn and really wanted the girl back. He was begging me that I send some people to "take care" of the Moroccan guy. I didn't want to make scandals and to start a war for a prostitute. But at some point my friend said that I am afraid of the Moroccan guy, and that is why I don't want to go and take his woman back. That was the end for me. I wasn't afraid of the guy at all. It was a ridiculous thing to say. But, man, when he said that, I just got up and said, "Let's go right now, let me show you how afraid I am!"
>
> I didn't go there to take the girl. It was just to show my friend what I am capable of doing. We went to the Moroccan guy's bar. I wanted to kill this guy. My Albanian friend found his girl and left with her, and I wanted to find the guy. But I think someone told him that we were coming so he ran away.
>
> A couple of days after the incident, I was at my house and my mother told me that two people were looking for me, and that they didn't look like any of my friends. I knew it was the police. There were fifty police officers, special forces . . . surrounding my house. . . . They said I had kidnapped a girl and almost killed her. A setup.
>
> Thinking about it, I should have ignored my friend's provocations, but at that time, hey, I didn't want to take shit from anyone. We do all for our friends. (interview, Kosovo, 2007)

The obligation of ethnic Albanian people to maintain solidarity applies not only to affiliates and their families, but at least in principle to all Albanian brothers. Besmir was an alleged supporter of the KLA during the Kosovo conflict, and he continued to be supportive of the ex-KLA fighters even after he was released from prison. His "Robin Hood" mentality resembles that of other Kosovo Albanian "godfathers." In the Kosovo context, being loyal to your own kind appears to be highly valued. During one interview, Besmir explained:

> I don't care about politics. However, I have been helping the KLA fighters financially during the war, because I believe in my people and my country. I also wanted so

much to be in Kosovo while the conflict was going on. But I couldn't, because at that time I was in prison. P [another notorious Kosovo Albanian offender] is also helping the KLA fighters. Even now he helps forgotten KLA veterans . . . buying food, medicines . . . for them. There are some disabled people. . . . For example, my friend Gjon here was a KLA fighter himself . . . but look at him now! He doesn't get any money, and he has no job. He has to work for twenty-five euros per day in a discotheque. The current government doesn't care about the fighters. Nothing has changed since the Milošević regime. All these people that are now in power are the mafia. They care only about their own interests. (interview, Kosovo, 2007)

Because of their friend-enemy discourse and distrust of outsiders, ethnic Albanians have long considered loyalty to one's own kind a key virtue. People are not judged by the means they use to achieve certain goals, but rather by their charisma and exaggerated sense of honor, loyalty, and solidarity. An Albanian who acts honorably toward his compatriots, who remains loyal to them and gives them both moral and material support, is highly valued in this society.

The conflicts in the Balkan region allowed charismatic criminals to flourish within a dysfunctional society. Many of the distinctive features of the Balkan conflicts are attributable to the use of irregular combat groups, or paramilitaries. These criminal combatants simultaneously protected and exploited their compatriots, trading both gunfire and consumer goods with their "enemies." In this manner they were able to enrich themselves while also serving their own causes.

During the postconflict period, local communities in the Balkans relied on homegrown criminals for protection. Many of these criminals quickly gained the admiration and respect of their communities by shifting attention away from their brutal crimes and turning it toward all they had done for the good of their society. Although the crimes committed by these "patriotic bandits" caused more social harm than good, the short-term rewards for the people they protected made these criminals heroes in their eyes. Police sources and confidential files from international police agencies show that the most powerful ethnic Albanian organized crime figures made sacrifices for their compatriots during the Balkan conflicts in order to obtain power and operate without hindrance.

The real acts of solidarity among Albanian criminals, particularly when their accomplices are arrested or imprisoned, can be observed in court cases. When one notorious Albanian smuggler of illegal immigrants was imprisoned in 2003 in Belgium, his ex-wife continued to receive money from criminal groups in Albania and the United Kingdom, the destination of his illegal human "cargo." This appears to be a typical scenario within the Albanian context.

However, the duty to be loyal to imprisoned members of a criminal organization works both ways. The imprisoned member should also remain loyal to his group. While the free members take care of the imprisoned man's family, he remains silent about the group's crimes. This is an important aspect of the principle of reciprocal solidarity. As Besmir reported: "I was put in jail for six months, awaiting my trial. Then I was unjustly sentenced to fifteen years' imprisonment. All because of my friends. Some got three months in detention before trial, and some got two years. [But] I never said a word against my friends or against anyone else. I am not a coward" (interview, Kosovo, 2007)

Paoli (2003, 86) reports a similar attitude among Italian mafiosi: "The duty of solidarity among affiliates is supreme, especially toward members who are on the run or in prison. This kind of duty constitutes a basic feature of the mafia community." Today, according to Paoli (2003), the prestige and authority of any mafia figure is measured by his ability to provide assistance to fugitives, to support the expenses of imprisoned members and their families, and to guarantee these prisoners short-term sentences by intimidating or corrupting judges. Although they are not formally written, similar rules apply to ethnic Albanian organized crime groups. Police records show that many Albanian criminals do support their imprisoned affiliates and do intimidate and corrupt judges in order to ensure shorter prison sentences for them.

GLORIFYING MEN OF (DIS)HONOR?

While it is often believed that the principle of generalized reciprocity obliges Italian mafia chiefs to behave altruistically toward those in the organization's lower ranks, it also enables them to exploit their subordinates in order to achieve their own short-term goals. Paoli (2003, 83) explains: "Bound by mafia fraternization contracts, the 'soldiers' of both Cosa Nostra and the 'Ndrangheta have no choice other than to comply with the orders of their superiors, no matter how 'evil' these may be."

Mafia chiefs are not the only exploitative actors. There are many cases of subordinates breaking the code of silence for their personal benefit. Joe Valachi was one of the first to betray the *omertà*. In 1963 he spoke publicly about the existence of the Italian mafia and testified before the US Congress. Among the most famous mafia *pentiti* is Tommaso Buscetta, the first important state witness against La Cosa Nostra. Buscetta helped Judge Giovanni Falcone to understand the inner workings of the Cosa Nostra; the Sicilian Mafia Commission, or *Cupola;* and the leadership of the Sicilian mafia.

Although being disloyal is not common among members of clan-based ethnic Albanian organized crime groups, it is naïve to believe that Albanian groups are based on absolute solidarity. Loyalty, mutual respect, and hierarchy may not exist in all groups. In general, criminals are not trustworthy people. They make money through deception and crime, and they take advantage of others. The fact that they break codes of silence and occasionally cooperate with police officials or other enemies should not come as a surprise. Generally speaking, while the code of silence is often respected within ethnic Albanian organized crime groups for different reasons, it is not adhered to as strictly as the media and some scholars have reported.[14]

Experts participating in a workshop on ethnic Albanian organized crime groups stressed the distinction between Albanian organized crime groups operating in the Balkan countries and those operating elsewhere in Europe.[15] The group agreed that in Western Europe, ethnic Albanians generally stay closer to one another, place a greater value on the concept of secrecy, and keep a lower profile than groups operating in the Balkans. In Western Europe, at least, it appears that Albanian groups are more cautious. Because they often operate in closed social networks, it is hard to infiltrate them. In the Balkan countries, where society sometimes reinforces criminality, Albanians want to flaunt their wealth. They seek public recognition of how rich and powerful they are, both within criminal circles and among ordinary people. This is how groups within Albania gain "reputation" and impose their influence on other groups. Such attitudes make the groups less secretive and easier to infiltrate.

Macedonian law enforcement official Vladimir Sharovic gave several examples of how ethnic Albanian members of organized crime groups, when pressured by the police, exposed their criminal associates, including their own relatives. Such cooperative attitudes, according to police officials, depend on the "deals" police officials can offer offenders in different countries. One official argued that when "offered a really good deal, Albanians start to talk. No discussion about that" (interview, Macedonia, 2008). Gus Xhudo further explained the US situation: "Prison doesn't scare Albanian offenders. They don't care if they are in prison, so why talk? Deportation on the other hand, from my experience, may affect their decision to talk" (interview, New York, 2014).

Albanian prosecutor Olsjan Cela stated: "I don't understand this myth surrounding Albanian organized crime groups and their code of silence. Every time Albanians are imprisoned, it is probably because they talked too much over the phone and said everything about the group, their crimes and methods. Where is the secrecy here? They are the most talkative criminals ever, and they have still not learned from their mistakes" (Arsovska and Sartorius 2008).

Numerous examples from the United States, starting in the mid-1970s, also demonstrate that when presented with a favorable deal, many Albanian criminals will take it. For example, recall the testimonies of Shestani and Rrapo against the Krasniqi brothers.

The case of John Edward Alite, aka Johnny Alletto, also illustrates this point.[16] As explained in chapter 3, Alite was a friend and crew leader for John A. Gotti in the 1980s and 1990s, but because his family is Albanian, not Italian, Alite could not become a made member of the Gambino organization.

After his relationship with Gotti and the Gambino leadership soured in 1994, Alite was asked to move to Tampa, Florida, and then, as federal racketeering indictments were handed down for his group's activities in the Tampa area, he fled to Rio de Janeiro. He lived there for ten months before authorities arrested him. He served two years in prison in Brazil while fighting extradition, but was eventually handed over to federal authorities in Tampa, Florida, for trial in 2006.

After being extradited from Brazil, Alite was convicted of several counts of murder, racketeering, and other charges stemming from his activities with the Gambino organization in Florida. The maximum penalty for the charges was life in prison—but Alite agreed to testify in the trial of Gambino family enforcer Charles Carneglia, who was found guilty of four murders and is serving a life sentence. "John Alite provided information that materially contributed to the conviction of numerous members and associates of the Gambino organized crime family," assistant US attorney Roger Burlingame wrote to the judge (Marzulli 2011).

After the successful trial against Carneglia, federal prosecutors made Alite a witness in their unsuccessful racketeering trial against Gotti. They charged that Gotti ordered the murders of George Grosso and Bruce Gotterup, whom prosecutors said were part of the drug ring that Gotti and Alite operated in Queens (Gendar and Siemaszko 2009). But after eleven days of deliberations, the jury was deadlocked and the judge declared a mistrial. After the trial, jurors said they had not trusted prosecution witnesses, particularly Alite (Porpora and Mcshane 2009; Feuer 2009).

Alite has kept a low profile since he was released from prison in 2012, after completing a hundred-month sentence for his part in Gotterup's murder. He did not deliver a conviction against Gotti Junior, whose trial ended in a hung jury, but his testimony did result in guilty pleas by other crew members. "Every day I walk out the door I check out everything," Alite told *Daily News* reporter John Marzulli in 2013. "I'm not going to be one of those guys who gets killed in the street if I can help it, but I'm not gonna go live in Utah.

"I get up at 6:30 now looking for work; I get depressed, I go to therapy," he said about working construction. "I'm trying to keep pushing forward.

"I know there's guys on the street who want me," Alite added. "They're patient. They want me to get comfortable. I know how easy it is to get somebody" (Marzulli 2013).

Despite the number of Albanian defectors, we must acknowledge the evidence pointing to the secretive nature of Albanian organized crime groups. Secrecy, overall, remains an important attribute of the Albanian criminal subculture.

· · ·

The boundaries of ethnic Albanian organized crime groups are not as clearly defined as originally believed. Group membership often shifts. Members of Albanian criminal subcultures neither undergo ritual ceremonies nor sign fraternization contracts in order to become members. Ethnic Albanian organized crime groups are formed more spontaneously than, for example, the Sicilian Cosa Nostra, although they should not be viewed as ad hoc coalitions.

Albanian organized crime groups have selectively utilized some prominent cultural themes that originate in a wider cultural context in order to justify criminal behavior, bring order to the criminal organization, and neutralize moral proscriptions. The values and norms implicit in the fluid subcultures of delinquency depart from conventional traditions; however, the relationship between a subculture of delinquency and the wider cultural context should not be summarized in terms of opposition.

Like ordinary citizens, ethnic Albanian criminals neither know all aspects of their customary Kanun laws nor respect these codes in equal measure. Consequently, it would be wrong to argue that the original Kanun is the code of conduct followed by ethnic Albanian organized crime groups. The Kanun is an old, customary code. It has never been a "mafia code" applied by criminal organizations. Albanian criminal organizations selectively use elements of this social code for their own criminal purposes. Some codes have been rationally applied or rejected by the criminal groups, while others have been strongly embedded in their mindset, leading them to act in sometimes irrational ways. The impact of the media and popular culture also has been significant in shaping criminal views and affecting decision-making processes.

Criminals often fuel and exploit elements of the mythology surrounding them in order to gain a reputation within criminal circles and to increase their power of intimidation. The codes applied by Albanian criminal subcultures have taken on a life of their own and are only partially affected by traditional and popular culture. Practice also shows that many of the codes applied by these groups do not necessarily serve their best interests. Despite their tough image, Albanian "sensation-gatherers" are affected by a series of emotions, including fear and pride. Illegal forms of excitement represent a break with the banalities of everyday life, particularly for the younger generation of offenders. Some Albanian organized crime figures inhabit a world where old normative systems are manipulated during the act of transgression.

The behavior of some Albanian organized crime figures has led some Western European law enforcement officials to describe Albanian offenders as irrational, and Albanian society as criminogenic. But these offenders' actions cannot be predicted by looking only at Western normative rationality—that is to say, calculation of losses and gains based purely on economic terms or normative interests. Examples of so-called irrational behaviors include being vengeful and extremely violent when there is no need for such measures; being preposterously secretive about certain crimes, even when confronted with hard evidence; exposing wealth and drawing attention to oneself; choosing a life-term prison sentence rather than providing information to officials; helping associates although doing so likely will land you in jail; needlessly getting involved in risky crimes with low rewards; recklessly spending all your profits; threatening law enforcement agents; and having no regard for human life. Emotions, passions, culture, social networks, and power are all extremely important behavior-shaping factors in the Albanian context.

Finally, culture is not a static phenomenon. The culture(s) of various ethnic Albanian criminal organizations, as well as their conduct norms, might change as the sociocultural context in which they operate changes. This is not always the case with Albanian organized crime groups; it appears that many Albanians tend to stick to old habits and not learn from their mistakes. For example, the recent developments in Albania, where a series of mafia-style attacks have killed or injured prosecutors, judges, and businessmen, illustrate that some Albanian offenders continue to use extreme violence.

Nevertheless, some groups have indeed adjusted to a new environment. According to Western European law enforcement agencies, in order to reduce the social impact of their crimes, certain ethnic Albanian crime groups in Western Europe have tended to use less violence during the past ten years, particularly against law enforcement officials and ordinary citizens.

Today, Albanians take advantage of their violent image, which allows them to use less violence than before. This more moderate approach has enabled some groups to maintain a slightly lower profile. Many Albanian offenders have started to treat their prostitution victims as partners-in-crime, giving them more money and freedom. This observed pattern of behavior indicates that at least some ethnic Albanian organized crime groups are able to adjust to the external environment and the sociocultural context in which they operate.

Chapter 6

SEX, GUNS, AND EXTORTION

The Albanian is not born of a womb, but of a [rifle's] trigger.
—ALBANIAN PROVERB

Ethnic Albanian organized crime groups have been actively involved in criminal activities such as trafficking of women for sexual exploitation, extortion, and selling and buying illicit firearms. It also appears that they have used cultural values other than valor, mutual aid, and secrecy to justify these crimes, to negate the intent of their actions, and to dehumanize their victims.

Careful examination of the cultural influences behind some common Albanian criminal activities may help to clarify the sensationalized relationship between culture and organized crime. For example, according to traditional Albanian culture, male honor is closely linked to the possession of firearms and the courage to use them. It is considered a dishonor for a man not to possess his own weapon, or to have his weapons taken away. Does this cultural attitude encourage Albanians to get involved in the arms trade?

In addition, the Kanun places great importance on the submissive role of women in Albanian society, as well as on the masculinity of men. Albanian society has a long patriarchal history in which women are taught to obey their husbands. Should one blame the Kanun laws for the increased involvement of Albanians in trafficking women for sexual exploitation?

Earlier I argued that we should differentiate between decision-making processes rooted in interests and those driven by values. From a rational choice perspective, the rationalization process includes the immediate need for criminal gain, the risk of apprehension, the severity of punishment if caught, and the (potential) value of the criminal enterprise. This approach, however, does not necessarily acknowledge that values and emotions associated with sociocultural and political factors may significantly affect human decision-making processes. Also, it doesn't acknowledge that male and female decision strategies may vary significantly. With this in mind, let's elaborate on the subtle yet dynamic relationship between culture, both traditional and popular; emotions; gender; and select Albanian organized crime activities.

TAKEN

"Eight years ago, I was kidnapped from my village in north Albania," said Drita, an Albanian woman now in her late twenties. "A man from a nearby village who I saw a couple of times before I was kidnapped did this" (interview, Belgium, 2008).

Drita explained that she did not know the man very well, but she did talk to him a few times before the incident she described. She insisted that she was kidnapped and denied accusations made by other people in her village that an Albanian man seduced her into leaving her village and her family. "He brought me first to Italy and then to Belgium. Once in Belgium, I ended up in the prostitution market in Antwerp. I was abused, beaten, sold, and resold. It was horrible what I had to go through." There was much sadness in Drita's eyes.

> I was saved by Payoke [a victim shelter] in Antwerp in 2003. They got me out of the brothels. I stayed a couple of nights in the shelter and Patsi [the director] said she would help me, and she did. The police helped me, too. Now I am enrolled in a school program here in Belgium. I have a normal job.
>
> I go to Albania from time to time because I have a daughter there. She is ten years old now. She was left behind with the family of my husband. However, my husband and his family don't want to have anything to do with me. They think I left them and escaped with another man. My husband's family never liked me, and I am sure they have convinced everyone that I just left them all because I didn't care. Even my daughter seems to think I left her.
>
> We were very poor, that is true; but I would never leave my two-year-old daughter like that. Never.

In 2008 Drita was still fighting a custody battle, trying to prove to the Albanian courts that she was a victim of human trafficking and not an irresponsible mother. Her story is not unique. Many Albanian women who are the victims of human trafficking are rejected by their families after being repatriated to their home countries. Also, many women are not as "lucky" as Drita; they die at the hands of their exploiters as a result of abuse or overdose.

Women from Albania are not the only ones who have been kidnapped by Albanian traffickers. One of the biggest human trafficking cases in Great Britain involved Albanian Luan Plakici, introduced in chapter 3. He lured women from Eastern Europe with the promise of money and jobs in the West, then kidnapped them and smuggled them into Britain with false passports. Plakici even married one of the teenagers, but on her wedding night she was forced to sell her body to other men.

After clearing immigration, the women usually were taken to a flat in north London before being supplied to brothels. Any dissent resulted in beatings, rape, and warnings that their families back home were in danger. Plakici's exploitation was exposed thanks to a twenty-four-year-old Romanian woman who escaped from a flat, jumped over a garden fence, and flagged down a police car (McKillop and Wilson 2003).

A nineteen-year-old Russian said to have links to Plakici also fled a brothel, in Glasgow, Scotland. A student from St. Petersburg, she said she had been abducted, drugged, and raped after responding to a newspaper advertisement for dancers while on holiday in Brussels. She told of being sold to three pimps in London, of being forced to return to prostitution within a week of having an abortion, and of being sold to an Albanian in Glasgow, where she was forced to have sex with his friends, as well as with customers (McKillop and Wilson 2003).

Plakici's victims were warned that escape was futile. They were told that they had no option but to work as prostitutes, entertaining as many as twenty men each day, seven days a week, in order to pay back their eight-thousand-pound "travel bill." The women were sold—or contracted out—to Albanians operating across the United Kingdom.

After a two-month trial at Wood Green Crown Court, in north London, Plakici was convicted of fifteen offenses, including seven counts of human trafficking. During the trial he admitted facilitating the illegal entry into the United Kingdom of between fifty and sixty young women who were lured from loving families with promises of a wealthier life.

The involvement of Albanians in human trafficking captured the world's attention, and in 2008 an English-language French action thriller called *Taken* was released. The film further reinforced the violent image of Albanian traffickers in Europe and beyond.

In the film, an American man travels to Europe to rescue his teenage daughter and her friend, who have been abducted by violent Albanian traffickers shortly after arriving for a vacation in Paris. The man learns that, as a virgin, his teenage daughter is very valuable on the black market. Although he eventually locates his daughter, her friend is found dead of an overdose (together with other captive teens), and he discovers that a French intelligence officer has been cooperating with the violent Albanian trafficking ring.

The movie became quite popular, and in 2012 *Taken 2* was released. Like the *Godfather* movie series for the Italian mafia, *Taken* has had a significant impact on the public image of Albanian traffickers. Some European NGOs that work on trafficking issues have noted that the movie accurately depicts the violent methods of Albanian human traffickers, who traditionally have engaged in kidnappings and used extreme violence against their victims. However, an Albanian organized crime offender from New York, involved in traditional mafia activities such as illegal gambling and extortion, clarifies:

> During my trial *Taken* hurt me a lot. The jury put me in the same basket with human traffickers and abusers of teenage kids. People who do the prostitution thing must not have kids. I have daughters. To think of someone doing that to them makes me sick. So there are those who get involved in human and drug trafficking and hurt kids, but those are the younger criminals, not me for sure. I was very upset that the name of the FBI unit that investigated my case was called "Balkan unit—Prostitution and Drugs." I wasn't involved in either of those things but they put me in this same category. (interview, New Jersey, 2014)

In the following sections, I will elaborate on the role of culture in selecting, on the one hand, more modern types of criminal activities, such as human trafficking for sexual exploitation, and on the other hand, more traditional mafia-type activities, such as extortion and arms trade.

TRAFFICKING, EXPLOITATION, AND SUBORDINATION

The Woman Is a Sack

In the mid-1990s, ethnic Albanian offenders in Europe developed a reputation for being some of the most notorious pimps and traffickers of women and children for sexual exploitation. Until about 1998 it was common for Albanian women to be trafficked by Albanian men from their own localities.[1] Victim databases from Belgium, the United Kingdom, France, and Italy confirm this trend. For years, Albania, Kosovo, and Macedonia were regarded as source and transit countries for trafficked women, but more recently they also have come to be regarded as countries of destination.

An investigation of sixty court files from Belgium show that about 85 percent of the trafficking cases from the 1990s and early 2000s involved family-based criminal groups coming originally from southern Albania and western Macedonia, areas populated mainly by ethnic Albanians. A smaller number of groups were from northern Albania and Kosovo. One police report noted that the trafficking of women for sexual exploitation is frequently associated with criminal groups from the city of Berat, in south-central Albania. A Belgian liaison officer explained that the Berat groups were recruiting local women almost exclusively and turning them to prostitution. It is estimated that in the period between 1992 and 2007, more than four hundred girls from Berat were traded and worked as prostitutes throughout Europe and beyond. Some 15 percent of these girls were minors, according to a law enforcement official interviewed in 2007.

The number of Albanian prostitutes abroad has been estimated at thirty thousand, but until 1998 Albanian authorities were reluctant to admit that many were victims of trafficking (Renton 2001; Hysi 2005). "The Albanian state and the police have ignored this crime, and I fear that these wealthy men will get off. There is a lot of pressure and money to set them free," said Gjin Lleshi, the father of several trafficked children (Renton 2001, 3).

A 2005 study by the Ministry of Public Order of Albania indicated that more than five thousand Albanian women and girls were trafficked into prostitution in the last decade. The Albanian Council of Ministers sets the figure at eight thousand. Yet according to the Italian press, there are almost fifteen thousand Albanian prostitutes in Italy and another six thousand in Greece (Hysi 2005: 548). More than 30 percent of them are under eighteen years old.[2]

The Italian Ministry of Interior reported that 168 foreign prostitutes were killed in 2000, mainly Albanian and Nigerian women murdered by their pimps (Hysi 2005). In Italy in the late 1990s, around 20 percent of imprisoned Albanians were being held for prostitution-related offenses (Jamieson and Sily 1998).

Sources indicate that ethnic Albanian offenders control more than 75 percent of the prostitution network in London and other cities in the United Kingdom (Bennetto 2002). Police raids on brothels in London's Soho section found that approximately 70 percent of the women working there were Albanian or Kosovo Albanian. Nearly a decade ago it was predicted that Russian organized crime would seek to exert influence over the British vice trade. Instead, Albanian gangs have taken control.

Around the turn of the twenty-first century, ethnic Albanian criminal groups began to expand and become involved in buying Romanian and Moldovan women in the Balkans. They smuggled these women into Albania through Montenegro and Kosovo, then moved them to Italy and other Western European destinations.[3]

The victims of ethnic Albanian criminal groups often were kept as virtual slaves while their families in Albania or Kosovo were subjected to various forms of retaliation. As illustrated in the Luan Plakici case, they often reported experiencing abuse, such as being raped or beaten.[4]

In addition to extreme violence, criminal groups use other methods to recruit women for prostitution. Most often, Albanian victims have been taken in with a promise of marriage—the traditional "lover-boy" method. Police files from Belgium show that Albanian pimps often married the Albanian women they brought to Western countries for prostitution, especially during the 1990s. Upon their arrival in Italy, the husband would convince the girl to prostitute herself by claiming that he couldn't find a job to support them. Alternatively, he might sell her to another pimp. Albanian girls who have fallen victim to this ruse often refer to their shock at their husband's sudden transformation from loving spouse to violent pimp (Renton 2003, 20–21). A nineteen-year-old Albanian victim of trafficking explained: "I was 17 when I left my home, seeking a new and worthy life with my boyfriend. I thought he loved me but after leaving home he sold me" (Ekonomi et al. 2006, 48).

A Belgian report based on a victim database with 1,101 trafficking victims (CEOOR 2006) shows that two-thirds of the victims had received a promise of marriage. In one case, police found a fifteen-year-old Albanian girl in a prostitution bar in Brussels. Her family wanted her to marry in Italy, yet once she arrived there, she discovered that her intended was already married to another girl. Friends of her family then brought her to Belgium, where she was made to work in a prostitution bar.

In another case, an arranged marriage left a twenty-five-year-old Albanian victim with a husband who abused and deceived her. When she became pregnant, her husband refused to accept the child, and he sold his wife to a prostitution ring. She was taken to Belgium, but she refused to work as a prostitute. After two weeks the traffickers sent her back to Albania, where she was held against her will for two months. In January 1999 she was transported again to Belgium and forced to work as a prostitute to reimburse the traffickers for her travel expenses, including the forged documents she was given.[5]

Another case file, also discussed in a report by the NGO Save the Children (Renton 2003), describes a fifteen-year-old schoolgirl, Marjana, from the north of Albania, who fell in love with a man named Xhevdet. He promised to marry her and take her to Italy to start a new life. Although she did not want to go, Xhevdet and his older brother persuaded her and another girl from Shkodra. When the girls arrived in Italy, they were told that the marriage plans were over, and both were forced to become prostitutes. Meanwhile, Marjana's sister, Klodeta, was abducted by neighbors in north Albania and taken to become a prostitute in Belgium. Marjana and Klodeta's elder sister, Marta, went to the police and reported the names of her sisters' traffickers. Word got back to the criminals, who confronted the girls' twelve-year-old brother, a handicapped boy named Tonin. He was told that if the family persisted in pursuing the matter with the authorities, Marta would be taken as well.

On May 31, 2000, the girls' father, Gjin, returned home to find the walls splattered with blood and no sign of Marta. The next day her dismembered body was found in bags in the nearby river. Gjin claims that no forensic evidence was gathered at the crime scene and no autopsy was conducted. Both traffickers were arrested the following day, but although they were charged with trafficking and drug offenses, no murder charges have been filed (Renton 2001, 4).[6]

Sometimes trafficked Albanian women are relatives of their Albanian pimps and traffickers, or they come from the same locality. A number of reports based on victims' statements explain that "Albanian families are not lacking in responsibility for inducing their daughters into prostitution. On the condition that the prostitution does not become common knowledge, it is sometimes the very parents who convince their daughters to follow boy-friends, cousins or acquaintances, even while knowing or imagining that they will be led into prostitution" (Becucci 2004).

If police checks in Western Europe locate trafficked women, they typically are sent back to their families. According to the International Organization for Migration, in some cases, women are being returned to family members who trafficked them in the first place, or to the very same situation from which they were trafficked. This often simply leads to the re-trafficking of these women (IOM/ IMCM 2002). In other cases the women were rejected by the families. According to one Albanian trafficking victim: "I was caught by the French police and after staying for a month in camp I have returned to Albania. At the Rinas airport the Albanian policemen were waiting. They behaved nicely and I wasn't scared. On the contrary, my family was a problem; my relatives didn't accept me back into my home."

Albanian and Roma girls have been kidnapped in the Balkans, too. In the Belgian court case "HP," the victim was kidnapped in Albania in 1997, when she was only sixteen years old. She was kept isolated for twenty days in a house where she was continually raped, beaten, and threatened by the traffickers. Later she was transported to Italy and then to Belgium, where she was forced to prostitute herself. A Belgian victims database shows that 17 percent of Albanian trafficking victims had been kidnapped or recruited against their will. When compared to victims of other nationalities, this number is significantly higher.

A Belgian liaison officer who has handled a number of trafficking cases while living and working in Tirana explained that traffickers from northern and southern Albania operate differently:

> Trafficking of women and children for sexual exploitation is a typical activity of Albanian criminal groups. However, both women-trafficking and cannabis production is associated more with southern Albania. Traffickers usually come from the south. When women are kidnapped in the north of Albania, people try to find women with no brothers and fathers, because they are afraid of vendetta. Blood revenge is more common in the north.
>
> Southerners know that if they kidnap the sisters and daughters of northern Albanian men, these men will take revenge later on. These men are more likely to defend the honor of their women. (interview, Albania, 2008)

Another horror is linked to the Kosovo conflict: Albanian criminal groups in the late 1990s started recruiting, and at times kidnapping, young women from refugee camps for the purpose of prostitution. In April 1999, employees of an Italian NGO working in Tirana noted that unidentified armed men had been entering refugee camps to "choose the best merchandise" from among the undernourished and desperate women sheltered there. Mauro Valeri, coordinator of this Italian NGO, pointed out in 1999 that Albanian girls generally were aware of what could happen to them in Italy. "[So] organized crime is tapping young refugee women who are unaware of the situation," he said. "The outbreak of the war meant a marked increase in the number of prostitutes in Italy coming from Albania, Montenegro, Macedonia, and Kosovo" (*Zenit* 1999).

Valeri also explained that certain Albanian organized crime groups were targeting adolescents just twelve or fourteen years old. In some instances, their families were paid money, or payments of five to seven thousand dollars were made directly to the recruiters or kidnappers. Elizabeth Rehn, a former Finnish defense minister who also served as UN undersecretary general and special rapporteur for human rights in the former Yugoslavia, similarly reported: "There is a marketplace outside Skopje [Macedonia] where women step out around a stage naked, and brothel keepers just point fingers to make a selection. Women are sold like cattle on the market, and they are kept like slaves. Very few are paid, and if so, only a minute fraction of what their owners get for them" (Boustany 2003, 16).

Since 2000, the increase in ethnic Albanian-run prostitution networks in Western countries has been alarming. Thousands of young ethnic Albanian or Eastern European women have been duped into emigrating with the lure of a job and money. When they arrive in Western countries, they are repeatedly beaten and raped by Albanian traffickers who force them into prostitution. Why is this occurring? What roles do culture and sociocultural confusion play in neutralizing the effects of these devastating crimes in the eyes of the offenders?

Gender, Culture, and the Kanun

The wider sociocultural context from which ethnic Albanian criminal groups emerge plays a unique role in enabling those criminals to justify their brutal crimes against women. It also explains why women sometimes accept their role as victims. According to the Kanun, families must be patrilineal (meaning that wealth is inherited through a family's men) and patrilocal (meaning that after marriage, a woman moves into the household of her husband's family). Customarily, marriages were also agreed on, often at birth or in early childhood. When a woman is deemed eligible to marry, she moves out of her parents' home and into her husband's. There she becomes the property of her husband's family (Çiuli 1996). In traditional Albanian society, women are taught to obey their husbands or male relatives and accept submissive roles. Although according to the Kanun, "Blood follows the finger" (that is, the person who commits a murder incurs a blood feud) (Fox 1989, 172), this law does not include women. Article 28 states that the husband "purchases a woman's labour and cohabitation, but not her life," and that the blood of a woman is not equal to the blood of a man (Fox 1989, 38). Article 29 of the Kanun explains the gender dynamics within the family: "A woman is known as a sack, made to endure as long as she lives in her husband's house. Her parents do not interfere in her affairs, but they bear the responsibility for her and must answer for anything dishonorable that she does. . . ." (Fox 1989, 38). As Fox explains, parents have killed daughters who have dishonored their husbands. (Fox 1989, 180).

Further, according to the Kanun (article 33), a man has the right to counsel and correct his wife, to beat and bind his wife when she scorns his word and orders, and to beat and publicly humiliate his wife if she disobeys him (Fox 1989, 42). He can kill her for two reasons: infidelity or betrayal of hospitality. The Kanun further provides: "If a husband beats his wife, he incurs no guilt . . . and her parents may not make any claims on him because of the beating. If a man beats his wife bloody, and she complains to her parents, the man must give an explanation" (Fox 1989, 38). Additionally, the value of a woman is said to be equal to half a man, or a dog (Baban 2004).

Numerous sources show that in this traditional context, women often have duties rather than rights (Binder 1991; Minnesota Advocates for Human Rights 1996). Gender-based subordination has been deeply embedded in the conscious-ness of Albanian men and women, and it was generally regarded as a natural con-sequence of biological differences between the two sexes (Hafizullah 1992, 32). The transition to democracy in Albania showed that "women are suffering both as a result of the general economic and political crises which continue to grip Albania and because of a resurgence of traditional male attitudes" (Gjipali and Ruci 1994, 32). The man still occupies the role of father-boss at home (Paluca-Belay 2003).

Today, the Kanun continues to influence the attitudes of many ethnic Albanians (although, as explained previously, it does not have the force of law). Statistics from the end of World War II found that most Albanian women were illiterate, because the patriarchal tradition of the country had made them a social class with no dignity (Çiuli n.d.). The communist government supposedly gave women total equality with men: the right to vote, equal salaries, and so forth. However, equality cannot be legislated. It can be achieved only when the economic, social, cultural, and psychological dimensions of a society have been transformed.

Research shows that in 2008, Kosovo ranked 0.76 on the Gender Development Index (GDI), the lowest in the Balkan region. Gender disparity in Kosovo remains an issue of concern. Although girls today are more likely to go to school than they were in the past, they are still underrepresented at all levels of the educational system. Women also are disadvantaged in the economic sector; their rate of unem-ployment is alarming. Of those women who are a part of the labor force (only 28 percent of Kosovo's population), just 12 percent have a permanent full-time job and only 6 percent are business owners (Gashi 2009).[7] In Albania, women's sala-ries are between 20 and 50 percent those of men, who own 92 percent of all prop-erty and approximately 84 percent of gross domestic product (Amnesty International 2006). In fact, in some parts of northern Albania, the terrible eco-nomic situation has led to the creation of "sworn virgins:" women that have assumed a male identity and live as men; according to the Kanun, they are equiva-lent to men (McDonald 2014). Sworn virgins vow to remain celibate for the rest of their lives in the company of twelve witnesses, and they dress and act as Albanian men do. Importantly, unlike women, sworn virgins are permitted to own property and work outside the home. This is, in large measure, the reason for their existence. Fatos Tarifa, an expert on Albanian culture and social issues, however, also points out, that in many cases women became sworn virgins in response to the hardships placed on their men via blood feuds (McDonald 2014).

Domestic violence continues to be viewed as a private matter, as if a woman who denounces her batterer betrays and shames her family. The media rarely reports incidents of domestic violence, and the criminal justice system continues to show sympathy toward perpetrators, so women are hesitant to report abuse to authorities. Moreover, women in Kosovo and many parts of Albania remain financially dependent on their husbands, and they often fear losing their children if they report abuse.

The oppressive communist regime in Albania did not allow for cultural development, especially when compared to Western countries. Many men still feel they have the right to treat women as their own personal property, which they can sell, rape, and even kill (Amnesty International 2006). According to Amnesty International, at least a third of all women in Albania are estimated to have experienced physical violence within their families. The following is one of many stories of abuse reported by Amnesty International:

> [Around 7pm] he took the meat cleaver when I was lying on the settee, and held it against the front of my neck, just because I called my sister, and he said, "Why did you call your sister, you wanted to ask about your brother-in-law and not your sister." So he beat me very badly. I was horrified. I was pregnant just in my first months. Then he took the cleaver, and with all the force of his upper hand pushed my head to one side and put the cleaver to my neck. I don't know how I didn't die from the shock. He was interrogating me trying to find out who I liked or if I had someone else. I didn't answer his questions as I was very afraid and didn't want to make any mistake as I knew it could end very badly. Then he took the electrician's pincers and pulled at my new blouse trying to get at my breast and destroyed the blouse with the pincers; then he took my hair and cut it with a bread knife; then he tried to gouge my eyes out with his finger; then he put his fist in my mouth with as much pressure as he could. I passed out at about 4.30 am. (Amnesty International 2006)

Despite this, research indicates that the original wording of the Kanun is not being respected in contemporary Albanian society. On one hand, although the Kanun of Lek Dukagjini makes female subordination culturally acceptable in many Albanian settings, prostitution goes against all moral values promoted by this code. The closer one follows the customary Albanian code, the less acceptable prostitution becomes. In fact, in traditional Albanian society, prostitution and infidelity have been regarded as some of the most disgraceful and shameful acts women can engage in. On the other hand, Western media, combined with a liberal Western values system, has made prostitution more common and female subordination less acceptable in contemporary Albania. Contradictions arise when different cultural codes and values emerging from both traditional and Western cultures are applied improperly by people who have insufficient knowledge of them.

Albanian traffickers have no doubt constructed their own value system by selecting varying elements from other cultural systems. The exploiters justify their behavior by referring simultaneously to contradictory themes that emerge from both traditional and popular culture. They have enabled themselves to prostitute and subordinate women by perceiving prostitutes, and often women in general, as worthless cattle. Albanian offenders have devalued women by treating them as merchandise. A Kosovo-Albanian offender once told me: "Albanians from Albania are crazy. I have some Albanian friends, pimps, but married with families. But what they have done to some prostitutes even I cannot comprehend. The nastiest things you can imagine. When they are together, they torture women. Prostitutes are worthless for them . . . dirty objects" (interview, Kosovo, 2007).

Even some official authorities have joined brutal trafficking networks, reinforcing their criminal behavior. According to a UK Home Office report, "The police in Albania often were involved directly or indirectly in trafficking. Few police officers and other government officials were prosecuted for trafficking during the year. Lawyers and judges were also manipulated and bribed, permitting traffickers to buy their way out of punishment if arrested" (UK Home Office 2004).

Some Albanian women have stayed silent about their misfortunes, either out of fear or because they have accepted their traditionally submissive role. Consequently, they have become easy targets for Albanian traffickers.

It is interesting to note that ethnic Albanian pimps and traffickers are often the relatives or husbands of trafficked and prostituted women. Why has this been the case? Before marriage, an Albanian woman's honor is defended by her family, mostly by her father or brothers. It is the male line of her family that decides her fate. Women are expected to be obedient to their fathers, and within their families they are dependent on the decisions men make for them. So when cousins and nephews participate in exploitive prostitution rings, the women in their families do as they are told.[8] Well-established emotional bonds often allow Albanian offenders to maintain strict control over their victims. The exploiters treat their victims, who are often their relatives, as belongings.

According to the Kanun, after marriage it is the husband's duty to defend the honor of his wife. Women lose part of their being after marriage, because they are expected to be obedient to their husbands. They exist and function only through the agency of their husbands, and as a result they do not dare go against their husband's demands. In many Albanian villages even today, once a woman is married, her husband reigns over her. This traditional gender value is overemphasized in contemporary ethnic Albanian society, particularly among criminal groups that trade in and exploit women. Italian researcher Stefano Becucci (2004) explains:

The recruitment strategies that are based on a sentimental relationship between exploiter and victim are particularly widespread in the ambit of Albanian prostitution. Sentimentally bonded to the exploiter, Albanian women have enormous difficulties freeing themselves from the prostitution circuit. Although they are subjected to brutal violence every day, the sentimental relationship and the fear that their families will discover the true nature of their activities abroad stop the girls from denouncing their pimps. A further impediment is the continual threats of retaliation towards family members back in Albania if the women do not obey their exploiters. Threats which are particularly credible and efficient considering that in many cases the victim and the exploiter come from the same locality in Albania.

One should note, however, that marriage and creating sentimental bonds between pimps and prostitutes is common not only among ethnic Albanian organized crime groups. As journalist Ruth Hopkins (2005) writes, "Since time immemorial, women have been manipulated into prostitution. In the days of yore, pimps who not only earned a living off a prostitute but also had a relationship with her were called *voosbinkies*, 'tough machos.'" The interesting fact, though, is that these fairly emotional exploiter-victim relationships are emphasized more within the ethnic Albanian context than any other. Victim databases show that emotional relationships are most common between Albanian victims and Albanian traffickers, and less common with victims of other nationalities (CEOOR 2005, 2007; EU Hippokrates Report 2001). As illustrated above, selective use of certain elements of the Kanun by Albanian criminals and their victims might explain the phenomenon.

Despite this, when they are arrested and brought to justice, ethnic Albanian offenders do not use the cultural argument to justify their behavior. They are aware of the consequences of their brutal actions, so the arguments they use in front of the authorities or the general public are often quite different from those used to break personal moral bonds with the law. The following are quotes from some of my 2006–2008 interviews with ethnic Albanian offenders from Kosovo, Albania, and Macedonia:

In our culture, prostituting women is absolutely unacceptable; I would never dare to abuse and prostitute women; if you know our culture you would be able to understand that.

I was falsely accused of hitting, trafficking, and prostituting women. I can beat up a guy at any time if he deserves it, but hitting and abusing women is not my thing. I protect women, I do not beat them.

In our culture, it is no man's business to mingle in another man's private affairs. The man himself can hit the woman, but not his friend or anyone else.

The woman was lying. We have never raped her or beaten her. I swear. Women are highly respected in our culture. The Kanun does not permit us to do that.

Some Albanian criminal groups frequently use cultural themes to make their arguments stronger, and offenders commonly deny their crimes (this is called the "cultural defense"). Criminals' use of different neutralization techniques in front of different audiences shows that culture often serves as a tool in the hands of the manipulative and innovative offenders. There are grounds to postulate that some elements of the Kanun laws, specifically those regarding the subordination of women, are used to justify trafficking-related crimes in the Albanian context. However, as noted earlier in this chapter, traditional organized crime figures argue that it is the younger generation of Albanians that engage in human trafficking and that more traditional offenders would see such acts as highly disrespectful and intolerable. An organized crime figure from Albania, serving a twenty-seven-year prison sentence in the United States, notes: "I put traffickers of women on the same level as child molesters. Makes me sick" (interview, New Jersey, 2014).

ALBANIAN WOMEN AND ORGANIZED CRIME

Another important gender dimension is the involvement of Albanian women in organized crime activities. In the Balkan context, while the gender composition of Slavic criminal groups remains blurry, Albanian organized crime groups are known to be composed almost exclusively of men. Even Albanian recruiters in human trafficking networks traditionally have been men who used kidnapping or the "lover-boy" approach to recruit victims. For example, 93 percent of the Albanian traffickers operating in Italy between 1996 and 2003 were male, and just 7 percent were female (UNODC 2009). Also according to a study based on fifty-four penal cases related to human trafficking from the district of Tirana, Shkoder, and Vlore in Albania (during the period from 2000 to 2003), we know that criminality is most prevalent among eighteen- to twenty-five-year-olds, followed by those aged twenty-six to thirty-five. Defendants have an average of eight year of education and are usually male (Ekonomi et. al. 2006, 49).

In the past, women were rarely the main traffickers, and they were seldom given the status of "partner," with access to finances. This was particularly true of Albanian women—they appeared always to be the victims. Only occasionally did trafficked Slavic women manage to rise within the criminal network. The case of an ethnic Albanian trafficker and pimp, Dilaver Bojku Leku, from Macedonia, illustrates the nature of this business in a Balkan context. Together with his male accomplice, Leku kept about one hundred Moldovan women locked in brothels, and he forced them to have sex with at least ten clients a day. When interviewed, the women reported that the "owners" frequently treated one "slave" better than the others. To survive, this favored woman had become the pimp's lover—and so she rose within the hierarchy. The girls called the pimp "Papa" and his mistress "Mama." Mama lived with the girls, and she became Papa's spy, informing on anyone who plotted to escape. The women said they acted submissively and tried to negotiate for better conditions with their captor rather than trying to retaliate or escape.[9]

After 2003 authorities began to see an increasing number of situations in which ethnic Albanian men cooperated with women, particularly those of Slavic descent (e.g., women from Bulgaria, Ukraine, Romania, Moldova, and Bosnia-Herzegovina). According to police files, for example, Naser Kelmendi, one of the most notorious Kosovo-Albanian drug traffickers, involved his Slavic mistress, Anna (pseudonym), in running an international drug trafficking network in Kosovo, Bosnia-Herzegovina, Montenegro, and Western Europe. Law enforcement officials observed that Anna often traveled between Bar and Sarajevo, allegedly transferring large sums of money from Bosnia to Montenegro. According to confidential intelligence reports from 2009, a majority of Kelmendi's properties in Bar and Ulcinj, in Montenegro, were registered under Anna's name. Kelmendi's wife is ethnic Albanian, and police agencies have reported that she is not directly involved in his criminal businesses. The police say it is typical for Albanian male offenders to have mistresses of other ethnicities, while being married to ethnic Albanian women who take care of their children.

Another interesting case is that of the Pink Panther group—a name INTERPOL has given to an international network of jewel thieves responsible for some of the most audacious thefts in criminal history. The Pink Panthers have robbed 120 stores in twenty different countries (Allen 2009; Fleishman 2009). INTERPOL estimates that there are several hundred thieves in the group, and many come from Serbia and Montenegro (Samuels 2010). Interestingly, the women in this group appear to hold important positions.

In an interview with Havana Marking, director of the 2013 documentary *Smash and Grab,* one of the key members of the Pink Panthers, an ethnic Albanian man from Montenegro, explained: "The women in the Panthers have to be exceptional. . . . You can have only one in each gang, and we have higher requirements for the women because they have the leading roles. They have to do the main job. . . . They enter, they record, and they bring the plan. That means the woman has to be intelligent, she has to be beautiful, and she has to love money."[10]

Investigated cases from Belgium also show that ethnic Albanian offenders have worked closely with Dutch and Belgian women since the late 1990s. Kosovo-Albanian organized crime figure Viktor Hoxha, for instance, was involved in extortion and racketeering at Belgian nightclubs. According to police, the women who worked as waitresses and bartenders in these nightclubs were on the criminal network's payroll. Belgian law enforcement officials said the women allegedly were "in love" with the Albanian boss and were involved in the business voluntarily. They appeared to be active partners-in-crime, although Belgian social workers, including victim shelter director Patsy Sorensen, argued that the women were victims because they were abused if they didn't "do their job properly" (interview, Belgium, 2007).

Albanian networks operating in Belgium and the Netherlands also have cooperated with Dutch and Belgian women as they transport cocaine from the Netherlands to Italy. Instead of using Albanian men as drivers to transport cocaine, the Albanians had women take on the job—and they often went undetected.[11] However, social workers pointed out that the women transporting the cocaine also worked in the prostitution market in Belgium and the Netherlands. Many of them were drug users, dependent on the traffickers for money and for their supply of drugs.

There are no significant cases of ethnic Albanian women leading transnational criminal networks or being partners with Albanian male traffickers. Instead, Albanian women have been identified as victims of human trafficking, especially during the 1990s, or as the wives of male offenders. Very rarely—usually in cases when their companion has been imprisoned—some of these women act as "interim" figures within the criminal network and assist their husbands. An interviewed Albanian offender noted that he cannot see Albanian women leading criminal organizations but, according to him, they would do all that is needed for their husbands: "After I lost my appeal I told my [American Albanian] wife, 'Go on with your life. I will be here for the next twenty years. You didn't chose this life, I did.' And she said, 'I really hope you are joking. I said I would love you in good times and in bad times. I am not going anywhere. Anything you need, I am here. And she has been here for me for the past ten years" (interview, New Jersey, 2014).

Also, in the case of robber Alket Rizaj, discussed in chapter 3, Rizaj's girlfriend, Soula-Aspasia Mitropia, helped organize his Hollywood-style helicopter escape from a Greek prison. And when guards opened fire, Rizaj's girlfriend fired back with an automatic rifle to protect her man.

Although Albanian women seldom have been involved in crime, their participation is somewhat greater now than during the communist era. Authorities report a slight increase in the number of homicides committed by Albanian women, as well as in the number of cases of theft, counterfeiting, drug trafficking, and kidnapping of children for sale or exploitation that involve women. Research indicates that in most of these cases the women are accomplices and not the main perpetrators (Paluca-Belay 2003). At times, women also have been involved in cases of swindling and fraud, taking on the special role of a manager of a private company. Falsification or counterfeiting—that is, the partial or complete exchange of documents with false information for the purpose of profit—appears to be another sphere where female criminality emerges in Albania. However, active female involvement in smuggling activities, armed robbery, illegal cultivation, and similar crimes remains rare (Paluca-Belay 2003).

Nevertheless, ethnic Albanian women have been among those involved in organized crime in the United States. In the Thaqi case, described in chapter 3, a couple of women had important roles. Twenty-eight-year-old Valter Memia and his forty-year-old wife, Lauretta Lokaj, both Albanian, were among the organization's more than thirty-seven members. Lauretta, a wholesale distributor for a drug-dealing cell within the organization, and another co-defendant, Magdalena Nikollaj allegedly were primarily responsible for laundering drug proceeds for the syndicate by transporting bulk cash and wiring money to co-conspirators in Canada. Prosecutors added that Lokaj also distributed oxycodone for the syndicate and had her own customer base. Court documents noted that Thaqi had been married to Lokaj before Memia married her (US Department of Justice 2011).

Although it appears that Albanian women have had only peripheral roles in transnational organized crime, working in the shadows of their husbands, one should be aware that women's presence in organized crime activities has not been systematically recorded in official documents. For example, Clare Longrigg, elaborating on cultural stereotypes in Italy, recalls a 1983 court ruling in which a Palermo judge declared that women could not be guilty of money laundering because they are not autonomous and are anyway too stupid to take part in "the difficult world of business" (1998, xv), even though it was clear that women often had an active role in laundering funds (Puglisi 2005). As a result, scholars in the past have concluded that organized crime is sexually segregated, because when the stakes are high and the risk is great, women are more likely to remain in gender-defined roles as wives or mothers, disconnected from crime (Steffensmeier and Allan 1996).

We should also recognize that female participation in transnational organized crime activities varies across sociocultural and historical space. There are gender-related variations in socialization across regions and countries, and various racial and ethnic groups may have different norms for femininity and masculinity (Arsovska and Allum 2014). The differences in norms lead to different experiences, interests, and wants, which subsequently affect the positions women hold in organized criminal activities. It is apparent that Albanian women have not been very active in organized crime activities, partially due to culture and for context-specific reasons; however, we must acknowledge the overall lack of reliable data in this area.

PROTECTION RACKETS AND EXTORTION
The Business of Extortion

Extortion has long been associated with organized crime and traditional mafia-type organizations. Indeed, it often has been described as the defining activity of organized crime, as well as the core activity of the traditional Italian mafia. When extortion is committed on a regular basis, it can turn into a protection racket, an institutionalized practice in which tribute is collected on behalf of a criminal group that, in exchange, claims to offer physical protection from other such groups.

Extortion racketeering takes the form of a business activity consisting of the sale and provision of protection; it is an industry that produces, promotes, and sells private protection (Gambetta 1993). Organized crime groups sometimes prepare the territory by generating a demand for security and protection through a high level of insecurity and uncertainty. Useful in describing extortion racketeering as a mafia crime is the distinction drawn by Anton Block ([1974] 1988) between enterprise syndicate/group and power syndicate/group, where the latter is a criminal group mainly involved in extortion as a form of territorial control. Extortion racketeering enables organized crime groups to gain control over a specific territory, or even political power.

The regular use of extortion consolidates a mafia culture. Entrepreneurs or shop owners who have to deal with the "mafia" gradually become used to its presence in their territory. Extortion is, in fact, an easy crime to carry out and an easy way to make money rapidly: it does not require a high initial investment, it carries low maintenance costs and, in areas where the state's protection is not regarded as adequate or reliable, it is a low-risk operation (Paoli 2003, 165).

Extortion and protection rackets are criminal activities commonly associated with ethnic Albanian organized crime groups, both in the Balkans and in Western countries. Sometimes these activities are hidden under the pretense of semilegal private security companies, and offenders act either on their own or on behalf of their criminal groups. The criminal organizations of Alex Rudaj and Oliger Merko in the United States are just two examples of organized crime groups dealing in extortion and racketeering offenses. These criminal groups, according to law enforcement agents, were involved in a pattern of racketeering activity that included conspiracy to commit murder, extortion, money laundering, witness intimidation, loan sharking, extortionate debt collection, obstruction of justice, and document fraud.[12] Similarly, in New York City, the group led by Redinel Dervishaj worked together with NYPD officer Besnik Lakatura and extorted money from restaurant owners in Astoria.

The criminal group led by Viktor Hoxha in Belgium, according to court documents, also was involved in extortion and protection rackets. Hoxha and his gang extorted money from discotheques and clubs, and they allegedly sold protection to wealthy club owners, whose decision to buy private protection was not always voluntary.[13]

In the last fifteen years, extortion and extortionate debt collection have become typical for Albanian crime groups in the Balkans. In October 2008, Vladimir Sharovic of Macedonia's Ministry of Interior and the former head of the Unit against Violent and Serious Crime, stated that a growing problem with ethnic Albanian groups in Macedonia in the previous decade was the increase in violent crimes such as armed robberies, murders, kidnappings, and extortion. The vio- lence exerted by these groups drove growth in the legal and illegal private security sectors. A history of recent conflict; rising rates of petty crime; relatively ineffective policing; and relatively high levels of poverty, unemployment, corruption, and the problems inherent in building an efficient rule of law are all factors that contrib- uted to the rise of protection rackets in the Balkans.

A decade after the cessation of conflict in Kosovo, the territory still suffered from a number of perceived and real security problems that generated demand for private security services (ISSR 2006; SEESAC 2005). Even today, although to a lesser degree, Kosovo and Macedonia continue to be affected by ethnic division and intense political rivalry, which contribute to an atmosphere of constant low- level insecurity. Many businesses have been robbed at gunpoint, and businesspeo- ple have been kidnapped for ransom.

Private security companies also have been involved in political and business corruption. In particular, it has been alleged that some private security companies threatened small-business owners at shopping centers when those shop and bar owners did not pay the security company to guard their businesses. When burgla- ries took place, the guards protecting other properties in the shopping center claimed not to have seen anything amiss. In addition to private security compa- nies, organized crime groups and individual actors have taken their share of this profitable extortion racket.

Victims of extortion have reported abuses by ethnic Albanian criminal groups. For example, in Kosovo, Albanian extortionists claimed they could pass on mes- sages to the relatives of individuals who disappeared during the Kosovo conflict. Facilitating such "contact," however, would come at a price. The extortionist would tell the victim's family that their relative was still alive and being forced to work in a highly guarded location. Once family members were convinced that their rela- tive was alive, the extortionist would ask for a sum of money to pay off the "guards." Gradually, the amount of money the extortionist demanded would increase, but the promised phone calls would not occur (Ahmetaj and Carew 2004).

The most common method of extortion applied by ethnic Albanian organized crime groups is asking for protection money, or *gjoba*. One of the main functions of criminal groups in Albania was to provide "protection" to ordinary citizens who did not trust the state, particularly around the turn of the century.[14] These groups provided protection most often in towns with a high concentration of people and resources. They demanded money and threatened to destroy property. Armed criminal groups regularly extorted bar and shop owners not only in Albania, but in Kosovo and Macedonia as well. If their demands were not met, bar owners might be shot and killed immediately. One instance of this occurred in July 1999, when a dozen men armed with Kalashnikov assault rifles called at the Sahati bar in the center of Shkoder. The bar's owner, Ibrahim Isufi, was waiting for them. In the ensuing shootout, five of the gang members were killed and three of Isufi's relatives were wounded. As a result, Isufi's male relatives went into hiding, fearing revenge from the families of the dead gangsters (International Crisis Group 2000a).

As described in chapter 2, the notorious Kosovo Albanian offender whom I call Besmir extorted people from the Kosovo diaspora, allegedly collecting money to finance the Kosovo Liberation Army (KLA). When people did not pay their "taxes," his criminal group threatened them, sending an unmistakable message by leaving bullets in front of their doors.

Various sources point out that extortion was Kosovo's most robust industry during and after the 1998–1999 conflict (Cullen 2000; Ahmetaj and Carew 2004). According to interviews with Kosovars conducted from 2006 to 2008, most cafés, restaurants, and shops make some form of payment. Most business owners simply shrug and pay the mobsters—some of them former members of the KLA who have morphed from freedom fighters into shakedown artists. "There is no law here," says John Foreman, a former British soldier who has worked in the Balkans for seven years and runs a bar in Prishtina (Cullen 2000). Foreman claims he has been threatened repeatedly by former KLA members who demand that he pay them three thousand dollars a month for the privilege of doing business. They have followed him home, telling him he is a dead man. Men who Foreman says are former KLA fighters often burst into the bar and threaten Albanian and Serbian customers and bartenders, ignoring the foreign patrons. Foreman says "he expects to get a bullet in his head" for obstinately refusing to pay off the extortionists (Cullen 2000).

Hospitality, Tough Guys, and Extortion

The Kanun stipulates that the life of a guest should be placed before one's own life, stating, "An offence against a father, a brother, and even a cousin without heirs may be forgiven, but an offence against a guest is not forgiven" (Fox 1989, 136).

Other articles in the Kanun emphasize the importance of guests, and hospitality in general, for Albanian families.

Article 602. The house of the Albanian belongs to God and the guest.

Article 603. At any time of the day or night, one must be ready to receive a guest with bread and salt and an open heart, with a fire, a log of wood, and a bed.

Article 610. A weary guest must be received and surrounded with honor. The feet of a guest are washed.

Article 629. If your guest commits an evil act while under your protection [i.e., in your house], you are responsible for it.

Article 636. You must pay for any damages done by your guest, even if you are obliged to place the bell of your flock on a beam [i.e., sell your sheep] or sell your oxen or your water rights.

Article 638. You must pay, and, if you can obtain something from your guest by way
of restitution, all the better for you: otherwise, the loss is yours: "I had and I
gave," says the Kanun.

In a survey of 864 ethnic Albanians, the respondents were asked their opinion
of the following statement from the Kanun: "If a guest enters your house, even
though he may be in a blood feud with you, you must welcome and honor him by
offering food, shelter, and an open heart." The respondents' opinions were divided,
as they were on many other sensitive questions: 38 percent agreed with the statement and 42 percent disagreed. This indicates that despite the overall sociocultural
confusion in Albania, many Albanians still deeply respect the institution of the
guest. In Albanian society the guest is often described as a "demigod."[15]

In order to justify extortion of innocent people, most frequently bar owners,
some criminals have taken advantage of the cultural themes of hospitality and the
guest. For example, some ethnic Albanian criminals claim to have been dishonored by the bar or shop owners whom they have extorted. According to the Kanun,
an "owner" of a "house" (in the modern context, a bar or similar facility) has to
respect the demands of his or her guest. If he does not, he has displayed dishonor
and blood may be taken. The Albanian regard for the guest rises above all other
human relationships, even the ties of kinship (Kadare 1998, 78). The famous Albanian writer Ismail Kadare explains that the reason for this perhaps "lies in the
democratic character of this institution. Any ordinary man, on any day, can be
raised to the lofty station as a guest" (Kadare 1998, 82).

Today, this regard for hospitality is not always a positive element of the Kanun—
at least not in the way it sometimes is interpreted. In Macedonia, Kosovo, and
Albania, innocent bar owners ("hosts") have been killed by Albanian criminals
who perceive that they have suffered some sort of injustice while they were a
"guest," or customer, in a particular bar. "You have to pay because you have dishonored me" is a customary demand in the Balkan region. The "guest-host" cultural
theme has been exploited by ethnic Albanian offenders to extort money from victims, to deny the rights of the victim, and to justify criminal actions.

Perhaps criminals expect that when they ask for *gjoba* or any other favor from
a host, that favor should be granted without question. When this does not occur,
offenders may deny their victim or may harm or even kill the host.

In order to start an argument that will justify their criminal behavior, offenders
often use the cultural themes of honor and hospitality. The holy guest/demigod
neutralization technique also is used in revenge killings.

The brutal 2005 murder in Macedonia of bar owner Mile Petkovic, described in
the previous chapter, seems to have been revenge for the death of one of the killers'
brothers, who had been murdered a few months earlier in Petkovic's bar. In the
language of the Kanun, although he was innocent of the man's death in his estab-

lishment, Petkovic was the "owner of the house" (since it was his bar); therefore, he was automatically answerable to his guests, and any harm done to them while in his "house" could be repaid only by taking the blood of the host.

Moreover, the Kanun also elaborates on the importance of personal property to Albanian families. One of the articles explains that "whomever violates someone's house must pay fine of 500 *grosh* to the Banner and double compensation to the owner for any stolen articles" (Fox 1989, 60). An offender involved in extortion, loan sharking, and illegal gambling, whom I interviewed in 2014, noted:

> If you put hands on my property, I have the right to put hands on you. I am all about respect, but if you don't respect my property, I have no respect for you. The FBI turned this into an extortion case but I don't believe I did anything wrong, except maybe not pay taxes. I worked hard for that money, why should I give a chunk of it away? I was a super in a building, a handyman, a busboy, a waiter, but of all the jobs I had, running the machines was the hardest work of all. It was mentally tough, and I was exhausted. You have to understand that gamblers are worse than crackheads, and you need to take care of your property, and be tough when needed. (interview, New Jersey, 2014)

Also to justify their actions, in some Western countries, offenders have blamed national governments of extortion. The argument put forward by Alex Rudaj and Basri Bajrami, both involved with gambling and extortion, is that the U.S. and Belgian governments respectively had been extorting money from them by trying to collect taxes. This behavior could be explained by David Matza's neutralization technique, which he describes as a "condemnation of the condemners" (Matza 1990). Offenders see the condemners (in this case governments) as hypocrites, or are reacting out of personal spite. According to Matza they shift the blame to others, repressing the feeling that their acts are wrong.

The business of extortion and private protection appears to appeal to ethnic Albanian criminals for several reasons: it displays the criminal's masculinity (the culture of tough machos); it is a group activity in which the behavior of the criminal actor is continually reinforced by the group to which he or she belongs (the audience effect); it is an activity that often involves vulnerable victims who are easy to extort (the easy target); and, above all, it allows criminals to neutralize their deviant behavior by referring to cultural themes of honor, respect, and hospitality (the honor culture).

OWNING GUNS, OWNING PRIDE

The Illicit Arms Trade in the Balkans

The increase in arms trafficking in the Balkans is closely related to the regional wars that took place during the 1990s in Yugoslavia. The wars left vast quantities of weapons outside government control. Before its breakdown, Yugoslavia maintained one of the largest armies in Europe. As a matter of policy, the entire population was engaged in armed resistance, armament production, and civil defense. For decades, Yugoslavia spent a large share of its annual gross domestic product on the production of weapons. The arms industry was one of its most flourishing economic sectors (Kauer 2007, 82). In fact, about 90 percent of Yugoslavia's arms were produced domestically as a result of Yugoslave statesman Josip Broz Tito's doctrine of self-sufficiency and nonalignment (Bromley 2007, 4).

As the wars in the Balkans started, these arms stockpiles became the primary source of weapons for paramilitary and militia organizations. One of the international community's first reactions to the Yugoslav wars was the 1992 arms embargo, imposed on all six republics: Bosnia, Croatia, Macedonia, Montenegro, Serbia (including Kosovo and Vojvodina), and Slovenia. This embargo seemed to have little effect on Serbia, which maintained control of the Yugoslav Army and its weapons. But the embargo badly hurt the defense forces of Bosnia, Croatia, and Kosovo. In order to push for their independence, these republics engaged in various alliances with foreign state and nonstate actors for the importation of weapons.

As a result, organized crime became a necessity for the survival of the Bosnian state and Kosovo. As the conflict progressed, Bosnian Serbs received military supplies from Serbia, while Bosnian Croats received help from Croatia. The majority of the groups supplying weapons to Bosniaks, frequently referred to as Bosnian Muslims, came from Islamic countries, especially Iran, Turkey, Sudan, and Saudi Arabia (Wiebes 2006). In the early 1990s, Bosnia's first weapon-smuggling channels appear to have been set up by the head of the KOS (Counter-Intelligence Service), Aleksandar Vasiljevic, a Bosnian Serb (CSD 2004). Throughout the past two decades, actors with diverse profiles—from state officials to ordinary citizens—have been involved in the arms trade in Bosnia.

Research indicates that illegally owned weapons in Kosovo already far exceeded the number of registered weapons in 1989, and throughout the tumultuous 1990s events in neighboring countries created an influx of even more illegal arms. The 1998–1999 conflict further contributed to a "small arms and light weapons" problem in Kosovo, and it left both the Albanian majority and the Serbian minority suspicious of security providers. Before and during the conflict Kosovo was a Serbian municipality, rather than a semiautonomous republic. The reserves of the Kosovo Territorial Defense had been taken away after 1981, and weapons supplies in Kosovo were limited. In order to achieve their secessionist goal, ethnic Albanians relied heavily on weapons illegally trafficked from abroad, especially from neighboring Albania (Zaborskiy 2007; Quin et al. 2003).

Between 1944 and 1985 Albania was under the communist rule of Enver Hoxha, who placed a strong emphasis on weapons supplies and a powerful army. After the fall of communism in Albania, large numbers of weapons remained in circulation throughout the country. During the collapse of the pyramid schemes in Albania in

March 1997, described in chapter 2, at least 38,000 handguns, 226,000 Kalashnikov rifles, 25,000 machine guns, 2,400 antitank rocket launchers, 3.5 million hand grenades, and 3,600 tons of explosives disappeared.

Many of these armaments reappeared during the Kosovo conflict (Michaletos 2006), and most ended up in the hands of the KLA. The border towns of Bajram Curri and Tropoje in northern Albania served as illegal arms bazaars for local arms traders and KLA supporters (Zaborskiy 2007; Quin et al. 2003).

Paradoxically, while Albania was supplying low-cost, Chinese-manufactured assault rifles to the KLA, Serbia was supplying expensive, Yugoslavian-made pistols to Kosovo (Khakee and Florquin 2003). In 2001, some of these weapons were transported to Macedonia, where a number ended up in the hands of ethnic Albanian nationalists closely linked to the KLA, including the Albanian National Army and the National Liberation Army.

In addition to readily available weapons, these postcommunist countries had a vast network of people who previously had worked for the military services, the secret security services, and the police. These individuals were well connected and had the know-how to become arms traders. The abolition of the Albanian secret service Sigurimi in 1991, for instance, left about ten thousand agents unemployed. In Bosnia, some fifty thousand people who were directly or indirectly employed by arms factories also lost their jobs.

Today, although the Balkan conflicts are officially over, it appears that arms trafficking for terrorist, criminal, and other purposes once again is flourishing in the wider region. Weapons collection campaigns did not result in people handing in illegal weapons; instead, they changed the way people stored their guns. In Albania, "weapons collectors [noted] that people were not simply hiding guns under their beds, but in more ingenious or awkward-to-reach places" (Saferworld 2009, 6). This may bring about a decrease in "impulse" or accidental use of weapons, but it most likely will have negative long-term consequences for the postconflict reconstruction agenda. Cash-for-weapons "buy-back" programs also have been ineffective and associated with negative consequences (Saferworld 2009).

In November 2007, Macedonian police seized large numbers of weapons and munitions hidden in bunkers in the village of Prvce, in western Macedonia. This was the third major confiscation of weapons in this area within two months. Many weapons were found close to the towns of Tetovo and Kumanovo, hidden mainly in bunkers or buried underground. In October of the same year the Macedonian police arrested eight ethnic Albanians, who were using seven horses to carry fifteen coffins filled with munitions, army uniforms, AK-47s, bombs, sniper rifles, and guidelines for military training in written Albanian (see figure 20).

Recent statistics indicate that many weapons remain in domestic circulation throughout the Balkans. For example, surveys suggest that ethnic Albanians still keep firearms in their households. Black market arms dealers satisfy the needs of

FIGURE 20. Macedonian police display weaponry confiscated in Skopje during "Operation Mountain Storm" in November 2007. Charges have been submitted against seventeen members of a criminal group headed by Ramadan Shiti and Lirim Jakupi, who a few months earlier escaped from Dubrava prison in Kosovo. Source: Macedonian Ministry of Interior.

local customers (Zaborskiy 2007; Saferworld 2009). The UN Small Arms Survey (Khakee and Florquin 2003; Mustafa 2005) estimated that there are between 330,000 and 460,000 small arms and light weapons in Kosovo, some 300,000 of them unlicensed. A poll conducted by an international NGO suggested that two out of three households in Kosovo still have a gun, and some households have more than one. Also, the perception among 58 percent of the Kosovo population surveyed (out of 1,200 respondents) by the Association for Democratic Initiative was that people in Kosovo possess weapons and that almost two-thirds of weapons possessed are illegal (Haziri 2003). A survey by the United Nations Development Program (UNDP) produced evidence that one in five school students in Kosovo is armed.

Over time, weapons collection programs in Kosovo have resulted in a decreasing number of arms. Likewise, although between 2003 and mid-2007 about 20,000 weapons were destroyed in Macedonia, more than 15 percent of Macedonia's two million inhabitants (about 330,000 people) still possess weapons, and 170,000 of them possess weapons illegally. Firearms play a crucial role in the execution of violent crimes, and they represent power, masculinity, and, above all, honor for many Albanians, both offenders and ordinary citizens.

During a conference on ethnic Albanian organized crime, Haxhi Krasniqi, deputy director in Kosovo's Directorate against Organized Crime, said that trafficking of weapons remained a major problem in Kosovo. He explained that huge numbers of weapons were still in civilian hands. In September 2008 Kosovo police arrested six people, all believed to be linked to the trade in illegal weapons. The arrests were part of a series of coordinated actions with police in neighboring Albania, where authorities arrested five people and seized fifteen guns, as well as ammunition. This makes it clear that the demand for small arms and light weapons is still high in the Balkan region, making the illicit firearms market an especially profitable one.

Gun Culture

Gun culture is a system of values or cultural elements, preferences, and attitudes that favor possession or use of arms among certain social groups or communities. In trying to define it, the South Eastern Europe Small Arms Control (SEESAC) noted: "Gun culture is the cultural acceptance of gun ownership in situations where the principal motivation or justification for it is not for utilitarian or economic reasons but because their society has a set of values and norms that deem it acceptable behavior. A simple example would be when a man carries a gun, primarily not for hunting or for protection, but because his 'culture' interprets his behavior as a sign of masculinity and status" (SEESAC 2006, 1). Societies or communities for which gun culture is characteristic feature a widespread acceptance of possession of modern firearms or traditional cold weapons.

The most severe consequences of an active gun culture, such as spikes in homicide and other types of violence, have been recorded in regions where people are in the midst of transitional periods characterized by confusion and lack of order. During the rapid postcommunist change and the uncertain modernization processes of the 1990s, many people in the Balkans were left between tradition and modernity, in a liminal stage of disorientation. One way to counteract this feeling of confusion was to find broader cultural paradigms that could normalize life situations. Being "tough" is one culturally appropriate way to do this, because toughness situates behavior in a historical context of wars and the fight for independence. Being considered tough can legitimize men's independence, strong-mindedness, strength of will, vigilance, and willingness to stand up against "enemies." "Fighting fire with fire" seems to have become the quintessential mark of being a man (or even a woman) in the Balkans. An individual's skills in using a weapon also earned that person respect and a better position in society (Cvetkovic 2006).

As noted earlier, weapons possession is an integral part of the concept of honor in traditional Albanian culture. In the Balkan region, there is a romantic attachment to arms as objects of great symbolic and cultural value. Guns often are fired into the air in celebration at weddings or births, an act that may confirm the existence of "gun culture."

The role of the Kanun also should be mentioned here, because Kanun articles place enormous emphasis on the importance of firearms. In both Albania and

Kosovo, male honor is closely linked to the possession of firearms and the courage to use these weapons. The importance of guns as symbols of power, protection, and pride is also clear in many Albanian and Kosovar proverbs—for example, "The rifle is asking daily, either for the life of another, or for the owner's life," and "An Albanian with a gun never fears anyone." A southern Albanian proverb admonishes, "You can kill an Albanian, but you cannot make him give up his gun." An Albanian cultural belief holds that a man who is disarmed also loses his honor, and he would prefer death to a loss of honor (SEESAC 2006, 7). Cultural proverbs also represent guns as part of social and national identity: "The gun protects your head, the gun protects the fatherland" (from Kosovo), and "an Albanian loves his rifle as much as [he loves] his wife" (from Albania).

In personal interviews with ethnic Albanian offenders, the fascination with firearms was obvious. The offenders talked proudly about their guns. One of them presented a videotape showing his use of weapons. He reported that for one wedding alone, he spent more than one thousand euros on ammunition. The video footage showed him and several of his friends at the wedding, shooting automatic guns and Kalashnikovs for hour after hour. While shooting they received the full attention of an interested audience, including young children. As the celebration ended, older members of the crowd complimented one of the offenders on his shooting skills. "Guns are very important for us," he said at the end of the interview. "They fascinate me" (interview, Kosovo, 2007).

Participants in the Saferworld Survey (2009) also mentioned history, tradition, and culture in relation to weapons ownership in Kosovo. However, when respondents were asked about the importance of different factors that caused people to keep their weapons (rather than handing them in to the authorities), 74 percent felt that the tradition requiring men to have weapons was not so important (Saferworld 2009). References to tradition as a reason for carrying weapons were more frequent among older respondents, however. Younger respondents appear to have their own reasons, which may be linked to popular culture.

BEYOND THE KANUN: POP CULTURE, INSECURITY, AND ALBANIANISM

Because of a unique interplay of administrative and law enforcement failures, human trafficking, extortion, and arms trafficking continue to exist in the Balkan region and remain typical activities of ethnic Albanian organized crime groups.

Popular Culture and Organized Crime

Popular culture plays an important role in explaining aspects of Albanian criminality. Global communication and the popular media certainly have contributed to the positive image of both tough-guy mafia figures and guns.[16] The effect of pop culture has been particularly powerful in regions where people experience culture conflict, socio-cultural confusion, and lack of order. Journalist Kevin Heldman (2011a) noted: "The members of the Krasniqi crew . . . practiced shooting at gun ranges, and then shot their weapons in a coffee shop and, another time, from a car going down the highway in celebration after a drug deal. They bought gun after gun, with accessories—Glocks, silencers, shotguns, 9 mms, semi-automatics, hollow-point bullets, bulletproof vests."

In Kosovo Albanian Viktor Hoxha's favorite television series, the American show *24*, Jack Bauer is a highly proficient Counter Terrorist Unit agent with an ends-justify-the-means approach, regardless of the perceived morality of his actions. He is violent, loves his weapons, and uses terror tactics to pry information out of suspects. He is also regarded as a superhero.

Marshall McLuhan, who has studied the notion of liminal beings through media theory, refers to objects of technology as extensions of the human body. Today the tendency to ascribe personal characteristics and create our identity through the objects we buy is quite common. One blatant example, described by Cvetkovic (2006), is the MTV show *Pimp My Ride,* where young people whose car has been "pimped" often comment that the new style reflects their personality, or changes it, or brings it to another level. Such media-promoted creation of personal identities, or at least of some important personal traits, through external objects can help to explain some aspects of gun-related behavior in Balkan societies. In Yugoslavia, for instance, the role of the army, its legitimization and symbolic meaning, was, among other means, created and perpetuated by the media for years. Numerous TV series and films, some involving high-profile foreign actors, promoted some sort of gun culture within a collective framework, such as the people's struggle against fascism or for freedom.

Some young people in the Balkans seem to be fascinated by the fast and rebellious lifestyle of certain organized crime figures. For example, when Alket Rizaj and Vassilis Paleokostas used a helicopter to escape from a high-security prison in Greece, as described in chapter 3, some Greeks hailed them as modern-day Robin Hoods.[17] News reports have fueled their notoriety, saying they offered loot to the poor and vowed never to harm members of the public during their thefts.

While the government scrambled to put on a show of force and vowed to prevent further escapes, some Greeks cheered the escaped inmates. Within hours, hundreds of people had joined more than a dozen fan clubs for Paleokostas on Facebook: "Paleokostas-Korydallos: 2–0" was one of the most popular. The preexisting "Paleokostas you must escape again (Greek Prison Break)" site gained eight hundred more members, taking the total number of members to more than forty-five hundred. Similarly, the Balkan Pink Panthers posted YouTube videos of their notorious robberies of jewelry stores around the world and were praised for their "amazing work" in online blogs. "Respect. You have to give it to them," a fascinated fan of the Pink Panthers commented on the YouTube video of their Dubai robbery. And another blogger added: "Nice job. . .They should be the new cast of OCEAN 14."[18]

Fear and Social Trauma

In many conflict-prone regions and regions with a long and intense history of armed fighting, a liminal stage of armed violence becomes fixed, making arms possession as well as extortion rackets a way of life. When conflicts and armed violence take on a more permanent character, a so-called conflict mentality emerges. This is a condition of fear and social trauma, both of which are expected outcomes of being exposed, directly or indirectly, to prolonged periods of violence, fighting, and instability.

The decade-long war campaign in the Balkans (1991–2001) is considered a liminal period that left many people insecure, distrustful, disoriented, and afraid of state institutions, as well as of other people in general. Experience shows that in the Balkan region, the demand for weapons is fueled by precisely that continued perception of insecurity. Because of the region's turbulent history of wars and invasions, many Balkan people do not trust their government and do not feel confident about the ability of state institutions to provide peace and order (Saferworld 2009; Cvetkovic 2006). Historically, the state has intruded in people's lives, so institutional forms of justice remain untrusted and questionable. As Dukajin Gorani, director of the Human Rights Center at Prishtina University in Kosovo, explains: "It is commendable that KFOR [Kosovo Force] is trying to collect weapons, but it is an impossible task. Kosovars have learned from the Kosovo Liberation Army that you get international attention if you have a gun. In our lifetime the rule of law has never achieved anything; only guns have provided a measure of justice. So you stick to your gun" (Farnam 2003).

According to a survey with twelve hundred respondents conducted by the Association for Democratic Initiative, trust in state institutions such as the police, judiciary, official army, and paramilitaries is extremely low among various ethnic groups in the Balkans, particularly among ethnic Albanians (Haziri 2003, 15). Despite some recent skepticism among people in Kosovo and Bosnia regarding the power of weapons to ensure safety, focus groups and informant interviews suggest that they are not prepared to give up their firearms just because the war is over. Recurring riots, sparked by frustration and anger, decade-long lawlessness, growing criminal-political ties, and the disappearance of money made many ethnic Albanians suspicious of their government's ability to protect them. As one informant noted, "There is an increase in people's awareness that they should not own firearms, but the security situation is as it is," so people do not feel safe without them (Saferworld 2009). Extended violence over ethnic identity, territory, and survival, as well as distrust in authorities, has created a sense that weapons are needed—and created demand for private "protection" as well.

Patriotism, Pride, and Duty

As noted earlier, most Yugoslav republics and autonomous provinces were distrustful of politicians representing superior republics or countries, such as Serbia.

This was particularly true in the case of Kosovo. Therefore, in order to achieve their goals and push for independence, various political actors and emerging paramilitary groups appealed to patriotic sentiments. With the introduction of political pluralism at the beginning of the 1990s, new political establishments in the region needed a base or ideology that would provide legitimacy and justify their parties' politics. Everyone seems to have found a solution in nationalism and "retraditionalization," promoting the presocialist past as the source of inspiration. This involved the creation and reinforcement of historical myths about Balkan warriors who moved their countries toward prosperity only through wars.

Criminal-political ties were quickly established. For example, selling and buying guns was closely linked to ethnic survival, national pride, and national duty. Arms dealers, often called "patriotic bandits," were proud to supply the paramilitary structures in their countries, as well as their compatriots, with much-needed weapons. By appealing to patriotic sentiments, many arms traffickers gained support and won respect because their activities were seen as supporting the right cause. In this way, weapons were glorified as tools for independence and freedom, and closely linked to the regional rise in nationalism and patriotism. In Kosovo, it is said that "if you don't fight, nobody will sing a song for you."

In Kosovo, the KLA and its supporters were in great need of weapons during the 1998 conflict. That need was met by patriotic bandits such as Princ Dobroshi, a Kosovo-Albanian drug trafficker described in chapter 2, in whose apartment authorities found a machine pistol, a telescopic rifle with a silencer, a handgun, and a banknote counter. The Czech special services (BIS) stated that part of the drug money Dobroshi earned went toward buying arms for the KLA. Nevertheless, Dobroshi was respected by many of his compatriots in Kosovo, particularly former KLA fighters. Likewise, Agim Gashi, an Albanian drug trafficker from Kosovo, had ties with politicians in his homeland. Gashi supplied his brothers in Kosovo with Kalashnikov rifles, bazookas, and hand grenades.

Extortion rackets also took on a patriotic flavor. Initially this illicit market flourished because of the demand for protection and security; people did not trust their governments and did not trust one another. In this environment, those providing "private protection" often felt they were contributing to their country's well-being. Some groups took money from their compatriots to support political parties, while others felt good about providing a service that was in high demand. Many extortion rackets also had political support. Basically, the situation in the Balkans allowed criminals to hide behind a patriotic disguise and give political excuses for their illicit activity.

· · ·

Unlike organized crime activities that deal in commodities such as drugs or smuggled cigarettes, which can be viewed as economic in nature, criminal activities such as arms dealing, human trafficking, and extortion are indisputably linked to issues of power.

In addition to power, culture—both traditional and popular—appears to be very important in shaping behavior within the Balkan context. Therefore, the impact of traditional and pop culture on the evolution, structure, and behavior of ethnic Albanian organized crime groups should not be disregarded. In fact, culture (or sociocultural confusion) can help to explain why gun trafficking is still flourishing in the region, and it can shed some light on the nature of the arms trafficking market. For example, the Albanian Kanun laws place enormous emphasis on the importance of firearms, and they closely link male honor to the possession of firearms and the courage to use them.

Although prostitution is not encouraged by traditional Albanian culture, some criminal figures have misused cultural elements to justify their actions. Crimes by and against women also have been shaped by the gender inequality inherent in traditional Albanian patriarchy, and patriarchal controls have led many Albanian women to accept submissive roles in their households and in society.

Popular culture has contributed to sociocultural confusion in the Balkan region. Despite law enforcement efforts, the problems of illicit firearms and extortion remain unresolved. For example, although authorities have tried to exert a greater degree of control over gun ownership during the postconflict reconstruction period, the general populace still holds onto its weapons. A lack of trust compounds this problem: Because of the region's turbulent history, Balkan people often do not trust state institutions. In the Balkans, fear and the so-called conflict-mentality foster a general feeling that it is good to have a gun around the house for self-protection, and a belief that widespread gun ownership will protect them from injustice.

Certainly not all illicit transfers are thick with meaning; many resemble simple market transactions grounded on cost–benefit calculations. Also, one must acknowledge that there are significant differences between younger and older Albanian offenders, and between offenders involved in drug and human trafficking activities and those involved in more traditional forms of organized crime. Yet despite such observation there is no doubt that Albanian organized crime activity can be understood much better when we also examine cultural attitudes, the region's sociopolitical complexity, and emotions.

Chapter 7

CONCLUSION

Dangerous Hybrids? What Now?

The more you can increase fear of drugs and crime, welfare mothers, immigrants and aliens, the more you control all the people.
—NOAM CHOMSKY

Albanian criminal organizations have become more active in the United States and Europe since the mid-1980s. At first, with a few exceptions, these organizations in the United States were involved in low-level crimes, including ATM burglaries, home invasions, and bank robberies. Later, ethnic Albanian offenders affiliated themselves with the established families of La Cosa Nostra (LCN) in New York, acting as low-level participants in activities such as gambling, extortion, violent witness intimidation, and even murder. As Albanian communities became better established in the United States, these criminal groups expanded to lead and control their own organizations, particularly those involved in drug trafficking.

In Europe, Albanian organized crime groups have been heavily involved in human smuggling and human trafficking, often for sexual exploitation. They first started to make money by trafficking women from Albania and other Eastern European countries, and they soon controlled the prostitution markets in various Western European cities. Then, as the criminal groups grew in size and power, some reinvested their "dirty money" in the highly profitable drug market. The rest often was spent on members' luxurious lifestyles, or was sent back to the offenders' countries of origin to support family members, political parties, or local businesses.

While several Albanian crime groups have been active in the United States and Europe, none has yet demonstrated the established criminal sophistication of traditional LCN and Sicilian mafia organizations. However, the Albanian groups have proven themselves capable of adapting to expanding criminal markets and becoming involved in new activities, echoing the historical growth of other organized crime groups.

As a result of the violent operational methods of some Albanian organized crime groups, they came to the attention of law enforcement agencies and were recognized as a serious threat to Western societies. Starting around 1998, stories about Albanian crime began to figure prominently in the media, and various myths arose. This chapter summarizes some of the key findings about the causes, culture, nature, and expansion of Albanian organized crime groups, and it contrasts a number of myths with their underlying realities. More importantly, this chapter looks to the future of Albanian organized crime as it tries to answer the question: What now? Does Albanian organized crime pose a threat after all, and if it does, how should we respond?

MYTHS VERSUS REALITIES

This book has examined some commonly held beliefs about the so-called Albanian mafia and promised to make sense of the mythology surrounding the topic of ethnic Albanian organized crime. Certain myths or stereotypes appear to have some basis in truth, but in other cases, a broad gap exists between myth and reality (see table 6).

Structure and Membership

A decade-long research project indicates that there is no single, ethnically homogeneous Albanian or Balkan "mafia," structured hierarchically like the traditional LCN or the Sicilian mafia. During the 1990s, many ethnic Albanian criminal groups survived through turbulent times because of their similarities, their mutual respect, and their close ties built on personal trust. Contrary to common belief, no strict hierarchy exists within ethnic Albanian criminal groups, and there are no "Kanun-based" godfathers. Rather, Albanian organized crime groups, for practical reasons of language and culture, are organized around ethnic groups and friendship ties. Often, family ties play a role, but the membership of a group is rarely exclusively Albanian. Albanian organized crime groups are not clearly defined or organized, and are instead centered around a "core group" of a few central "leaders" who are often of ethnic Albanian origin. However, these crime groups cooperate with offenders of Italian, Greek, and other nationalities, and the structure of the extended group frequently is based on ties of friendship. The group structure tends to be mainly horizontal, with some charismatic individuals taking the lead but not being considered permanent "bosses."

The activities of these groups often are project-based, and membership frequently shifts. Members of Albanian criminal subcultures do not undergo ritual ceremonies in order to join the group. The boundaries of ethnic Albanian organized crime groups are not as clearly defined as originally believed. Ethnic Albanian organized crime groups are formed more spontaneously than, for example, the

TABLE 6 Myths versus realities

Myths	Realities
The traditional Albanian "culture of violence" and the customary Kanun laws have led to a drastic increase in organized crime in Albania.	The rapid expansion of Western norms and values in the Albanian territories has caused a "culture conflict" and sociocultural confusion within the society. In particular, materialistic values emerging from the Western value system, in combination with weak social and state institutions, have turned some Albanians toward criminal innovation. While many people dreamed of instant gratification, the social structure in Albania could not offer people legitimate opportunities to earn money quickly and fulfill those dreams.
The Albanian mafia is the new Sicilian mafia.	Despite some cultural similarities, Albanian organized crime groups are significantly different from the Italian mafia and La Cosa Nostra. Once members of Albanian organized crime groups are arrested, the group loses continuity and no longer exists.
There is one nationwide Albanian mafia.	There is no evidence to support such claims.
Albanian crime groups are hierarchically structured.	Loosely connected "core" groups (horizontal, fluid structures) and solidarity brotherhoods are the norm.
Albanian crime groups are homogenous organizations based on blood ties.	Ethnic ties play an important role, and sometimes brothers and cousins work together, but this doesn't mean that the groups are composed exclusively of ethnic Albanians; at the periphery one finds associates of different ethnicities, and friendship ties are very strong.
Albanian criminals adhere to ancient Albanian customary Kanun laws.	The Kanun code is not a "mafia" code; criminals may use their own interpretations of some cultural themes to justify their behavior, but in general, Albanian criminals do not respect or follow the Kanun laws.
Albanian crime groups are extremely violent.	Members can be violent, and violence has been one of the core characteristic of many Albanian-speaking organized crime groups.
Albanian crime groups are highly secretive and impossible to infiltrate.	The clan-based structure of Albanian society, Albanians' general distrust of state institutions, and the fear of reprisal make some of these groups hard to infiltrate, but this doesn't mean that specific codes of secrecy are strictly followed; in return for lesser sentences, many Albanian criminals have become defectors and testified against their associates in court. They also tend to talk over the phone and be careless in discussing their crimes.
Albanian crime groups are hyper-sophisticated, rational, and able to easily adjust to changing environments.	In general, Albanian organized crime has graduated from providing simple criminal services or high-risk, low-profit activities to working within the highest echelons of international organized crime and running independent criminal organizations. There has certainly been some advancement over time; however, this study concludes that such adaptation has not occurred on the group level. Groups may be dismantled permanently after operating for several years, and then new groups emerge. There is no continuity. Rather than fitting the stereotype of a highly adaptive, hyper-sophisticated mafia group, this study suggests that overall most Albanian criminal organizations are neither operationally highly sophisticated, nor particularly protean.

TABLE 6 *(continued)*

Myths	Realities
The Albanian mafia is able to move easily across territories and gain control of foreign territories.	There is little evidence that Albanian organized crime is a strategically transplanted entity or a rational bureaucracy that has been able to move its "business" successfully to foreign territories. These criminal groups do not appear to resemble multinational corporations that open outposts in Western countries, nor is there a nationwide Albanian mafia.
Politicians in the country of origin (Albania and Kosovo) control the Albanian mafia.	Organized crime figures maintain ties to the Balkan region and their countries of origin; however, this does not mean that groups in the Balkan region control Albanian criminal organizations abroad. The Balkan region remains a safe haven for some of these groups. Groups have been supporting political processes in their country of origin and often maintain close ties with politicians, but there is no evidence that political leaders control these organizations abroad.

LCN or the Sicilian mafia, although they should not be viewed as entirely ad hoc coalitions. There is no evidence that any Albanian organized crime group has found a way to replicate itself after its key members have been imprisoned; in other words, these groups lack continuity.

Kanun Laws

Although the Albanian traditional culture does not directly cause violent and organized crime, some prominent cultural themes, originating in the wider cultural context, have been selectively utilized by Albanian organized crime groups to neutralize moral prescriptions, justify criminal behavior, keep the membership stable, avoid direct and frequent conflict with the law, and bring order to the criminal organizations. The values and norms implicit in the fluid subcultures of delinquency depart from conventional traditions, but the relationship between a subculture of delinquency and the wider cultural context should not be summarized in terms of opposition. Like ordinary citizens, ethnic Albanian criminals neither know all aspects of their customary Kanun laws, nor do they respect these codes equally. The original Kanun is a cultural code meant to bring order. It is not the code of conduct followed by ethnic Albanian organized crime groups, and it has never been a "mafia code."

Self-selected and modified Kanun elements have served as neutralization mechanisms, helping criminals to order their behavior and justify their actions. Practice, however, shows that many of these codes have not been rationally applied by the ethnic Albanian organized crime groups, since they have not necessarily served the groups' best interests. Some codes have been beneficial for the groups' establishment and development, while others have been disadvantageous.

Extreme Violence

Albanian organized crime groups have proven ready and able to use violence. This does not imply that all groups use extreme violence frequently; however, some groups have used unnecessary violence against rival groups, victims, and even police officers and judges. Use of violence remains an important characteristic of these groups, and although it may have been on the decrease during the past eight years, at least in Western Europe, one cannot conclude that Albanian organized crime groups are not violent.

According to Western European law enforcement agencies, some Albanian crime groups have tended to use less violence in recent years, particularly against law enforcement officials and ordinary citizens, in order to reduce the social impact of their crimes. It is important to note that they have built their reputation in the criminal underworld already, so at times they may not need to use extreme violence to prove a point. However, if their reputation is not recognized, these groups have demonstrated that they are ready to use violence.

Secrecy

Although disloyalty is uncommon among members of clan-based ethnic Albanian organized crime groups, it is naïve to believe that the bonds between members of Albanian groups are based on absolute solidarity. In general, offenders are not trustworthy people. They make money through deception and crime, and the assumption is that they take advantage of others. The fact that they break their own "codes of silence" and occasionally cooperate with police officials or other enemies should not come as a surprise. Generally speaking, while the "code of silence" is respected within ethnic Albanian organized crime groups, it is not adhered to as strictly as the media and some scholars have reported. It is not unusual to find defectors in Albanian criminal organizations, particularly if the offenders are asked to testify in court in return for a reduced sentence. Also, many Albanian offenders do not seem to care about long-term consequences; these groups frequently are dismantled because members "talk too much" and fail to keep a low profile.

Criminal Evolution and Sophistication

European law enforcement agencies and popular media have depicted ethnic Albanian criminals as a "dangerous breed" posing a serious threat to society because they have graduated from providing simple criminal services to working within the highest echelons of international organized crime. We certainly can observe an evolution of Albanian organized crime groups over time, particularly when we examine the type of criminal activities in which they are involved and the scope of their operations. In particular, these groups have come to dominate some important criminal markets, including aspects of the international drug market.

They have established direct contact with criminals in the supply countries and move large quantities of heroin, cocaine, and marijuana across borders.

However, in terms of structure, infiltration, and level of violence there has been only limited advancement. For example, Western European law enforcement officials report that those Albanian organized crime groups that managed to learn lessons from other groups have developed sophisticated structures and operational methods, become specialized, and manage to keep a lower profile. However, this same development has not been observed across countries, and these changes remain country-specific.

Also, after operating successfully for several years, most Albanian criminal organizations have been dismantled and their members imprisoned. It is nearly impossible to observe the advancement of a single criminal organization over time because no Albanian criminal organization has managed to survive in its totality for a long period. Moreover, there is no evidence that Albanian organized crime groups around the world have moved noticeably into economic, high-profit/low-risk, sophisticated nonviolent crimes. This study suggests that, overall, most Albanian criminal organizations are neither operationally sophisticated nor particularly protean, but they are certainly daring, highly motivated, and ready to engage in risky behavior.

Transatlantic Connections, Political Ties, and "Mafia" Migration

Although organized crime figures maintain ties to the Balkan region and their countries of origin, this does not mean that groups in the Balkan region control Albanian criminal organizations abroad. The Balkan region remains a safe haven for some of these groups, but one should bear in mind that some Albanian groups established themselves abroad after escaping justice in Albania or Kosovo. There is little evidence that Albanian organized crime is a strategically transplanted entity or a rational bureaucracy that has been able to move its "business" successfully to foreign territories. It does not appear that these criminal groups resemble multinational corporations, or that there is a nationwide Albanian mafia. On the contrary, the mobility of the groups seems to be functional and project-based, and there is no "one size fits all" explanation of criminal mobility.

Organized crime groups composed of ethnic Albanians are often created after the migrants arrive in new territories. Although most migrants do not commit crimes, some join preexisting criminal organizations or, with time, form their own smaller groups. Study results indicate that the desire for fast cash, immediate gratification, and a luxurious lifestyle makes organized crime an attractive choice for some immigrants.

Finally, criminal-political ties in the Balkans were very strong during the 1990s, and they still exist today. Offenders try to bribe politicians, judges, and police officers, and although this may not be as easy as it was in the 1990s, it still occurs on a regular basis. Criminals bribe politicians to ensure immunity from prosecution or because they need some specific favor in order to perform their activities.

Yet this is not to say that politicians in the Balkan region have control over Albanian groups operating abroad.

LIMINALITY AND THE BUTTERFLY EFFECT

There is no single factor that explains why some individuals become involved in organized or violent crime, or why crime is more prevalent in some communities than in others. This book has explored the roles of sociopolitical, economic, and cultural codes, as well as the role of emotions and situations, as it seeks to explain deviant behavior in general and organized crime in particular.

The findings first illustrated that, contrary to media accounts, it is not the traditional Albanian "culture of violence and crime" and customary Kanun laws that have led to an increase in organized and violent crime in Albania, Kosovo, and Macedonia. The rapid expansion of Western norms in the Albanian territories has caused sociocultural confusion within the society. Materialistic values, in particular those emerging from the Western value system, in combination with weak social and state institutions, have turned some Albanians toward criminal innovation. The social structure in Albania could not offer people, particularly younger individuals, legitimate opportunities to earn money quickly, yet at the same time many dreamed of instant gratification and fast money. The demoralizing effects of poverty in today's capitalist society, where money stands against a range of emotions, also has contributed to increased emotional arousal and vulnerability to crime.

A breakdown of norms and loosened social controls encouraged the development of unstable, dynamic systems going through a period of drastic change. The lack of clear norms also enabled offenders to use neutralization techniques and justifications in an attempt to provide noncriminal images of their actions. On the whole, the lack of belief in and respect for the system in general further weakened the moral bond between citizens and the state and its agencies. After the fall of communism, many social institutions, clans, and families in the Balkan region failed to uphold order within their own macro or meso settings. Older clan or family members have always had a great deal of social authority within the household; however, after the 1990s, their position of power has weakened considerably. Many emergent criminal groups seem to be created by younger, socially confused men. And even if the fathers have not explicitly encouraged the behavior of these delinquents, many have neither denounced their deviant behavior nor taken measures to counter it.

In a 1963 paper for the New York Academy of Sciences, Edward Lorenz quoted an unnamed meteorologist's assertion that a single flap of a single seagull's wings would be enough to change the course of all future weather systems on Earth. By 1972, Lorenz had examined and refined that idea for a talk entitled "Predictability: Does the Flap of a Butterfly's Wings in Brazil Set off a Tornado in Texas?" The example of a system as small as a butterfly being responsible for creating a large and distant system, such as a tornado, illustrates the impossibility of making accurate predictions for complex systems.

This is one interesting way to make sense of human behavior, including organized crime, particularly during periods of liminality. This theory (known as chaos theory), addresses the behavior of dynamical systems that are highly sensitive to initial conditions—what is popularly known as "the butterfly effect." When the macro system (the state) is already unstable (in this case, undergoing rapid social change and internal conflicts), small differences in initial conditions yield widely diverging outcomes for the dynamical micro systems (people).

This doesn't mean that chaos equals disorder. In general, chaos theory is not about disorder; it is about very complicated systems of order that could be shaken by some unexpected external factor or situation. In human behavior, one can certainly see how small changes could render behavior extremely unpredictable. People interpret the situations they face and then act accordingly. Through the lens of symbolic interactionism, reality is seen as social, developed interaction with others. People do not respond to this reality directly, but rather to the social understanding of reality. During periods of rapid change, and during liminal periods, these interpretations of "social reality" vary even more because people are part of a multiloyalty system and have no clear norms and rules to follow.

Even if liminality lasts for a substantial period of time, in the end it must eventually dissolve, for it is a state of great intensity that cannot exist eternally without some sort of structure or authority to stabilize it, at least temporarily. Equilibrium—which doesn't mean complete order—must be achieved eventually or the system will cease to exist. People cannot live forever in a state of fear, insecurity, social trauma, and intense emotions. The social structure eventually must provide comfort to distrustful people and lead to a degree of stability and trust. Yet the existence of a liminal period must be acknowledged by policy makers who propose quick solutions and top-down anti-organized crime measures, inspired by rational choice theory, in specific regions. There is no quick fix to complex problems.

APPROPRIATENESS OF RESPONSE
AND THE DOMINO EFFECT

Albanian organized crime has attracted a lot of attention in recent years. Albania has been depicted as a criminogenic society, and Albanian people as dangerous. But these sensational labels cannot do justice to this ethnic group; they lead only to emotional arousal and higher levels of seclusion and unpredictability.

Part of symbolic interactional theory is the concept of the looking-glass self, or the self-fulfilling prophecy. This social psychological concept, created by Charles Horton Cooley in 1902, states that an individual's sense of self grows out of society's interpersonal interactions and the perceptions of others. The term refers to people shaping their self-concepts based on their understanding of how others perceive them. Because people conform to the imagined perceptions of others, it's difficult to act differently from how one thinks one is perpetually perceived. Cooley described society, then, as an interweaving and interworking of mental selves. Identity, or self, is thus the result of the concept in which we learn to see ourselves as others do (Yeung and Martin 2003).

One never stops modifying one's self unless all social interactions cease or change. So with the self-fulfilling prophecy in mind, we, as a society, should not immediately regard organized crime figures as our "enemies," because by doing so we encourage more sophisticated criminal structures to emerge. Labeling, criminalizing, and imprisoning people leads to the establishment of friend-enemy discourse and to the creation of more advanced and hostile criminal structures. For example, farmers growing opium poppies or cannabis should not be labeled immediately as "drug traffickers." Instead, they should be included in policy discussions and peace-making processes, and their needs should be understood before policies are made. Dialogue with nonstate actors is often essential. As the famous quote goes, "Keep your friends close and your [perceived] enemies closer." In fact, you may even realize that you have more in common with your "enemies" than you think. People rarely do bad things because they are "evil" themselves. The question is, would people do what they do if they had equally rewarding alternatives? Positive situations and positive reinforcement can change people's lives, just as negative experiences can lead to their destruction.

To continue this train of thought, organized crime should not be perceived as a sinister entity threatening the civil world but rather as a social problem—an outcome of various sociocultural, political, and economic developments. First, it is not a new phenomenon; historical studies show that organized crime has existed as an integral part of many societies, including many Western societies, for centuries. Although organized crime is a threat recognized by societies in the Balkans, it is not as significant as other, more pivotal threats. Many Balkan people feel that, in comparison to issues such as economic underdevelopment and unemployment, organized crime is not a major threat to their own security, despite the pressure of Western countries to identify it as such. In fact, practice shows that organized crime, leading to the growth of the "gray economy," often has served the interests of people living in poor countries, enabling them to make profits and survive.

There is no quick fix to the organized crime problem, and one can argue that it's naïve to assume a society can "fight" organized crime with nothing more than police officers, prosecutors, special units, and judges (see figure 21).

This argument goes hand in hand with another essential aspect of the "fight" against organized crime—tackling the demand side. What exactly is happening in our society that there is so much demand for certain "forbidden" goods? What can

FIGURE 21. Training of "razors," or Albanian special forces that fight against smuggling of arms and drugs (Shkodër, Albania, 1997). Copyright © Laurent Piolanti.

we do to reduce this demand, and is such a reduction necessary? The Western world has focused for too long on the supply countries. It is true that organized crime, in its various forms, appears to be more likely to form and strengthen in societies too unstable to enforce the rule of law. However, Western countries have externalized the problem of organized crime to Third World countries, presenting organized crime primarily as an external security threat rather than an internal one.

Despite the fact that the European Union and the United States have put enormous pressure on the Western Balkans to combat organized crime, most of the criminal activities in Western countries are committed by their own nationals. For example, a report published by UNODC (2008) studied the nationalities of heroin trafficking arrestees in fifteen European countries in 2004. Only 4 percent were from Albania, and 2 percent were from Serbia and Montenegro. Approximately 10 percent were from Africa, but 68 percent were from Western Europe.

In conclusion, this book does not claim that all organized crime activities are so thick with meaning. What this book strongly recommends is for policy makers to take into equal consideration culturally enriched and socially embedded factors that may have an impact on various illicit markets; to avoid sensational reporting that externalizes local problems and threats; to study more carefully the actual social harm caused by organized crime; and, most importantly, to focus on the demand side of organized crime and to try to understand why there is a demand for certain products.

So, although the threat posed by ethnic Albanian organized crime groups should not be underestimated, neither should it be overinflated. If we see organized crime groups as movements for some type of change—whether political, economic, or cultural—rather than as "enemies" or "evil and uncivilized minds," we may have better long-term results in dealing with these complex issues.

PREFACE

1. These are translations from several Macedonian newspapers, mainly *Utrinski Vesnik* (The morning news), but also *CNN World* and the *Los Angeles Times*.

2. In June 2013 the minister of interior, Ljube Boshkovski, was prosecuted and charged with the assassination of Marjan Tushevski and his driver. He was given a prison sentence of twelve years. Nine people, including police officers as well as the minister's security chief, were charged and sentenced to prison. The police are still searching for six other suspects involved in this case, three of whom are Serbian nationals. The opposition claims that the criminal justice process was not just, and that the minister was imprisoned because of his different political views (Dimovski 2012; *Time.mk* 2012; *MKnews* 2012; *Mkinfo* 2013). The name of another figure linked to the criminal underworld, Orce Korunovski, a Macedonian businessman who was later assassinated in a restaurant in Bulgaria, was also closely linked to the assassination of Marjan. He was also suspected of having ordered the killing (Dimovski 2012).

AUTHOR'S NOTE

1. In *The Drowned and the Saved,* Levi describes the gray zone in this way: "The hybrid class of the prisoner-functionary constitutes its armature and at the same time its most disquieting feature. It is a gray zone, poorly defined, where the two camps of masters and servants both diverge and converge" (Levi 1989, 42).

1. INTRODUCTION

1. See Xhudo (1996); Galeotti (2001); Boyes and Wright (1999); Fleishman (1999), as well as reports and threat assessments published by INTERPOL, Europol, and the United Nations between 2003 and 2011.

2. See Ruscica (1998); Milivojevic (1995); Viviano (1994); Prentice (1999); Stefanova (2005); Alexe (1998); Kitsantonis and Brunwasser (2006).

3. See Binder and Mendenhall (2003); Viviano (1999); Cilluffo and Salmoiraghi (1999); Bennetto (2002); Raufer and Quéré (2002; 2006); Lallemand (2007); Michaletos (2006).

4. A Human Rights Watch report published in November 2003 said that similar problems plague other Balkans nations, noting that official corruption contributed to the operation of more than two hundred brothels in Bosnia-Herzegovina alone.

5. Research by the International Organization for Migration and the data provided by several NGOs, including the Coalition All for Fair Trials, show that the ethnic composition of those in in Macedonian prisons for specific offences is as follows: 55 percent Albanians, 36 percent Macedonians, and 9 percent other ethnic groups. This information is based on charges and court cases in the fields of human trafficking, migrant smuggling, organizing a criminal group, and mediation of prostitution (Gotovski 2011).

6. See Galeotti (2001); Ilievski and Dobovšek (2013).

7. See Ruscica (1998); Boyes and Wright (1999); Milivojevic (1995); Alexe (1998).

8. Due to the high levels of ethnic homogeneity among Albanian criminal groups, the word "ethnic" is often used in relation to Albanian organized crime (in, for example, Europol and INTERPOL reports).

9. Congressional Statement, Ralf Mutschke, Assistant Director, Criminal Intelligence Directorate International Criminal Police (see www.russianlaw.org/Mutschke.htm).

10. Ethnic Albanian Alex Rudaj of Yorktown, New York, is the alleged boss of the Rudaj organization. The group was involved mainly in extortion and illegal gambling.

11. Some writers have argued that the typical structure of an Albanian mafia group is that of a family clan, referred to as a *fis*, and that several Albanian mafia families have an executive committee known as a *bajrak* (Heldman 2011b; Xhudo 1996).

12. For participant observation and ethnographic research, see the work of Pistone and Woodley (1987); Ianni and Reuss-Ianni (1972); Chambliss (1988); Mieczkowski (1986).

13. This database was created with Stef Janssens, researcher at the Interculturalism Migration and Minority Research Centre (IMMRC), University of Leuven, and human trafficking analyst at the Centre for Equal Opportunities and Combating Racism in Belgium.

14. This research was conducted with the partial support of a CERGE-EI: GDN Grant and with the help of two research institutes: one from Albania (Albanian "Viewpoint"), and the other from Kosovo (Kosovo Law Centre).

2. WHY WE DO WHAT WE DO

1. Aldo Bare was found guilty of the premeditated murder of two or more persons, with the complicity of Genc Kashari and Artur Daja, and was sentenced to twenty-three years in prison for these crimes alone. Then he was found guilty of the premeditated murder of Xhevat Demiri, and sentenced to life in prison; guilty of the premeditated murder under

criminal organization orders of Nimet Zeneli, and sentenced to twenty-five years in prison; and guilty of the attempted murder under criminal organization orders of Gramoz Selamani, and sentenced to twenty-five years in prison. Bare also was found guilty of creating a crime organization, for which he was sentenced to eight years in prison. See more on Bare in Likmeta (2011) and *Tirana Observer* (2012).

2. Information about Petrit's testimony was provided by the Refugee Review Tribunal of Australia (December 5, 2007), the *BBC Monitoring* (July 27, 2006), and the *Albanian New Agency* (July 27, 2006).

3. This extract is taken from an Albanian court document that I was given by the Tirana prosecution office (2012). The text has been streamlined.

4. See the case of Stanislava Cocorovska, who was responsible for trafficking half a ton of cocaine from Venezuela to Greece, via Bar in Montenegro, Kosovo, and Macedonia.

5. The information presented here is primarily based on a thirty-minute documentary about the life of Basri Bajrami, specifically an exclusive interview with Basri Bajrami in 2009, prepared by Macedonian TV show *Kod* (with Snezana Lupevska), and interviews with politicians familiar with his case. See www.youtube.com/watch?v=pPuRw_hccWY.

6. Satisficing is a decision-making strategy that entails searching through the available alternatives until an acceptability threshold is met. This is contrasted with optimal decision making (maximization), an approach that specifically attempts to find the best alternative available.

7. See Hayward (2007); Holbrook and Hirschman (1986); Wood (1998).

8. Other criminologists who share Katz's view include Hayward (2007); Presdee (2000); Ferrell, Hayward, and Young 2008; Young 2007.

9. The butterfly effect, first described by Edward Lorenz (1972), vividly illustrates the essential idea of chaos theory. If chaos theory were true, a single flap of a single seagull's wings would be enough to change the course of all future weather systems on Earth.

10. See Anastasijevic (2006); UNODC (2008); CSD (2004).

11. See more info on Banda Mustafaj at *InfoArkiv* (http://arkivamediatike.com): "Rrëfimi i Halit Bajramit: Unë, njeriu i Hazbiut në bandën e Xhevdet Mustafës" (August 12, 2011a); "Xhevdet Mustafa, sot 29 vite nga zbarkimi në Divjakë, zbulohet biseda me kunatin e Hazbiut" (September 25, 2011b); "Nëna e Xhevdetit, misioni i pamundur në negociatat me të birin në rrethim" (June 8, 2014).

12. One such group was the gang of Pusi i Mezinit (Banda e Pusit të Mezinit). The Gang of Gaxhai (Banda e Gaxhait) was another criminal group, created in March 1997 in the city of Vlore.

13. Committees of Public Salvation, or Salvation Committees (Komiteti i Shpëtimit Publik), were organizations set up during the 1997 rebellion in Albania to usurp the functions of the Albanian state.

14. The Otranto tragedy took place on March 28, 1997, when the Albanian ship *Kateri i Radës* sank in a collision with the Italian naval vessel *Sibilia* and eighty-three Albanians lost their lives.

15. See more on the KLA (collection of articles) at www.kosovo.net/kla7.html.

16. See Troebst (1998).

17. A German intelligence report (Bundesnachrichtendienst 2005, 11), cited in Jonsson (2013), added: "[Haliti] is connected to money laundering, drug-, weapons-, human and

fuel smuggling, trade in women and the prostitution business and belongs to the inner circle of the Mafia."

18. The *Detroit News* (August 7, 2012) reported that Tomo Duhanaj, an illegal immigrant, was charged with running a loan-sharking business in the United States that charged exorbitant rates to the local Albanian community. Duhanaj was one of the KLA fundraisers during the war.

19. This operation resulted in 124 arrests, mostly of Albanians, but also of Italian, German, Tunisian, Spanish, and Turkish nationals.

20. Interestingly, in these "business" transactions the patriot Gashi spoke Serbo-Croatian. In one telephone conversation intercepted by Italian police, Gashi was overheard admonishing his Turkish heroin suppliers to continue shipments during Ramadan—"a violation of religious rules for the sake of a more important cause: 'To submerge Christian infidels in drugs'" (Williams 2005, 61).

21. In 2002, Haridinaj's brother Daut was convicted with four other men of kidnapping, torturing, and killing four former members of FARK, the armed wing of the Democratic League of Kosovo (LDK). Since then, three key witnesses and two policemen investigating the case have been murdered (Xharra 2005).

22. See Bundesnachrichtendienst (2005, 22), cited in Jonsson (2013): "In the Decani region the clan-based structure of the Haradinajs engages in the entire spectrum of criminal, political and military activities that influences all of Kosovo."

23. The KPC was created on September 21, 1999, through the promulgation of UNMIK Regulation 1999/8. It was a result of the need to disarm the KLA, which was stipulated by UNSCR 1244 and rejected by the Kosovo Albanians. So, basically, the KLA was transformed into the KPC. The KPC had no role in defense, law enforcement, internal security, or any other law and order tasks.

24. Nazim Bllaca has confessed to being a former hit man for SHIK. Bllaca is being indicted for murder, attempted murder, and involvement in organized crime, and he has served as a trial witness against two other KLA soldiers (McAllester 2011).

25. See Babanovski (2002); Daskalovski (2004); Raufer and Quéré (2006).

26. The aim of the Ohrid Agreement was to end the hostilities between the Albanian National Liberation Army (NLA) and the Macedonian government. According to the agreement, any language spoken by over 20 percent of the population in Macedonia becomes co-official with the Macedonian language on a municipal level.

27. Johan Tarchulovski, an ethnic Macedonian, was sentenced on July 10, 2008, to twelve years in prison by the ICTY. He was held responsible for the actions of the Macedonian police in Ljuboten, where three Albanian civilians were murdered and several properties were damaged.

28. The Albanian customary criminal law is encoded in the following canons: The Code of Lekë Dukagjini (collected and codified by Shtjefën Gjeçovi), Shkodër, 1933; The Canon of Skenderbeu (collected and codified by Dom Frano Ilia), Milot, 1993; The Canon of Labëria (codified by Dr. Ismet Elezi), Tiranë, 2006; and the Canon of Mountains, which was applicable in the nine mountains of the Malësia e Madhe e Mbishkodrës to the Gjakova Highlands, Malësia e Madhe, and the Kosovo Field (see Elezi 2003).

29. Fifty-four countries were surveyed during the 1995–1999 survey cycle, and about forty countries were surveyed during the 1999–2004 cycle. In Albania, 1,000 people were

surveyed during the 1999–2004 cycle, and 999 during the 1995–1999 cycle. More info on the WVS can be found at www.worldvaluessurvey.org/WVSOnline.jsp.

30. Bell (1953) believed that for a certain segment of the American population, criminality had become a normal way of life.

31. According to official Albanian statistics, GDP per capita was estimated at $4,500 dollars in 2002–2003.

3. ON THE RUN

1. See Varese (2011); Hobbs (1998); Gambetta (1994).

2. See Shelley (1999; 2006); Castells (2000); Williams (2001).

3. A three-count indictment was unsealed in federal court in Brooklyn, New York, charging Redinel Dervishaj, Besnik Llakatura, and Denis Nikolla with Hobbs Act extortion conspiracy, attempted Hobbs Act extortion, and brandishing a firearm in relation to the extortion.

4. See Shelley (1999; 2006); Castells (2000); Williams (2001).

5. See Shelley (1999; 2006); Castells (2000); Galeotti (2005); Leman and Janssens (2007).

6. Data on immigrants in Greece is from the 2001 census. It is difficult to estimate the exact number of Albanian immigrants (documented and undocumented), and available numbers range from six hundred thousand to more than one million (see Barjaba 2004).

7. This estimate is provided by Istituto nazionale di statistica: La popolazione straniera residente in Italia (October 16, 2006) (see Barjaba 2004).

8. Reports also indicate that approximately four hundred thousand ethnic Albanians have left Kosovo as a result of the conflict in 1998.

9. This information was presented at the international expert workshop "Ethnic Albanian Organized Crime Groups: Real or Perceived Threat?" Belgian Federal Police, October 2–3, 2008 (see Arsovska and Sartorius 2008).

10. Members include Xhevdet Lika, Skender Fici, Xhevdet Mustafa, Mehmet Bici, Vuksan Vulaj, Gjon Barisha, Luan Lika, and Dujo Saljanin (whom Lika was later to murder after a falling out). In January 1985, Xhevdet Lika was convicted on one count of conspiracy to import heroin, one count of conspiracy to distribute heroin, one count of conspiracy to violate the RICO statute, five substantive counts of heroin distribution, and one count of operating a continuing criminal narcotics enterprise. The district sentenced Lika to life imprisonment on his continuing criminal enterprise (United States of America Appellee, v. Luan Lika, Skender Fici, Nazif Vrladu, Bari Drishti, Mehmet Bici, Anver Kalbas, Stella Millaj, Defendants, Xhevdet Lika, Defendant-appellant, 2003).

11. See Fikret Korac v. United States of America, 93 CR 848 (2011).

12. See Nardino Colotti v. United States of America, 11 Civ. 1402 (2012).

13. See US Attorney's Office press release, "US Charges Violent Albanian Organized Crime in Groundbreaking Racketeering Indictment," October 26, 2004. Available at www.justice.gov/usao/nys/pressreleases/October04/rudajindictpr.pdf.

14. See Nardino Colotti v. United States of America, 11 Civ. 1402 (2012); US District Court, Southern District of New York, USA vs. Alex Rudaj et al. (2004) Redacted Indictment, p. 3. Case 1:04 CR011110

15. See United States of America v. Korac et al., 1:01 CR 01127 (2003).

16. See Boomgaarden and Rens (2009); Christoph (2012).

17. See Antonopolous, Tierney, and Webster (2008); King and Mai (2004); Schwandner-Sievers (2008); Paoli and Reuters (2008).

18. See Bernburg (2009); Hagan (1973); Winfree and Abadinsky (2010).

4. IRON TIES

1. In personal interviews, law enforcement officials from INTERPOL and from Belgium (Laurent Sartorious, Francois Farcy), the Netherlands (Rene Bulstra), Italy (Rosario Aitala), and other European countries reported that in most cases ethnic Albanian (or Albanian-speaking) organized crime groups are structured around their families and ethnic communities.

2. The structure of Albanian organized crime groups was discussed during an expert workshop on Albanian organized crime that took place in Belgium (Belgian Federal Police—Brussels) in October 2008 (see Arsovska and Sartorius 2008).

3. The term "lover boy" is frequently used to describe young men who pick up vulnerable girls, form emotional relationships with them, and, after some time, force the girls to work in prostitution. It was the most common recruitment method used by Albanian pimps and traffickers during the 1990s.

4. The brothers also personally seduced Albanian girls in Albania and Moldovan girls in Italy. After the victims were seduced, they were treated brutally. Luzlem was a "lover boy" himself, responsible for selling the trafficked victims in Italy and Belgium. He accompanied the girls when they asked for asylum.

5. This case is based on a Belgian court file. Together with researcher Stefan Janssens I reviewed numerous human trafficking (court and police) files from Belgium, and we developed a comprehensive database based on these files files. See Arsovska and Janssens 2009.

6. These numbers were cited in a report prepared by Transcrime Center in Italy and are based on interviews with several Albanian law enforcement officials.

7. This quote is from an interview with the Belgian newpaper *Le Soir* and was republished by the periodical *Albania* on May 26, 2007.

8. A large number of petrol stations were built on the south-north route in Albania. These stations served as a cover for the oil smuggling business.

9. All of these case descriptions are based on confidential police reports acquired in the period from January to April 2009.

10. This case description is based on an internal police report from 2009.

11. See von Lampe and Johansen (2004); Ianni and Reuss-Ianni (1972); Kleemans and van de Bunt (1999).

12. This case description is based on a Belgian court file, 2003. See also Leman and Janssens (2006) for more information on this case.

13. Some of the members of the Krasniqi organization were Bruno Krasniqi, Saimir Krasniqi, Elton Sejdaris, Erkliant Sula, Skender Cakoni, Gjovalin Berisha, Nazih Nasser, Plaurent Cela, Gentian Nikolli, Shkelzen Balidemaj.

14. This case description is based on an internal police report from 2009.

15. When I refer occasionally to the concept of "brotherhood" in this book, I do not mean ritual brotherhood with clear, rigid boundaries; instead I use the term to indicate semi-flexible groups composed of ten to thirty men who are in some way kin to one another. These members have spontaneously formed bonds of friendship among themselves without undergoing specific ritual ceremonies.

16. On June 25, 1997, the Greek newspaper *Republica* (translated by the Albanian Telegraphic Agency) stated that the Albanian Mafia from southern Albania is in close cooperation with three hundred Greek citizens who are suspected of running illegal trafficking in this area.

17. Muolo has been accused of several murders, concealing corpses, possession of firearms, and extortion.

18. From 1992 to 1995, the UN sanctions imposed on neighboring Yugoslavia offered an immediate opportunity: organizing smuggling channels to supply Yugoslavia with oil. As many as two hundred boats would make a nightly trip from Zeta, in Montenegro, to Vraka, in Albania.

19. The punishments listed in the Kanun (Fox 1989, 16) include the following: (a) deprivation of food; (b) forbidding the bearing of weapons; (c) fettering or imprisonment in the house; and (d) depriving the disobedient one of his share in the household, in order to drive out the dishonor and danger.

20. Based on personal interviews with Belgian and Norwegian law enforcement officials in 2006, 2007, and 2008.

5. VIOLENCE, HONOR, AND SECRECY

1. See, for example, Xhudo (1996); Raufer and Quéré (2006); Goodnough (1994); Hartocollis (2005).

2. Dajti is facing charges for executing police officers Siamir Duçkollari, Altin Dizdar, Fatos Xhani, and Kastriot Feskaj during a failed police operation to arrest him on August 7, 2009.

3. This information is based on court transcripts provided by the Tirana prosecution office in 2012 and has been slightly adjusted to follow the format of the book. See also *Gazeta Shqiptare* (2009); *Shekulli* (2009).

4. This is an extract from the StreetGangs.com forum (2008). It has been slightly adjusted to follow the format of the book.

5. See Sutherland (1939); Wolfgang and Ferracuti (1967); Cohen (1955); Cloward and Ohlin (1960).

6. For example, see the testimonies of *pentiti* Stefano Castagna and the Sicilian witness Gaspare Mutolo (Paoli 2003, 65).

7. These and similar statements can also be found in court transcripts as well as US Department of Justice press releases on the Rudaj case (October 2004). See also *The Johnsville News* 2004; Fahim and Feuer (2006); Campanile (2004).

8. The Dutch owners recruited girls via advertisements, and the sex bar in Rotterdam had recruitment sites in Belgium, the Netherlands, and France. During the trial, the manager reported that during the last two years she had seen about a thousand girls. This section is based on analyzed court and police files from Belgium. See also Arsovska and Janssens (2009).

9. Similar to the way Albanian criminals have manipulated the concept of *besa,* Nigerian organized crime groups have used the concept of *voodoo (juju),* and Chinese Triads have used their "culture of honor" principles in exploiting their victims. Many Nigerian girls have taken an oath before going to Western Europe. The criminals threaten the oath takers with divine retribution if they break their oaths.

10. The nature of Albanian organized crime was discussed during an expert workshop on Ethnic Albanian Organized Crime (Real or Perceived Threat) at the Belgian Federal Police—Brussels, October 2008 (attended by thirty international experts on Albanian organized crime). In general, law enforcement experts from several European countries agreed that *besa* today doesn't have much meaning to Albanian criminal organizations. This was confirmed during personal conversations with Albanian prosecutors Osljan Cela, Argila Coca, and Ardian Visha, as well as with law enforcement official Vladimir Sharovic, who agreed that promises are easily broken in criminal organizations. See Arsovska and Sartorius (2008).

11. This observation has been confirmed during numerous interviews with both offenders and law enforcement officials. See Arsovska and Sartorius (2008).

12. This statement is based on a personal interview with Vladimir Sharovic, police officer from Macedonia, during an expert workshop in Belgium (October 3, 2008).

13. Nedzmedin Ajeti was a former commander of the National Liberation Army and died after a fight in the bar Brus (Chancharevic 2009).

14. See Raufer and Quéré (2000; 2006); Cilluffo and Salmoiraghi (1999); Lucic (1988).

15. See Arsovska and Sartorius (2008).

16. See also *Mob Talk* documentary, Fox 29 TV, October 23, 2009, available at www.myfoxphilly.com/story/17540196/mob-talk-john-alite.

6. SEX, GUNS, AND EXTORTION

1. The arguments in this section are mainly based on investigative police files on human trafficking cases from Belgium and interviews with law enforcement officials. Experts from the Payoke victim shelter in Belgium were also interviewed, as were experts from the trafficking unit of the Center for Equal Opportunities and Combating Racism in Belgium. See also Hippokrates Project (2001).

2. These data were presented by participants at a seminar on international trafficking of women and children that took place in Tirana, Albania, in 1998; see also Koja (1998).

3. Some of the observations regarding the operational methods of the traffickers, discussed in this section, are based on personal interviews with Belgian law enforcement officials (August and September 2006), a Dutch law enforcement official (February 2006), and representatives from victim shelters (Patsy Sorensen and Stef Janssens, April 2007).

4. See Hysi (2005, 546); IOM/IMCM (2002, 10); Hippokrates Project (2001); CEOOR (2005, 2006); Boustany (2003).

5. Cases are based on a report provided by Belgian victim shelter Payoke; see Hippocrates Project (2001, 15).

6. This case is based on a report by the organization Save the Children. See Renton (2001).

7. Since 2010, there have been some positive developments for women in Kosovo. For example, a woman was elected president of Kosovo in 2011.

8. See Becucci (2004); International Crisis Group (2000a); Renton (2001).

9. This section is based on personal interviews with Macedonian law enforcement officials and with Patsy Sorensen, director of the Belgian victim shelter Payoke (2007 and 2008).

10. *Smash and Grab: The Story of the Pink Panthers* is a 2013 documentary by Havana Marking about the international jewel theft network known as the Pink Panthers.

11. This observation is based on personal interviews with law enforcement officials from Belgium and the Netherlands conducted between February 2008 and July 2009. See also Arsovska and Sartorius 2008.

12. For more information on Alex Rudaj, see the FBI Organized Crime webpage and the US Department of Justice press release (October 26, 2004), available at www.justice.gov/usao/nys/pressreleases/Octobero4/rudajindictpr.pdf.

13. I have interviewed four law enforcement officials during 2006 and 2007 that have been working on this case. The police file also was reviewed.

14. See Gambetta (1993) on the Sicilian Mafia and its business of private protection.

15. This term was used by the famous Albanian writer Ismail Kadare (1998) in his novel *Broken April*.

16. See Katz (1990); McGrew et al. (1992); Squires (2000).

17. The video of the escape can be found at *Huffington Post* (2009).

18. YouTube videos of the Dubai robbery s well as the viewers' comments can be found at www.youtube.com/watch?v=aj4nNtHWiyU and www.youtube.com/watch?v=_MQAjI-IQbjM.

REFERENCES

Adams, J. 2008. "Three Germans Detained Related to Attack on EU Office in Kosovo." *Christian Science Monitor,* November 24.

Ahmetaj, K., and M. Carew. 2004. *A High Price for Dreams.* Prishtina: *UNMIK, OMPF.* www.unmikonline.org/pub/focuskos/oct2004/focuskosaffair1.htm.

Albanese, J. 1994. "Models of Organised Crime." In *Handbook of Organized Crime in the United States,* edited by R. J. Kelly, K. Chin, and R. Schatzberg, 77–89. Westport, CT: Greenwood Press.

———. 2000. "The Causes of Organised Crime." *Journal of Contemporary Justice* 16 (4): 409–423.

Albeu (2010). "Ç'ka mbetur nga Kadriovski?" December 28. www.albeu.com/maqedoni /cka-mbetur-nga-kadriovski/27334/

Albini, J. L. 1971. *The American Mafia: Genesis of a Legend.* New York: Appleton-Century Crofts.

Alexe, V. 1998. "Albanian Terrorists of KLA Pay Weapon in Heroin." *Romania Libera* 12, July 30."

Aliu, F. 2012. "Krasniqi: Kosovo MPs are Scared of SHIK." *Balkan Insight Pristina,* August 6.

Allen, P. 2009. "Three Suspected Pink Panther Gang Members Arrested in Monaco." *The London Daily Telegraph,* June 20.

Allum, F., and S. Gilmour. 2012. *Routledge Handbook on Transnational Organized Crime.* New York. Routledge.

Alston, P. 2010. "The Blood Feud Phenomenon in Albania." UN Press Release (Report by UN Special Rapporteur on Extrajudicial Executions), February 23.

Amnesty International. 2006. *Albania: Violence against Women in the Family: "It's Not Her Shame."* 19 April.

Anastasijevic, D. 2006. "Organized Crime in the Western Balkans." *HUMSEC Working Paper,* European Commission.

Andelman, D. A. 1994. "The Drug Money Maze." *Foreign Affairs* 73 (4): 94–108.

Anderson, E. 1999. *Code of the Street: Decency, Violence, and the Moral Life of the Inner City.* New York: W. W. Norton & Company.

Anderson, S. E., and G. Howard G., eds. 1998. *Interrogating Popular Culture: Deviance, Justice, and Social Order.* Guilderland, NY: Harrow & Heston.

Annese, J. M. 2010. "Career Criminal Tied to Bank Job." *Staten Island Advance,* March 3. www.silive.com/news/index.ssf/2010/03/career_criminal_tied_to_bank_j.html.

———. 2011. "Staten Island Garage Housed $10M-a-Year Pot Operation, Authorities Allege." *Staten Island Advance,* August 12.

Antonopoulous, G., J. Tierney, and C. Webster. 2008. "Police Perceptions of Migration and Migrants in Greece." *Criminal Law and Criminal Justice* 16 (1): 353–378.

Arlacchi, P. 1986. *Mafia Businesses: The Mafia and the Spirit of Capitalism.* London: Verso.

Arsovska, J., and F. Allum, F. 2014. "Introduction: Women and Transnational Organized Crime." *Trends in Organized Crime* 17 (1–2): 1–15.

Arsovska, J., and M. Craig. 2006. "'Honourable' Behaviour and the Conceptualisation of Violence in Ethnic-Based Organised Crime Groups: An Examination of the Albanian Kanun and the Code of the Chinese Triads." *Global Crime* 7 (2): 214–246.

Arsovska, J., and S. Janssens. 2009. "Human Trafficking and the Police: Good and Bad Practices." In *Strategies against Human Trafficking: The Role of the Security Sector,* edited by Cornelius Friesendorf, 169–211. Geneva: DCAF and Austrian National Defence Academy.

Arsovska, J., and P. Kostakos. 2008. "Illicit Arms Trafficking and the Limits of Rational Choice Theory: The Case of the Balkans." *Trends in Organized Crime* 11 (4): 352–387.

Arsovska, J., and L. Sartorius. 2008. "Ethnic Albanian Organized Crime: A Real or Perceived Threat." International Expert Workshop. Brussels, Belgian Federal Police, October 2–3. www.law.kuleuven.be/strafrecht/BijlagenENGenNEDL/EACG_WORK-SHOP_FINAL_PROGRAM_OCT%202008.pdf.

Arsovska, J., and P. Verduyn. 2008. "Globalisation, Conduct Norms and 'Culture Conflict': Perceptions of Violence and Crime in an Ethnic Albanian Context." *British Journal of Criminology* 48 (2): 226–246.

Asale, A. 2003. "The Racial Economies of Criminalization, Immigration and Policing in Italy." *Social Justice* 30 (3): 48–62.

Ashley, D. G. 2003. "Eurasian, Italian, and Balkan Organized Crime." Testimony of Grant D. Ashley, Assistant Director, Criminal Investigative Division, FBI, US Senate, October 30.

Baban, A. 2004. *Domestic Violence against Women in Albania.* Tirana: UNICEF Report.

Babanovski, I. 2002. *ONA teroristicka paravojska vo Makedonija.* Skopje: Veda.

Babic, J. 2001. "MORH [Defense Ministry of Croatia] Protects Arms Dealers Who Smuggle Weapons to ETA and IRA." *Nacional,* 24 July.

Bacelli, A. n.d. "Zbulohen dokumentet e CIA-s dhe FBI-se per Xhevdet Mustafen." *Shqiperia.com.* www.shqiperia.com/lajme/lajm/nr/9174/Zbulohen-dokumentet-e-CIA-s-dhe-FBI-se-per-Xhevdet-Mustafen

Baldwin-Edwards, M. 2004. "Albanian Emigration and the Greek Labor Market: Economic Symbiosis and Social Ambiguity." *South-East Europe Review* 1 (1): 51–66.

Balkanforum 2013. "Gambino Clan and the Albanian Muslim Mafia." Balkanblog.org, October 15. http://balkanblog.org/2013/10/15/gambino-clan-and-the-albanian-muslim-mafia/.

Barbes, E. J. 1999. "2 Cleared on Some Counts in 1996 Slayings at Scores." *New York Times,* January 31.

Barjaba, K. 2004. "Albania: Looking beyond Borders." *Immigration Policy Institute,* August 1.

Barron, B. 2000. "Albanian Mafia Steps Up People Smuggling." *BBC News Online,* August 3. http://news.bbc.co.uk/2/hi/europe/863620.stm,

Basha, D. 2013. "Globalization and the Rise of Salafism in Kosovo." MA Thesis, The New School.

Bauman, Z. 1997. *Postmodernity and Its Discontents.* Cambridge: Blackwell Publishing.

Bazargan, D. 2003. "Balkan Gun Traffickers Target UK." *BBC News,* 5 December.

BBC. 2000. "Kosovo Gripped by Racketeers." April 5.

———. 2003a. "Prison for Sex Slave Gang Leader." December 22.

———. 2003b. "EU Targets Balkan Crime." June 21.

———. 2005. "UN Court Acquits Top Kosovo Rebel." 30 November.

———. 2008a. "Serbian Arms Industry Expects to Thrive on Major Gun Making Deal with Iraq." *SEESAC/BBC Monitoring Service,* 10 March.

———. 2008b. "Macedonian Police Arrest Alleged Leader of Organized Criminal Gang." Macedonian Information Agency (MIA), October 22.

———. 2010. "Macedonian Police Seize Eight Tons of Illegally Distributed Cigarettes." Macedonian Information Agency (MIA), October 31.

BBC Monitoring. 2005. "Italian Report Warns of Threat by Rise of Albanian Mafia." December 26.

BBC World Broadcasts. 1993a. "Tanjug: Albanian Bandits Raiding Villages in Western Macedonia." December 15.

Beccaria, C. (1764) 1996. *On Crimes and Punishment.* Translated by Jane Grigson. New York: Marsilio Publishers.

Becker, G. 1962. "Irrational Behavior and Economic Theory." *Journal of Political Economy* 70 (1): 1–13.

———. 1976. *The Economic Approach to Human Behavior.* Chicago: University of Chicago Press.

Becucci, S. 2004. "Human Trafficking in Italy." Unpublished paper presented at the CIROC Conference, Amsterdam, Netherlands, June 2004.

Bell, D. 1953. "Crime as an American Way of Life." *The Antioch Review* 13: 131–154.

Bennetto, J. 2002. "Albanians 'Taking Over London Vice.'" *The Independent,* November 25. http://www.independent.co.uk/news/uk/crime/albanians-taking-over-london-vice-605315.html.

Bernburg, J. 2009. "Labeling Theory." In *Handbook on Crime and Deviance,* edited by M. D. Krohn., G. P. Hall and A. J. Lizotte, 187–207. New York: Springer.

BETA. 2001. "BETA: Profile of Macedonia's NLA Leader Ali Ahmeti." *Balkan Human Rights List,* August 2.

Binder, D. 1991. "The Land of Talkative Men and Toiling Women." *The New York Times,* April 23.

Binder, D., and P. Mendenhall. 2003. "Sex, Drugs and Guns in the Balkans: Ethnic Albanian Rebels Benefit From Sex Slavery." *MSNBC*, December 11.

Black, D. 1993. *The Social Structure of Right and Wrong.* San Diego: Academic Press.

Block, A. (1974) 1988. *The Mafia of a Sicilian Village 1860–1960: A Study of Violent Peasant Entrepreneurs.* Long Grove, Illinois: Waveland Press.

Bogdanich, W. 2003. "Stealing the Code: Con Men and Cash Machines; Criminals Focus on A.T.M.'s, Weak Link in Banking System." *The New York Times.* August 3.

Boomgaarden, H., and E. Rens. 2009. "How News Content Influences Anti-Immigration Attitudes: Germany, 1993–2005." *European Journal of Political Research* 48 (4): 516–542.

Boustany, N. 2003. "Taking Aim at Exploitation, Enslavement Of Women." *The Washington Post,* October 1.

Boyes, R., and E. Wright. 1999. "The Times: Drugs Money Linked to Kosovo Rebels." *The Times of London,* March 24.

Bozinovich, M. n.d. "The New Islamic Mafia." Serbianna.com, http://www.serbianna.com /columns/mb/028.shtml.

Bregu, Z. 2005. "Albania: Crime Wave Alarms Bosses." Institute for War and Peace Reporting (IWPR'S Balkan Crisis Report), No. 428, September 6.

Bromley, M. 2007. "UN Arms Embargoes: Their Impact on Arms Flows and Target Behaviour. Case Study: Former Yugoslavia, 1991–96." Stockholm: Stockholm International Peace Research Institute.

Brunnwasser, M. 2011. "Death of War Crimes Witness Casts Cloud over Kosovo." *The New York Times,* October 6.

Bureau of Democracy, Human Rights and Labour. 2006. *Country Reports on Human Rights Practices: Macedonia.* March 8.

Burrell, I. 2001. "Albanian Mafia Takes Control of Soho Vice Scene." *The Independent,* June 18.

Camaj, M. 1989. *The Code of Lekë Dukagjini.* Translated by Leonard Fox. Compiled by Shtjefën Gjeçov. New York: Gjonlekaj Publishing Company.

Campanile, C. 2004. "Albania Mafia Broken—Feds Charge 22 Here." *New York Post,* October 27.

Castells, M. 2000. *End of Millennium.* Oxford: Blackwell Publishers.

Cencich, J. 2013. *The Devil's Garden: A War Crimes Investigator's Story.* Washington, DC: Potomac Books.

CEOOR. 2005. *Belgian Policy on Trafficking in and Smuggling of Human Beings: Shadows and Lights.* Brussels: CEOOR Publication.

———. 2006. *Annual Report Human Trafficking.* Brussels: CEOOR Publication.

Chambliss, W. 1988. *On the Take: From Petty Crooks to President.* Bloomington: Indiana University Press.

Chambliss, W., and E. Williams. 2012. "Transnational Organized Crime and Social Sciences Myths." In *Routledge Handbook of Transnational Organized Crime,* edited by F. Allum and S. Gilmore, 52–64. London: Routledge.

Chancharevic, O. 2009. "Се вжештува скопското подземје" ("The underground in Skopje is heating up"). *Nova Makedonija,* August 1.

Christoph, V. 2012. "The Role of Mass Media in the Integration of Migrants." *International Mind, Brain and Education Society* 6 (2): 97–105.

Chu, Y. K. 2000. *The Triads as Business*. London: Routledge.

Cilluffo, F., and G. Salmoiraghi. 1999. "And the Winner is . . . The Albanian Mafia." *The Washington Quarterly* 22 (4): 21–25.

CIR (Center for Investigative Reporting). 2009. "Naser Kelmendi: From Kosovo Inmate to Sarajevo Businessman." N°18, November 20.

Çiuli, D. 1996. "Women in Albania: Opportunities and Obstacles."*Mediterranean Review* 3 (2).

Clarke, R. V., and M. Felson, eds. 1993. *Routine Activity and Rational Choice*. Advances in Criminological Theory 5. New Brunswick, NJ: Transaction Press.

Cleland, W. A., S. Kondi, D. Stinson, and P. M. Von Tangen, eds. 2006. *Internal Security Sector Review (ISSR) Kosovo*. Pristina: UNDP.

Cloward, A. R., and E. O. Ohlin. 1960. *Delinquency and Opportunity: A Theory of Delinquent Gangs*. New York: Free Press.

Cobain, I. 2002. "Albanians Take Over Organised Crime." *The Times*, November 26.

Cohen, A. K. 1955. *Delinquent Boys: The Culture of the Gang*. New York: Free Press.

Cohen, E. L., and M. Felson. 1979. "Social Change and Crime Rate Trends: A Routine Activity Approach." *American Sociological Review* 44 (4): 588–608.

Collins, R. 2008. *Violence: A Micro-Sociological Theory*. Princeton, NJ: Princeton University Press.

Council of the European Union. 2003. *EU Action against Organized Crime in the Western Balkans*. No. 14810/03 CRIMORG 88, Brussels, December 2.

Cressey, D. R. 1969. *Theft of the Nation: The Structure and Operations of Organized Crime in America*. New York: Harper and Row.

CSD (Center for the Study of Democracy). 2004. *Partners in Crime: Analysis*. Report 13. Sofia: CSD.

Cullen, K. 2000. "A Year after Kosovo War, UN Is Facing a Quagmire." *Boston Globe*, March 19.

Curtis, G., and T. Caracan. 2002. *The Nexus among Terrorists, Narcotics Traffickers, Weapons Proliferators, and Organized Crime Networks in Western Europe*. Washington DC: Federal Research Division, Library of Congress.

Cvetkovic, V. 2006. *Serbian Society and Gun Culture*. Pristina: OSCE.

Daily Mail. 2010. "Pictured: The Albanian Immigrant Gang Free Pose with High-Powered Machine Guns on Bebo and YouTube." January 8. www.dailymail.co.uk/news /article-1241578/Sickening-pictures-immigrant-gang-posing-high-powered-weapons-rapping-killing.html

Daskalovski, Z. 2004. *The Macedonian Conflict of 2001: Problems of Democratic Consolidation*. Sindelfingen: Libertas.

del Ponte, C., and C. Sudetic. 2008. *La caccia: Io e i criminali di guerra* (The hunt: Me and the war criminals). Milan: Giangiacomo Feltrinelli Editore.

DeStefano, A. M. 1985. "Giuliani and Kosovo-Albanian Drug Mafia in NYC." *Wall Street Journal*, September 9.

Dimovski, S. 2012. "Macedonia's Boskoski Charged with Assisting Murder." Balkaninsight, October 19.

Donnelly, F. 2013. "Staten Island Cop and Friend Who Fatally Stabbed Man Last Year Are Accused of Shaking Down Queens Restaurateur." Silve.com News, December 3. www .silive.com/news/index.ssf/2013/12/staten_island_cop_and_pal_who.htm.

Douglas, M. 1985. *Risk Acceptability According to the Social Sciences.* New York: Russell Sage Foundation.

Durham, E. M. 1909. *High Albania.* London: Edward Arnold.

Durkheim, E. 1965a. *The Division of Labor in Society.* Translated by George Simpson. New York: Free Press.

———. 1965b. "The Normal and the Pathological." *The Rules of the Sociological Method,* edited by George E. G. Catlin and translated by Sarah A. Solovay and John H. Muller, 65–73. New York: Free Press.

Eide, E. 1994. "The Determinants of Crime." In *Economics of Crime: Deterrence and the Rational Offender,* edited by E. Eide, 7–85. Bradford, JK: Emerald Group Publishing Limited.

Ekonomi, M., E. Gjermeni, E. Danaj, E. Lula, and L. Beci. 2006. *Creating Opportunities for Women in Albania.* Tirana: Gender Alliance for Development Center.

Elezi, I. 2003. *Knowledge on the Pan-Albanian Customary Law.* Pristina: University of Prishtina.

European Council. 2003. *A Secure Europe in a Better World: European Security Strategy* (document adopted at the European Council in Brussels on December 12). France: The EU Institute for Security Studies.

European Stability Initiative. 2008. *The Albanian Renaissance.* ESI Briefing, European Parliament, May 21.

Europol. 2011. *Octa 2011: EU Organised Crime Threat Assessment.* www.europol.europa.eu/sites/default/files/publications/octa_2011_1.pdf.

Eurostat 2007. *Living Conditions in Europe. Data 2002–2005.* Brussels: European Commission.

Fahim, K., and A. Feuer. 2006. "Beating Them at Their Own Game; Albanian Groups Are Muscling into Mob Land, Officials Say." *The New York Times.* January 3.

Falcone, G., with M. Padovani. 1992. *Men of Honour: The Truth about the Mafia.* London: Warner.

Farnam, A. 2003. "Gun Culture Stymies the UN in Kosovo." *The Christian Science Monitor,* September 26.

FBI. 2006. "Not Your Average Syndicate: The Rise and Fall of an Albanian Organized Crime Ring." *FBI Press Release,* March 29.

———. 2009. "Albanian Organized Crime." *FBI Podcasts and Radio,* November 27. www.fbi.gov/news/podcasts/inside/albanian-organized-crime.mp3/view.

———. 2013. "New York City Police Officer and Criminal Associates Charged with Extorting Queens Restauranteur." *FBI Press Release,* December 3.

Ferrell, J. 1998. "Culture, Crime and Cultural Criminology." In *Interrogating Popular Culture,* edited by S. E. Anderson and J. G. Howard, 1–16. New York: Willow Tree Press.

Ferrell, J., K. Hayward, and J. Young. 2008. *Cultural Criminology: An Investigation.* Los Angeles: SAGE.

Feuer, A. 2007a. "Officer Is Accused of Serving as Gang's Driver and Lookout." *The New York Times,* July 19.

———. 2007b. "Informant Returns to Court, This Time Facing Charges." *The New York Times,* July 28.

———. 2009. "A 4th Mistrial in Federal Prosecution of John A. Gotti." *New York Times,* December 1.

Filkins, Dexter. 2001. "In the Bronx, Ethnic Mix Breeds Tensions at School." *New York Times,* February 12.

Fitsanakis, J. 2008. "German Intelligence Active in Kosovo." *IntelNews,* November 29. http://intelnews.org/about/latest-analysis/content/analysis001/

Fleishman, J. 1999. "Italy Battling a New Wave of Criminals—Albanians Refugees Are Cutting into the Mafia Turf." *The Philadelphia Inquirer,* March 15.

———. 2009. "Balkans' Pink Panther Jewel Thieves Smash Their Way into Myth." *Los Angeles Times,* July 29. www.latimes.com/la-fg-balkan-panthers29-2009jul29-story.html#page=1.

Flikins, D. 2001. "In the Bronx, Ethnic Mix Breeds Tensions at School." *The New York Times,* February 12. www.nytimes.com/2001/02/12/nyregion/in-the-bronx-ethnic-mix-breeds-tensions-at-school.html.

Fox, L. trans. 1989. *The Code of Lekë Dukagjini/Kaunui I Lekë Dukagjinit.* Compiled by Shtjefën Gjeçov. New York: Gjonlekaj Publishing Company.

Galeotti, M. 1998. "The Albanian Connection." *Jane's International Policing,* December 2.

———. 2001. "Albanian Gangs Gain Foothold in European Crime Underworld." *Jane's Intelligence Review* 13: 25–27.

———, ed. 2005. *Global Crime Today: The Changing Face of Organised Crime.* London: Routledge.

Galliher J. F., and J. A. Cain. 1974. "Citation Support for the Mafia Myth in Criminology Textbooks." *American Sociologist* 9: 68–74.

Gambetta, D. 1993. *The Sicilian Mafia: The Business of Private Protection.* Cambridge, MA: Harvard University Press.

Gashi, G. V. 2009. *Poverty and Gender Equality: UNDP Development and Transition Report.* Vienna: UNDP.

Gazeta Shqip Online. 2011. "Terrorist in the US, Humanitarians in Kosovo." November 24.

Gazeta Shqiptare Online. 2009. "Haxhiu: Aldo Bare e mbante në dorë kokën e prerë të Tur Dajës." September 5. www.balkanweb.com/gazetav5/newsadmin/preview.php?id=64978.

Gendar, A., and C. Siemaszko. 2009. "Mob Turncoat John Alite Testifies He Got Nails Done with John Gotti Jr. after Drug Dealer's Murder." *Daily News,* October 1.

Gendercide Watch. 2002. *Honour Killings and Blood Feuds.* www.gendercide.org/case_honour.html.

Gërxhani, K., and A. Schram. 2000. "Albanian Political-Economics: Consequences of a Clan Culture." MA thesis, Catholic University of Leuven, Belgium.

Ghosh, P. 2012. "Tip of the Iceberg: French Police Arrest Albanian Heroin Traffickers, but Balkan Criminal Gangs Tighten Grip across Europe." *International Business Time,* October 16.

Giddens, A. 1971. *Capitalism and Modern Social Theory: An Analysis of the Writings of Marx, Durkheim and Max Weber.* Cambridge: Cambridge University Press.

Gjipali, S., and L. Ruci. 1994. *The Albanian Woman: Hesitation and Perspectives, Gains and Losses: Women and Transition in Eastern and Central Europe.* Bucharest: European Network for Women's Studies.

Gjonça, A. 2001. *Communism, Health and Lifestyle: The Paradox of Mortality Transition in Albania, 1950–1990.* Westport, CT: Greenwood Press.

Goldstein, J., and M. Secret. 2013. "Police Officer Charged in Queens Extortion Racket." *New York Times,* December 3.

Gonzalez, G. 1992. "Just Boys Being Boys, or Vicious Gangs?" *New York Times,* January 16.

Goodnough, A. 1994. "Albanians Seek Strength in Unity." *New York Times,* July 17. www.nytimes.com/1994/07/17/nyregion/neighborhood-report-central-bronx-albanians-seek-strength-in-unity.html.

Gotovski, M. 2011. *Monitoring na sudski predmeti od oblasta na trgovijata so luge i ilegalna migracija vo Makedonija 2010 godina.* Skopje: NVO.

Graham, P. 2000. "Drug Wars: Kosovo's New Battle." *National Post* (The Center for Peace in the Balkans), April 13.

Grutzpalk, J. 2002. "Blood Feud and Modernity." *Journal of Classical Sociology* 2 (2): 115–134.

The Guardian. 2013. "Kosovo Police Arrest Suspected Balkan Drug Boss Naser Kelmendi." May 6.

———. 2014. "Grenades Fired at Albanian Police during Cannabis Crackdown." June 16.

Habermas, J. (1962) 1989. *The Structural Transformation of the Public Sphere: An Inquiry into a Category of Bourgeois Society.* Cambridge, MA: Polity Press.

Hafizullah, E. 1992. "Development Strategies and Women in Albania." *Economic and Political Weekly* 27 (19): 999–118.

Hagan, J. 1973. "Labeling and Deviance: A Case Study in the Sociology of the Interesting." *Social Problems* 20 (4): 447–458.

Hajdinjak, M. 2002. *Smuggling in South East Europe, The Yugoslav Wars and the Development of Regional Criminal Networks in the Balkans.* Sofia: Center for the Study of Democracy.

Hall, A., and J. Philips. 2000. "Albanian Mafia Sells Babies in Germany." The Center for Peace in the Balkans, July 1. www.balkanpeace.org/index.php?index=article&articleid=9828.

Hamzaj, B. 2000. *A Narrative about War and Freedom: Dialog with the Commander Ramush Haradinaj.* Prishtina: Zari.

Hartocollis, A. 2005. "Albanian Gang Portrayed as Aspiring Mafiosi." *New York Times,* December 20.

Hasluck, M. 1954. *The Unwritten Law in Albania.* Cambridge: Cambridge University Press.

Hayward, K. J. 2004. *City Limits: Crime, Consumer Culture and the Urban Experience.* London: GlassHouse Press.

———. 2007. "Situational Crime Prevention and Its Discontents: Rational Choice Theory Versus the 'Culture of Now.'" *Social Policy and Administration* 41 (3): 232–250.

Hayward, K., and M. Yar. 2006. "The 'Chav' Phenomenon: Consumption, Media and the Construction of a New Underclass." *Crime, Media and Culture* 2 (9): 9–28.

Haziri, L. 2003. *Arms in Macedonia: Survey.* Association for Democratic Initiatives. Skopje: AD.

Heinemann-Grüder, A., and W.-C. Paes. 2001. *Wag the Dog: The Mobilization and Demobilization of the Kosovo Liberation Army,* Bonn International Centre for Conversion (BICC), Brief no. 20.

Heldman, K. 2011a. "The Big Trial: An Albanian-American Crime Story, from 15 Mile Road to Pearl Street." *The New York Capital,* June 9.

———. 2011b. "The Streets of Tirana and the Roots of Albanian-American Organized Crime." *Capital New York,* June 14.

Hill, P. B. E. 2003. *The Japanese Mafia.* Oxford: Oxford University Press.

Hippokrates Project. 2001. *Research Based on Case Studies of Victims of Trafficking in Human Beings in 3 EU Member States, i.e. Belgium, Italy and The Netherlands, Commission of the European Communities* (Project JAI/2001/HIP/023). http://ec.europa.eu/justice_home/daphnetoolkit/files/projects/2001_010/int_trafficking_case_studies_be_it_nl_hippokrates.pdf.

Hobbs, D. 1998. "Going Down the Glocal: The Local Context of Organised Crime." *Howard Journal of Criminal Justice* 37 (2): 407–422.

Hoffman, W., and L. Headley. 1993. *Contract Killer: The Explosive Story of the Mafia's Most Notorious Hitman Donald "Tony the Greek" Frankos.* New York: Kensington Publishing.

Holbrook, M. B., and E. C. Hirschman. 1986. "The Experimental Aspects of Consumption: Consumer Fantasies, Feelings and Fun." *Journal of Consumer Research* 9: 132–140.

Hopkins, R. 2004. "Human Trafficking in Albania." Unpublished paper presented at Center for Information and Research on Organized Crime (CIROC), Amsterdam, Netherlands, June.

———. 2005. "Slavenhandel op de Wallen" (Slave trade in the red light district). *NRC Handelsblad,* October 1. http://vorige.nrc.nl/nieuwsthema/mensenhandel/article2178819.ece/Slavenhandel_op_de_Wallen.

Horvath, A., T. Bjørn, and H. Wydra. 2009. "Introduction: Liminality and Cultures of Change." *International Political Anthropology,* 2 (1): 3–4.

Hoxha, A. 2008. "Altin Dardha, si i shpëtoi atentatit në korrik 1997." *Gazeta Shqiptare Online,* November 19. www.balkanweb.com/gazetav5/newsadmin/preview.php?id=47864.

Huffington Post. 2009. "Vassilis Paleokostas, Alket Rizaj: Greeks Hunt For Convicts Who Escaped By Helicopter." March 9. www.huffingtonpost.com/2009/02/23/vassilis-paleokostas-alke_n_169227.html.

Huisman, S. 2004. *Public Administration, Police and Security Services, Corruption and Organised Crime in Albania.* Unpublished paper presented at Center for Information and Research on Organized Crime (CIROC), Amsterdam, Netherlands, June.

Human Rights Watch. 2003. "Albania: Human Rights Developments." *World Report 2003.* www.hrw.org/wr2k3/europe1.html].

Hysi, V. 2005. "Organised Crime Control in Albania: The Long and Difficult Path to Meet International Standards and Develop Effective Policies." In *Organised Crime in Europe: Concepts, Patterns and Control Policies in the EU and Beyond,* edited by C. Fijnaut and L. Paoli, 963–987. Rotterdam: Springer.

Ianni, F. A. J., and E. Reuss-Ianni. 1972. *A Family Business.* New York: Russell Sage.

Ilievski, A., and B. Dobovšek. 2013. "Operation of the Albanian Mafia in the Republic of Macedonia." *Journal of Criminal Justice and Security* 15 (2): 190–202.

Immigration and Refugee Board of Canada. 1994. *Macedonia: Information on Whether Harassment or Extortion Is Used by Albanians to Force Macedonian Landowners to Sell Their Lands, and the Protection Available to Victims of Such Extortion.* MCD18868.E. UNHCR Refworld, November 1.

Internal Police News. 2009. "German Diplomat Arrested for Espionage in Kosovo." March 19.

International Crisis Group. 2000a. *Albania: State of the Nation.* Europe Report No 87, 1 March. www.crisisgroup.org/en/regions/europe/balkans/albania/087-albania-state-of-the-nation.aspx.

————. 2000b. *What Happened to the KLA?* Europe Report no. 88, March 3. www.crisis-group.org/en/regions/europe/balkans/kosovo/088-what-happened-to-the-kla.aspx.

————. 2001. *Bin Laden and the Balkans: The Politics of Anti-Terrorism.* Europe Report no. 119, November 9.

————. 2010. *The Rule of Law in Independent Kosovo.* Europe Report no. 204, May 19. www.crisisgroup.org/~/media/Files/europe/balkans/kosovo/204%20The%20rule%20of%20Law%20in%20Independent%20Kosovo.pdf.

IOM/IMCM (International Organization for Migration/International Catholic Migration Commission). 2002. *Research Report on Third Country National Trafficking Victims in Albania.* Tirana: IOM/IMCM.

Nebiu, S. 2003. *Fakti,* March 19, 7. Reported also by the International Organization for Migration (IOM), Skopje.

————. 2004. "Changing Patterns and Trends of Trafficking in Persons in the Balkan Region." Geneva: IOM.

ISSR (Institute for Social Science Research). 2006. *Kosovo Internal Security Review.* Prishtina: Rrota.

Jacques, E. Edwin. 1995. *The Albanians: An Ethnic History from Prehistoric Times to Present.* Jefferson, NC: McFarland & Company.

Jamieson, A., and A. Sily. 1998. "Migration and Criminality: The Case of Albanians in Italy." *Ethnobarometer Programme Working Paper Number 1.* CSS/CEMES Publication.

Jarvis, G. 2000. "The Rise and Fall of Albania's Pyramid Schemes." *IMF Finance and Development* 37 (1). www.imf.org/external/pubs/ft/fandd/2000/03/jarvis.htm.

JIR (Jane's Intelligence Review). 1999. "KLA Action Fuelled NATO Victory." *Jane's Defence Weekly,* June 16.

————. 2007. "Jane's Sentinel Security Assessment—The Balkans." *Jane's Defence Weekly* June 13.

————. 2009. "Networking Sites—Criminal Group Expands across the Balkans." *Jane's Intelligence Review* 21 (12): 43–47.

Johnson, B. A. 2012. "Sam Zherka: People Love Him, Politicians Hate Him." *New Britain City Journal,* November 29.

The Johnsville News. 2004. "The Rudaj Organization aka: The Albanian Mafia." November 2. http://johnsville.blogspot.com/2004/11/rudaj-organization-aka-albanian-mafia.html.

Jolis, B. 1997. "Honour Killing Makes a Comeback." *Albanian Life* 57 (1): 25–35.

Jonsson, M. 2013. "The Kosovo Conflict: From Humanitarian Intervention to State Capture." In *Political Economy of Armed Conflict in Eurasia,* edited by C. Svante and M. Jonsson, 177–199. Philadelphia: University of Pennsylvania Press.

Kadare, I. 1998. *Broken April.* Chicago: New Amsterdam Books.

Kamm, H. 1982. "Firefight on Albania Coast Stirs Speculations on Internal Woes." *The New York Times,* October 16.

Katona, G. 1975. *Psychological Economics.* New York: Elsevier.

Karadaku, L. 2011. "Major Drug Bust in Albania." *Southeast European Times,* March 31.

Kasapi, J. 2013. "Dritan Dajti Threatens Court Members: I'll Exert Pressure on Your Relatives." *Albanian Screen,* June 18.

Katz, J. 1990. *Seductions of Crime: Moral and Sensual Attractions in Doing Evil.* New York: Basic Books.

Kauer, E. 2007. "Weapons Collection and Destruction Programmes in Bosnia and Herzegovina." In *Small Arms—Big Problem: A Global Threat to Peace, Security and Development*, edited by Peter Hazdra, 81–103. Vienna: Schriftenreihe der Landesverteidigungsakademie.

Kenny, M. 1999. "When Criminals Out-Smart the State: Understanding the Learning Capacity of Columbian Drug Trafficking Organizations." *Transnational Organized Crime* 5 (1): 97–119.

KFOR (Kosovo Force). 2004. *Target Folder Xhavit Haliti, Secret Rel USA KFOR and NATO*. March 10. www.mafialand.de/Members/juergen/pdf/kosovo%20-%20Haliti%20Xhavit.pdf.

Khakee, A., and N. Florquin. 2003. *Kosovo and the Gun: A Baseline Assessment of Small Arms and Light Weapons in Kosovo*. Geneva: UNDP and Small Arms Survey.

King, R., and N. Mai. 2004. "Albanian Immigrants in Lecce and Modena: Narratives of Rejection, Survival and Integration." *Population, Space and Place* 10 (6): 455–477.

Kinsella, D. 2006. "The Black Market in Small Arms: Examining a Social Network." *Contemporary Security Policy* 27 (1): 100–117.

Kitsantonis, N., and M. Brunwasser. 2006. "Baby Trafficking is Thriving in Greece – Europe." *New York Times*, December 18. www.nytimes.com/2006/12/18/world/europe/18iht-babies.3939121.html?pagewanted=all.

Klebnikov, P. 2000. "Heroin Heroes." *Mother Jones*, January–February. www.motherjones.com/politics/2000/01/heroin-heroes.

Kleemans, E. R., and G. H. van de Bunt. 1999. "The Social Embeddedness of Organized Crime." *Transnational Organized Crime* 5 (1): 19–36.

Koha Ditore. 2008. "Police Smash Weapons Trafficking Ring in Kosovo, Albania." Top Channel. September 22.

Koja, G. J. 1998. "8000 Albanian Girls Work as Prostitutes in Italy." HURINet (The Human Rights Information Network), July 25.

Kokalari, G. 2007. "Mafia Report in Albania." Albanian-Canadian League Information Service, June 10.

Kosic, A., and K. Phalet. 2006. "Ethnic Categorization of Immigrants: The Role of Prejudice, Perceived Acculturation Strategies and Group Size." *International Journal of Intercultural Relations* 30 (1): 769–782.

Krug, E. G., L. Dahlberg, J. A. Mercy, A. Zwi, and R. Lozano, eds. 2002. *World Report on Violence and Health*. Geneva: World Health Organization.

Kulish, N., and S. Mekhennet. 2008. "Small Blast in Kosovo Chafes Bond with Germany." *New York Times*, November 24.

Laing, P. 2012. Albanian Crime Gangs Top List of Most Feared Foreign Gangsters. *Deadline News*, January 15.

Lallemand, A. 2007. "La Mafia Albanese Choisit la Belgique." *Le Soir*, May 9.

Lawson, C., and D. Saltmarshe. 2000. "Security and Economic Transition: Evidence from North Albania." *Europe-Asia Studies* 52 (1): 133–148.

Leman, J., and S. Janssens. 2006. "Human Smuggling and Trafficking From/via Eastern Europe: The Former Intelligence and the Intermediary Structures." *Kolor Journal on Moving Communities* 6 (1): 19–40.

———. 2007. "Travel Agencies as a Linking Element for Human Smuggling and Trafficking from Eastern Europe." *Migration Studies* 44 (166): 443–459.

Levi, P. 1989. *The Drowned and the Saved.* New York: Vintage.

Lewis, P. 2011. "Report Identifies Hashim Thaci as 'Big Fish' in Organized Crime." *The Guardian,* January 24.

Likmeta, B. 2011. "Albania's Aldo Bare to Receive New Trial." *Balkan Insight,* October 11.

———. 2013a. "Albania Is Europe's Most Homophobic Country, Survey Says." *Balkan Insight Tirana,* March 23.

———. 2013b. "Europe's Marijuana Capital Isn't Amsterdam." *Global Post,* August 16.

London Daily News. 2009. "Albanian Hit Men on Hire in London for 5,000." March 17.

Longrigg C. 1998. *Mafia Women.* London: Vintage.

Lorenz, E. 1972. "Predictability: Does the Flap of a Butterfly's Wings in Brazil Set Off a Tornado in Texas?" Unpublished paper presented at the American Association for the Advancement of Science, 139th Meeting. http://eaps4.mit.edu/research/Lorenz/Butterfly_1972.pdf.

Lucic, V. D. 1988. *Tajne Albanske Mafije.* Belgrade: Kosmos.

Lupevska, S. 2009. "The Life of Basri Bajrami: An Exclusive Interview with Basri Bajrami." Macedonian TV show *Kod,* Channel 5. www.youtube.com/watch?v=pPuRw_hccWY.

Lupsha, P. A. 1983. "Organised Crime in the United States." In *Organised Crime: Cross-Cultural Studies,* edited by R. J. Kelly, 32–57. Totowa, NJ: Rowman and Littlefield.

Lushnje, G. A. 1997. "Albanian 'Financiers' Fail to Play the Game." *The Independent,* February 6. www.independent.co.uk/news/world/albanian-financiers-fail-to-play-the-game-1277155.html.

Macedonia's State Election Commission. 2012. Election results. Retrieved from www.sec.mk/index.php/arhiva.

Maddux, M. 2012. "DEA Has Uncovered Mob-Linked Drug Smuggling Ring That Bribed Doormen." *New York Post,* February 3. http://nypost.com/2012/02/03/dea-has-uncovered-mob-linked-drug-smuggling-ring-that-bribed-doormen/.

Malcolm, N. 1998. *Kosovo: A Short History.* New York: New York University Press.

Marty, D. 2010. "Inhuman Treatment of People and Illicit Trafficking in Human Organs in Kosovo." Council of Europe, Committee on Legal Affairs and Human Rights, December 12.

Marzulli, J. 2011. "John A. (Junior) Gotti's 'Rat' Buddy John Alite Gets 10-Year Prison Sentence." *New York Daily News,* April 27.

———. 2013. "Former Pal of John A. (Junior) Gotti Will Read Statement at Sentencing of Gambino Mobster John Burke Implicating Mob Honcho in 1991 Murder." *New York Daily News,* January 23.

Matza, D. 1990. *Delinquency and Drift.* New Brunswick: Transaction Publishers.

McAllester, M. 2011. "Kosovo's Mafia: Assassinations and Intimidations." *The Global Post,* April 5.

McAllester, M., and J. Martinovic, J. 2011. "Kosovo's Mafia: A Hotbed of Human Trafficking." *Global Post,* March 29. www.savekosovo.org/default.asp?p=5&leader=0&sp=569.

McCabe, G. 2013. "Schoolboy Who Fled Kosovo for Scotland Became Underworld Druglord." *Daily Record,* February 10.

McClear, S. 2001. "Albanians and Their Culture: A Study of Their Defining Character and Uniqueness." MA thesis, California State University.

McDonald, G. 2014. "Human Trafficking in Albania." *Stanford Journal of Public Policy Online,* February 9. http://sites.duke.edu/sjpp/2014/human-trafficking-in-albania-part-one/.

McFadden, R. D. 1999. "Two Brothers Convicted in Slayings at Strip Club." *The New York Times,* May 29.

McGarvey, B. 2002. "Pole-Vaulting: Another Group of Eastern-European Gunsels Makes its Mark." *City Paper,* December 18.

McGrew, T., S. Hall, and D. Held, eds. 1992. *Modernity and Its Futures: Understanding Modern Societies.* Cambridge: Polity.

McKillop, J., and I. Wilson. 2003. "Rags to Riches Rise of a Sex-Slave Trader Merciless Albanian Made £ 3m Trafficking Women to UK." *Herald Scotland,* December 23.

McKinna, A. 2011. "The War Crimes Case against Fatmir Limaj and Lingering Problems for Kosovo's Transitional Justice." *Balkanalysis,* October 13.

McPherson M., L. Smith-Loving, and M. J. Cook. 2001. "Birds of a Feather: Homophily in Social Networks." *Annual Review of Sociology* 27: 415–444.

McQuail, D. 2005. *McQuail's Mass Communication Theory.* 5th ed. London: Sage.

Mendenhall, P. 2001. "Infiltrating Europe's Shameful Trade in Human Beings." *MSNBC,* June 1.

Merton, K. R. 1938. "Social Structure and Anomie." *American Sociological Review* 3 (5): 672–682.

Messner, S. F., and R. Rosenfeld. 2001. *Crime and the American Dream.* Belmont, CA: Wadsworth.

Michaletos, I. 2006. "Shape of the Albanian Organized Crime." Research Institute for American and European Studies.

Michilli, E. A. 2014. "Ruthless Criminals or Hardworking Migrants? Perceptions of Ethnic Albanians in Western Societies and the Role of Media." MA thesis, John Jay College of Criminal Justice, CUNY.

Mieczkowski, T. 1986. "Geeking and Throwing Down: Heroin Street Life in Detroit." *Criminology* 24: 645–666.

Milivojevic, M. 1995. "The Balkan Medellin." *Jane's Intelligence Review* 7 (2): 67–69.Miller, R. 2010. "Gojcaj Found Guilty in Danbury Murder Trial." *News Times,* November 5.

Mincheva L., and T. D. Gurr. 2010. "Unholly Alliances: Evidence of the Linkages between Trans-State Terrorism and Crime Networks: The Case of Bosnia." In *Transnational Terrorism, Organized Crime and Peace Building,* edited by W. Benedek et al., 265–286. London: Palgrave.

Minnesota Advocates for Human Rights. 1996. *Domestic Violence in Albania.* April. Minnesota: MAHR.

Misztal, B. A. 1996. *Trust in Modern Societies: The Search for the Bases of Social Order.* Cambridge: Polity Press.

MKD Online. 2012. "Власта од 2001 година знае кој го уби син ми!" (The government from 2001 knows who killed my son." July 24. www.mkd.mk/46587/crna-hronika/vlasta-od-2001-godina-znae-koj-go-ubi-sin-mi-marjan-tusevski.

MKinfo. 2013. "Александар Василевски - Нинџа: Ја обелоденува вистината за убиството на Марјан Тушевски" (Aleksandar Vasilevski-Ninja: Telling the truth about the murder of Marjan Tushevski). February 6. http://mkinfo.mk/makedonija/kriminal/item/3007-aleksandar-vasilevski-nindza-ja-obelodenuva-vistinata-za-ubistvoto-na-marjan-tushevski.

MKnews. 2012. "Uapsen telohranitelot na Boshkovski" (Boshkovski's bodyguard arrested). July 24. http://mkd-news.com/uapsen-telohranitelot-na-boshkovski-se-raschistuva-ubistvo-od-2001-koj-beshe-marijan-tushevski/.

Mortimer, M., and A. Toader. 2005. "Blood Feuds Blight Albanian Lives." *BBC World Service,* September 23.

Murusic, J. S. 2011. "Macedonia Abandons Hague Cases." Balkaninsight.com, July 20. www.balkaninsight.com/en/article/macedonia-passes-amnesty-for-hague-cases.

Mustafa, A. 2005. "Armed to the Teeth." *Institute for War and Peace Reporting* 470, September 6.

Mutschke, R. 2000. "The Threat Posed by the Convergence of Organized Crime, Drugs Trafficking and Terrorism." Congressional Statement by Assistant Director, Committee on the Judiciary Subcommittee on Crime. Interpol, December 13 (see www.russianlaw.org/Mutschke.htm).

MSF (Médecins Sans Frontières). 2014. *Violence against Kosovar Albanians, NATO's Intervention 1998–1999.* MSF Case Studies, June 20.

Nelan, B. W. 1997. "The Ponzi Revolution." *Time,* March 17. http://content.time.com/time/magazine/article/0,9171,986050,00.html.

Nellas, D. 2009. "Vassilis Paleokostas and Alket Rizai: Greece's Most Wanted Men Stage Helicopter Prison Escape—Again." *The World Post,* February 22.

Nelli, H. S. 1981. *The Business of Crime: Italians and Syndicate Crime in the United States.* Chicago: University of Chicago Press.

New York Post. 2008. "'04 Chief Chopper' Arrested." March 12.

———. 2012. "'Gangster' Sought in Groom Slay." March 20.

New York Times. 1985. "The City; Head of Drug Ring Gets Life in Prison." March 14.

Nikolic-Ristanovic, V. 2008. "Potential for the Use of Informal Mechanisms and Responses to the Kosovo Conflict." In *Restoring Justice After Large Scale Conflicts,* edited by I. Aertsen, J. Arsovska, H.-C. Rohne, K. Vanspauwen, and M. Valinas M., 157–182. Cullompton: Willan Publishing.

Nimoni, G. 2011. "How Witness X's Diary Unlocked Kosovo's Klecka Case." *Balkan Insight,* October 20.

Oakes, R. T. 1997. "The Albanian Blood Feud." *Journal of International Law and Practice* 6: 177–198.

O'Donnell, J. S. 1995. "Albania's Sigurimi: The Ultimate Agents of Social Control." *Problems of Post-Communism* 42 (6): 18–23.

Owen, F. 2012. "Chris Paciello Ratted on Mob Bosses, New Documents Show." *Miami New Times,* March 8.

Paluca-Belay F. 2003. "Women in Organized Crime in Albania." In *Women and the Mafia: Female Roles in Organized Crime Structures,* edited by G. Fiandaca, 139–149. New York: Springer.

Paoli, L. 2002. "The Paradoxes of Organized Crime." *Crime, Law and Social Change* 37: 51–97.

———. 2003. *Mafia Brotherhoods: Organized Crime, Italian Style.* New York: Oxford University Press.

Paoli, L., and C. Fijnaut, eds. 2005. *Organised Crime in Europe: Concepts, Patterns and Control Policies in the EU and Beyond.* Rotterdam: Springer.

Paoli, L., and P. Reuter. 2008. "Drug Trafficking and Ethnic Minorities in Western Europe." *European Journal of Criminology* 13 (5): 13–32.

Passas, N., ed. 1995. *Organised Crime.* Sudbury, MA: Dartmouth Publishing Company.

————. 2000. "Global Anomie, Dysnomie, and Economic Crime: Hidden Consequences of Neoliberalism and Globalization in Russia and around the World." *Social Justice* 27 (2): 16–44.

Pavia, W. 2011. "Juicehead, the Bear, Big Brian: Meet the New Albanian Mob." *The Times*, July 19.

Pearce, F., and M. Woodiwiss, eds. 1992. *Global Crime Connections: Dynamics and Control*. London: Macmillan.

Pearson, O. 2006. *Albania in the Twentieth Century, A History*. Vol. 3, *Albania As Dictatorship and Democracy*. London: I. B. Tauris.

Pistone, J. D., and R. Woodley. 1987. *Donnie Brasco: My Undercover Life in the Mafia*. New York: New American Library.

Poggioli, S. 2010. "Radical Islam Uses Balkan Poor to Wield Influence." *NPR*, October 25.

Popovski, K. 2006. "Полицијата ги крие убијците на мојот син Марјан Тушевски!" (The police is hiding the killers of my son Marjan Tushevski). *Utrinski Vesnik*, no. 912, October 16.

Porpora, K., and L. McShane. 2009. "Prosecution Case against Junior Gotti Wasn't Credible, Juror Says." *New York Daily News*, December 2.

Potter, G. W., and P. Jenkins. 1985. *The City and the Syndicate: Organizing Crime in Philadelphia*. Lexington, MA: Ginn Press.

Prato, G. 2004. "The Devil Is Not as Wicked as People Believe, Neither is the Albanian." In *Between Morality and the Law: Corruption, Anthropology and Comparative Society*, edited by I. Pardo, 69–85. Aldershot: Ashgate Publishing.

Prentice, E. A. 1999. "Kosovo Is Mafia's 'Heroin Gateway to West.'" *The London Times*, July 24.

Presdee, M. 2000. *Cultural Criminology and the Carnival of Crime*. London: Routledge.

President's Commission on Law Enforcement and Administration of Justice. 1967. *The Challenge of Crime in a Free Society*. Washington: United States Government.

Preston, J. 2006. "6 Convicted of Racketeering after Muscling in on Mob." *The New York Times*, January 5.

Puglisi, A. 2005. *Donne, Mafia e AntiMafia*. Palermo: DG Editore.

Quin, D., V. Jovanovski, A. Petruseva, N. Miftari, A. Mustafa, and J. Xharra. 2003. *Albania, Kosovo and Macedonia: Armed to the Teeth*. Institute for War and Peace Reporting, November 27.

Raufer, X. 2002. "At the Heart of the Balkan Chaos: The Albanian Mafia." http://www.xavier-raufer.com/site/At-the-heart-of-the-Balkan-chaos.

————. 2003. "A Neglected Dimension of Conflict: The Albanian Mafia." In *Potentials of Disorder: Explaining Conflict and Stability in the Caucasus and in the Former Yugoslavia. New Approaches to Conflict Analysis*, edited by J. Koehler and K. Zurcher, 62–75. Manchester: Manchester University Press.

————. 2007. "Albanian Organized Crime." In *Long March to the West: Twenty-First Century Migration to Europe and the Greater Mediterranean Area*, edited by M. Korinman and J. Laughland, 397–406. Portland: Vallentine Mitchell.

Raufer, X., and S. Quéré. 2000. *La Mafia Albanaise, une Menace pour l'Europe: Comment est née cette Superpuissance Criminelle Balkanique*. Lausanne: Favre.

————. 2006. *Kodot na zloto: Albanska Mafia*. Skopje: Di-Em.

————. 2007. "Albanian Organized Crime." In *Long March to the West: Twenty-First Century Migration to Europe and the Greater Mediterranean Area,* edited by M. Korinman and J. Laughland, 397–406. Portland: Vallentine Mitchell.

Reid, S., and A. Martin. 2009. "80 Foreign Murderers Welcomed to Britain: Albanian Killers Allowed to Stay Despite Being on Interpol 'Wanted' List." *Daily Mail,* January 23.

Renton, D. 2001. *Child Trafficking in Albania.* Tirana: Save the Children.

Repa, J. 2000. "Europe's Drug Gangs." *BBC News Online,* June 15.

Reuter, P. 1983. *Disorganized Crime: The Economics of the Visible Hand.* Cambridge, MA: The MIT Press.

————. 1985. *The Organization of Illegal Markets: An Economic Analysis.* New York: US National Institute of Justice.

Robbins, T. 2005. "The Mob's Multimillion-Dollar Batter, The Feds Say This Albanian Tough Guy Swings for John Gotti's Old Team." *The Village Voice,* February 15.

Rock, P. 2012. "Sociological Theories of Crime." In *The Oxford Handbook of Criminology,* 5th ed., edited by Rod Morgan, Mike Maguire, and Robert Reine, 39–81. Oxford: Oxford University Press.

Roth, R. 2002. "Guns, Gun Culture, and Homicide: The Relationship between Firearms, the Uses of Firearms, and Interpersonal Violence." *The William and Mary Quarterly* 59 (1): 223–240.

Ruscica, R. 1998. "Albanian Mafia, This Is How It Helps the Kosovo Guerrilla Fighters." *Corriere della Sera* (Milan), October 15.

Saferworld. 2009. *Ready or Not? Exploring the Prospects for Collecting Illicit Small Arms and Light Weapons in Kosovo.* London: Saferworld.

Sagramoso, D. 2001. *The Proliferation of Illegal Small Arms and Light Weapons In and Around the European Union: Instability, Organised Crime and Terrorist Groups.* London: Saferworld/Centre for Defence Studies.

Salerno, R., and J.S. Tompkins,. 1969. *The Crime Confederation: Cosa Nostra and Allied Operations in Organized Crime.* New York: Doubleday.

Salla, M. 1995. "Kosovo, Non-Violence and the Break-Up of Yugoslavia." *Security Dialogue* 26 (4): 427–438.

Samuels, D. 2010. "The Pink Panthers: A Tale of Diamonds, Thieves, and the Balkans." *The New Yorker* 86 (8): 42–72.

Scepanovic, I. 2002. "Arms Smuggling: Four Suspects Released." *The Irish News,* October 17.

————. 2004. "Court Jails Man over 50 'Real IRA Grenades.'" *The Irish News,* February 16.

Schemer, C. 2012. "The Influence of News Media on Stereotypic Attitudes towards Immigrants in a Political Campaign." *Journal of Communication* 62 (5): 739–757.

Schram, J. 2011. "ID-Theft Raps for 'Gym Rat.'" *New York Post,* April 29.

Schwandner-Sievers, S. 1999. "Humiliation and Reconciliation in Northern Albania: The Logics of Feuding in Symbolic and Diachronic Perspectives." In *Dynamics of Violence,* edited by G. Elwert, S. Feustchtwang, and D. Neubert, 133–152. Berlin: Duncker and Humblot.

————. 2008. "Albanians, Albanianism and the Strategic Subversion of Stereotypes." *Anthropological Notebooks* 14 (2): 47–64.

Schwarz, P. 2008. "Kosovo's Dirty Secret: The Background to Germany's Secret Service Affair." *World Socialist Website,* December 1. www.wsws.org/en/articles/2008/12/koso-do1.html.

SEESAC (South Eastern Europe Small Arms Control). 2005. *SALW and Private Security Companies in South Eastern Europe: A Cause or Effect of Insecurity?* Belgrade: SEESAC.

———. 2006. *The Rifle Has the Devil Inside: Gun Culture in South Eastern Europe.* Belgrade: SEESAC.

Sellin, T. 1938. *Culture Conflict and Crime.* New York: Social Science Research Council.

Seper, J. 1999. "KLA Finances Fight with Heroin Sales: Terror Group Is Linked to Crime Network." *The Washington Times,* May 3.

Shala, S. 2007. "Trafficking in Human Beings Is Being Redeveloped." Organization for Security and Co-operation in Europe, press release (translated from *Koha Jone*), September 4.

Shaw, C., and H. McKay. 1942. *Juvenile Delinquency and Urban Areas.* Chicago: University of Chicago Press.

Shekulli. 2009. "Aldo Bare shëtiste me kokën e Dajës në dorë." September 5. http://arkivame-diatike.com/lajme/artikull/iden/302927/titulli/Aldo-Bare-shetiste-me-koken-e-Dajes-ne-dore.

Shelley, L. 1999. "Identifying, Counting and Categorizing Transnational Criminal Organizations." *Transnational Organized Crime* 5 (4): 1–18.

———. 2006. "The Globalization of Crime and Terrorism." *EJournal USA,* 42–45.

Siebert, L., and A. Little, A. 1997. *Yugoslavia: Death of a Nation.* London: Penguin Books.

Simon, H. A. 1982. *Models of Bounded Rationality.* Cambridge, MA: MIT Press.

Simons, M. 2000. "Balkan Gangs Stepping Up Violence, Dutch Say." *New York Times,* November 30.

Small Arms Survey. 2005. *Weapons at War.* Oxford: Oxford University Press.

———. 2009. *Shadows of War.* Cambridge: Cambridge University Press.

———. 2012. *Moving Targets.* Cambridge: Cambridge University Press.

Smith, C. D. 1980. "Paragons, Pariahs, and Pirates: A Spectrum-Based Theory of Enterprise." *Crime and Delinquency* 26: 358–386.

———. 1991. "Wickersham to Sutherland to Katzenbach: Evolving an 'Official' Definition for Organized Crime." *Crime, Law and Social Change* 16: 135–154.

Smith, C., and D. Sagramoso. 1999. "Small Arms Trafficking May Export Albania's Anarchy." *Jane's Intelligence Review* 11 (1): 24–26.

Smith, K. 2009. "'Junior' Gleeful When Describing Murder: Witness." *New York Post,* September 30.

Sorensen, P. 2003. *Organised Crime.* European Parliament Publication.

Southerton, D. 2002. "Boundaries of 'Us' and 'Them': Class, Mobility and Identification in a New Town." *Sociology* 36 (1): 171–193.

Squires, P. 2000. *Gun Culture Or Gun Control? Firearms, Violence and Society.* London: Routledge.

Standing, A. 2003. "Rival Views on Organised Crime." *Monograph,* 77.

Stefanova, R. 2004. "Fighting Organised Crime in a UN Protectorate: Difficult, Possible, Necessary." *Southeast European and Black Sea Studies* 44 (2): 257–279.

Steffensmeier D., and E. Allan. 1996. "Gender and Crime: Toward a Gendered Theory of Female Offending." *Annual Review of Sociology* 22: 459–487.

Sterling, C. 1994. *Thieves' World: The Threat of the New Global Network of Organized Crime.* New York: Simon & Schuster.

264   REFERENCES

Sullivan, S. 2004. *Be Not Afraid, For You Have Sons in America: How a Brooklyn Roofer Helped Lure the US into the Kosovo War*. New York: St Martin's Press.

Sutherland, E. H. 1939. *Principles of Criminology*. Philadelphia: J. B. Lippincott.

Sykes, M. G., and D. Matza. 1957. "Techniques of Neutralization: A Theory of Delinquency." *American Sociological Review* 22 (6): 664–670.

Taleski, D. 2011. "From Bullets to Ballots: Guerilla to Party Transformation in Macedonia." Central European University, Political Science Doctoral Seminar. http://politicalscience .ceu.hu/node/19819.

Time.mk. 2012. "Police arrests 9 tied to Janev and Tushevski murder in 2001." July 24. www. time.mk/cluster/714fa2e66a/devetmina-uapseni-za-ubistvoto-na-marjan-tusevski-od-2001-ta.html.

Tirana Observer. 2012. "Mbyllet Historia e Kapobandës Aldo Bare, Ja Vrasjet e Bujshme te 97tes." July 17.

Top Channel. 2011. "Prosecution, Life to Prison for Tufa." November 26. http://top-channel. tv/english/artikull.php?id=3326.

Troebst, S. 1998. *Conflict in Kosovo: Failure of Prevention? An Analytical Documentation, 1992–1998*. ECMI Working Paper no. 1. www.ecmi.de/uploads/tx_lfpubdb/working_ paper_1.pdf.

Tsaliki, L. 2008. "How does the word Albanian make you feel?" A case study in the representation of the Albanian ethnic minority within the Greek media. Conference paper, September 21–23, London School of Economics, U.K.

Turner, V. 1967. *The Forest of Symbols: Aspects of Ndembu Ritual*. Ithaca: Cornell University Press.

UK Home Office. 2004. *Albania Country Report*. UK: Country Information and Policy Unit.

UNDP. 2000. *Albanian Human Development Report 2000*. Tirana: UNDP Albania.

UNICEF Report. 2000. *Mapping of Existing Information on Domestic Violence in Albania*. Tirana: National Committee of Women and Family of Albania and UNICEF.

UNMIK. 2004. *Combating Human Trafficking in Kosovo: Strategy and Commitment*. Prishtina: UN Publication.

UNODC. 2002. *Results of a Pilot Survey of Forty Selected Organized Criminal Groups in Sixteen Countries*. Global Programme against Transnational Organized Crime. Vienna: United Nations Office on Drugs and Crime. https://www.unodc.org/pdf/crime /publications/Pilot_survey.pdf.

———. 2008. *Crime and Its Impact on the Balkans*. Vienna: UNODC.

———. 2009. *Global Report on Trafficking in Persons*. Vienna: UNODC.

———. 2011. *Corruption in the Western Balkans: Bribery as Experienced by the Population*. Vienna: UNODC.

UN Palermo Convention. 2000. *UN Convention against Transnational Organized Crime*. www.uncjin.org/Documents/Conventions/dcatoc/final_documents_2/convention_ eng.pdf.

US Department of Justice. 2005. *Albanian Crews*. Intelligence Report, MAGLOCLEN.

———. 2011. "37 Alleged Members and Associates of an International Ethnic-Albanian Organized Crime Syndicate Arrested." Press release, July 13. www.justice.gov/usao/nye /pr/2011/2011jul13.html.

Vaknin, S. 2010. *Corruption and Financial Crime.* Skopje: A Narcissus Publications Imprint.

Valinas, M., and J. Arsovska. 2008. "A Restorative Approach for Dealing with the Aftermath of the Kosovo Conflict: Opportunities and Limits." In *Restoring Justice after Large Scale Conflicts,* edited by I. Aertsen, J. Arsovska, H.-C. Rohne, K. Vanspauwen, and M. Valinas, 183–213. Cullompton, UK: Willan Publishing.

Van Gennep, A. (1909) 1960. *The Rites of Passage.* Chicago: University of Chicago Press.

Varese, F. 2011. *Mafias on the Move: How Organized Crime Conquers New Territories.* Princeton, NJ: Princeton University Press.

Vest. 2001. "Ubistvo Pred Svedoci Vo Skopskata Naselba Taftalidge" (Murder in front of witnesses in Skopje). July 12. http://star.vest.com.mk/default.asp?id=11488&idg=2&idb= 305&rubrika=Crna+Hronika

———. 2005. "Policijata Nema Osomniceni Ama Istragata Napreduva" (Police has no suspects but the investigation continues"). June 27. http://star.vest.com.mk/default.asp?id= 99517&idg=5&idb=1500&rubrika=Crna+Hronika.

Viviano, F. 1994. "Drugs Paying for Conflict in Europe, Separatists Supporting Themselves with Traffic in Narcotics." *San Francisco Chronicle,* June 10.

———. 1999. "KLA Linked to Enormous Heroin Trade." *San Francisco Chronicle,* May 5.

von Lampe, K., and P.O. Johansen. 2004. "Criminal Networks and Trust: On the Importance of Expectations of Loyal Behaviour in Criminal Relations." In *Organised Crime, Trafficking, Drugs: Selected Papers Presented at the Annual Conference of the European Society of Criminology,* edited by S. Nevala and K. Aromaa, 102–114. Helsinki: European Institute for Crime Prevention and Control, Series 42.

Waldmann, P. 2001. "Revenge without Rules: On the Renaissance of an Archaic Motif of Violence." *Studies in Conflict and Terrorism* 24: 435–450.

Weber, M. 1978. *Economy and Society: An Outline of Interpretive Sociology.* Berkeley: University of California Press.

Wiebes, C. 2006. *Intelligence and the War in Bosnia: 1992–1995.* Studies in Intelligence History. Berlin: Lit Verlag.

Williams, P. 1994. "Transnational Criminal Organisations and International Security." *Survival* 36 (1): 96–113.

———. 2001. "Transnational Criminal Networks." In *Networks and Netwars: The Future of Terror, Crime, and Militancy,* edited by J. Arquilla and D. Ronfeldt, 61–99. Santa Monica, CA: Rand Publications.

———. 2009. *Criminals, Militias, and Insurgents: Organized Crime in Iraq.* Strategic Studies Institute, United States Army War College.

Williams, P.L. 2005. *The Al Qaeda Connection: International Terrorism, Organized Crime, and the Coming Apocalypse.* New York: Prometheus Books.

Winfree, L., and H. Abadinsky. 2010. *Understanding Crime: The Essentials of Criminological Theory.* Belmont, CA: Cengage Learning Press.

Wolfgang, M.E., and F. Ferracuti. 1967. *The Subculture of Violence: Towards an Integrated Theory in Criminology.* New York: Tavistok.

Wood, M. 1998. "Socio-Economic Status, Delay of Gratification and Impulse Buying." *Journal of Economic Psychology* 19: 295–320.

Wood, N. 2000. "US Fears Terrorist Attack in Kosovo." BBC News, April 3. http://news.bbc .co.uk/2/hi/europe/700435.stm.

World Bank. 2010. *Albanian Country Governance Review.* Washington DC: World Bank.

World Value Survey. 2002. *World Value Survey: Material Possessions and Hard Work.* http://www.worldvaluessurvey.org/WVSDocumentationWV4.jsp.

Wortley, S. 2009. "The Immigration-Crime Connection: Competing Theoretical Perspectives." *International Migration and Integration* 10 (4): 349–358.

Xharra, J. 2005. "Kosovo's Intelligence Services Come In from the Cold." *Balkan Investigative Research Network,* December 23.

Xhudo, G. 1996. "Men of Purpose: The Growth of the Albanian Criminal Activity." *Frank Cass Journal* 2 (1): 1–20.

Yeung, K., and J. L. Martin. 2003. "The Looking Glass Self: An Empirical Test and Elaboration." *Social Forces* 81 (3): 843–879.

Yinger, M. J. 1960. "Contraculture and Subculture." *American Sociological Review* 25: 625–635.

Young, J. 2007. *The Vertigo of Late Modernity.* London: Sage.

Zaborskiy, V. 2007. "Small-Arms, Big Problem—Light Weapons Trafficking in Albania." *Jane's Intelligence Review,* September 14.

Zenit. 1999. "Refugees Abused by Organized Crime: Kosovo Women Enticed or Forced Into Prostitution." *Daily Catholic News* 10 (80), April 23. www.dailycatholic.org/issue/archives/1999Apr/80apr23,vol.10,no.80txt/apr23nv6.htm

Zhelyazkova, A. 1999. *The Three Albanian Communities and Their Perspectives.* Sofia: International Center for Minority Studies and International Relations.

Zickel, R., R. W. Iwaskiw, eds. 1994. *Albania: A Country Study.* Washington, DC: Federal Research Division of the United States Library of Congress.

INDEX

CPSIA information can be obtained at www.ICGtesting.com
Printed in the USA
LVOW11s0907120916

504230LV00008B/19/P